New Testament Commentary

New Testament Commentary

Exposition
of the
Epistle of James
and the
Epistles of John

Simon J. Kistemaker

BAKER BOOK HOUSE
Grand Rapids, Michigan 49506

Copyright 1986 by
Baker Book House Company

ISBN: 0-8010-5469-9

Second printing, November 1986

Library of Congress Catalogue Card Number: 85-73720

Printed in the United States of America

Scripture references are from the Holy Bible: New International Version. Copyright ©
1973, 1978 by the International Bible Society. Used by permission of Zondervan Bible
Publishers.

Contents

Contents

Abbreviations

ASV	American Standard Version
Bauer	Walter Bauer, W. F. Arndt, F. W. Gingrich, and F. W. Danker, *A Greek-English Lexicon of the New Testament,* 2d ed.
Bib	*Biblica*
BS	*Bibliotheca Sacra*
CBQ	*Catholic Biblical Quarterly*
CTJ	*Calvin Theological Journal*
I Clem.	First Epistle of Clement
EDT	*Evangelical Dictionary of Theology*
EvQ	*Evangelical Quarterly*
ExpT	*Expository Times*
GNB	Good News Bible
HTR	*Harvard Theological Review*
Interp	*Interpretation*
ISBE	*The International Standard Bible Encyclopedia,* rev. ed., edited by G. W. Bromiley, 1979–.
JB	Jerusalem Bible
JBL	*Journal of Biblical Literature*
JETS	*Journal of the Evangelical Theological Society*
JTS	*Journal of Theological Studies*
KJV	King James Version
LCL	Loeb Classical Library edition
LXX	Septuagint
MLB	The Modern Language Bible
Moffatt	The Bible: A New Translation by James Moffatt
NAB	New American Bible
NASB	New American Standard Bible
NEB	New English Bible
Nes-A1	Eberhard Nestle; Kurt Aland, rev., *Novum Testamentum Graece,* 26th ed.
NIDNTT	*New International Dictionary of New Testament Theology*
NIV	New International Version

NKJV	New King James Version
NovT	*Novum Testamentum*
NTS	*New Testament Studies*
RSV	Revised Standard Version
RV	Revised Version
SB	H. L. Strack and P. Billerbeck, *Kommentar zum Neuen Testament aus Talmud und Midrasch*
ScotJT	*Scottish Journal of Theology*
SWJournTheol	*Southwest Journal of Theology*
Talmud	The Babylonian Talmud
TDNT	*Theological Dictionary of the New Testament*
TR	Textus Receptus: *The Greek New Testament According to the Majority Text*
Thayer	Joseph H. Thayer, *Greek-English Lexicon of the New Testament*
Tyn H Bul	*Tyndale House Bulletin*
WJT	*Westminster Theological Journal*
ZPEB	*Zondervan Pictorial Encyclopedia of the Bible*

Exposition
of the
Epistle of James

Introduction

Outline

A. Is This an Epistle?
B. What Are the Characteristics of the Epistle?
C. Who Were the First Readers?
D. Who Wrote This Epistle?
E. What Is the Theological Message of James?
F. When and Where Was the Epistle Written?
G. What Is the History of the Epistle?
H. How Can James Be Outlined?

A. Is This an Epistle?

James begins his letter with an address and a greeting (1:1), employs the personal pronouns *you* and *we* throughout his epistle, and frequently appeals to the readers by calling them "my dear brothers" or "my brothers." He does not list any names of the addressees, he provides no personal information about them, and he fails to mention any details concerning himself. He concludes his epistle without a benediction and final greetings.

This letter, then, is not a personal document but rather a general epistle. The general epistles in the New Testament (those of Peter, John, and Jude, and the Epistle to the Hebrews) and other letters, preserved for centuries in the sands of Egypt but recently uncovered, have this same literary form. Some scholars wish to make a distinction between the terms *epistle* and *letter*. They maintain that letters display temporality, whereas epistles show permanence and universality.[1] Others, however, regard the terms as synonyms.

1. A Discourse

If we use the term *letter* or *epistle*, we have to describe what the word means. Is a letter equivalent to a discourse or to a sermon? First, then, is the Epistle of James a discourse? Scholars have pointed out that this epistle resembles a diatribe. A diatribe, a discourse marked by irony, satire, and name-calling, was common in Hellenistic circles. In Greek diatribes and in James's epistle scholars have detected similarities in the use of rhetorical questions, examples from nature and history, verbal witticisms, the use of alliteration and assonance, analogies, short sayings, and quotations.[2]

---

1. See, among others, Adolf Deissmann, *Bible Studies,* trans. Alexander Grieve (1923; reprint ed., Winona Lake, Ind.: Alpha, 1979), pp. 45–51. Also see Walter W. Wessel, *ISBE,* vol. 2, p. 961.

2. Refer to Martin Dibelius, *James: A Commentary on the Epistle of James,* rev. Heinrich Greeven, trans. Michael A. Williams, ed. Helmut Köster, Hermeneia: A Critical and Historical Commentary on the Bible (Philadelphia: Fortress, 1976), p. 1. Compare James Hardy Ropes, *A Critical and Exegetical Commentary on the Epistle of James,* International Critical Commentary series (1916; reprint ed., Edinburgh: Clark, 1961), pp. 10–18. Also consult Peter H. Davids, *The Epistle of James: A Commentary on the Greek Text,* New International Greek Testament Commentary series (Grand Rapids: Eerdmans, 1982), p. 23.

Even though similarities are obvious (see, for example, the sequence of short questions, rhetorical questions, and commands in 4:1–10), the fact remains that James is not a Hellenist but a Jew. James is an inspired author who in his epistle presents God's revelation. Because of the sacred content of this letter, bitter sarcasm, irony, and name-calling—characteristic features of Hellenistic diatribes—are absent. Therefore, we conclude that the Epistle of James ought not to be considered a discourse in the sense of a diatribe. If it is not a discourse, can we call the letter a sermon?

2. A Sermon

The apostle Paul instructs the church at Colosse to read the letter he sent them and to exchange it with the letter he sent to the church at Laodicea (Col. 4:16). And in his first epistle to the church at Thessalonica, he tells the believers, "I charge you before the Lord to have this letter read to all the brothers" (I Thess. 5:27). Letters addressed to churches and to individuals were written *"to be read aloud in the churches."*[3] Presumably, the letter James addressed to "the twelve tribes scattered among the nations" (1:1) was read in the worship services as a sermon from Pastor James.

The Epistle of James can be divided into two parts that are nearly equal in length; the first two chapters consist of fifty-three verses and the last three of fifty-five verses. The two parts, in effect, are two successive sermons that disclose common themes. After the greeting, the first sermon introduces and concludes with the topic *faith* (1:3; 2:26). The second begins with the observation that we who teach will be judged, for all of us stumble in what we say (3:1–2), and ends with the counsel to turn a sinner from the error of his way (5:20). In short, James's epistle consists of two sermons.

Moreover, Jewish sermons from the early centuries of our era reveal striking similarities to the letter James wrote to his scattered flock. These sermons include the use of dialogue, the method of addressing a synagogue audience with the term *brothers*, and the numerous subjects mentioned in the letter of James.[4]

The probability that James addressed the synagogue audience (2:2) of his day with sermon material that eventually became his epistle cannot be ignored. This epistle embodies characteristics of a sermon, but because of the address and greeting at the beginning of the letter, it is not a sermon but an epistle.

B. What Are the Characteristics of the Epistle?

Primarily the characteristics of this letter are stylistic and cultural in form.

---

3. P. B. R. Forbes, "The Structure of the Epistle of James," *EvQ* 44 (1972): 148.

4. Concludes Wessel, "The variety of the material in the Epistle is paralleled by that found in the Jewish synagogue sermons." *ISBE*, vol. 2, p. 962.

1. Stylistic Characteristics

First, although the epistle is written in Greek that compares favorably with the best in the New Testament (that is, the Greek of the Epistle to the Hebrews), its literary style shows a distinct Hebraic coloring. Here is a sample of Hebraic parallelism:

James 1:9	*James 1:10a*
the brother	but the one
in humble circumstances	who is rich
ought to take pride	should take pride
in his high position	in his low position

Other examples are in 1:15, 17, 19–20, 22–23; 2:22; 4:7, 10.[5]

Next, the letter is replete with imperatives. By one count, there are fifty-four occurrences.[6] The frequent use of the imperative is an indication that the writer is a person who speaks with authority and who commands respect from the members of the church. At the same time he demonstrates his loving pastoral concern for the addressees.

Third, the author communicates his message effectively with numerous examples and comparisons taken from nature and human life. In the first chapter, for example, he refers to wind and waves, to the rising sun and the scorching heat, to the plant and its blossom, to heavenly lights and shifting shadows, to the look in the mirror, and the taming of the tongue. The style of this epistle is engaging; it captures and holds the attention of the reader because the imagery is natural.

And last, James links sentences and clauses by repeating a verb or a noun. Even in translation, this stylistic characteristic is evident. Note this sample taken from 1:13–15:

> When tempted, no one should say, "God is tempting me." For God cannot be tempted by evil, nor does he tempt anyone; but each one is tempted when, by his own evil desire, he is dragged away and enticed. Then, after desire has conceived, it gives birth to sin; and sin, when it is full-grown, gives birth to death.

2. Cultural Characteristics

James and his readers are thoroughly familiar with names taken from Old Testament history: Abraham, Isaac, Rahab, Job, and Elijah. Inclusion of these names is a preliminary indication that James addresses his letter to Jewish-Christian readers.

---

5. Franz Mussner in his commentary *Der Jakobusbrief*, 2d ed., Herder Theologischer Kommentar zum Neuen Testament series (Freiburg: Herder, 1967), pp. 30–31, lists a number of parallelisms taken from the Greek text. They are 1:5, 9, 13; 3:9; 4:8, 9; 5:4.

6. I have counted only true imperatives and not the participles that take the place of the imperative. Expanding the use of the imperative, C. Leslie Mitton in *The Epistle of James* (Grand Rapids: Eerdmans, 1966), p. 235, mentions sixty occurrences.

Throughout his epistle, James alludes to all three parts of the Old Testament canon—Law, Prophets, and Wisdom literature. By directing the attention of his readers to the whole law, he exhorts them to keep it (2:10). Moreover, in regard to exercising patience in the face of suffering, the author tells them to take the prophets as an example (5:10). And by reminding them of Job's perseverance, he alludes to Wisdom literature (5:11).

These references indicate that the Old Testament was a book the author and the readers knew well. James and the recipients of his letter belonged to the twelve tribes (1:1). They were the people God had chosen "to inherit the kingdom" (2:5). They were the people who called Abraham their father (2:21).

James also remarks on the "autumn and spring rains" (5:7). This is a description that fits the climate of Israel and not the other countries surrounding the Mediterranean Sea. The writer, therefore, reveals that he lives in Israel and that the readers also find their origin there.

C. Who Were the First Readers?

The readers were Jews, as the address of the letter clearly indicates: "to the twelve tribes scattered among the nations" (1:1). The designation *twelve tribes* is a biblical reference to Israel (Exod. 24:4; Matt. 19:28; Luke 22:30; Acts 26:7; Rev. 21:12) that should be understood figuratively, not literally. James addresses representatives of these twelve tribes who, because of Christ's work, are now the new Israel.

In fact, James calls the readers brothers who are "believers in our glorious Lord Jesus Christ" (2:1). They are Jewish Christians who live "scattered among the nations" (1:1), but nevertheless know that they are God's people. In his epistle James provides no evidence that he is addressing Gentile Christians. The readers of this epistle are exclusively Jewish, with the exception of the rich oppressors James rebukes (5:1–6).

The recipients of this epistle are Jews; they come together for worship in a "meeting"—a translation of the word *synagogue* (2:2). They are called "adulterous people" (4:4); the original Greek has the term *adulteresses* (4:4), which is obviously an Old Testament figure that relates to the marriage contract God (as husband) has with Israel (his wife). They understand the Hebrew term *Sabaoth,* which the New International Version translates "Almighty" (5:4). And they call the elders of the church to visit and pray with the sick (5:14). However, the church has no overseers. The expression *overseer* (see Acts 20:28; Phil. 1:1; I Tim. 3:2; Titus 1:7; I Peter 2:25) finds its origin in that part of the Christian church which has a membership of Gentile origin. The term *elder,* by contrast, is reminiscent of the leaders in Israel who were called elders, and therefore reflects Jewish influence.

These Jews, then, are Christians. The writer introduces himself as "a servant of God and of the Lord Jesus Christ" (1:1). In addition to addressing the readers as brothers who believe in Jesus Christ (2:1), he writes that God has chosen "to give *us* [the author and the readers] birth through the word of truth" (1:18, italics added). The readers belong to Jesus, whose noble name is slandered (2:7).

These Jewish Christians have been scattered among the nations. Although the expression *scattered* appears only in John 7:35, James 1:1, and I Peter 1:1, it has a verbal parallel in the written account of the persecution of the church in Jerusalem. After Stephen's death, the Jerusalem church was scattered throughout Judea, Samaria (Acts 8:1), and even as far as Phoenicia, Cyprus, and Antioch (Acts 11:19). From Acts, then, we know that the scattered Christians were Jews who had been driven from Jerusalem.

If we assume that James wrote his epistle to the Jewish Christians who were persecuted following the death of Stephen, then the conclusion is that this epistle dates from the first part of the first century. Furthermore, these people were Jewish Christians whose native tongue was Greek and who found a refuge in Greek-speaking countries north of Israel: Phoenicia, Cyprus, and Syria.

James wrote a pastoral letter to these scattered believers who, before the persecution, belonged to the church at Jerusalem.[7] He knew that they were living in poverty while they were employed by rich landowners who exploited them. Some of them were merchants, but all experienced hardship. James ministered to their needs by writing them a pastoral letter.

D. Who Wrote This Epistle?

The introductory greeting informs the reader that James is "a servant of God and of the Lord Jesus Christ" (1:1). This greeting in itself provides little information about the identity of the author. Who is he? What does the New Testament say about James?

1. Evidence from the New Testament

Name

The New Testament lists a number of men who are called James. They are the son of Zebedee (Matt. 10:2 and parallels; Acts 1:13; 12:2); the son of Alphaeus (Matt. 10:3 and parallels; Acts 1:13); James the younger (Mark 15:40); the father of Judas (not Iscariot [Luke 6:16; Acts 1:13]); the brother of Jude (Jude 1); and the half brother of Jesus who became the leader of the Jerusalem church (Matt. 13:55; Mark 6:3; Acts 12:17; 15:13; 21:18; I Cor. 15:7; Gal. 1:19; 2:9, 12). If the brother of Jude (Jude 1) and James the half brother of Jesus are the same person, the number is reduced to five men bearing that name.

a. "James the son of Zebedee." James and his brother John received the

---

7. Refer to F. W. Grosheide, *De Brief aan de Hebreeën en de Brief van Jakobus* (Kampen: Kok, 1955), p. 330.

name *Boanerges,* which means "Sons of Thunder" (Mark 3:17). Apart from the lists of apostles in the Gospels and Acts, his name appears in Acts 12:2, where Luke informs the reader that King Herod Agrippa I "had James, the brother of John, put to death with the sword." This happened in A.D. 44 during the Feast of Unleavened Bread. If James the son of Zebedee had written the Epistle of James, we would have expected more internal and external information. Instead of calling himself "a servant of . . . Jesus Christ," he would have used the title *apostle of Jesus Christ.* The early church would have received and treasured the epistle as an apostolic writing.

b. "James the son of Alphaeus." We know this apostle only from the lists of the apostles in the Gospels and Acts. The New Testament is silent on the life and labors of this person. If this apostle had composed the epistle, he would have given further identification. Also, the church would have kept the memory alive, had this epistle been written by an apostle.

c. "James the younger." According to the Gospel of Mark (15:40), James, his brother Joses, and his sister Salome are children of Mary. James is identified as "the younger"—a reference to his age or stature. We know nothing about the life of James the younger. His mother presumably was the wife of Clopas (John 19:25).[8]

d. "James the father of Judas." Nothing is known about this particular person, except that he was the father of the apostle Judas (not Iscariot).

e. "James the [half] brother of the Lord." The Gospel writers mention him as one of the sons of Mary, the mother of Jesus (Matt. 13:55; Mark 6:3). During Jesus' earthly ministry, he and his brothers did not believe in Jesus (John 7:5). James became a believer when Jesus appeared to him after the resurrection (I Cor. 15:7). After Jesus' ascension, he was present with his brothers and the apostles in the so-called upper room (Acts 1:14). He assumed leadership of the Jerusalem church after Peter's release from prison (Acts 12:17), spoke with authority during the assembly at Jerusalem (Acts 15:13), was recognized as the head of the church (Gal. 1:19; 2:9, 12), and met Paul to hear his report on missions in the Gentile world (Acts 21:18). Tradition teaches that this influential and esteemed leader wrote the epistle.

Objections to the traditional view that James, the brother of Jesus, wrote the epistle have come in the form of the following arguments:

a. A Galilean whose native tongue was Aramaic could not have composed a letter in cultured Greek. This objection, however, is not formidable in view of the pervasive Greek influence in Galilee. James's linguistic ability is not known, but the possibility of being bilingual is not remote.[9] "The real issue must be one of education, for since Galilee was a region with many Greek cities and non-Jews and since there is extensive evidence

---

8. Consult E. F. F. Bishop, "Mary (of) Clopas and Her Father," *ExpT* 73 (1962): 339.
9. Refer to Donald Guthrie, *New Testament Introduction* (Downers Grove: Inter-Varsity, 1971), p. 748.

of the use of Greek by Jews throughout Palestine, there is no reason to suppose that James could not speak Greek fluently."[10] Even the issue of education is unconvincing; consider, for example, that an uneducated cobbler named John Bunyan wrote *Pilgrim's Progress*, which is considered a classic work. The objection that James could not have composed a letter seems unfounded.

b. James calls himself a servant, not a brother of Jesus. If he were the leader of the Jerusalem church, he could have indicated this in the introductory greeting. However, in their addresses the other writers of New Testament epistles often omit references to themselves and to their office.[11] Moreover, James regarded his relationship to Jesus not physically as his brother but spiritually as his servant. Throughout the epistle, the authority of the author's status in the church is unmistakable and undeniable. Known to the readers of his document, James is not compelled to identify himself as leader of the church in Jerusalem.

Language

If we assume that James, the leader of the Jerusalem church, is the author of the epistle, we must examine the speech he delivered during the assembly held in Jerusalem and the letter which he composed at that time (Acts 15:13–29). For instance, he calls Peter Simeon (in the Greek, Acts 15:14), a name that occurs again only in II Peter 1:1. "From this we gather that the actual words of the speaker are recorded either in their original form or in a translation; and it becomes thus a matter of interest to learn whether there is any resemblance between the language of our Epistle and that of the speech said to have been uttered by James, and of the circular [letter] containing the decree, which was probably drawn up by him."[12]

Moreover, we find similarities when we compare the choice of words and the structure of sentences (as reported by Luke in Acts) with the Epistle of James. James begins his speech with the familiar address *brothers*, an expression he employs frequently in his epistle. Consider the following words and phrases that even in an English translation show resemblance:

---

10. Davids, *James*, p. 11. Also consult J. N. Sevenster, *Do You Know Greek?* (Leiden: Brill, 1968), pp. 190–91.

11. Although Paul usually introduces himself as an apostle in his epistles, this is not the case in Phil. 1:1; I Thess. 1:1; and II Thess. 1:1. In his epistles, John does not identify himself as an apostle.

12. Joseph B. Mayor, *The Epistle of St. James* (reprint ed., Grand Rapids: Zondervan, 1946), p. iii. Mayor calls attention to the resemblance between the two hundred and thirty words James spoke and wrote during the Jerusalem Council and the Epistle of James. "It [is] a remarkable coincidence that . . . so many should reappear in our Epistle, written on a totally different subject."

"Greetings" (Acts 15:23; James 1:1)

"Brothers, listen to me" (Acts 15:13) and "Listen, my dear brothers" (James 2:5)

"The remnant of men may seek the Lord, and all the Gentiles who bear my name" (Acts 15:17) and "Are they not the ones who are slandering the noble name of him to whom you belong?" (James 2:7)

Even though we cannot be absolutely certain concerning the authorship of the epistle, the internal evidence appears to point in the direction of James, the half brother of Jesus.

2. External Evidence

Eusebius, the church historian of the fourth century, quotes Hegesippus when he relates that James "used to enter alone into the temple and be found kneeling and praying for forgiveness for the people, so that his knees grew hard like a camel's because of his constant worship of God."[13] As leader of the Jerusalem church, James had earned the respect of both the Christian and the Jew.

Nevertheless, this pious man known as James the Just met a violent death, which is decribed by the Jewish historian Josephus. After Governor Festus (Acts 24:27–26:32) died in A.D. 62, Emperor Nero sent Albinus to Judea as Festus's successor. But before Albinus had arrived in Jerusalem, a high priest named Ananus, who was young and inexperienced, had convened the judges of the Sanhedrin. He accused James, the brother of Jesus, and others of breaking the law. James was sentenced to be killed by stoning.[14] James met his death, however, at the hands of priests who threw him from the roof of the temple. He survived the fall, but they began to stone him until a laundryman beat him to death with a club.[15]

E. What Is the Theological Message of James?

The Epistle of James appears to be a collection of sayings and thoughts loosely put together. It differs from those epistles Paul has written in which he first develops a doctrinal issue—for example, Christology in Colossians—and then concludes with a section on practical application. By contrast, James presents a series of exhortations and numerous admonitions that reflect an ethical rather than a doctrinal emphasis. Even though these exhortations seem to be loosely connected, James shows progress and development in his presentation.

Typically, James introduces a subject in summary fashion which he afterward augments. Some of these subjects are faith, testing, wisdom (1:2–5); restraining the tongue; controlling anger, and submission to God (1:19–20). He returns to some topics to discuss them more fully:

---

13. Eusebius *Ecclesiastical History* 2. 23. 6.
14. Josephus *Antiquities* 20 (LCL, 197–200).
15. Eusebius *Ecclesiastical History* 2. 23. 18.

testing and temptation (1:12–15); keeping the law in faith (1:22–2:26); restraint of the tongue (3:1–12); earthly and heavenly wisdom (3:13–18); living in harmony with the will of God (4); and exercising patience through prayer (5). Because James often reverts to discussing items he has mentioned already (compare 4:8 with 1:8; 5:11 with 1:12), his epistle does not lend itself to separate divisions of topics. To treat every topic would make this introduction proportionately too lengthy. I must choose a few subjects and leave the rest for discussion in the commentary itself.

James seems to leave the impression that he is familiar with the oral gospel of Jesus but not with the books of the New Testament. "No case can be demonstrated for literary dependence on our gospel of Matthew (or indeed on Luke and John)."[16] Had he been acquainted with the written Gospel accounts and with the epistles, James would have been more theologically than ethically oriented in his epistle. True, he presents theology, but it is implicit rather than explicit. James depends on the preaching of Jesus, discusses the topic *faith and works* independently of Paul's teaching, and writes on submission to God in a more elementary form than that which Peter presents in his epistles.

In his epistle, James echoes the tone and tenor of Jesus' preaching recorded in the Gospels. The parallel between the Sermon on the Mount (Matt. 5:3–7:27; Luke 6:20–49) and verses, clauses, phrases, and words in the letter of James is remarkable.[17] Here are a few verses to illustrate this point:

Matthew	*James*
5:7 "Blessed are the merciful, for they will be shown mercy."	2:13 Judgment without mercy will be shown to anyone who has not been merciful.
5:19 "Anyone who breaks one of the least of these commandments . . . will be called least in the kingdom of heaven."	2:10 Whoever keeps the whole law and yet stumbles at just one point is guilty of breaking all of it.
6:19 "Do not store up for yourselves treasures on earth, where moth and rust destroy."	5:2–3 Moths have eaten your clothes. Your gold and silver are corroded. . . . You have hoarded wealth.

---

16. J. A. T. Robinson, *Redating the New Testament* (Philadelphia: Westminster, 1976), p. 125.

17. Mayor has compiled a complete list of all the verbal resemblances between the Epistle of James and the synoptic Gospels. Choosing from the most striking parallels that Mayor indicates, I list only those parallels for Matt. 5–7: 5:3—James 2:5; 5:7—James 2:13; 5:11, 12—James 1:2; 5:10, 11; 5:34–37—James 5:12; 6:11—James 2:15, 16; 6:19—James 5:2, 3; 6:22—James 4:4, 8; 6:34—James 4:13, 14; 7:1—James 4:11, 12; 5:9; 7:7, 8—James 1:5; 4:3; 7:16—James 3:10–13, 18; 1:21; 7:21–23—James 1:26, 27; 2:14–26; 3:13, 14; 7:24—James 1:22–25. See Mayor's *James*, pp. lxxxv–lxxxvii.

From a literary point of view, scholars generally acknowledge that James is not quoting from but alluding to the synoptic Gospels. The choice of words, the syntax, and the structure of the sentences differ, so that it is safe to say that James relies on the spoken word and conveys allusions to the written gospel.[18] On the basis of these numerous allusions to the teaching of Jesus, we venture to say that James had heard Jesus preach on many occasions and therefore had become familiar with his teachings. With "eyewitnesses and servants of the word" (Luke 1:2), James participated in receiving and delivering the message of Jesus.

If we are able to detect the direct teachings of Jesus in James's epistle, is it possible to formulate a Christology? The answer is affirmative.

1. Christology

The Epistle of James is devoid of references to the life, suffering, death, and resurrection of Jesus. Although the doctrine of the resurrection is the substratum of apostolic preaching and a basic theme in the Book of Acts, in his epistle James pays no attention to this redemptive event. He is interested in proclaiming the gospel of Christ not so much in terms of his person as in terms of the practical and ethical application of his teachings.[19]

The epistle contains only two direct references to Jesus Christ. The first one is in the address: "James, a servant of God and of the Lord Jesus Christ" (1:1). The second is in the discussion on faith, where James calls the recipients "believers in our glorious Lord Jesus Christ" (2:1).

Besides including these direct christological testimonies, James refers indirectly to Jesus by employing the term *Lord* eleven times.[20] However, I hasten to point out that in the case of a few of these references this term is equivalent to the name *God* (3:9; 5:4, 10, 11).

When James calls Jesus "Lord," he wants his readers to think of the ascended Christ. The names of God and Jesus are parallel to each other in the address (1:1); the intent is to emphasize that the exalted Lord is divine. Furthermore, James attributes divine acts to Jesus: he forgives sin (5:15), heals the sick (5:14–15), and as the Judge is standing at the door (5:9).

James furnishes still another allusion to Jesus. He tells the readers that the rich "are slandering the noble name of him to whom you belong" (2:7).[21] That noble name belongs to "our glorious Lord Jesus Christ"

---

18. Says Davids, "Collectively, these allusions argue that the author was someone saturated with the teaching of Jesus and that the work was written before its author contacted written gospel traditions." See *James*, p. 16.

19. Refer to C. E. B. Cranfield, "The Message of James," *ScotJT* 18 (1965): 182–93.

20. See 1:7; 3:9; 4:10, 15; 5:4, 7, 8, 10, 11, 14, 15.

21. Richard N. Longenecker adds that this is a "reference to blaspheming the name of Jesus." *The Christology of Early Jewish Christianity*, Studies in Biblical Theology, no. 17, 2d series (Naperville, Ill.: Allenson, 1970), p. 45.

(2:1). Note that James describes the Lord as "glorious" (in the Greek, "the Lord of glory"). This term reminds the reader of the glory of God that filled the tabernacle in the desert (see Exod. 40:35), and resembles the descriptions of Jesus that John provides in the prologue of his Gospel. John confesses, "We have seen his glory, the glory of the one and only Son, who came from the Father, full of grace and truth" (John 1:14). The expression *glory* indicates that Jesus has fulfilled the Old Testament promises that God himself would come to live with his people. In Jesus Christ, God has revealed his glory.[22]

And last, the early church understood the phrase *our glorious Lord Jesus Christ* to mean that Jesus had ascended to heaven where he reigns with God in heavenly glory.

In his epistle James discloses his Christology not directly but indirectly, and thereby seems to reveal an early stage of doctrinal development in the Christian church. If we assume that the church in the first part of the first century had no fully developed doctrine of Christ, we may conclude that the letter appears to reflect an early period in the history of the church.

2. Prayer

James, who reportedly spent much time in prayer, acquaints his readers with this subject in at least three places in his epistle. In the introductory part of his epistle, he exhorts them to ask God for wisdom (1:5–7). When he rebukes them for their sin of quarreling and fighting, he points out that they do not receive anything from God because they are asking him for goods they want to use for their personal pleasures (4:2–3). And if there is sickness or if sin has been committed, James counsels the readers to offer prayer so that the sick person may be made well and sin may be forgiven (5:14–16).

In these three passages, James instructs his readers that genuine prayer must be based on trust and faith in God. God answers prayer only when the believer asks in faith. In response to the believer's request, God generously will grant the gift of wisdom, supply man's material needs, and heal the sick. The prayer of a person who is right with God "is powerful and effective" (5:16). The example is that of Elijah, whose prayers influence the course of nature (5:17–18).

Indirectly James touches on prayer in still more places. Prayer is also praise. "With the tongue we praise our Lord and Father," writes James (3:9). Prayer is coming near to God (4:8) and humbling oneself before the Lord (4:10).

The similarity between the words of Jesus and the Epistle of James on

---

22. Consult B. B. Warfield, *The Lord of Glory* (1907; reprint ed., Grand Rapids: Zondervan, n.d.), p. 265. And refer to Franz Mussner, " 'Direkte' und 'indirekte' Christologie im Jakobusbrief," *Catholica* [Münster] 24 (1970): 111–17.

the subject *prayer* is unquestionable. Jesus teaches that prayer based on faith is able to move mountains (Matt. 17:20; 21:21; Luke 17:6). Says he, "If you believe, you will receive whatever you ask for in prayer" (Matt. 21:22). Other writers of the New Testament, among them the author of Hebrews, stress the same truth. Paul puts it rather pointedly: "Everything that does not come from faith is sin" (Rom. 14:23).

3. Faith

One of the first topics James introduces in this epistle is faith: "the testing of your faith develops perseverance" (1:3). And when a person approaches God in prayer, "he must believe and not doubt" (1:6).

Especially in the second chapter of his letter, James develops the subject *faith*. In the original Greek, this noun appears predominantly in chapter 2; that is, of the sixteen occurrences in the entire epistle,[23] thirteen are in the second chapter. In addition, the chapter has three occurrences of the verb *to believe* (2:19 [2 times], 23). This indeed is the chapter on faith in the Epistle of James.

The recipients of the letter are called "believers in our glorious Lord Jesus Christ" (2:1). The person who is materially poor is spiritually rich in faith (2:5) and heir to God's kingdom.

In the section on faith and deeds, James asserts that faith which "is not accompanied by action, is dead" (2:17, 26), for faith that is dead is no faith. Therefore, he illustrates his teaching with a reference to the historical account of Abraham offering his son Isaac on Mount Moriah. He proves that Abraham's works result from the patriarch's active faith.[24] Works, then, are an essential part of faith.

4. Law

For James, the law of God gives the believer freedom (1:25; 2:12), is summarized as "the royal law" ("Love your neighbor as yourself," 2:8), and must be kept (4:11). Concludes Peter H. Davids, "In each of these passages the validity of the law is not argued, but simply assumed."[25]

Parallels between the Epistle of James and the teaching of Jesus on the law are recognizable. The person who does what the law requires by looking intently into it, declares James, "will be blessed in what he does" (1:25). Jesus observes, "Not everyone who says to me, 'Lord, Lord,' will enter the kingdom of heaven, but only he who does the will of my Father who is in heaven" (Matt. 7:21). The person who puts Jesus' words into practice is a wise man (Matt. 7:25; and see Luke 6:47). James depicts the second part of the summary of the law—"Love your neighbor as your-

---

23. Refer to 1:3, 6; 2:1, 5, 14 (2 times), 17, 18 (3 times), 20, 22 (2 times), 24, 26; 5:15.
24. Donald Guthrie, *New Testament Theology* (Downers Grove: Inter-Varsity, 1981), p. 599.
25. Davids, *James*, p. 47. Also see his "Theological Perspectives on the Epistle of James," *JETS* 23 (1980): 102.

self"—as royal (2:8). Asked by an expert in the law to identify the greatest commandment in the law, Jesus teaches the summary:

> " 'Love the Lord your God with all your heart and with all your soul and with all your mind.' This is the first and greatest commandment. And the second is like it: 'Love your neighbor as yourself.' " [Matt. 22:37–39]

James instructs the readers not to criticize or judge a brother, for that is the same as criticizing or judging the law. "When you judge the law, you are not keeping it, but sitting in judgment on it" (4:11). The words are an echo and an expansion of those spoken by Jesus, "Do not judge, or you too will be judged. For in the same way you judge others, you will be judged" (Matt. 7:1–2).

The Epistle of James breathes the spirit of Christ in respect to the law. True, James presents not a full-fledged doctrine of law and salvation but the teaching that God "gives grace to the humble" (4:6). It is for Paul to present the church the doctrine of justification by faith and not by works.

5. Faith and Works

A comparison of Romans 4 and James 2 discloses an apparent similarity in the choice of the words *faith* and *works* and the quotation from Genesis 15:6, "Abram believed God, and it was credited to him as righteousness" (Rom. 4:3; James 2:23). What is the relationship between Paul's presentation of faith and works in Romans and that of James in his epistle?

Some commentators maintain that James wrote his epistle to criticize Paul's teaching on faith and works. Paul, they say, was misunderstood by the church because he separated the concepts *faith* and *works*. James saw a danger in the teaching Paul set forth, namely, that of faith without works. Therefore, because some Christians misunderstood the phrase *without works*, James wrote his letter to affirm the teaching that faith results in works.[26]

Other scholars are of the opinion that James wrote his epistle before Paul began his writing career.[27] That is, after the Epistle of James began to circulate in the early church, Paul wrote his letter to the Romans to present a better understanding of the significance of faith without works.

Both James and Paul develop the topic *faith and works*, each from his own perspective, and each for his own purpose.

James uses the word *faith* subjectively in the sense of trust and confidence in the Lord. This active faith gives the believer perseverance, certainty, and salvation (1:3; 2:14; 5:15). Faith is the believer's active involve-

---

26. For example, consult Dibelius, *James*, pp. 29, 178–80.
27. Refer to Robinson, *Redating the New Testament*, pp. 127–28. Robinson writes, "As a reply to Paul's position James' argument totally misses the point; for Paul never contended for faith *without* works." Also consult Theodor Zahn, *Introduction to the New Testament*, 3 vols. (Edinburgh: Clark, 1909), vol. 1, p. 143.

ment in the church and in the world. Through faith he receives wisdom (1:5), righteousness (2:23), and healing (5:15).

Paul, on the other hand, often speaks of faith objectively. Faith is the instrument by which the believer is justified before God (Rom. 3:25, 28, 30; 5:1; Gal. 2:16; Phil. 3:9). Faith is the means by which the believer takes hold of the merits of Christ. Because of these merits, man is justified before God. Justification, then, comes as a gift from God to man—a gift which he appropriates in faith.[28] Justification is God's declaration that God has restored the believer through faith to a right relationship with himself.

In his discussion of faith and works, James appears to write independently of Paul's letter to the Romans. James approaches the topic from a point of view that is more practical than theological. In effect, his approach is elementary, direct, and consequential.

Paul's discussion represents an advanced stage of the teaching relating to faith and works. Because the approach of James varies significantly from that of Paul, we conclude that he wrote his epistle independently of Paul's teaching and perhaps prior to the composition of Romans.

6. Trials and Submission

Two topics that both James and Peter pursue are those of trials and submission. This similarity raises questions. Did Peter depend on the Epistle of James when he wrote his own epistle? Did James borrow from I Peter? Or did both authors derive their material from a common source?

Before we attempt to answer these questions, we must take note of at least three facts. First, with respect to resemblances and parallels, the Epistle of James is short and I Peter elaborate. The hermeneutical rule "The shorter reading is likely to be the original" has merit, for a writer who borrows material tends to lengthen his presentation. Next, James addresses his letter exclusively to Jewish Christians; Peter writes to Gentile Christians (see I Peter 1:18; 2:10, 12; 4:3). And last, James and Peter share a common heritage of culture, training, and purpose. Undoubtedly, their intimate fellowship in Jerusalem contributed to interdependence in the writing of their respective epistles.

Numerous are the resemblances between the Epistle of James and the First Epistle of Peter.[29] Both authors allude to and quote two identical passages from the Old Testament. The first one is from Isaiah 40:6–8:

> "All men are like grass,
>   and all their glory is like the flowers of the field.

---

28. Consult Grosheide, *Jakobus*, p. 336. Also refer to Louis Berkhof, *Systematic Theology* (Grand Rapids: Eerdmans, 1953), p. 520.

29. Choosing only the resemblances that Mayor indicates as the most striking parallels, I list the following passages of I Peter 1:1—James 1:1; 1:3—James 1:18; 1:6—James 1:2; 1:12—James 1:25; 1:23—James 1:18; 2:1—James 1:18; 2:11—James 4:1; 2:12—James 3:13; 5:4—James 1:12; 5:5, 6—James 4:6, 7. Mayor, *James*, pp. cvi–cvii.

> The grass withers and the flowers fall,
> because the breath of the LORD blows on them . . . .
> The grass withers and the flowers fall,
> but the word of our God stands forever."

James alludes to this passage (1:10–11) and Peter quotes parts of it verbatim (I Peter 1:24). The second quotation is from Proverbs 10:12, "Love covers over all wrongs." Both James and Peter quote this verse (James 5:20; I Peter 4:8).

Also, we must note a few parallels in the two epistles to see how each writer unfolds a specific topic. From a look at parallels we are able to determine who gives the fuller account of that topic. Here are a few parallel verses to illustrate the themes *trials* and *submission*.

James 1:2	*I Peter 1:6*
Consider it pure joy,	In this you greatly rejoice,
my brothers, whenever you	though now for a little while
face trials of many kinds.	you may have had to suffer grief
	in all kinds of trials.

James indicates that the man who perseveres under trial will receive the crown of life (1:12). Peter exhorts his readers not to be surprised when they endure painful suffering (4:12) and not to be ashamed when they suffer as a Christian (4:16).

James 4:6–7, 10	*I Peter 5:5–6*
	Young men, in the same way
	be submissive to those who
Scripture says:	are older . . . because,
"God opposes the proud	"God opposes the proud
but gives grace to the humble."	but gives grace to the humble."
Submit yourselves, then	
to God. . . . Humble yourselves	Humble yourselves, therefore,
before the Lord,	under God's mighty hand,
and he will lift you up.	that he may lift you up
	in due time.

Whereas James exhorts, "Resist the devil, and he will flee from you" (4:7), Peter is expansive in his exhortation and in his description of the devil. He admonishes the readers to "be self-controlled and alert." He explains his admonition by saying, "Your enemy the devil prowls around like a roaring lion looking for someone to devour." And last, he tells the believer to "resist [the devil], standing firm in the faith" (I Peter 5:8–9).

These two examples illustrate the conciseness of James's style and the expansiveness of Peter's. Although this observation alone by itself is nothing more than the proverbial straw in the wind, it seems to favor the theory that the Epistle of James was written before the letter of Peter. An early date for this epistle is more likely than one that is late.

17

F. When and Where Was the Epistle Written?

1. Date

James wrote his epistle after he became the leader of the church in Jerusalem in A.D. 44 and before he met a martyr's death in A.D. 62.

The two terminal dates for determining the time when the Epistle of James was written can be verified. We begin with the earliest possible date on which the epistle could have been written. The Jewish Christians who were driven from Jerusalem because of the persecution that resulted from the death of Stephen were scattered (Acts 8:1). They "traveled as far as Phoenicia, Cyprus, and Antioch" (Acts 11:19). This probably happened during the early part of the fifth decade. Also in those years, James assumed prominence in the church at Jerusalem. When Peter was released from prison in A.D. 44 (the year King Herod Agrippa I died [Acts 12:23]), James took Peter's place as head of the church.

In his letter, James addresses "the twelve tribes scattered among the nations" (1:1). He fulfills his role as pastor even toward former members now living in dispersion. He writes his letter to all the Christians in dispersion, because from his point of view at that period in the history of the church, there were no Gentile Christians.[30] The last possible date for the composition of the Epistle of James is A.D. 62, the year of James's death. That date can be ascertained because Festus had died and his successor Albinus was on his way to Judea to assume his role as governor.[31]

The epistle itself lacks references to time or to specific circumstances that aid the reader in establishing a date. If we survey the content of James's epistle and analyze the indirect references to the culture and conditions of the age in which the author wrote, we are able to determine the approximate date when the letter was composed.

James gives no indication of a division between Jewish Christians and Jews, which is rather pronounced in the Gospels and the Epistles. For instance, Matthew records the words of Jesus that admonish the believer not to be like the hypocrites who "love to pray standing in the synagogues" (6:5). And John, in his Gospel, repeatedly refers to the opposition as "the Jews," even though Jesus and the disciples themselves were Jews. Paul also faced organized resistance to the message of Christ, not so much from Gentiles as from Jews.

The Epistle of James, however, mirrors a time of relative tranquility within the Jewish community in the fourth and fifth decades of the first

---

30. Zahn in his *Introduction to the New Testament*, vol. 1, p. 77, observes, "It is to be remembered, however, that there was a time when . . . the believing Israel constituted the entire Church."

31. Refer to Eusebius *Ecclesiastical History* 2. 23. 21; Josephus *Antiquities* 20 (LCL, 197–203). F. F. Bruce states that "Festus governed from 59 until his death in 61." See his *Commentary on the Book of Acts*, New International Commentary on the New Testament series (Grand Rapids: Eerdmans, 1960), p. 474.

century. The recipients of his epistle attend the worship services in their local synagogue (2:2; see the Greek). To be sure, these recipients endured economic hardship and religious harassment from people who slandered the noble name of Jesus (2:7). They were oppressed, not because they were Jews, but because they were poor.[32]

Whereas Paul and Peter in their epistles make a distinction between Gentile Christians and Jewish Christians, James addresses only Christians who belonged to the twelve tribes (1:1) and who called Abraham their ancestor (2:21). Because nothing in the Epistle of James hints at the Jewish-Gentile controversy that precipitated the general meeting of apostles and elders at Jerusalem (Acts 15), the letter probably was composed before that council meeting. Scholars believe the council met in A.D. 49.

Moreover, the epistle reflects a time in which the church seems to be in its initial stages of development. James says little about the organization of the church. True, the term *elders* occurs in connection with the healing of the sick (5:14). But James fails to note or comment on the ruling and teaching ministry of the elders. Even though he mentions teachers in relation to restraining the tongue (3:1), he does not link them to a ministry in the church. He does not allude to a caring ministry of the deacons to the poor. And the sacraments of the Lord's Supper and baptism are not discussed. These omissions seem to reflect an initial stage of a developing church. Although this is an argument from silence, the cumulative evidence points in the direction of a date in the middle of the fifth decade. A date that falls halfway between the time James succeeded Peter as leader in the Jerusalem church and the convening of the council at Jerusalem seems judicious.

2. Place

The author of the epistle provides no information about his domicile, yet he alludes to climatic conditions that pertain to Israel. His remark that the farmer patiently waits "for the autumn and spring rains" (5:7) fits only the Palestinian region. Countries to the south and east of Israel, or even Syria to the north, do not experience the recurring cycle of autumn and spring rains peculiar to Israel. James also notes "the scorching heat" (1:11) that prevails in his native land, and acquaints the reader with the produce of the land: figs and olives (3:12).

G. What Is the History of the Epistle?

For more than a century and a half after it was written, the Epistle of James was not circulated and failed to gain publicity. Perhaps because it was addressed to a limited group of Jewish Christians, the letter remained

---

32. Consult Robinson, *Redating the New Testament*, p. 121.

unnoticed in the Gentile Christian church.[33] The fact that James was not an apostle resulted in the neglect the church displayed in respect to his letter. The church applied the rule that unless a book was apostolic it could not be canonical.

The Muratorian Canon, which presumably dates from A.D. 175, fails to list the Epistle of James. Writers in the second century vaguely allude to it. Clement of Alexandria reportedly commented on the epistle about A.D. 220, even though there are no quotes from it in his extant writings.[34] Also in the first decades of the third century, Origen quotes the Epistle of James in his commentary on the Gospel of John (John 19:6). Origen refers to the epistle as Scripture, and mentions James by name.

One hundred years afterward, historian Eusebius reports that the Epistle of James was used publicly in the churches. Some people at the time considered it a spurious document and the historian himself places it in the category of disputed books. Nevertheless, Eusebius refers to this epistle as Scripture and ascribes it to "the holy apostle," whom he repeatedly calls the Lord's brother.[35] After describing the martyrdom of James, he says,

> Such is the story of James, whose [epistle] is said to be the first of the Epistles called Catholic. It is to be observed that its authenticity is denied, since few of the ancients quote it, as is also the case with the Epistle called Jude's, which is itself one of the seven called Catholic; nevertheless we know that these letters have been used publicly with the rest in most churches.

The Council of Carthage in A.D. 397 officially recognized the Epistle of James as canonical. In A.D. 412, the church in Syria included it with I Peter and I John in the authorized version known as the Syriac Peshitta. Except for the Syrian church, the East acknowledged the epistle as canonical sooner than the West. Influential leaders, including Jerome, were instrumental in acquainting the church in the West with the Epistle of James.

During the time of the Reformation, Erasmus voiced doubts that James, the brother of Jesus, wrote the epistle. He thought that James, because of his Jewish background, could not have written Greek of the quality the epistle exhibits. Martin Luther added his own reservations by observing that the epistle teaches little about Christ, is not apostolic, stresses law instead of gospel, and opposes Paul on the doctrine of faith

---

33. Mayor, in *James,* p. lxix, concludes, "The Epistle was probably written at Jerusalem and addressed to the Jews of the Eastern Dispersion; it did not profess to be written by an Apostle or to be addressed to Gentile churches, and it seemed to contradict the teaching of the great Apostle to the Gentiles."

34. Consult Eusebius *Ecclesiastical History* 6. 14. Also see Alfred Wikenhauser, *New Testament Introduction* (New York: Herder and Herder, 1963), p. 474.

35. Eusebius *Ecclesiastical History* 2. 23.

1

Perseverance

1:1–27

Outline

1 1 James, a servant of God and of the Lord Jesus Christ,
To the twelve tribes scattered among the nations:
Greetings.

A. Greetings
1:1

The Epistle of James belongs to the category of biblical writings called general Epistles—Hebrews, James, I Peter, II Peter, I John, II John, III John, and Jude. Some of these epistles, however, lack an address; in the case of Hebrews and I John, the name of the author is also missing. James gives us his name, the names of the addressees, and his greeting. Compared with the other canonical letters, the Epistle of James, too, appears to be a genuine epistle.

1. James, a servant of God and of the Lord Jesus Christ, To the twelve tribes scattered among the nations: Greetings.

The heading of the epistle varies from "The General Epistle of James" (KJV, RV) to "The Letter of James" (RSV and other translations) to "James" (NIV). Scholars maintain that the headings of New Testament books were added later, presumably in the second century.

Manuscript evidence for the heading of James is varied. For example, some manuscripts (P, 33, 1739, and others) have this superscription: "The General Epistle of James the Apostle." Others are even more elaborate: "The General Epistle of the Holy Apostle James." And still others simply say "The Epistle of James."

The early church, especially in the East (Egypt), applied the following general rule: "A book has to be apostolic to be canonical." Was James an apostle? Actually, he did not meet the requirements which were applied to Joseph Barsabbas and Matthias (Acts 1:23). Apostles had to be disciples of Jesus from the time of his baptism to the day of his ascension. But James had not believed in Jesus (John 7:5) until Jesus appeared to him in the forty-day period between Jesus' resurrection and ascension (I Cor. 15:7).

Then, some scribes in earlier centuries of the Christian era tried to avoid the problem of the canonicity of James's epistle. They called James an apostle in the heading of the epistle. But headings, merely the work of man, are not inspired. The church at the local level accepted the epistle as canonical, and in time church councils acknowledged its canonicity.

Is the letter of James an epistle? The church has always regarded it as an epistle. In other words, the voice of tradition speaks forcefully in its favor. The address carries the name and status of the writer. Also, the author addresses the recipients by identifying them as "the twelve tribes scattered among the nations." The introduction to the epistle, then, is the equivalent of an envelope that shows the names and addresses of sender and recipients. Questioning whether the document is an epistle, however, is valid. We would expect, for instance, that the writer would say something about himself in the epistle. The last chapter ends somewhat abruptly without the customary greetings. In fact, disregarding the introductory verse (1:1), the reader finds the beginning of the letter as abrupt as its ending. Yet this writing bears the marks of a letter because of the direct manner of address.[1] The author speaks to his hearers and readers. For example, he uses the imperative mood fifty-four times. He has a definite group of people in mind when he writes his letter. We note the following points:

a. "James." The writer identifies himself by the common name *James*. (In the Greek, it is "Jakobos.") The frequent appearance of this name in the New Testament attests to popular use. James, the brother of John, son of Zebedee, was killed (Acts 12:1–2). James, the son of Alphaeus (Matt. 10:3 and parallels), James the father of the apostle Jude (not Iscariot [Acts 1:13]), and "James the younger" (Mark 15:40) are virtually unknown. Jude mentions that he is the brother of James (Jude 1), and last there is James, the brother of Jesus.

Scholars agree that the writer of the epistle is the brother of Jesus (Matt. 13:55). James became the leader of the mother church in Jerusalem after the departure of Peter (Acts 12:17), was one of the spokesmen at the Council of Jerusalem (Acts 15:13–21), and was a "pillar" to whom Paul reported his missionary experience (Gal. 2:2, 9; Acts 21:18–19).

James identifies himself as "a servant of God and of the Lord Jesus Christ." This designation reminds us of Jesus' words: "The Son of Man did not come to be served, but to serve" (Matt. 20:28).[2] James could have said that he was the Lord's brother. Instead he uses the term *servant* in all humility, even though he occupies a position of authority in the church.[3] James is a willing and obedient servant of God and of the Lord Jesus Christ. Actually, he is a slave, not of necessity and force but by choice. He acknowledges Jesus as Lord of his life.

---

1. Peter H. Davids calls the letter "a literary epistle, i.e., a tract intended for publication, not an actual letter, e.g., the epistles of Paul to specific churches." *The Epistle of James: A Commentary on the Greek Text,* New International Greek Testament Commentary series (Grand Rapids: Eerdmans, 1982), p. 24.

2. Klaus Hess, *NIDNTT,* vol. 3, p. 546; Rudolf Tuente, *NIDNTT,* vol. 3, p. 598.

3. Paul, Peter, and Jude also use the expression *servant* in the introductions to their respective epistles. See Rom. 1:1; Gal. 1:10; Phil. 1:1; Titus 1:1; II Peter 1:1; Jude 1.

b. "Twelve tribes." That the letter of James is the most Jewish of all the New Testament epistles becomes evident already in the address: "To the twelve tribes scattered among the nations." James addresses his epistle to people of Jewish descent who live outside of Israel "among the nations." They are the Jews in dispersion (John 7:35).

After the deportation of the ten tribes from Israel to Assyria (II Kings 17:6) and the exile of the two tribes to Babylon (II Kings 25:11), and at times afterward, thousands of Jews lived outside the borders of their homeland. Luke enumerates all of the places in the first-century world where "God-fearing Jews from every nation" resided (Acts 2:5, 9–11). These devout Jews came to Jerusalem for the Feast of Pentecost, heard the gospel of Jesus Christ, became converts, and returned to their places of residence. Those who stayed in Jerusalem were persecuted and driven away after the death of Stephen (Acts 8:1; 11:19).

James addresses the Jewish Christians who live in places other than Jerusalem. Also, Peter sends his first epistle "to God's elect, strangers in the world, *scattered* throughout Pontus, Galatia, Cappadocia, Asia and Bithynia" (I Peter 1:1; italics added). James, however, is more general. He writes to Jewish believers living in dispersion.[4] We have no indication that he specifically refers to Gentile Christians anywhere in his epistle. Nevertheless, the message of his letter speaks to them, too.

c. "Greetings." Both the address to spiritual Israel in dispersion and the simple greeting seem to point to an early stage in the development of the church. As far as scholars are able to determine, the epistle may be the oldest of the twenty-seven New Testament books. Perhaps James wrote the epistle before the Council of Jerusalem met in A.D. 49. Apparently, James wrote the letter that the council sent to the Gentile believers in Antioch, Syria, and Cilicia; he began that letter with the same succinct salutation: "Greetings" (Acts 15:23). The similarity is undeniable. James employs the Greek manner of saluting the readers, for Claudius Lysias writes the same word in his letter to Governor Felix (Acts 23:26).[5]

Practical Considerations in 1:1

If anyone knew Jesus well, James would probably be the one. James and Jesus grew up together in the same family; they ate together, played together, and worked together. After his resurrection, Jesus appeared to James, who at the time

---

4. Sophie Laws cautiously states, "If the main intention of the address is to define the community theologically in its Christian character, the question whether its members are of Jewish origin remains undecided." See her *Commentary on the Epistle of James*, Harper's New Testament Commentaries (San Francisco: Harper and Row, 1980), p. 48.
5. Paul's greetings reflect a standard formula of the early church: "Grace and peace to you from God our Father and from the Lord Jesus Christ" (e.g., Rom. 1:7). Peter, John, and Jude in their respective epistles address their readers with the same formula (with minor variations).

was alone (I Cor. 15:7). If there was one person who could rightfully call Jesus "my brother," it was James.

James refrains from boasting. In all humility he calls himself "a servant of God and of the Lord Jesus Christ." Jesus is not ashamed to call us his brothers and sisters (Heb. 2:11). We, however, do well to follow the example of James and call ourselves servants of God and of our Lord Jesus Christ.

Greek Words, Phrases, and Constructions in 1:1

Ἰάκωβος—this is the Hellenized form of the Old Testament name Ἰακώβ.

τῇ διασπορᾷ—from the compound verb διασπείρω (I scatter), this noun implies either that the readers were being scattered (a scattering) or that they had been scattered (a dispersion).

χαίρειν—the present active infinitive occurs three times in the New Testament at the opening of a letter (Acts 15:23; 23:26; James 1:1) and means "greetings." The form λέγει needs to be supplied; that is, James says, "Greetings."[6] The infinitive is imperatival.

---

2 Consider it pure joy, my brothers, whenever you face trials of many kinds, 3 because you know that the testing of your faith develops perseverance. 4 Perseverance must finish its work so that you may be mature and complete, not lacking anything. 5 If any of you lacks wisdom, he should ask God, who gives generously to all without finding fault, and it will be given to him. 6 But when he asks, he must believe and not doubt, because he who doubts is like a wave of the sea, blown and tossed by the wind. 7 That man should not think he will receive anything from the Lord; 8 he is a double-minded man, unstable in all he does.

9 The brother in humble circumstances ought to take pride in his high position. 10 But the one who is rich should take pride in his low position, because he will pass away like a wild flower. 11 For the sun rises with scorching heat and withers the plant; its blossom falls and its beauty is destroyed. In the same way, the rich man will fade away even while he goes about his business.

B. Trials
1:2–11

1. Testing of Faith
1:2–4

Pressures in our technological age are too great for many people. They cannot cope with the difficulties they meet from day to day. They seek to escape from the treadmill of trying incidents that confront them. Escape in many instances is impossible, especially when people cannot control these incidents. Thus the sacred writer, addressing persecuted Jewish Christians, reaches out to all people throughout the centuries. He says,

---

6. Erich Beyreuther and Günter Finkenrath, *NIDNTT*, vol. 2, p. 358. Also consult Hans Conzelmann, *TDNT*, vol. 9, p. 367; and see A. T. Robertson, *A Grammar of the Greek New Testament in the Light of Historical Research* (Nashville: Broadman, 1934), p. 394.

2. Consider it pure joy, my brothers, whenever you face trials of many kinds, 3. because you know that the testing of your faith develops perseverance.

James writes his epistle to Jewish Christians who have been driven from their homes and possessions. He addresses people who suffer because they are exploited by the rich, dragged into court, and slandered for believing in the noble name of Jesus (2:6–7). To these people James directs a pastoral letter in which his first admonition is to rejoice.

a. "Consider it pure joy." What a strange way of addressing the recipients of this letter! James lives safely and securely in Jerusalem, and he addresses Jewish Christians who have lost house and home because of hardship and persecution. James appears to be out of touch with reality. He seems to be ignorant of the daily trials the people face. And some may say that he is a typical pastor who knows how to make sermons but is unaware of the suffering his people experience on a day-to-day basis.

James, however, is not unaware of the trials his people face. He himself had witnessed the death of Stephen, the persecution that followed, and the scattering of the Jerusalem church throughout Judea and Samaria (Acts 8:1). He knows his task as a pastor. He speaks words of encouragement. He exhorts the people to rejoice. In this respect he finds support in the apostolic admonitions of Paul and Peter:

> Not only so, but we also rejoice in our sufferings, because we know that suffering produces perseverance. [Rom. 5:3]

> In this you greatly rejoice, though now for a little while you may have had to suffer grief in all kinds of trials. [I Peter 1:6]

James repeats the thought Jesus expresses in the last beatitude: "Blessed are you when people insult you, persecute you and falsely say all kinds of evil against you because of me. Rejoice and be glad, because great is your reward in heaven" (Matt. 5:11–12; and see Luke 6:22–23). Therefore, James tells the readers, "Do not become embittered because of adversities, but rather rejoice."

b. "My brothers." To make his appeal more intimate and at the same time direct, the author addresses his readers as his "brothers." This expression places the writer on the same level as that of the readers. He is one of them and one with them. Because of the repeated occurrence of this address, the letter is most personal (1:2, 16, 19; 2:1, 5, 14; 3:1, 10, 12; 4:11; 5:7, 9, 10, 12, 19).

What is the meaning of the term *brothers?* In a nationalistic sense, all Jews are brothers. That was true in ancient times (Exod. 2:11; Deut. 15:3; Matt. 5:47; Acts 13:26) and is still true today.[7] But this concept is not what

---

7. James Hardy Ropes, *A Critical and Exegetical Commentary on the Epistle of James*, International Critical Commentary series (1916; reprint ed., Edinburgh: Clark, 1961), p. 131. Also consult Simon J. Kistemaker, *The Parables of Jesus* (Grand Rapids: Baker, 1980), p. 167, n. 3: "When a Jewish soldier loses his life in armed conflict, the nation mourns because a *brother* has died."

the author has in mind. He addresses Jewish Christians, for *they* are his spiritual brothers.[8] In New Testament times, as well as today in many Christian circles, the word *brother* refers to a fellow believer.

c. "Trials of many kinds." Trying circumstances are the adversities God uses to test the faith of the believer. These trials can come in a variety of ways and forms. No believer has received the guarantee that he will live a trouble-free and peaceful life. Everyone experiences difficulties, problems, and pains of one kind or another. No one can escape them, because man does not control the circumstances that cause the difficulties.

James says, in effect, that the Christian literally falls into a trying situation. That is, God places the believer, sometimes rather suddenly, in a predicament that is designed to test his faith in God. The believer may not even realize that he has stumbled into a test. Quite often at a later time the believer begins to understand why God tested him.[9] When his eyes are opened, he sees the goodness and the grace of God that fill him with joy and happiness. Therefore, James exhorts his readers to consider the trials causes for pure joy. The Christian ought to see the hand of God in all of life. Wrote William Cowper:

> God moves in a mysterious way
> His wonders to perform;
> He plants his footsteps in the sea,
> And rides upon the storm.
>
> Deep in unfathomable mines
> Of never failing skill,
> He treasures up his bright designs
> And works his sovereign will.

d. "Testing of . . . faith." Why should the Christian be filled with pure joy every time God tests him? Says James, "Because you know that the testing of your faith develops perseverance." The verb *know* is the key word. The believer knows that the trials he endures do not come to him by chance. He believes that everything comes to him by the hand of God. As Zacharius Ursinus confesses in a sixteenth-century catechism:

> All things, in fact, come to us
> not by chance,
> but from his fatherly hand.[10]

---

8. "The employment of the name *brother* to designate the members of the Christian communities is illustrated by the similar use, made known to us by the Papyra." See Adolf Deissmann, *Bible Studies,* trans. Alexander Grieve (1923; reprint ed., Winona Lake, Ind.: Alpha, 1979), pp. 87–88.

9. Walter Schneider and Colin Brown, *NIDNTT,* vol. 3, p. 801.

10. In answering question 27 (on providence) of the Heidelberg Catechism, Ursinus, assisted by Caspar Olevianus, describes God's providence by saying that it includes "the almighty and ever present power of God by which he upholds, as with his hand, heaven and earth and all creatures . . .—all things, in fact, come to us, not by chance, but from his fatherly hand."

God stands behind every trial and test. He wants us to know this by experience, so that we not only see his hand but also feel it. We place our hand in the hand of God. Then, in every adversity that we face, we keep our trust in our heavenly Father, for we know that he sends us these trials to test our faith. We believe that he is in complete control of every situation. And God gives us exactly what we need: joys and sorrows, trials and triumphs. An Arabic proverb succinctly states, "Sunshine alone creates deserts." Consider it pure joy when dark clouds gather above your head; they will give you showers of blessings. These showers cause your life of faith to develop and grow.

e. "Perseverance." "The testing of your faith develops perseverance," says James. The term *testing* is a further explanation of the expression *trials* in the preceding verse ("whenever you face trials of many kinds"). We note a parallel between the Epistle of James and the First Epistle of Peter at this point. Peter reminds his readers that they "had to suffer grief in all kinds of trials." He continues, "These have come so that your faith— of greater worth than gold, which perishes even though refined by fire— may be proved genuine" (I Peter 1:6–7).

The believer experiences a testing in the sense of a refining process. That is, his faith is being refined, much the same as gold is subjected to the smelter's fire (Prov. 27:21). As the goldsmith removes impurities that are foreign to the metal, so God purifies the believer's faith from sin. Gold, however, is an inanimate quantity that is and remains passive through the refining process. Man's faith can never be passive. It is active. Faith, as James points out in his epistle, must be accompanied by action; otherwise it is dead (2:17).

The verb *develop* in the Greek actually conveys the meaning *to work something out completely*. For example, Paul uses the same verb in his exhortation to the Philippians: "Continue to work out your salvation with fear and trembling" (2:12). The testing of your faith continues to work out perseverance, writes James.

Perseverance is a quality in man that demands admiration. "Positively, steadfastness, constancy and perseverance are among the noblest of manly virtues."[11] This quality, exemplified by Job, has nothing in common with resignation. Some people think that, because they are unable to avoid trying circumstances, they should resign themselves to them. They adopt the slogan *Whatever will be, will be.* But whereas resignation is passive, perseverance is active. Resignation results in defeat; perseverance, in triumph. The Christian perseveres by looking to Jesus, the author and perfecter of his faith (Heb. 12:2; also see Rom. 5:3–5).

The believer trusts in God for help, aid, strength, and comfort. He knows that God always responds to faith and provides the means to sus-

---

11. Ulrich Falkenroth and Colin Brown, *NIDNTT*, vol. 2, p. 772. Also consult Friedrich Hauck, *TDNT*, vol. 4, p. 588.

tain the period of testing. The believer who possesses the virtue of steadfastness clings to God in faith, persists in doing God's will, and cannot be
diverted from his avowed purpose to serve his God.

**4. Perseverance must finish its work so that you may be mature and
complete, not lacking anything.**

James repeats the noun *perseverance* to demonstrate that this concept is important to the message of the epistle. By repeating the term, James alludes to
the teaching of Jesus, who on two different occasions taught his disciples,
"But he who stands firm to the end will be saved" (Matt. 10:22; 24:13).

We cannot hasten perseverance. It needs time. For example, a patient
receives the encouraging news from his physician that his broken leg is
healing satisfactorily. Daily the doctor visits the patient and each time tells
him virtually the same thing. The patient realizes that he must obey
orders not to put pressure on the injured leg, even though it is supported
by a cast. The healing process must run its normal course. Should the
patient abruptly end this process, the results would be disastrous. Paul
asked the Lord to remove the thorn in his flesh. "Three times I pleaded
with the Lord to take it away from me," writes Paul. "But he said to me,
'My grace is sufficient for you, for my power is made perfect in weakness' " (II Cor. 12:8–9). Note the term *perfect*, for James uses the same
word. "Let patience [perseverance] have her perfect work" (KJV). That is,
do not interfere with God's plan for your life. Persevere in your trials, so
that the work God has begun in you may be brought to completion. As
David prayed in one of his psalms,

> The Lord will fulfill his purpose for me;
>   your love, O LORD, endures forever—
>   do not abandon the works of your hands. [Ps. 138:8]

Parallelism is one of the Semitic features in the Epistle of James. Note
that verse 4 repeats the thought of the preceding verse and thus explains
its meaning.[12] Here is the parallel:

> The testing of your faith completely works out the virtue of persever-
> ance.

> Let perseverance work out its course completely.

Just as a fruitproducing plant must be allowed to finish its complete
growing period, so perseverance must be given its full term.

a. "Mature and complete." James has a penchant for linking words or
concepts, preferably by repeating the same term. A literal translation
illustrates this: "And let endurance have its perfect result, that you may be
perfect and complete, lacking in nothing" (NASB).

---

12. R. C. H. Lenski, *The Interpretation of the Epistle to the Hebrews and of the Epistle of James*
(Columbus: Wartburg, 1946), p. 526.

What does "perfect" mean? Certainly it does not mean "without sin." In 3:2 James writes, "We all stumble in many ways. If anyone is never at fault in what he says, he is a perfect man, able to keep his whole body in check." James intends to convey the concept of wholeness, that is, "not lagging behind in any point."[13] Addressing the Philippians, Paul also uses the expression *perfect*. The New International Version translates it "mature": "All of us who are mature should take such a view of things" (Phil. 3:15). With respect to the readers of Paul's and James's letters, the term *perfect* means "mature."

A synonym of "mature" is the word *complete*. In the name of Jesus, Peter healed the lame man who daily sat begging at Solomon's Colonnade. Luke writes that this beggar was given *complete* healing (Acts 3:16). The crippled man's feet and ankles became strong so that he functioned as a complete human being without handicap.

b. "Not lacking anything." The phrase *not lacking anything* is synonymous with the preceding term *complete,* which expresses the concept that all parts are functioning. Although both terms state the same concept, the first does so positively; the second, negatively. If, then, we have received all the necessary parts that make us mature and complete and if God has given us all things so that we lack nothing, we should be able to endure the trials God is giving us. And because God has fully equipped us, we are able to persevere in faith.

Practical Considerations in 1:2–4

Verse 2

Suppose the house burns down or the medical analysis reveals terminal cancer. Should a Christian shout, "Praise the Lord!" when calamity strikes? Christians meet frustrations, difficulties, and adversities. They often stumble upon circumstances. Instead of praising God, many Christians have become cynical, skeptical, and even depressed because of these trials. To them and to all believers, James declares: Consider it pure joy when God tests your faith. Remember Job, who triumphed in faith and received God's richest blessings.

Verse 3

A person who is accepted by the admission office of a college or university can say, "I am a student." But until that person takes tests and examinations, no one can actually affirm that he is a student worthy of that name. The only way to determine the worth of a student's work is to see his performance on his examination. Dispensing with examinations would hinder the professors and the school administration in determining the student's ability.

---

13. Reinier Schippers, *NIDNTT,* vol. 2, p. 63. Says Donald W. Burdick, "The statement that 'perseverance must finish its work' indicates progress and development, the result of which may well be described as maturity." *James,* vol. 12, the *Expositor's Bible Commentary,* ed. Frank E. Gaebelein, 12 vols. (Grand Rapids: Eerdmans, 1981), p. 168.

Greek Words, Phrases, and Constructions in 1:2–4

Verse 2

πᾶσαν χαράν—the noun χαράν is an allusion to the infinitive χαίρειν of the preceding verse. The modifying adjective πᾶσαν conveys the meaning *full* or *pure*.

ἡγήσασθε—as an aorist middle imperative of ἡγέομαι (I lead, guide; think, consider), the verb denotes "deliberate and careful judgment."[14]

πειρασμοῖς—the author displays choice alliteration in the phrase πειρασμοῖς περιπέσητε ποικίλοις. The noun derives from πειράζω (I try, test; tempt). It refers to trials that come to man from the outside. Temptations affect man's inner being (see James 1:13–15).

περιπέσητε—the second person plural second aorist active subjunctive from the compound περιπίπτω (I fall in with and am surrounded by [trials]; consult Luke 10:30 and I Clem. 51:2).

Verse 3

γινώσκοντες—the present active participle from γινώσκω (I know) expresses cause and provides the evidence for the exhortation of the main verb in verse 2. Moreover, the verb γινώσκω refers to experiential knowledge, while its synonym οἶδα connotes innate knowledge (e.g., 3:1).

τὸ δοκίμιον—this noun from δοκιμάζω (I test, try, approve) is equivalent to the articular present infinitive τὸ δοκιμάζειν and suggests and action or a process.[15]

κατεργάζεται—as a deponent middle verb in the present tense, the form is compound with a perfective (or intensive) meaning.

ὑπομονήν—this noun occurs thirty-two times in the New Testament, sixteen of which appear in Paul's epistles and three in the Epistle of James (1:3, 4; 5:11).

Verse 4

ὁλόκληροι—although this adjective appears only twice in the New Testament (I Thess. 5:23; James 1:4), its meaning is clear. The compound adjective derives from the adjective ὅλος (whole) and the noun κλῆρος (lot). That is, everything the believer needs has fallen to him by lot. Thus he is complete in every respect. Writes Peter H. Davids, "That is, perfection is not just a maturing of character, but a rounding out as more and more 'parts' of the righteous character are added."[16]

λειπόμενοι—this is the present passive participle of λείπω (I leave), not the middle. With the prepositional phrase ἐν μηδενί, it means "lacking."

---

2. Asking for Wisdom
1:5–8

Characteristically, James introduces a topic rather briefly and then returns to it later. In this particular section, he speaks about the need for

---

14. Thayer, p. 276.

15. C. F. D. Moule, *An Idiom-Book of New Testament Greek*, 2d ed. (Cambridge: At the University Press, 1960), p. 96. And see Robert Hanna, *A Grammatical Aid to the Greek New Testament* (Grand Rapids: Baker, 1983), p. 416.

16. Davids, *James*, p. 70.

wisdom; in chapter 3 he delineates two kinds of wisdom—one from heaven and the other from earth.

5. If any of you lacks wisdom, he should ask God, who gives generously to all without finding fault, and it will be given to him.

James demonstrates the art of writing by linking key words and phrases. In verse 3 he stresses the word *perseverance;* he puts it last in the sentence to give it emphasis. In verse 4, "perseverance" is the first expression he uses. The last phrase in verse 4 is "not lacking anything"; the first clause of the next phrase repeats this verb, "If any of you lacks wisdom." The writer knows how to communicate effectively in simple, direct prose.

Note these points:

a. *Need.* The clause *if any of you lacks wisdom* is the first part of a factual statement in a conditional sentence. The author is saying to the reader: "I know you will not admit it, but you need wisdom." James tackles a delicate problem, for no person wants to hear that he is stupid, that he makes mistakes, and that he needs help. By nature man is independent. He wants to solve his own problems and make his own decisions. Eighteenth-century German theologian John Albert Bengel put it rather succinctly: "Patience is more in the power of a good man than wisdom; the former is to be exercised, the latter is to be asked for."[17] Man has to overcome pride to admit that he needs wisdom. But wisdom is not something he possesses. Wisdom belongs to God, for it is his divine virtue. Anyone who admits the need for wisdom must go to God and ask him. James appeals to the individual reader and hearer. He writes, "If *any* of you lacks wisdom" (italics added). This approach is tactful, for he could have said, "Everyone lacks wisdom." But by saying "any of you," James gives the reader a chance to examine himself, to come to the conclusion that he needs wisdom, and to follow James's advice to ask God.

b. *Request.* The believer must ask God for wisdom. James implies that God is the source of wisdom. It belongs to him.[18]

What is wisdom? Both the Old and the New Testaments seek to explain this term. Solomon expresses it in typical Hebraic parallelism. Says he, "For the LORD gives wisdom, and from his mouth come knowledge and understanding" (Prov. 2:6). Solomon equates wisdom with knowledge and understanding.

Also, the New Testament states that the Christian receives wisdom and that knowledge comes from God (see, for instance, I Cor. 1:30).[19] True, we make a distinction between wisdom and knowledge when we say that knowledge devoid of wisdom is of little value. Observes Donald Guthrie,

---

17. John Albert Bengel, *Gnomon of the New Testament,* ed. Andrew R. Fausset, 5 vols., 7th ed. (Edinburgh: T. and T. Clark, 1877), vol. 5, p. 5.

18. Spiros Zodhiates observes that wisdom "among the Jews was primarily recognized as an attribute of God, and later became identified with the Spirit of God." *The Epistle of James and the Life of Faith,* vol. 4, *The Behavior of Belief* (Grand Rapids: Eerdmans, 1966), p. 33.

19. Jürgen Goetzmann, *NIDNTT,* vol. 3, p. 1032.

"If wisdom is the right use of knowledge, perfect wisdom presupposes perfect knowledge."[20] To become mature and complete, the believer must go to God for wisdom. God is willing to impart wisdom to anyone who asks humbly. God's storehouse of wisdom is infinite, and he will give this gift "generously to all without finding fault."

c. *Gift*. God is not partial. He gives to everyone, no matter who he is, because God wants to give. Giving is a characteristic of God. He keeps on giving. Every time someone comes to him with a request, he opens his treasury and freely distributes wisdom. Just as the sun continues to give light, so God keeps on giving wisdom. We cannot imagine a sun that fails to give light; much less can we think of God failing to give wisdom. God's gift is free, without interest, and without the request to pay it back. It is gratis.

Moreover, God gives "without finding fault." When we ask God for wisdom, we need not be afraid that he will express displeasure or will utter reproach. When we come to him in childlike faith, he will never send us away empty. We have the assurance that when we ask for wisdom, it "will be given" to us. God never fails the one who asks in faith.

6. But when he asks, he must believe and not doubt, because he who doubts is like a wave of the sea, blown and tossed by the wind.

Once again James repeats key words. Note the verb *to ask* in verses 5 and 6, and the verb *to doubt* in the successive clauses of verse 6. Moreover, in verse 6 the writer brings out contrast which he embellishes with an illustration.

a. *Contrast*. First, by implication James teaches that God desires sincerity of heart. God gives generously without reservation; therefore he expects the believer to come to him in prayer without reservation. A motto of the sixteenth-century Genevan reformer John Calvin was, "I offer my heart to you, O Lord, promptly and sincerely." So God wants the believer to request wisdom with sincerity and trust. To be sure, God does not want the contrast of faith and doubt in man's heart.

Next, faith and doubt cannot reside in man at the same time. When man believes, he does not doubt. And when he is in doubt, he lacks faith. The contrast, then, is evident in the instability man reveals: today he believes; tomorrow he doubts. The writer of Hebrews in his chapter on faith simply states, "And without faith it is impossible to please God, because anyone who comes to him must believe that he exists and that he rewards those who earnestly seek him" (Heb. 11:6).

Last, when Jesus caused the fig tree to wither quickly and his disciples asked him about this, he replied: "I tell you the truth, if you have faith and do not doubt, not only can you do what was done to the fig tree, but also you can say to this mountain, 'Go throw yourself into the sea,' and it will be done. If you believe, you will receive whatever you ask for in

---

20. Donald Guthrie, *New Testament Theology* (Downers Grove: Inter-Varsity, 1981), p. 95.

prayer" (Matt. 21:21–22). Faith, therefore, is able to move mountains by the power God gives the person who puts his full trust in God.

When man prays to God with a heart filled with doubt, God does not answer him. When he expresses doubt in God's ability to help, man indicates that he wants to be independent of God. Without divine wisdom man wavers; he is like a wave of the sea and is without stability. God's relation to the Christian who puts his confidence in him never wavers.[21]

b. *Illustration.* James grew up in Nazareth, about thirty kilometers from both the Lake of Galilee and the Mediterranean Sea. The sight of the rolling waves was not unfamiliar to him. Thus he applies this imagery to the man who doubts. "He who doubts is like a wave of the sea, blown and tossed by the wind." The sea is always full of waves; and when the wind blows, the waves move almost rhythmically in rushing sequence. When the wind changes direction, the waves alter their course accordingly. Also, the upward and downward movements of the waves create crests and troughs. In short, the picture of the sea painted by James is one of instability and restlessness. So James portrays the man who doubts. That man is like the heaving waves of the sea, unsettled and unstable. He lacks the wisdom that he desperately needs to give direction to his life. But because the man doubts, God withholds wisdom from him. God expects his people to come to him in faith; then he rewards them for seeking him. If man doubts, however, he will not receive the Lord's blessing.

7. That man should not think he will receive anything from the Lord; 8. he is a double-minded man, unstable in all he does.

We readily confess that our faith is weak and timid at times. We struggle with periods of doubt. Are we the people James addresses? Are we tossed about as the waves of the sea? Do we forfeit God's blessing because we are weak in faith?

Briefly let us consider Abraham, the father of believers. His faith was not always unfailing and strong. He had his moments of doubt and despair. Yet Abraham received the promise of God, and God blessed him.

What then is James saying? He is not referring to the person who wards off doubt, but rather to the one who is double-minded and unstable. The double-minded man actually has two personalities or two souls. One says that he will try "religion"—if it does not do any harm, it may do some good. The other says that he has no need of God because he wants to be independent and self-sufficient. A person who doubts does not expect to receive anything from God. James, then, observes that a doubter "should not think he will receive anything from the Lord."

James calls the person who doubts "that man." The wording exhibits disdain; that man doubts the truthfulness of God's power and promises. He asks God for wisdom but doubts whether God will give it to him. One

---

21. Burkhard Gärtner, *NIDNTT,* vol. 1, p. 505. Also consult Friedrich Büchsel, *TDNT,* vol. 3, p. 949.

moment he prays, but the next moment he ignores God. His prayer—if it is prayer—is not supported by faith.

When the father of the epileptic said to Jesus, "I do believe; help me overcome my unbelief!" (Mark 9:24), Jesus heard his prayer of faith. He healed the man's son by casting out the demon. Note, however, that this man struggled with his weak faith and asked for help. He received it.

God wants us to pray to him because he wants to be our God. As God himself is unchangeable in all he says and does (Mal. 3:6; Heb. 6:17–18), so he expects his people to be the same. He detests instability, double-mindedness, and doubt. He desires that we pray to him and believe that he will answer. Near the end of his letter James writes, "The prayer of a righteous man is powerful and effective" (5:16). God blesses the righteous because they are his people.

But the double-minded man should not think that God will bless him. That man goes his own way, makes his own decisions, and lives his own life—apart from God. If he does not pray to God in childlike trust, God cannot grant him the gift of wisdom. Therefore, when God refuses his request, the cause is not God's unwillingness but man's doubt.

Practical Considerations in 1:5–8

Verse 5

If you are a teacher, you may have received the best training available to equip you for your task. You may have a talent to communicate well. And you may enjoy your vocation. But if you fail to ask God daily for wisdom to meet the challenge of your profession, you cannot be most effective.

Ask God for wisdom and he will give generously without finding fault. Ask in faith and you will see the difference in your life. "Ask and it will be given to you; seek and you will find; knock and the door will be opened to you" (Matt. 7:7).

Verse 6

Is doubt always sinful? Not necessarily. For instance, when doubt appears in the form of perplexity, it is not sinful. When the "God-fearing Jews from every nation under heaven" (Acts 2:5) heard the apostles preach the gospel on the day of Pentecost in Jerusalem, they were "amazed and perplexed" (Acts 2:12). They were at a loss to comprehend the meaning of the outpouring of the Holy Spirit. After Peter delivered his Pentecost sermon, about three thousand people believed. Others, however, made fun of the apostles by calling them drunkards (Acts 2:13). These people refused to accept God's truth because they doubted. Doubt, then, expressed as unbelief, is sin.

Greek Words, Phrases, and Constructions in 1:5–8

Verse 5

εἰ—the first clause of the condition introduced by the particle εἰ depicts a simple fact. The verb λείπεται is the present passive indicative and shows the current state. The verb controls the genitive case of σοφίας (wisdom).[22] Derived from λείπω (I leave), it means "to lack."

αἰτείτω—the second clause of the conditional sentence has the present active imperative of the verb αἰτέω (I ask). This verb implies the submissiveness of one who asks. It describes "the seeking of the inferior from the superior; of the beggar from him that should give alms; of the child from the parent; of the subject from the ruler; of man from God."[23]

τοῦ διδόντος θεοῦ—note the position of the present active participle—between the definite article and the noun. The participle becomes a descriptive adjective and indicates that continued giving is one of God's characteristics.

Verse 6

διακρινόμενος—the writer constructs his sentences and clauses by repeating key words. He repeats the verb αἰτέω, and within this verse he uses the present middle participle διακρινόμενος twice. The compound διά (through) and κρίνω (I judge) advances the idea of making a distinction between two persons, things, or thoughts. Thus, in the middle (as a reflective) it has the meaning "to be at odds with oneself, doubt, waver."[24]

ἔοικεν—a second perfect active from the classical verb εἴκω (I am like) is a durative present and occurs only in this form (see James 1:23).

Verse 7

μὴ οἰέσθω—the present middle imperative of the contracted form οἶμαι (I suppose, think) is negated by the particle μή. The prohibition in the present tense instructs the reader and hearer to stop thinking that he will receive something.

ὁ ἄνθρωπος ἐκεῖνος—the position of the demonstrative pronoun ἐκεῖνος (that one) expresses a degree of disdain (compare with Mark 14:21).[25] The noun ἄνθρωπος is generic.

λήμψεται—the future middle indicative of λαμβάνω (I receive).

Verse 8

δίψυχος—this is a combination of δίς (twice) and ψυχή (soul). As an adjective it derives from the verb διψυχέω (I am undecided, changeable).

ἀκατάστατος—the compound adjective derived from the privative ἀ (not), the preposition κατά (down), and the verb ἵστημι (I stand) conveys the impression of instability.

ἐν πάσαις ταῖς ὁδοῖς—literally translated "in all the ways," the phrase is a Hebraism referring to a person's conduct.

---

22. Robertson, *Grammar*, p. 518, classified the verb in the category of "verbs of missing, lacking, despairing."
23. R. C. Trench, *Synonyms of the New Testament* (1854; reprint ed., Grand Rapids: Eerdmans, 1953), p. 144.
24. Bauer, p. 185.
25. James B. Adamson, *The Epistle of James,* New International Commentary on the New Testament series (Grand Rapids: Eerdmans, 1976), pp. 94–95.

3. Taking Pride
1:9–11

As he does in other passages of this first chapter of his epistle, James mentions a topic in a sentence or two. Then in a later section or chapter he elaborates. Here he introduces the subject *pride.*

9. The brother in humble circumstances ought to take pride in his high position. 10. But the one who is rich should take pride in his low position, because he will pass away like a wild flower.

These two verses reveal parallelism and contrast common in the Psalms and the Proverbs. The parallel lies in the expression *take pride.* The phrases *brother in humble circumstances* and *one who is rich* show contrast. Also the adjectives *high* and *low* stand in opposition to each other.

Note that although James refrains from using the word *poor* in this verse, the intent to depict poverty is evident (compare 2:2, 3, 5, 6). The man in humble circumstances he designates "brother."

a. "The brother." Pastor James writes a letter to the Christians "scattered among the nations." He knows that many of them live in grinding poverty and fill the lowest-paying positions in society. These people need words of encouragement, for economic conditions are oppressive and perplexing. Thus, James exhorts the Christian brother "to take pride in his high position."

Although the brother lives "in humble circumstances,"[26] he should not only know his exalted position; he is even encouraged to take pride in it. The contrast is striking. How can an economically deprived Christian understand that he is highly exalted? Before he can boast of an honorable position, he must learn first to appreciate the significance of his status. That is, he should look not at material possessions, but at spiritual treasures. He must have an entirely different outlook on life. He views life not from the aspect of materialism but rather in relation to spiritual values. He knows that God himself has elevated the believer to a high rank.[27] He sees himself as a child of the King—a son or daughter of God.

As a member of God's royal family, the brother "ought to take pride" in his family tree. Proudly he points to his heavenly Father and to his brother Jesus Christ. The Christian has royal blood in his veins. Says James, "Listen, my dear brothers: Has not God chosen those who are poor in the eyes of the world to be rich in faith and to inherit the kingdom he promised those who love him?" (2:5). No wonder the Christian ought to take pride in his high position. He is heir of God's kingdom.

---

26. Quoting Prov. 3:34, both James and Peter use the adjective *humble* (James 4:6; I Peter 5:5). There the word signifies "humility as readiness for service." Walter Grundmann, *TDNT,* vol. 8, p. 23. In James 1:9, the expression *humble* refers to one who is financially poor. Also see Hans-Helmut Esser, *NIDNTT,* vol. 2, p. 263.

27. Davids, *James,* p. 76.

b. "The one who is rich." The counterpart to the "brother in humble circumstances" is the "one who is rich." James exhorts both to take pride in their respective positions.

Who is this rich person? This is an open question. Some interpreters wish to complete the parallel in verses 9 and 10 by inserting the word *brother:* "But the brother who is rich should take pride in his low position." Then both the poor and the rich are Christians.[28]

We note a few objections, however. First, although James explicitly calls the man in lowly circumstances a brother, he omits this term when he introduces the rich man. Next, James compares the rich man to a plant that withers and dies—he will fade away (v. 11). He adds no word of admonition and no call to repentance.[29] Then, in other parts of his epistle, James leaves the impression that the rich do not belong to the Christian fellowship (see 2:6–9; 5:1–6). And last, James addresses Christians who were persecuted and dispersed. They had lost their possessions and now lived in economically depressed conditions. They were oppressed by the rich in the areas where they had settled.

Moreover, we note that James speaks about the rich man but not about riches. He does not repudiate earthly possessions in order to rejoice in poverty. No, he teaches that God is the giver of "every good and perfect gift" (1:17). James is not concerned about riches but about the person who possesses them. I conclude, then, that the rich man is not a Christian.

How can the rich person "take pride in his low position"? The poor man boasts about his spiritual riches, but the rich man who has rejected God is spiritually blind and unable to see his "low position." He boasts about his material wealth, but earthly riches "pass away like a wild flower."

James resorts to irony. He is saying, "The rich man should take pride in his low position," viewed by the spiritually discerning brother. Earthly goods can be compared to the tides of the sea; they come and they go. James, however, uses an illustration taken from climate and landscape.

11. For the sun rises with scorching heat and withers the plant; its blossom falls and its beauty is destroyed. In the same way, the rich man will fade away even while he goes about his business.

The illustration finds an echo in the prophecy of Isaiah:

> "All men are like grass,
>   and all their glory is like the flowers of the field.
> The grass withers and the flowers fall,
>   because the breath of the LORD blows on them."
>   [40:6–7; also see Job 14:2]

---

28. Among the proponents of this view are Ropes, Adamson, Burdick, and Joseph B. Mayor.

29. F. W. Grosheide, *De Brief aan de Hebreeën en de Brief van Jakobus* (Kampen: Kok, 1955), p. 357. Davids observes that James did not consider the rich man "truly Christian, for he is given no future hope." See his commentary on *James*, p. 77.

The author describes the climatic conditions of Israel in a single sentence. The primary cause of drought is the scorching heat of the rising sun, especially when it is accompanied by the searing wind from the desert. That combination makes plants wither quickly, and blossom and beauty disappear within hours. When the so-called sirocco blows day and night from the east, the appearance of the landscape changes dramatically.

"In the same way, the rich man will fade away." Certainly man's earthly possessions can vanish in a remarkably short time. But the text does not say that riches will disappear. It says "man will fade away." In poetic form, this is the description of man in Psalm 103:

> Man is like the tender flower,
> And his days are like the grass,
> Withered where it lately flourished
> By the blighting winds that pass.
> —Psalter Hymnal

The rich man passes away "even while he goes about his business." The New International Version has given us an apt translation of a Semitic idiom.[30] Suddenly the life of the rich man comes to an end while he is busily engaged in making money. His riches are unable to prolong his life, for he departs and leaves his possessions behind.

Practical Considerations in 1:9–11

Verse 9

Mindful of Paul's admonition to do good to all people (Gal. 6:10), we seek to alleviate the needs of those who are poverty-stricken. But while it is one thing to give generously to the poor, it is another thing to associate with them. A person of financial means may have much more influence and respect than people who belong to the lower class of society. This person can demonstrate his willingness to help the needy, but not necessarily on a personal basis.

James, however, says that an impoverished brother occupies a high position. In other words, do not think too lightly of him! Also, the brother himself ought to be fully aware of the exalted position he occupies. He is a child of God.

Verse 10

In today's world we praise the rich who have gained positions of authority, and we pity the poor for living in deplorable conditions. The Bible says that the position of the rich who live without God is deplorable (Luke 12:20–21). But "the brother in humble circumstances" is exalted.

---

30. Bauer gives this translation of the idiom: "*the rich man on his* (business) *journeys* or more general *in his undertakings* or *pursuits*," p. 692.

Greek Words, Phrases, and Constructions in 1:9–11

Verse 9

καυχάσθω—the third singular present middle imperative of καυχάομαι (I boast) occurs once in this verse and by implication (in the original) is understood in verse 10 to complete the parallel. Here the word has a favorable connotation. By contrast, in James 4:16 it has an unfavorable meaning: "As it is, you boast and brag. All such boasting is evil."

ὁ ταπεινός—this adjective with the definite article follows the expression ὁ ἀδελφός (the brother). Its position in the sentence, then, is attributive and descriptive; it describes the social status of the one who is poor. Moreover, this expression has its counterpart in ὁ πλούσιος (the rich).

τῷ ὕψει αὐτοῦ—referring to rank, the definite article and noun with the possessive αὐτοῦ stand in contrast to ταπεινός (humble). Says Jürgen Blunck, this verse "paradoxically reverses all human relationships and in the faith exalts those who are lowly."[31]

Verse 10

ἐν τῇ ταπεινώσει—the author stresses key words and concepts which he repeats. From the adjective ταπεινός he goes to the noun ταπείνωσις. The noun denotes the experience of humiliation, not the state of humility. That is, the -σις ending reveals progress.

ἄνθος χόρτου—literally translated "a flower of grass," the expression means "a wild flower." James repeats it in a slightly different form in verse 11.

Verse 11

σὺν τῷ καύσωνι—in the Septuagint the noun καύσων (heat) usually indicates the scorching desert wind (sirocco) that comes from the east. In this verse, we cannot be sure whether James implied a reference to the sirocco. The preposition σύν (with) appears to point in that direction. Translators stay close to the text and render the phrase "with scorching heat."

ἐξέπεσεν—the aorist active indicative of ἐκπίπτω (I fall from) is descriptive of the falling of a withered flower. The aorists ἀνέτειλεν (rises), ἐξήρανεν (withers), ἐξέπεσεν (falls), and ἀπώλετο (is destroyed) reflect the Hebrew perfect. But classical and koine Greek know this characteristic, too, and call it the timeless aorist.[32] Compare also Isaiah 40:7 (LXX) and I Peter 1:24.

ἡ εὐπρέπεια τοῦ προσώπου—"the beauty of its face" is a Semitic idiom that is somewhat redundant. The translation *beauty* is sufficient.

πορείαις—the noun means "journeys" and has its synonym in ὁδοῖς (ways) in verse 8.

μαρανθήσεται—the first future passive indicative of μαραίνω (I fade, disappear) portrays the withering of plants, the dying of the wind, and the fading away of man.

---

31. Jürgen Blunck, *NIDNTT*, vol. 2, p. 200.
32. Robertson, *Grammar*, p. 837. Also see Hanna, *Grammatical Aid*, p. 416.

12 Blessed is the man who perseveres under trial, because when he has stood the test, he will receive the crown of life that God has promised to those who love him.

13 When tempted, no one should say, "God is tempting me." For God cannot be tempted by evil, nor does he tempt anyone;   14 but each one is tempted when, by his own evil desire, he is dragged away and enticed.   15 Then, after desire has conceived, it gives birth to sin; and sin, when it is full-grown, gives birth to death.

16 Don't be deceived, my dear brothers.   17 Every good and perfect gift is from above, coming down from the Father of the heavenly lights, who does not change like shifting shadows.   18 He chose to give us birth through the word of truth, that we might be a kind of firstfruits of all he created.

C. Tests
1:12–18

1. Sustaining the Test
1:12

James returns to the theme he introduced at the beginning of his epistle: perseverance under trial (vv. 2–4). He calls the persevering believer blessed and tells him that because of his love for God, the believer "will receive the crown of life."

The author displays a fondness for using key words. With these words he advances the flow of his epistle. In verse 12 he explains the meaning of the expressions *trial* and *test;* this leads him to an explanation of the verb *to tempt.* Verse 12, then, is introductory to the next section.

12. Blessed is the man who perseveres under trial, because when he has stood the test, he will receive the crown of life that God has promised to those who love him.

Note these points:

a. *Man.* The term *blessed* relates to the Beatitudes of Jesus. Matthew records a series of nine such statements (5:3–11) in the Sermon on the Mount. The complete expression—"blessed is the man"—appears frequently in Psalms, Proverbs, and the Prophets.[33]

The Jews were fond of using the word *blessed* (*makarios*). Both in the New Testament and in extrabiblical literature the word is common. For example, in the New Testament it occurs fifty times.[34]

Who is the man the Bible calls "blessed"? He is the person who finds complete happiness in God. He may be poor, meek, hungry, or persecuted—but he is happy. This appears to be a contradiction. From a worldly perspective only the rich and those who are secure can be happy. But Scripture says that "the man who perseveres [endures] under trial" is blessed.

b. *Test.* God tests man's faith to learn whether it is genuine and true.

---

33. Ps. 1:1; 32:2; 34:8; 40:4; 65:4; 84:5 (with minor variation); 94:12; 112:1; Prov. 8:34; Isa. 56:2; Jer. 17:7. Also see Job 5:17; Rom. 4:8.

34. Friedrich Hauck, *TDNT,* vol. 4, pp. 367–70. Consult Oswald Becker, *NIDNTT,* vol. 1, pp. 216–17.

For instance, we test the purity of a bowl made of lead crystal by lightly tapping the outer edge. Immediately we know its genuineness when we hear a reverberating, almost musical sound. We also know that the lead crystal bowl went through the fire when it was made.

Similarly, God tests the faith of man as, for example, in the case of Job. Faith that is not tried and true is worthless. God wants the believer to come to him in a time of trial so that he may give him the strength to endure. God is not interested in seeing the believer falter and fail; he wants him to endure, overcome, and triumph.

See how Peter encourages his readers to persevere: "But how is it to your credit if you receive a beating for doing wrong and endure it? But if you suffer for doing good and you endure it, this is commendable before God" (I Peter 2:20).

c. *Promise.* Why is the believer who perseveres during a time of testing happy? Because "he will receive the crown of life that God has promised to those who love him."

After his period of testing has ended, the believer will receive the crown of life. No one competing in games receives a crown until the race is over, and then only one person gets the crown (I Cor. 9:24–25). The phrase *the crown of life,* it seems, was a well-known idiom in the first century. It occurs in the letter addressed to the church in Smyrna: "Be faithful, even to the point of death, and I will give you the crown of life" (Rev. 2:10).

Writes R. C. Trench, the crown of life "is the emblem, not of royalty, but of highest joy and gladness, of glory and immortality."[35] The phrase, then, suggests fullness of life that God grants to those who endure the test of faith. God has promised this gift "to those who love him."

Man cannot earn the crown of life, for God gives it to him full and free. God asks that man place his complete confidence in him and love him wholeheartedly. To love God with heart, soul, and mind, and to love one's neighbor as oneself constitutes the summary of the Ten Commandments. Interestingly enough, James returns to that royal law, as he calls it, in the next chapter (2:8). However, James teaches that God chose man who then began to love him (2:5). John says the same thing when he writes, "We love because he first loved us" (I John 4:19). God comes first, then man.

Greek Words, Phrases, and Constructions in 1:12

δόκιμος—this adjective has its origin in the verb δέχομαι (I receive, accept) and means "accepted." It refers to something that has been tested and is genuine, for example, coins and metals. The word occurs seven times in the New Testament (Rom. 14:18; 16:10; I Cor. 11:19; II Cor. 10:18; 13:7; II Tim. 2:15; James 1:12).

ἐπηγγείλατο—from the compound verb ἐπαγγέλλομαι (I promise), the aorist

35. Trench, *Synonyms of the New Testament,* p. 80.

middle indicative lacks the subject. Scribes and translators have supplied the subject, either "Lord" or "God."[36] "In the style of rabbinical writings, where the word 'God' is sometimes to be supplied mentally, the earlier and better witnesses support the reading ἐπηγγείλατο, without a subject being expressed. Later witnesses, however, fill out what may have seemed a lacuna by adding either κύριος or ὁ κύριος or ὁ θεός."[37]

ἀγαπῶσιν—the present active participle of ἀγαπάω (I love) is the masculine dative plural as the indirect object of the verb *to promise* (see also Rom. 8:28).

---

2. Being Tempted to Desire
1:13–15

The pastor knows the human heart, for not everyone will endure the tests God places before him. Therefore, James warns his readers not to blame God but rather to understand the cause and the result of temptation.

13. When tempted, no one should say, "God is tempting me." For God cannot be tempted by evil, nor does he tempt anyone; 14. but each one is tempted when, by his own evil desire, he is dragged away and enticed. 15. Then, after desire has conceived, it gives birth to sin; and sin, when it is full-grown, gives birth to death.

The believer who passes the test is blessed, but the one who fails it is filled with remorse. The one who failed the test refuses to admit that he lacks faith in God. That is what Adam did in paradise when he fell into sin. He listened to Eve who in turn obeyed Satan. When God confronted them with their failure, Adam blamed Eve and Eve blamed the serpent (Gen. 3:12–13). In effect, Adam blamed God when he said, "The woman *you* put here with me—she gave me some fruit from the tree, and I ate it" (v. 12; italics added). No one should say, "God is tempting me."

a. "God cannot be tempted." James is not interested in explaining the origin of evil, for he knows that not God but Satan is called the tempter. Therefore he writes, "God cannot be tempted by evil, nor does he tempt anyone." He means to say that God, who created all things, is not the cause of evil. In his holiness God stands far above evil and cannot be influenced by it. James puts it this way: it is impossible for God to be tempted. Because of his perfection, God has no contact with evil, and evil is powerless to bring God into temptation.

Moreover, God does not tempt anyone. God hates evil and therefore does not lead anyone astray. "Do not say, 'Because of the Lord I left the

---

36. The translations that have the reading *the Lord* are KJV, NKJV, RV, ASV, NASB, NAB, JB. Those that have "God" are RSV, MLB, GNB, NEB, NIV. Moffatt circumvents the problem by translating the verb *to promise* in the passive, "which is promised to all who love Him."

37. Bruce M. Metzger, *A Textual Commentary on the Greek New Testament*, corrected ed. (London and New York: United Bible Societies, 1975), p. 679.

right way'; for he will not do what he hates. Do not say, 'It was he who led me astray'; for he has no need of a sinful man" (Sir. 15:11–12).

In the Lord's Prayer Jesus teaches the believer to pray, "And lead us not into temptation" (Matt. 6:13; Luke 11:4). Of course, in this petition Jesus does not say that God is tempting us, because that is impossible. Jesus teaches us that we must ask God to keep us from falling into temptation.[38] Who, then, tempts man? Scripture is plain on this point: Satan. To be precise, Satan has the name *the tempter* (Matt. 4:3; I Thess. 3:5). And Satan is amazingly successful in leading man into temptation and sin.

b. "Each [man] is tempted." Some people try to excuse sin by saying, "The devil made me do it." But this excuse does not hold, for man himself is responsible for his own sin. Temptation is universal; not one person escapes confronting it.[39]

"Each one is tempted when, by his own evil desire, he is dragged away and enticed." James uses an illustration taken from the art of fishing. A fish sees the lure and is tempted to strike. When the fish takes hold of the bait, it is suddenly dragged away and pays with its life for its innocence and ignorance.[40] But man cannot claim innocence and ignorance. James puts it pointedly: "Each one is tempted . . . by his own desire." He deprives man of any excuse to place the blame on someone or something else. He says, in effect, that the cause lies within ourselves. Note that James speaks of one's *own* desire. Our desires lead us into temptation, and if we are not controlled by the Spirit of God they lead us into sin.

The heart of man is deceitful, as Jeremiah prophesied (17:9). Jesus repeats the same thought when he describes the human heart in these words: "For out of the heart come evil thoughts, murder, adultery, sexual immorality, theft, false testimony, slander" (Matt. 15:19).

Is there an escape from temptation? Certainly. God has not forsaken us. He still hears and answers our prayer, "Lead us not into temptation, but deliver us from the evil one" (Matt. 6:13). And Paul writes these reassuring words: "God is faithful; he will not let you be tempted beyond what you can bear. But when you are tempted, he will also provide a way out so that you can stand up under it" (I Cor. 10:13).

---

38. Herman N. Ridderbos, *Het Evangelie naar Mattheüs*, 2 vols., Korte Verklaring der Heilige Schrift (Kampen: Kok, 1952), vol. 1, p. 136. Also consult F. W. Grosheide, *Het Heilig Evangelie volgens Mattheüs*, Commentaar op het Nieuwe Testament series (Kampen: Kok, 1954), p. 101; William Hendriksen, *Matthew*, New Testament Commentary series (Grand Rapids: Baker, 1973), pp. 336–37.

39. D. Edmond Hiebert, *The Epistle of James: Tests of a Living Faith* (Chicago: Moody, 1979), p. 105.

40. Consult Joseph B. Mayor, *The Epistle of St. James* (reprint ed., Grand Rapids: Zondervan, 1946), p. 54; A. T. Robertson, *Studies in the Epistle of James*, rev. and ed. Heber F. Peacock (Nashville: Broadman, 1959), p. 52. Also see R. V. G. Tasker, *The General Epistle of James: An Introduction and Commentary*, Tyndale New Testament Commentaries (Grand Rapids: Eerdmans, 1957), p. 46; and Curtis Vaughan, *James: A Study Guide* (Grand Rapids: Zondervan, 1969), p. 31.

c. "Desire . . . gives birth to death." James resorts to still another illustration. He takes the example of a living creature from the time of conception through birth and maturity to death. He depicts the scene in a few clauses which he places in parallel form:

then,	and when
after desire has conceived,	sin is full-grown,
it gives birth to sin;	it gives birth to death.

If God created desires within us, are they necessarily sinful? No, because they have been given to us so that we may live a balanced life. We have the desire to eat and to drink so that we may take care of our bodies. When we properly control our desires we live normal lives, but when we discard checks and balances, desires get out of hand and, so to speak, become pregnant.

James refrains from spelling out how desire conceives. Desire is able to conceive when man's will no longer objects but yields. When this takes place, conception begins and sin develops and eventually is born. Sin results in death (Rom. 7:5, 10, 13). Bengel writes, "Sin from its birth is big with death."[41]

Again, James refrains from telling us what he means by sin, but from the context we understand that he contemplates sin in the general sense of the word.

Sin leads to death. More graphically, Paul writes that "the wages of sin is death" (Rom. 6:23). Is death confined to physical death or does it include spiritual and eternal death?[42] James does not elaborate; he only stresses that sin leads increasingly to death. That is, sin progressively leads from physical death to spiritual death and to eternal death.

Practical Considerations in 1:13–15

Verse 13

God tests the believer to strengthen his faith. In his providence God allows Satan to tempt the believer. For instance, God permitted Satan to take away all Job's possessions, but Job praised God (Job 1:21). Satan tempted Job when Job's wife said, "Are you still holding on to your integrity? Curse God and die!" (2:9). That is, Satan used Job's wife to turn him against God. But Job stood firm in his faith and replied, "You are talking like a foolish woman. Shall we accept good from God, and not trouble?" (2:10). Job triumphed in faith and God blessed him accordingly (42:10).

---

41. Bengel, *Gnomon of the New Testament*, vol. 5, p. 7. Also consult Grosheide, *Jakobus*, p. 360.
42. Zodhiates, *The Behavior of Belief*, pt. 1, p. 73.

Verse 14

James counsels the believer to "resist the devil, and he will flee from you" (4:7). We are able to resist the devil by keeping our eye of faith fixed on Jesus, "the author and perfecter of our faith" (Heb. 12:2). How far will the devil flee? When will he return to tempt the believer again? The devil returns when the right moment comes. When Satan finished tempting Jesus, "he left him until an opportune time" (Luke 4:13).

Verse 15

The world readily makes sin a laughing matter, especially when sin pertains to sex. But sexual sins (prostitution, adultery, fornication, homosexual acts) should never be treated humorously. Sin is the cause of suffering and grief and it leads to destruction and death.

Greek Words, Phrases, and Constructions in 1:13–15

Verse 13

μηδεὶς . . . λεγέτω—the present imperative preceded by the negative substantive μηδείς conveys the implication that the readers asserted that God was tempting them.

ἀπό—the use of the preposition ἀπό with a passive verb is similar to ὑπό (Matt. 16:21; Acts 2:22; 4:36).[43] The preposition denotes the agent.

ἀπείραστος—the compound verbal adjective from the privative ἀ (not) and πειράζω (I tempt) expresses the passive voice, and "the idea of necessity" in the sense of inability.[44] The word occurs once in the Septuagint and once in the New Testament.

Verse 15

συλλαβοῦσα—from συλλαμβάνω (I seize, catch, conceive, support), this aorist participle in the nominative feminine denotes "to become pregnant."

ἀποτελεσθεῖσα—this aorist passive participle from the compound ἀποτελέω (I bring to completion) occurs only here (see Luke 13:32).

ἀποκύει—the author has a penchant for assonance—a noun, a participle, and a verb begin with the letter ἀ. From ἀποκυέω (I give birth to), the verb appears twice in the New Testament (James 1:15, 18).

---

3. Receiving Perfect Gifts
1:16–18

God is unable to tempt and to be tempted. Let no one ever think, not to mention say, that God originates temptations. If man entertains such an accusation, he sins against God. God is the giver of every good and perfect gift. And all his children can testify to God's goodness and love.

---

43. Hanna, *Grammatical Aid*, p. 416.
44. Robertson, *Grammar*, p. 1097. Also see Ropes, *James*, p. 155; Mayor, *James*, p. 51.

16. Don't be deceived, my dear brothers. 17. Every good and perfect gift is from above, coming down from the Father of the heavenly lights, who does not change like shifting shadows.

James is a pastor who fully understands the hearts of those who live scattered abroad far from home and former possessions. He knows that their lot is difficult, and that they have begun to direct their complaints to God. As a trained leader he counsels them by addressing them as "dear brothers," and he warns them not to be deceived.[45] He wants them to consider the person and the characteristics of God.

The readers ought to know that God does not send his children sorrow and grief to drive them from him. He gives them adversities so that they may come to him and rely fully on him. God has absolutely nothing in common with evil, for he abhors that which is not holy. Therefore, the readers ought not to think that God instigates evil. Never!

Yet, some Christians who are tested and tried lose perspective and question the providence of God. If God is almighty, why does he not prevent tragedy and calamity? Man can multiply the verbal and nonverbal accusations directed to God, but he ought not to do so. Instead he should direct attention to what God gives and who God is. In our study, then, let us note:

a. *God's goodness.* God is goodness personified; he is the fountain of all that is good, for goodness originates with him.[46] God gives by creating heaven and earth; God gives by sending his Son; God gives by pouring out his Spirit. The gifts God makes available to his people are good and perfect—every one of them. They include spiritual and material gifts.

All things come to us out of God's hand, for we receive both prosperity and adversity from him. God gives his people trials and tests that at times come in the form of calamity. Says the prophet Amos to the people of Israel, "When disaster comes to a city, has not the LORD caused it?" (3:6).

God is fully in control of every situation and knows what is best for his children. "If you, then, though you are evil, know how to give good gifts to your children, how much more will your Father in heaven give good gifts to those who ask him!" (Matt. 7:11; compare Luke 11:13).

b. *God's character.* James moves from speaking about the gifts to speaking about the giver, that is, about God himself. Good and perfect gifts come down from heaven, "from the Father of the heavenly lights." The writer encourages the reader to look up to the sky where he will see the brilliant light of the sun by day, the reflective light of the moon by night, and the twinkling stars. God is the creator of these heavenly lightbearers;

---

45. Compare these Scripture references: I Cor. 6:9; 15:33; Gal. 6:7; I John 3:7.

46. Guido de Brès, author of the sixteenth-century document (1561) known as the Belgic Confession, expressed his faith in the only God in these words: "We all believe in our hearts and confess with our mouths *that there is* a single and simple spiritual being, whom we call God—eternal, incomprehensible, invisible, unchangeable, infinite, *almighty;* completely wise, just, and good, *and the overflowing source of all good*" (art. 1).

he himself is nothing but light. "God is light; in him there is no darkness at all" (I John 1:5). Therefore, darkness cannot exist in the presence of God. In this light, God displays his holiness, goodness, love, integrity, and unchangeableness.

Note that James calls God the "Father" of lights and uses this figure of speech to illustrate God's absolute stability. God "does not change like shifting shadows." The being, nature, and characteristics of God are unchangeable (Mal. 3:6). As the earth, sun, moon, and stars move in their ordained courses, we observe the interplay of light and darkness, day and night, the longest and the shortest day of the year, the waning and the waxing of the moon, eclipses, and the movements of the planets. Nature is subject to variation and change. Not so with God! He is the Father of the heavenly lights, who is always light and does not change. He has an abiding interest in his children.

18. He chose to give us birth through the word of truth, that we might be a kind of firstfruits of all he created.

James designates God the Father of lights. By implication, however, he calls God our Father. Even though he omits the word *Father,* he employs the concept *to give birth.* Fatherhood is part of God's nature. He is the Father of Jesus Christ and through him is our Father.

a. "He chose to give us birth." The first verb in this sentence is "chose"; because of its position it receives emphasis. "We have been born of his saving will (Jas. 1:18), and because God himself is the unalterable one (cf. Jas. 1:17), his gracious will cannot be overthrown."[47] We did not choose him; rather, he chose us and saved us from death. He gave us new life in Christ Jesus.

In verse 15 James depicts sin giving birth to death. In verse 18 he states that God "chose to give us birth through the word of truth." God is our creator but also our redeemer.[48] In this verse the context favors the interpretation that God is our re-creator. He gives us new life through spiritual birth.

b. "Through the word of truth." Paul uses this expression a number of times (II Cor. 6:7; Eph. 1:13; Col. 1:5; II Tim. 2:15). It refers to the gospel, as Paul explains in his letter to the Colossians. When this gospel is proclaimed, God regenerates the sinner and reforms him into a "new creation" (II Cor. 5:17; Col. 3:10). Writes D. Edmond Hiebert, "There is no substitute for the proclamation of the gospel."[49]

---

47. Dietrich Müller, *NIDNTT,* vol. 3, p. 1018. Consult Gottlob Schrenk, *TDNT,* vol. 1, p. 632.

48. L. E. Elliott-Binns in "James 1:18: Creation or Redemption," *NTS* 3 (1957): 148–61, argues that the concept *regeneration* is absent from the Epistle of James. James, therefore, thinks of creation and not of redemption (see pp. 160–61). Ropes in *James* meets this argument by saying that "the figure of begetting was not used for creation, whereas it came early into use with reference to the Christians, who deemed themselves 'sons of God'" (p. 166). Also see Laws, *James,* p. 78; and Davids, *James,* p. 89.

49. Hiebert, *James,* p. 116.

c. "That we might be a kind of firstfruits." God created, regenerated, and renewed us. We are his handiwork, his prize possession. James says that we are "a kind of firstfruits." In Old Testament times, the first fruits were holy and belonged to God: the first-born of man and of cattle, the first produce from the vineyard, orchard, and field (see, for instance, Exod. 23:16; 34:22; Lev. 19:23–25; Num. 15:20–21; Deut. 18:4). However, already in the Old Testament the prophets began to use the expression figuratively. Jeremiah writes, "Israel was holy to the LORD, the firstfruits of his harvest" (Jer. 2:3). And in the New Testament, Christians are God's first fruits (Rom. 11:16; 16:5; I Cor. 16:15). In his epistle, James calls us "a kind of firstfruits of all [God] created." We belong to the countless multitude (symbolically represented as the 144,000) who "were purchased from among men and offered as firstfruits to God and the Lamb" (Rev. 14:4).

What an honor! We are God's first fruits and as such are holy. That is, God has chosen us from among all his creatures to be holy and has dedicated us to himself. We belong to God. Therefore, let no one ever think that God can lead us astray. That is impossible, for he is holy and we, his first fruits, share his holiness.

Practical Considerations in 1:17–18

Verse 17

The writer is a man who takes a keen interest in God's creation and observes the phenomena of nature. For example, he mentions the waves of the sea, the wind, the rising sun, the heat of the day, the flowers of the field, and the heavenly lights in the firmament. James knows that he is part of God's creation, that God upholds him, and that God's love is constant and unchangeable. God demonstrates this by giving good and perfect gifts. We hear the voice of Jesus when he speaks about the splendor of the lilies of the field: "If that is how God clothes the grass of the field, which is here today and tomorrow is thrown into the fire, will he not much more clothe you, O you of little faith?" (Matt. 6:30).

Verse 18

God not only has given us his creation so that with our physical eyes we can see his loving care. He also has entrusted to us his special revelation, that is, the word of truth. Through that word we know that we are privileged people. We are God's own people. We are that now. God has chosen us. What a privilege!

Greek Words, Phrases, and Constructions in 1:16–18

Verse 16

μὴ πλανᾶσθε—from πλανάω (I wander, go astray), the present middle imperative preceded by the negative particle μή indicates that some of the readers were deceiving themselves. In effect, the author says, "Stop doing this."

54

ἀγαπητοί—a verbal adjective that conveys a passive meaning. That is, the brothers are being loved.

Verse 17

πᾶσα δόσις—the adjective *every* precedes the noun δόσις and because of gender and emphasis it is repeated before the noun δώρημα. The ending of the word δόσις (-σις) shows progression, while that of δώρημα (-μα) depicts result. The first word, then, relates to the act of giving, the second to the gift itself.[50] However, we ought not to press the distinction, because James may have meant no more than to list two synonyms.

ἄνωθέν ἐστιν καταβαῖνον—the first word is an adverb from ἄνω (above) and the enclitic particle -θεν (from). The last word is the present active participle from καταβαίνω (I go down). The adverb and the participle explain one another and are virtually synonymous. Taken with the verb ἐστίν, the participle can be understood as a periphrastic construction.[51]

παραλλαγή—although the noun occurs only once in the New Testament, from extrabiblical literature we learn that the verb παραλλάσσω (I change) denotes the concept *strange, extraordinary*. The noun itself is seldom used as a technical term in astronomy.[52]

ἤ τροπῆς ἀποσκίασμα—there are many variants of this phrase; Bruce M. Metzger relates that "in the opinion of the Committee [of the United Bible Societies] the least unsatisfactory one is" the one given in the text.[53] Literally, the phrase means "or shadow of turning." The noun τροπή is a genitive of cause and means "a shadow because of change."

Verse 18

βουληθείς—first in the sentence, this aorist passive participle receives emphasis. God acted deliberately and freely "in conformity with the purpose (βουλήν) of his will" (Eph. 1:11).

λόγῳ ἀληθείας—the noun λόγος lacks the definite article. The expression ἀληθείας can be understood as an adjective: "a true [ἀληθής] word."[54]

τινα—in the sense of "so to say, a kind of," the indefinite adjective serves to moderate the noun ἀπαρχήν (first fruits).[55]

---

50. The NIV translators have taken the two nouns as synonyms. They combine them and translate: "every good and perfect gift." But other translations stay with the Greek text and even provide a literal version. For instance, the NEB has "all good *giving*, every perfect *gift*" (italics added). Consult Mayor, *James*, pp. 57–58.

51. The NEB is a good example. In this translation the verb form *is* has been eliminated: "every perfect gift, comes from above." Mayor (*James*, p. 58) separates the verb *is* from the participle; so does Moule, who writes that it "need not be periphrastic at all." Consult his *Idiom-Book of New Testament Greek*, p. 17.

52. Bauer, p. 620.

53. Metzger, *Textual Commentary*, pp. 679–80.

54. E. M. Sidebottom, *James, Jude, and 2 Peter*, Century Bible series (London: Nelson; Greenwood, S.C.: Attic, 1967), p. 32. Also see Grosheide, *Jakobus*, p. 362.

55. Bauer, p. 820. Also see Friedrich Blass and Albert Debrunner, *A Greek Grammar of the New Testament and Other Early Christian Literature*, trans. and rev. Robert Funk (Chicago: University of Chicago Press, 1961), sec. 310(1).

19 My dear brothers, take note of this: Everyone should be quick to listen, slow to speak and slow to become angry,   20 for man's anger does not bring about the righteous life that God desires.   21 Therefore, get rid of all moral filth and the evil that is so prevalent, and humbly accept the word planted in you, which can save you.

22 Do not merely listen to the word, and so deceive yourselves. Do what it says.   23 Anyone who listens to the word but does not do what it says is like a man who looks at his face in a mirror   24 and, after looking at himself, goes away and immediately forgets what he looks like.   25 But the man who looks intently into the perfect law that gives freedom, and continues to do this, not forgetting what he has heard, but doing it—he will be blessed in what he does.

26 If anyone considers himself religious and yet does not keep a tight rein on his tongue, he deceives himself and his religion is worthless.   27 Religion that God our Father accepts as pure and faultless is this: to look after orphans and widows in their distress and to keep oneself from being polluted by the world.

D. Agreements
1:19–27

1. Accepting the Word of God
1:19–21

James told his readers that God had given them spiritual birth through the word of faith, that is, the gospel (1:18). Now he tells them to live according to that word, whether it comes to them in written or spoken form. That word has been planted in their hearts and is able to save them.

19. My dear brothers, take note of this: Everyone should be quick to listen, slow to speak and slow to become angry, 20. for man's anger does not bring about the righteous life that God desires.

Throughout the letter in general and here in particular, James talks directly to his readers. He tells them what to do and what not to do. Here he says, "Take note of this."[56] And what should they know? In typical Semitic parallelism he states the proverb:

> Everyone should be
> > quick to listen
> > slow to speak
> > slow to become angry.

Speakers who have the talent to express themselves fluently and eloquently are much in demand. They receive recognition, admiration, and acclaim. James, however, puts the emphasis not on speaking but on listening. That is more important than speaking.

Listening is an art that is difficult to master, for it means to take an intense interest in the person who is speaking. Listening is the art of

---

56. Three translations are possible: "wherefore" (KJV) or "therefore" (NKJV), which is a reading based on late Greek manuscripts; "this you know" (NASB), which is a declarative sentence; and "take note of this" (NIV), which is the imperative. Translators favor the imperative reading.

closing one's mouth and opening one's ears and heart. Listening is loving the neighbor as oneself; his concerns and problems are sufficiently important to be heard.

James cautions his readers to be fully aware of the words they speak. In effect, he echoes the saying of Jesus, "But I tell you that men will have to give an account on the day of judgment for every careless word they have spoken. For by your words you will be acquitted, and by your words you will be condemned" (Matt. 12:36–37; consult Eccles. 5:1–2; Sir. 5:11).

When James says that we must be slow to speak, he does not advocate that we take a vow to be silent. Rather, he wants us to be wise in our speaking. Jewish proverbs prevalent in the days of James were these: "Speak little and do much"; "It is wise for learned men to be silent, and much more for fools"; "Even a fool is thought wise if he keeps silent" (Prov. 17:28).[57] Solomon said something similar in this proverb: "When words are many, sin is not absent, but he who holds his tongue is wise" (Prov. 10:19).

Careless words often accompany an angry mood. Of course, there is a place for righteous anger, but the psalmist tells us to know the limit of righteous anger: "In your anger do not sin" (Ps. 4:4; Eph. 4:26; and see Matt. 5:22). James pleads for restraint in respect to anger.

We have our excuses ready for being angry: too busy, too much pressure, a family trait, or even "I can't help it." James rules out excuses when he says, "Be . . . slow to become angry." That is, we must be able to give an account of every word we speak. "A quick-tempered man displays folly" (Prov. 14:29) and anger is sin (Eph. 4:31; Col. 3:8; Titus 1:7). An angry man listens to the voice of the evil one and not to the voice of God.

James is direct. Says he, "Man's anger does not bring about the righteous life that God desires." Anger hinders the prayers of a believer (I Tim. 2:8) and thus prevents him from promoting the cause of Christ. In effect, he has given "the devil a foothold" (Eph. 4:27). Consider Moses, who became angry with the Israelites but did not listen to the instructions God had given him. He showed disobedience and thus was not permitted to enter the Promised Land (Num. 20:10–12, 24; 27:14; Deut. 1:37; 3:26–27).

When we live the righteous life that God desires of us, we listen carefully and obediently to the Word of God. When we plan to do or say something, we ought to ask whether our actions and words promote the honor of God and advance the cause of justice and peace for our fellow man. When we permit anger to guide us, we are no longer guided by the law of God. "An angry man stirs up dissension, and a hot-tempered one commits many sins" (Prov. 29:22). Instead the believer ought to control his temper, pray for wisdom, and keep the law of God.

---

57. SB, vol. 3, p. 753.

21. Therefore, get rid of all moral filth and the evil that is so prevalent, and humbly accept the word planted in you, which can save you.

Here is the conclusion to this section: an uncontrolled tongue and temper drive a man deep into sin and far from God. Therefore, a spiritual housecleaning is needed so that God's Word, whether in written or spoken form, can enter man's life.

The verse teaches these points:

a. *A command.* "Get rid of all moral filth," says James. He uses the word *filth* figuratively to describe moral uncleanness (see Rev. 22:11). In the Old Testament the word appears in Zechariah 3:3–4 (LXX, with slight variation).[58] The high priest Joshua stood before the angel of the Lord and was dressed in filthy clothes. The angel commanded the ones standing before him to remove Joshua's filthy clothes, for they represented sin. And Joshua received clean clothes.

James orders his readers to get rid of all moral filth that soils their souls and to put aside prevailing evil that blights their lives (compare Eph. 4:22, 25, 31; Col. 3:8; I Peter 2:1).[59] He wants them to put away internal filth and external evil. He commands them to get rid of the evil that prevails around them and influences them.[60]

b. *An imperative.* When the house has been swept and dusted, it cannot remain empty (Matt. 12:43–45). Therefore, James tells his readers to receive the Word of God that has been planted in them. Note that they already had been given the message of salvation that as a plant had taken root in their souls. Once again, the writer resorts to an illustration from nature.[61] A plant needs constant care. If a plant is deprived of water and nurture, it will die. Thus if the readers who have heard the Word fail to pay attention, they will die a spiritual death. The Word needs diligent care and application, so that the readers may grow and increase spiritually.

"Humbly accept the word." James prompts them to receive the Word of God and tells them how to do so. They must accept it humbly, not in weakness but with meekness. As they accept the Word, their hearts must be free from anger, malice, or bitterness. Instead they ought to demonstrate gentleness and humility.

c. *A result.* The Word of God faithfully proclaimed and attentively received is able to save those who hear it. That Word has the power to transform lives because it is living and active (Heb. 4:12).

---

58. J. I. Packer, *NIDNTT*, vol. 1, p. 479.

59. Some translators and interpreters wish to make the noun *evil* the key word and have all the preceding words dependent on it. A somewhat literal translation is this: "Therefore, put aside all the filthiness and excess of evil." Consult Robert Johnstone, *A Commentary on James* (1871; reprint ed., Edinburgh: Banner of Truth Trust, 1977), p. 105. Ropes (*James*, p. 170) is of the opinion that this construction is not necessary.

60. Bauer, p. 650. Consult Theodor Brandt, *NIDNTT*, vol. 1, p. 731.

61. John Calvin, *Commentaries on the Catholic Epistles: The Epistle of James*, ed. and trans. John Owen (Grand Rapids: Eerdmans, 1948), p. 294.

The word *save* has a much deeper meaning in Scripture than we often give it. The verb *to save* implies not merely the salvation of the soul but the restoration of life. For example, when Jesus healed the woman who had suffered from a flow of blood for twelve years, he said to her, "Daughter, your faith has healed you" (Mark 5:34). The Greek actually says, "Your faith has saved you."[62] To save, then, means to make a person whole and complete in every respect. And that is what the Word of God is able to do for the believer. The gospel is the power of God working in everyone who believes (Rom. 1:16). The gospel saves!

Greek Words, Phrases, and Constructions in 1:19–21

Verse 19

ἴστε—some late Greek manuscripts have the reading ὥστε (for this reason), which is the word in the Majority Text. However, most translations adopt the reading ἴστε, which can be either the indicative or the imperative of the second person plural of οἶδα (I know).

ἔστω—the third person singular present active imperative of εἰμί (I am).

εἰς τό—with the infinitive the combination expresses purpose.

Verse 20

ἀνδρός—the writer uses this noun as a synonym of ἄνθρωπος (v. 19) for stylistic reasons (see 1:7–8). Note that all the nouns in this verse lack the definite article.

ἐργάζεται—from ἐργάζομαι (I produce). Based on a few Greek manuscripts the Majority Text has the compound verb κατεργάζεται (produce, NKJV). In translation the difference between these two forms in this text has disappeared.[63]

Verse 21

ἀποθέμενοι—the aorist middle participle of the compound verb ἀποτίθημι (I put away) has an imperatival connotation because of its dependence on the main verb δέξασθε, the aorist middle imperative of δέχομαι (I receive). The use of the aorist is ingressive.

τὰς ψυχὰς ὑμῶν—in this verse the term ψυχάς (souls) signifies man's life and is equivalent to "yourselves" or "you."

---

2. Listening Obediently
1:22–25

The tone and tenor of the writer's discourse resembles that of the Sermon on the Mount delivered by Jesus. For instance, Jesus concludes

---

62. William L. Lane, commenting on this incident, writes, "It was the profound experience of well-being which is related to salvation from God." See his *Gospel According to Mark*, New International Commentary on the New Testament series (Grand Rapids: Eerdmans, 1974), p. 194.

63. Martin Dibelius, *James: A Commentary on the Epistle of James*, rev. Heinrich Greeven, trans. Michael A. Williams, ed. Helmut Köster, Hermeneia: A Critical and Historical Commentary on the Bible (Philadelphia: Fortress, 1976), p. 110.

the sermon with the parable of the wise and foolish builders and says, "Therefore everyone who hears these words of mine and puts them into practice is like a wise man who built his house on the rock" (Matt. 7:24; also see vv. 21, 26). That same sentiment James expresses in these words:

22. Do not merely listen to the word, and so deceive yourselves. Do what it says.

In the next four verses, we see the following parts:

a. *A direct command.* The command has a negative and a positive part. "Do not merely listen. . . . Do what it says." Here is a more literal translation of the text: "But be doers of the word, and not hearers only, deceiving yourselves" (RSV). The New International Version reverses the order because in actual experience hearing comes before doing. Also, the phrase *and so deceive yourselves* applies only to hearing. Therefore, the choice to place the words *do what it says* separately at the end of the verse is commendable, for it shows emphasis.

First, let us look at the term *hearers.* This expression is closely linked to the word *disobedience* in the Greek. The writer of Hebrews joins the verb *to hear* and the noun *disobedience* in the same breath. "We must pay more careful attention, therefore, to what we have heard, so that we do not drift away. For . . . every violation and disobedience received its just punishment" (2:1–2). James also warns his readers to pay attention to the Word of God. If they neglect to hear God's message, they deceive themselves. They merely listen to the preaching of the gospel and at the conclusion of the worship service walk away as if the Word of God has nothing to say to them.

Next, to all of us James says, "Do what it says." The Christian faith is always active and stands in sharp contrast to other religions that practice meditation and general inactivity. In one of his epistles, John delineates the Christian's duty to be active. Says he, "Dear children, let us not love with words or tongue but with actions and in truth" (I John 3:18; also consult Ezek. 33:32).

23. Anyone who listens to the word but does not do what it says is like a man who looks at his face in a mirror 24. and, after looking at himself, goes away and immediately forgets what he looks like.

b. *A striking example.* A picture, especially one that portrays us as we are, is worth a thousand words. We see ourselves daily in the reflection in a mirror: before we leave the house in the morning, during the course of the day, and several times in the evening. Mirrors are part of life. But the repeated returns to the mirror establish the point that our memories are like sieves.

James uses the illustration of a mirror. In fact, his illustration approaches the parabolic form of speech Jesus used during his earthly ministry (compare Matt. 7:26). Mirrors in the first century were not made of glass but of metal that was polished regularly. The mirrors rested horizontally on tables so that the person who wished to see his reflection had to bend and look down. Then he would see but a poor reflection of himself (Job 37:18; I Cor. 13:12; II Cor. 3:18; Wis. 7:26; Sir. 12:11).

Here is the point of comparison. The person who looks into the mirror to see his own image and promptly forgets is like a person who hears the Word of God proclaimed but fails to respond to it. He sees his reflection in the mirror, quickly adjusts his external appearance, and walks away. He hears the gospel preached, makes minor adjustments, and goes his own way. But the gospel is unable to penetrate his heart and cannot change the internal disposition of man. The mirror is an object used to alter man's external appearance; the Word, however, confronts man internally and demands a response.

Why does a person forget what he looks like almost as soon as he walks away from the mirror? That seems incredible and yet it is true. Many people hear a sermon on a given Sunday and a week later cannot remember a single word of that sermon. The person who only listens to the Word goes away and fails to respond to its demands.

25. But the man who looks intently into the perfect law that gives freedom, and continues to do this, not forgetting what he has heard, but doing it—he will be blessed in what he does.

c. *A ready response.* Look at the contrast. The person whose ears and heart are open to what God has to say literally bends over to look into the law of God, much the same as he does when he looks into the mirror that is placed horizontally on a table. However, the difference is that while he studies the perfect law of God he does not walk away from it, as does the person who casts a fleeting glance into a mirror. He continues to look intently into the Word.[64] He meditates on it and obediently puts it into practice.

James resorts to using a synonym for the Word of God. He calls it the "perfect law" and causes the reader to recollect the content of Psalm 19. There David sings,

> The law of the LORD is perfect,
> reviving the soul.
> The statutes of the LORD are trustworthy,
> making wise the simple. . . .
> By them is your servant warned;
> in keeping them there is great reward. [vv. 7, 11]

The descriptive adjective *perfect* has an absolute, not a relative meaning. For instance, when Jesus says, "Be perfect, therefore, as your heavenly

---

64. Wilhelm Michaelis writes that the meaning of the main verb is "I stoop to see." He continues, "The bent over position may be modified by the situation of the observer or by that of what he is trying to see." *TDNT*, vol. 5, p. 814. Also see Luke 24:12; John 20:5; I Peter 1:12.

Father is perfect" (Matt. 5:48), he uses the adjective first in a relative sense (for man) and then in an absolute sense (for our heavenly Father).

Laws made and enacted by man are temporary and conditioned by culture, language, and location. By contrast, God's law is permanent and unchangeable. It applies to everyone at any time and in any situation. It is perfect.

Why is the law perfect? Because God's perfect law gives freedom and it alone sets man really free.[65] That is, the law of God through Jesus Christ sets man free from the bondage of sin and selfishness. Says Jesus, "So if the Son sets you free, you will be free indeed" (John 8:36; also consult Rom. 8:2, 15; Gal. 5:13). Within the boundaries of the law of God man is free, for there he lives in the environment God designated for him. When he crosses the boundary, he becomes a slave to sin. As long as he keeps the law, he is free.

And last, the man who continues to look into the perfect law and keeps it will be blessed. Why is that man happy? He knows that "the precepts of the LORD are right, giving joy to the heart" and "the commands of the LORD are radiant, giving light to the eyes" (Ps. 19:8; compare Ps. 119:1–3). He finds joy in his work, joy in his family, and joy in his Lord. He knows that God is blessing him in all that he does (John 13:17).

Doctrinal Considerations in 1:22–25

If the person who hears the gospel but does not respond to it forfeits salvation, then the one who acts in response to God's Word is not deceived but rather is blessed with salvation. It stands to reason that the person who acts in obedience to the Word of God gains salvation. He performs good deeds and God blesses him accordingly. Consequently, the question is whether salvation is still a free gift of God. Of course! Says Paul to the Ephesians, "For it is by grace you have been saved, through faith—and this not from yourselves, it is the gift of God—not by works, so that no one can boast" (Eph. 2:8–9).

What then are good works? They are the fruits of faith and expressions of gratitude to God for his saving work in Jesus Christ. Scripture clearly teaches that they cannot earn salvation for us or cleanse us from sin. Sixteenth-century Swiss theologian Heinrich Bullinger wrote in 1561 that the purpose of good works is "for the glory of God, to adorn our calling, to show gratitude to God, and for the profit of our neighbor."[66]

Greek Words, Phrases, and Constructions in 1:22–25

Verse 22

γίνεσθε—the present middle imperative of γίνομαι (I am, become) is the substitute for ἔστε (the present imperative of εἰμί) which never occurs in the New

---

65. Reinier Schippers, *NIDNTT*, vol. 2, p. 63.
66. The Second Helvetic Confession, chap. 16. Also see the Westminster Confession of Faith, chap. 16.

Testament. For that reason, γίνεσθε signifies "be" and not "become." In the second half of the sentence, the implied imperative is negated by the particle μή.

Verse 23

ὅτι—this conjunction expresses cause and introduces a parable.
ἔοικεν—see verse 6 and the Septuagint version of Job 6:3. This incomplete verb in the perfect has a present meaning.
τὸ πρόσωπον τῆς γενέσεως—"the face that nature gave him" is an apt translation.[67] The genitive is descriptive.

Verse 24

κατενόησεν—this aorist active indicative from κατανοέω (I observe carefully) and the perfect active indicative ἀπελήλυθεν, from ἀπέρχομαι (I go away); the aorist middle indicative ἐπελάθετο, from ἐπιλανθάνομαι (I forget); and the imperfect active indicative ἦν, from εἰμί (I am), are gnomic, that is, timeless. Therefore, the New International Version translates these verbs in the present tense.

Verse 25

ὁ δὲ παρακύψας—this verse shows contrast and parallelism to the preceding verse. The combination ὁ δέ introduces contrast, whereas the aorist active participle παρακύψας, from παρακύπτω (I bend over to see something better), is parallel to κατενόησεν (v. 24).
τόν—the definite article refers to νόμον (law) and is demonstrative and specific—"the perfect law that gives freedom."[68]
ἐν τῇ ποιήσει—instead of using the verb ποιέω (I do, make), James employs the nouns ποιητής (doer) and ποίησις (doing). The -σις ending denotes progress, so that this last noun reflects the characteristics of a verb form in the present tense.

---

3. Serving Religiously
1:26–27

What is practical Christianity? James gives a few examples of what the true Christian religion should be: keep your tongue in check, get your hands dirty helping people in need, and keep yourself clean from the filth of this world. In these two verses, James lists some examples that serve as checkpoints on one's religion.

26. If anyone considers himself religious and yet does not keep a tight rein on his tongue, he deceives himself and his religion is worthless.

In explaining the meaning and implication of serving God, James tells his readers first how not to serve God. Then in the next verse, he instructs them how to profess and practice their religion.

a. "If anyone considers himself religious." This is a simple fact conditional sentence that depicts life as it is. A person who attends the worship services in a Christian church may consider himself religious. To be sure,

---

67. Ropes, *James*, p. 176.
68. Robertson, *Grammar*, p. 780.

many people believe that church attendance, praying, or even fasting is the equivalent of being religious. Not so, says James, because such activity may be merely outward show. That is formalism, not religion.

What, then, is religion? Negatively, it is not what man construes it to be when he considers himself to be pious. Positively, religion comes to expression when man speaks with a bridled tongue.

b. "Yet does not keep a tight rein on his tongue." The author of this epistle introduces the subject of the tongue in the first chapter (1:19), mentions it here in connection with religion, and then returns to it more explicitly in the third chapter. There he compares the tongue to horses that have bits in their mouths so that they obey their masters. "No man can tame the tongue," James says. "It is a restless evil, full of deadly poison" (3:8). If man is able to bridle his tongue, "he is a perfect man" (3:2).

If man fails to keep his tongue in check, his religion is worthless. The unruly tongue engages in lying, cursing and swearing, slander, and filthy language.[69] From man's point of view the hasty word, shading of the truth, the subtle innuendo, and the questionable joke are shrugged off as insignificant. Yet from God's perspective they are a violation of the command to love the Lord God and to love one's neighbor as oneself. A breach of this command renders man's religion of no avail.

c. "He deceives himself and his religion is worthless." This is the third time that James tells his readers not to deceive themselves (1:16, 22, 26). As a pastor he is fully aware of counterfeit religion that is nothing more than external formalism. He knows that many people merely go through the motions of serving God, but their speech gives them away. Their religion has a hollow ring. And although they may not realize it, by their words and by their actions—or lack of them—they deceive themselves. Their heart is not right with God and their fellow man, and their attempt to hide this lack of love only heightens their self-deception. Their religion is worthless.

27. Religion that God our Father accepts as pure and faultless is this: to look after orphans and widows in their distress and to keep oneself from being polluted by the world.

Scripture is not a book with concise definitions that can be applied to specific instances. The Bible teaches us the way of life that is pleasing to God and to our neighbor. Thus, James gives us not a precise definition in this verse but rather a principle.

a. "Religion that God our Father accepts as pure and faultless." When James says "God our Father," he immediately introduces the family concept. We are God's children because he is our Father. He expects us to pay due respect and love to him, to our brothers and sisters in God's

---

69. Thomas Manton, *An Exposition on the Epistle of James* (reprint ed., London: Banner of Truth Trust, 1968), pp. 172–73.

household, and to all people (Gal. 6:10). Within the family of God love is the prevailing characteristic because God himself is love. God sets the example.

Here are a few random Scripture verses that illustrate this characteristic:

A father to the fatherless, a defender of widows,
is God in his holy dwelling. [Ps. 68:5]

The LORD watches over the alien
and sustains the fatherless and the widow. [Ps. 146:9]

He defends the cause of the fatherless and the widow, and loves the alien. [Deut. 10:18]

For the pagans run after all these things [physical needs], and your heavenly Father knows that you need them. [Matt. 6:32]

If, then, God sets the example, he expects his children to do what he does. If they follow God's example, they demonstrate religion that is "pure and faultless." These two adjectives show the positive (pure) and the negative (faultless) aspects; together they denote the essence of religion.[70] And how do we practice our religion? James gives two examples:

b. The first example pertains to the social circumstances and conditions of his day: "To look after orphans and widows in their distress." Social conditions in ancient times were such that orphans and widows were unprotected because they had no guardian and breadwinner. God himself, therefore, filled that role. He exhorted the Israelite to be a protector and provider for the orphan and the widow (for example, see Deut. 14:29; Ezek. 22:7; Acts 6:1–6).

The person who exhibits true religion visits the "orphans and widows in their distress." He puts his heart into being a guardian and provider, he alleviates their needs, and shows them the love of the Lord in word and deed (Matt. 25:35–40).

c. "To keep oneself from being polluted by the world." Even though James urges us to become socially involved in helping needy people around us, at the same time he warns us to stay away from a sinful world. Do we have to isolate ourselves from the world? No, we are always in the world but not of the world (John 17:14).

Therefore, we ought not to imitate the ways of the world; rather, we ought to practice godliness. Writing about the coming of the Lord and the end of the world, Peter says, "So then, dear friends, since you are looking forward to this, make every effort to be found spotless, blameless, and at peace with him" (II Peter 3:14; and see I Tim. 6:14). In a sense James repeats what he said earlier, "Get rid of all moral filth and the evil that is so

---

70. J. I. Packer explains the term *faultless* by saying that it "is used to express the purity of Christ as High Priest (Heb. 7:27), of our heavenly inheritance (2 Pet. 1:4), of sexual relations within marriage (Heb. 13:4), and of practical religion (Jas. 1:27); what it affirms in each of its applications is the absence of anything that would constitute guilt before God." *NIDNTT*, vol. 1, p. 448. Also consult Hans Währisch, *NIDNTT*, vol. 3, p. 925.

prevalent" (1:21). Members of God's family have the word *holy* written on their foreheads. They "know that friendship with the world is hatred toward God" (James 4:4). They love and serve the Lord truly and sincerely.

Practical Considerations in 1:26–27

Should the church stress the concept *religion* as James has developed it and make its requirements mandatory for anyone seeking to become a member of the church? Certainly! The church ought to teach the scriptural truth recorded in this section of the Epistle of James. The principle of pure and undefiled religion is to love God and the neighbor.

How much should the church become involved in social-welfare programs? Primary tasks of the church are to preach the gospel, to administer the sacraments, and to care for the poor. These tasks need to be kept in balance so that the church can function properly.

Should the church extend her care for the poor beyond the limits of her own community? Yes, in our shrinking world the refugees and homeless, the hungry and destitute, the sick and afflicted need our help wherever they are. We show the love of Jesus by reaching out to help them. Again, we must maintain balance and exercise discretion, remembering Paul's admonition, "Therefore, as we have opportunity, let us do good to all people, especially to those who belong to the family of believers" (Gal. 6:10).

Greek Words, Phrases, and Constructions in 1:26–27

Verse 26

εἰ—the sentence is a simple fact condition with the verb δοκεῖ (seems, considers) in the protasis and the understood verb *to be* in the apodosis. However, the clause ἀλλὰ ἀπατῶν καρδίαν αὐτοῦ (however he deceives himself) conveys the meaning of the verse much better when it is taken as part of the apodosis (NIV, GNB). The words, then, are parallel to the clause *his religion is worthless*. Other translations make this clause independent of the conditional sentence (NAB, NEB).

θρησκός—the adjective describes a person who is pious, God-fearing, and religious. The noun θρησκεία appears four times in the New Testament (Acts 26:5; Col. 2:18; James 1:26, 27) and means "the worship of God." It differs little from the noun λατρεία.[71]

χαλιναγωγῶν—the present active participle is a compound derived from χαλινός (bridle) and ἄγω (I lead).

μάταιος—this adjective from the verb ματαιόω (I make empty, worthless) describes the lack of truth in a hollow religion.

Verse 27

ἐπισκέπτεσθαι—the present middle infinitive of the verb ἐπισκέπτομαι (I look after, visit [in order to help]). The infinitive expresses purpose and is somewhat

---

71. Karl Ludwig Schmidt, *TDNT*, vol. 3, p. 156; Klaus Hess, *NIDNTT*, vol. 3, p. 551.

similar to the imperative which, in fact, some of the manuscripts have as a variant reading.

ἄσπιλον ἑαυτὸν τηρεῖν—the present infinitive τηρεῖν denotes purpose; the predicate adjective ἄσπιλον derives from the privative ἀ (un-) and the noun σπίλος (spot). One influential manuscript (P⁷⁴) has the reading ὑπερασπίζειν αὐτούς (to protect them). This reading, however, has not received the favor of most translators.[72]

Summary of Chapter 1

At first the content of chapter 1 appears to be a number of unrelated proverbial sayings that are connected only by catchwords. But upon closer examination, we realize that the writer introduces themes which he explains more fully in the rest of the chapter and the epistle. For example, after an introductory address (v. 1), the author lists the themes of testing of faith, gaining wisdom, and being rich (vv. 2–11).[73]

Then, in the next part of the chapter (vv. 12–25) he elucidates the theme of testing by expanding it to tempting (vv. 12–15); he mentions the generous gift of wisdom God gives and broadens it to include good and perfect gifts from the heavenly Father (vv. 5, 17–18); and he fortifies the humble brother's pride in a high position with the assurance that we are a kind of God's first fruits of all that he has created (v. 18).

The last segment of the chapter has the themes of keeping the tongue in check, putting the Word of God into practice, and living a spotless life in a polluted world (vv. 19–27). James returns to these themes in the succeeding chapters. In fact, scholars see in the three examples of pure religion—to bridle the tongue, to show mercy, and to keep oneself undefiled—an outline for the next four chapters.[74]

---

72. D. J. Roberts defends the variant reading by saying that it could be original because it agrees with the message of James, that is, "to protect them [the orphans and widows] in their affliction from the world." "The Definition of 'Pure Religion' in James 1:27," *ExpT* 83 (1972): 215–16. But B. C. Johanson disagrees. See "The Definition of 'Pure Religion' in James 1:27 Reconsidered," *ExpT* 84 (1973): 118–19.

73. Davids, *James*, p. 25.

74. Grosheide, *Jakobus*, p. 368.

2

Faith

2:1–26

Outline

2 1 My brothers, as believers in our glorious Lord Jesus Christ, don't show favoritism. 2 Suppose a man comes into your meeting wearing a gold ring and fine clothes, and a poor man in shabby clothes also comes in. 3 If you show special attention to the man wearing fine clothes and say, "Here's a good seat for you," but say to the poor man, "You stand there," or, "Sit on the floor by my feet," 4 have you not discriminated among yourselves and become judges with evil thoughts?

5 Listen, my dear brothers: Has not God chosen those who are poor in the eyes of the world to be rich in faith and to inherit the kingdom he promised those who love him? 6 But you have insulted the poor. Is it not the rich who are exploiting you? Are they not the ones who are dragging you into court? 7 Are they not the ones who are slandering the noble name of him to whom you belong?

8 If you really keep the royal law found in Scripture, "Love your neighbor as yourself," you are doing right. 9 But if you show favoritism, you sin and are convicted by the law as lawbreakers. 10 For whoever keeps the whole law and yet stumbles at just one point is guilty of breaking all of it. 11 For he who said, "Do not commit adultery," also said, "Do not murder." If you do not commit adultery but do commit murder, you have become a lawbreaker.

12 Speak and act as those who are going to be judged by the law that gives freedom, 13 because judgment without mercy will be shown to anyone who has not been merciful. Mercy triumphs over judgment!

A. Faith and the Law
2:1–13

1. Avoid Favoritism
2:1–4

All men are created equal. We have brought nothing into this world and we cannot take anything out of it. Before God we cannot boast of our possessions or achievements, for all that we have has been given to us by God. And God does not show partiality (Acts 10:34; Rom. 2:11; Eph. 6:9; Col. 3:25; I Peter 1:17). If God sets the example, we should follow in his footsteps.

1. My brothers, as believers in our glorious Lord Jesus Christ, don't show favoritism.

The appeal is personal: "my brothers." James uses this address rather frequently in his epistle, but here he is more specific. He calls the brothers "believers in our glorious Lord Jesus Christ."[1] The word *believers* is reminiscent of the beginning of the epistle, where James encourages the "brothers" to persevere in their faith (1:3). Now he tells them that they are believers in Jesus Christ. That is, he speaks of their personal subjective faith in Jesus—not of the faith that belongs to Jesus.

The writer places himself on a level with his readers and identifies with them when he says "our glorious Lord." He and the readers look to Jesus, who dwells in glory.

What is the meaning of the expression *our glorious Lord?* In one of Paul's epistles (I Cor. 2:8) the expression *Lord of glory* occurs. This is identical to the reference to "the God of glory" in Stephen's speech (Acts 7:2). Both titles are reminders of the glory of the Lord that settled upon and filled the tabernacle in the desert (Exod. 40:35). A possible interpretation is to take the words *of glory* and place them in apposition with *Jesus Christ:* "Jesus Christ, who is the glory, [that is,] of God."[2] This interpretation resembles John's testimony about Jesus living among the disciples: "We have seen his glory, the glory of the one and only Son, who came from the Father, full of grace and truth" (John 1:14).

The descriptive adjective *glorious* in this passage demonstrates contrast between the glory of our Lord Jesus Christ and the glitter of earthly riches. The brothers should not look at their fellow man and judge him merely by external appearance. Therefore, James admonishes his readers, "don't show favoritism." Don't look at a person's face, clothing, wealth, and position! Don't be biased in your judgment! "A just judge must not be influenced by personal prejudices, hopes, or fears, but by the single desire to do justice."[3]

In the next verses of this section, James spells out the reasons Christians should not show favoritism: if you do, you will "become judges with evil thoughts" (v. 4); God looks at the heart, not at the external appearance of man (v. 5); God has given man the law of loving one's neighbor as oneself (v. 8); and last, "mercy triumphs over judgment!" (v. 13).

James resorts to an illustration and says,

2. Suppose a man comes into your meeting wearing a gold ring and fine clothes, and a poor man in shabby clothes also comes in. 3. If you show special attention to the man wearing fine clothes and say, "Here's a good seat for you," but say to the poor man, "You stand there," or, "Sit on the floor by my feet," 4. have you not discriminated among yourselves and become judges with evil thoughts?

The term *religion* (1:26–27) immediately brings to mind anything that

---

1. Translations of this phrase differ. Here are a few examples: "the faith of our Lord Jesus Christ, the Lord of glory" (KJV, NKJV, RV, ASV); "your faith in our glorious Lord Jesus Christ" (NASB; NAB); "believing as you do in our Lord Jesus Christ, who reigns in glory" (NEB).

2. E. C. Blackman, *The Epistle of James* (London: SCM, 1957), p. 76.

3. Joseph B. Mayor, *The Epistle of St. James* (reprint ed.; Grand Rapids: Zondervan, 1946), p. 78.

pertains to the church. Perhaps this was the reason that James resorts to an example taken from the setting of a Christian church. Actually, the Greek for "meeting" (v. 2) is the word *synagogue*.[4] Even though James employs the expression *church* when he mentions "the elders of the church" (5:14), the term *synagogue* reveals something about the writer and the readers of his letter: they are of Jewish descent.[5]

a. "Suppose a man comes into your meeting." The author chooses the general term *meeting* that can mean either the worship service or a special gathering for official purposes. James does not specify the purpose of the meeting in question. Some scholars think that James portrays an assembly that meets for official, that is, judicial matters.[6] Common opinion, however, favors the concept of a worship service. The point of the example is to show that in a gathering of believers snobbery prevailed.

b. "A man . . . wearing a gold ring and fine clothes." Was the rich man a member of the church? Was he a visitor? Was he a government official or dignitary? We do not know. Perhaps he was a person with authority, and not a member of the local church. For instance, the centurion who built the synagogue in Capernaum presumably was a proselyte (Luke 7:2–5). The meetings of the church were open to the public, so that people of the community were given the opportunity to meet with Christians for worship and instruction (I Cor. 14:23–24).

c. "And a poor man in shabby clothes also comes in." The contrast is deliberate, for the rich man wears bright, shiny clothes; the poor man's clothes are dirty, shabby, and unsightly. He is poverty-stricken; the only clothes he has are the clothes he wears. Again, we do not know whether the man is a member of the church. Probably not. He also seems to be a visitor.

d. "If you show special attention." The emphasis in this particular section is on the external appearance of these two visitors. Only the apparel of the two men is significant. Of course, dress also reflects the status of

---

4. Of all the translations, only JB has the reading, "Now suppose a man comes into your synagogue."

5. Lothar Coenen comments on the word *synagogue* in James 2:2, "For the word would have been natural for a group which sprang from Jewish roots and which at least in the beginning counted itself a part of Judaism." *NIDNTT*, vol. 1, p. 296. On the other hand, Wolfgang Schrage shows that the word "is used not only for the assemblies, congregations, and synagogues of the Jews but also for the liturgical meetings and meeting-places of Christians. . . . For gatherings for worship it is common in the post-apostolic fathers" (e.g., Ignatius). *TDNT*, vol. 7, p. 840.

6. Consult the article by Roy Bowen Ward, "Partiality in the Assembly: James 2:2–4," *HTR* 62 (1969): 87–97. Also see James B. Adamson, *The Epistle of James*, New International Commentary on the New Testament series (Grand Rapids: Eerdmans, 1976), pp. 105–8; and Peter H. Davids, *The Epistle of James: A Commentary on the Greek Text*, New International Greek Testament Commentary series (Grand Rapids: Eerdmans, 1982), p. 109. Sophie Laws, however, expresses her reservations and doubts "if the terms in which James sketches his supposed situation will allow for so precise a definition of it." See her *Commentary on the Epistle of James*, Harper's New Testament Commentaries (San Francisco: Harper and Row, 1980), p. 101.

these two individuals: the one is rich and has influence; the other is poor and has nothing.

The immediate reaction of the church members is to pay deference to the rich man by showing him to a good seat. In the local synagogue of that day, scribes and Pharisees occupied the most important seats (Matt. 23:6; Mark 12:39; Luke 11:43; 20:46).[7] In the setting of the church that James depicts, the rich man receives a warm welcome and is ushered to a good seat, perhaps somewhat elevated. The poor man can either stand in the back section of the building or sit cross-legged on the floor. In fact, the text says, "Sit down by my footstool."

e. "Have you not discriminated among yourselves?" To ask the question is to answer it. Certainly, they discriminate and have "become judges with evil thoughts." Instead of looking at the incomparable glory of the Lord, they are staring at the splendor of a gold ring and fine clothes. Instead of honoring Jesus Christ, they are paying respect to a rich man and despising a poor man. And instead of accepting persons on the basis of faith in Christ, they are showing favoritism based on appearance and status.

James points not to officially appointed judges but to the members of the church. The congregation ought to realize the full extent of its sin of discrimination. It is not a sin that can be labeled insignificant. What is at stake, says James, is that justice is not being served because the believers' hearts are filled with evil thoughts. A judge whose thoughts are evil can never be impartial; the justice that he administers is a farce. Since time immemorial, justice has been depicted as a blindfolded lady who holds scales in her hand. The blindfold prevents her from seeing anyone so that she is able to serve impartially the cause of justice. Within the context of the Christian faith, practicing discrimination is the exact opposite of loving one's neighbor as oneself.

Whether James cites an actual incident that occurred in the church of his day or constructs an example of something that may happen is immaterial.[8] Of importance is that believers in Christ ought to shun the sin of discrimination. In short, "don't show favoritism."

Practical Considerations in 2:1–4

God loves the poor, watches over them, and provides for them. When the church of Jesus Christ proclaims the gospel and welcomes the poor into the

---

7. "The congregation sat in an appointed order, the most distinguished members in the front seats, the younger behind," writes Emil Schürer in *A History of the Jewish People in the Time of Jesus Christ* (Edinburgh: Clark, 1885), 2d div., vol. 2, p. 75.

8. Martin Dibelius believes that James "has merely contrived the event." *James: A Commentary on the Epistle of James*, rev. Heinrich Greeven, trans. Michael A. Williams, ed. Helmut Köster, Hermeneia: A Critical and Historical Commentary on the Bible (Philadelphia: Fortress, 1976), p. 135.

communion of the believers, does it show love and concern for them? When the poor hear the gospel of Jesus' love, the message of salvation, and the promise of God's constant care, and then experience a cold indifference, a lack of interest and concern from the members of the church, they feel slighted.

Today many church sanctuaries are partially filled during the worship services. The pews in these sanctuaries are padded, the worshipers sit in comfort, but the poor are absent.

The gospel must be proclaimed in word and deed to the poor. The loving heart of the believer is shown when he extends a helping hand. The love of the Lord Jesus, when it is genuinely extended to those who hear the gospel, effectively builds the body of Christ.

Greek Words, Phrases, and Constructions in 2:1–4

Verse 1

προσωπολημψίαις—derived from the noun πρόσωπον (face) and the verb λαμβάνω (I receive), this noun is a translation of the Hebrew *nasa panim* (he lifts up someone's face, he receives someone kindly). The Hebrew *panim* is a plural and the Greek translation appears as an idiomatic plural.[9] Paul uses the term in the singular (Rom. 2:11; Eph. 6:9; Col. 3:25), and James employs the verb προσωπολημπτεῖτε (you show favoritism) in 2:9.

τὴν πίστιν—the use of the definite article and the genitive τοῦ κυρίου indicate that the noun πίστιν (faith) is not the body of Christian doctrine; rather, it is *the* subjective faith that Christians have *in* the Lord (objective genitive).[10]

τῆς δόξης—in the Greek the sentence structure is difficult because of the combination of four genitives. The appellation Ἰησοῦ Χριστοῦ stands in apposition to τοῦ κυρίου; so does τῆς δόξης. On the other hand, δόξης can also be taken in the form of a descriptive adjective *glorious*. Whatever the choice, difficulties remain.

Verse 2

ἐάν—the particle introduces a conditional sentence that features the use of the subjunctive to express a hypothetical situation. Note that the tense of εἰσέλθῃ (from εἰσέρχομαι, I enter) is aorist to show single occurrence.

λαμπρᾷ—this adjective in the dative feminine singular describes the noun ἐσθῆτι (clothes) and is contrasted with the adjective ῥυπαρᾷ (dirty, filthy). The word λαμπρός, derived from the verb λάμπω (I shine), actually means "beaming, bright, shining." In this reference to a garment, it can indicate affluence or wealth.[11] See Luke 23:11 and Revelation 19:8.

---

9. A. T. Robertson, *A Grammar of the Greek New Testament in the Light of Historical Research* (Nashville: Broadman, 1934), p. 408.

10. "Faith in Jesus Christ is the distinctive act which makes a man a Christian." Consult James Hardy Ropes, *A Critical and Exegetical Commentary on the Epistle of James,* International Critical Commentary series (1916; reprint ed., Edinburgh: Clark, 1961), p. 187.

11. Hans-Christoph Hahn, *NIDNTT,* vol. 2, p. 486.

Verse 3

ἐπιβλέψητε—as part of the protasis of the conditional sentence, this aorist active subjunctive from ἐπιβλέπω (I look up to [with esteem]) is followed by the preposition ἐπί (upon) to stress the directive meaning of the verb.

τὸν φοροῦντα—the present active participle of the verb φορέω (I wear) indicates that the rich man regularly wore fine clothing.

σὺ κάθου—the use of σύ (you) in both this and the next imperatival sentence emphasizes the verbs. The aorist middle imperative κάθου is a contraction of κάθησο (sit). The addition of καλῶς (well) softens the tone to make it the equivalent of "please."

ὑπὸ τὸ ὑποπόδιόν μου—the preposition ὑπό denotes not "under" but "at" or "by." The reference to a footstool indicates that the "good seat" was elevated.

Verse 4

οὐ διεκρίθητε—a rhetorical question that demands a positive answer, the verb in the aorist passive is from διακρίνω (I differentiate) and with the noun κριταί (judges) is a play on words. The aorist passive with middle force and the words ἐν ἑαυτοῖς (among yourselves) show redundancy.

ἐγένεσθε—the aorist passive of γίνομαι (I become) is timeless.

---

2. Be Rich in Faith
2:5–7

From the example James turns to the principle: the poor are precious in God's sight. Jesus came to preach the gospel to the poor (Isa. 61:1; Luke 4:18; 7:22) and declared the poor blessed and heirs of the kingdom of God (Matt. 5:3; Luke 6:20).

5. Listen, my dear brothers: Has not God chosen those who are poor in the eyes of the world to be rich in faith and to inherit the kingdom he promised those who love him?

Once again James addresses the readers as brothers.[12] He tells them to give him their undivided attention: "Listen." He wants them to listen and take note. His tone of voice, however, is gentle, for he calls the readers "dear brothers" (1:16, 19).

a. *Chosen.* James asks a question that can be answered only in the affirmative. "Has not God chosen those who are poor?" Yes, of course, the Scriptures clearly teach that in his electing grace God chooses not on the basis of merit but because of his love toward his people (see, for instance, Deut. 7:7). God directs his love to the poor and needy, for his eye is always on them (Job 5:15–16; Ps. 9:18; 12:5; Prov. 22:22–23). This does not mean that all the poor are included and that God has chosen only the

---

12. Here are the places where James addresses the readers as brothers: 1:2, 16, 19; 2:1, 5, 14; 3:1, 10, 12; 4:11; 5:7, 9, 10, 12, 19.

poor. "For poverty and riches of themselves do not render any man good or evil."[13] Election is God's work, as Paul teaches. "He chose the lowly things . . . so that no one may boast before him" (I Cor. 1:28–29; and see Eph. 1:4).

b. *Confer.* James repeats the thought he expressed earlier (1:9) when he writes that "those who are poor in the eyes of the world [are] rich in faith." Not earthly riches but spiritual treasures count (Matt. 6:19–21; Luke 12:16–21). God looks not at man's material possessions that are void of stability, but at the confidence and assurance man places in God. Such faith God amply rewards. God demands faith, as the writer of Hebrews states eloquently: "Without faith it is impossible to please God, because anyone who comes to him must believe that he exists and that he rewards those who earnestly seek him" (11:6).

Note that James echoes words of Jesus recorded as beatitudes. Here is the parallel:

Luke 6:20	James 2:5
Blessed are you	Has not God chosen those
who are poor,	who are poor . . .
for yours is	to be rich in faith and
the kingdom of God.	to inherit the kingdom?

Who are the ones who are rich in faith? They are the believers whom God enriches with spiritual gifts. Observes John Calvin, "Since the Lord deals bountifully with all, every one becomes partaker of his gifts according to the measure of his own faith. If, then, we are empty or needy, that proves the deficiency of our faith; for if we only enlarge the bosom of faith, God is always ready to fill it."[14] And God will enrich the believers; they are the people who inherit his kingdom.

c. *Promised.* God has promised the kingdom to those who love him. Although the word *kingdom* appears only here in the Epistle of James, its parallel is "the crown of life that God has promised to those who love him" (1:12; and see Rom. 8:28). Jesus links the concepts *eternal life* and *kingdom* in his teachings (see especially Matt. 19:16, 24, 28–30; Mark 10:17, 23–25; Luke 18:18, 23–30).

Who inherits the kingdom? All those—whether rich or poor—who love the Lord. Says God, "I love those who love me, and those who seek me find me" (Prov. 8:17).

The references to inheriting the kingdom of God are many: Jesus reveals that in the judgment day the King will welcome his own and say,

---

13. John Albert Bengel, *Gnomon of the New Testament,* ed. Andrew R. Fausset, 5 vols., 7th ed. (Edinburgh: Clark, 1877), vol. 5, p. 14. Ropes comments, "Poverty and election coincide." See *James,* p. 193.

14. John Calvin, *Commentaries on the Catholic Epistles: The Epistle of James,* ed. and trans. John Owen (Grand Rapids: Eerdmans, 1948), p. 303.

"Come, you who are blessed by my Father; take your inheritance, the kingdom prepared for you since the creation of the world" (Matt. 25:34). And Paul discloses that the wicked will not inherit the kingdom (I Cor. 6:9–10; Gal. 5:19–21).

6. But you have insulted the poor. Is it not the rich who are exploiting you? Are they not the ones who are dragging you into court? 7. Are they not the ones who are slandering the noble name of him to whom you belong?

From the New Testament we learn that the early church consisted primarily of poor people, especially in Judea and Jerusalem (Acts 11:29–30; I Cor. 16:1–3). These people who themselves belonged to the lower class of society were paying homage to the rich and despising the poor. James condemns that uncharitable practice.

The charge James put to the readers of his epistle is serious. He states a fact: "you have insulted the poor" (see also I Cor. 11:22). The implication is that those who insult the poor insult Jesus Christ, the protector and guardian of the poor. They no longer champion the cause of Christ; by showing favoritism to the rich they have "sided with the devil against God."[15] What is the effect of this snobbery? In his teaching Jesus put it in these words: "He who is not with me is against me, and he who does not gather with me scatters" (Matt. 12:30).

James pointedly addresses the issue of favoritism. His intent is to root it from the soil of the early Christian church. He exhorts the believer to open his eyes, look at reality, and answer the following three questions:

a. *Who exploits you?* James answers this question in the latter part of his epistle where he rebukes the rich who oppress the poor. He mentions specific examples: "The wages you failed to pay the workmen who mowed your fields are crying out against you. The cries of the harvesters have reached the ears of the Lord Almighty" (5:4). From the general context of the situation that James describes we learn that the rich do not belong to the Christian community. Whether they were Jewish or Gentile people is inconsequential. They exploit people who are unable to defend themselves, including widows and orphans (compare Amos 8:4; Mic. 2:2; Zech. 7:10). From the writings of the Qumran community in the first part of the first century, we learn that even the priests in Israel were exploiting the poor.[16]

If Christians pay tribute to the rich who exploit and oppress the poor, they go contrary to the explicit teachings of Scripture. The Christians are in the wrong camp, for they are the ones who should defend the poor.

b. *Who drags you into court?* The New Testament provides a few striking examples of the apostles being taken to court by Jews and by Gentiles

---

15. Davids, *James*, p. 112.
16. Ernst Bammel has compiled specific references in his article on the poor in *TDNT*, vol. 6, p. 897. Also consult Hans-Helmut Esser, *NIDNTT*, vol. 2, p. 824.

(Acts 5:27; 16:19; 18:12). Influential rich Jews had the power to drag poor Christian Jews into court to malign them.[17] James refrains from being specific in his references to the rich. Whether Jewish or Gentile, these rich people were receiving honor and respect from the very Christians they were dragging into court. Were these Christians not tainted by the sin of favoritism, they would remain loyal to the poor, endure injustice, and thus demonstrate the mind of Christ (see, for example, I Peter 2:20). Instead, they honored the rich and insulted the poor.

c. *Who slanders Christ's name?* James is much more specific in this third question. He is calling the readers back to their senses. He asks them to tell him who the people are who slander the noble name of him to whom the readers belong. Both in the Old Testament and the New, God teaches that his people "are called by the name of the LORD" (Deut. 28:10; compare II Chron. 7:14; Isa. 43:7; Jer. 14:9; Amos 9:12). When James addressed the Jerusalem Council, he quoted Amos 9:11–12, where the prophet says that the Gentiles who bear the name of the Lord may seek him (Acts 15:17). The name *Jesus* became the substitute for the Old Testament name *Lord.*

Christians revere the name of Jesus—a name that James describes as noble. They are the ones who have to listen to rich people blaspheme the name of Jesus. If they keep silent while the rich slander that noble name, they themselves sin against the command not to take the name of God in vain (Exod. 20:7; Deut. 5:11). By keeping silent these people who belong to Jesus give assent to slandering the name of Jesus. They have turned against him by showing deference to the rich.

Practical Considerations in 2:5–7

Verse 5

Jesus identified with the poor because he himself experienced poverty from the day he was born in Bethlehem until the day he died outside of Jerusalem. Consequently, the poor promptly responded to Jesus' message. They still do today, for the church is growing rapidly among economically depressed people in numerous parts of the world. As a class, the poor place their faith in Jesus much more readily than do those who are rich. They are poor in material possessions but rich in faith. Because of their circumstances, the poor cannot put their trust in material possessions. Therefore they turn to Jesus who says, "Come to me, all you who are weary and burdened, and I will give you rest" (Matt. 11:28).

Verse 6

The rich are able to afford the help of lawyers to press a claim or file a suit. Check the records in court and the evidence will show that, generally, not the poor but the rich bring suit against others.

---

17. R. C. H. Lenski, *The Interpretation of the Epistle to the Hebrews and of the Epistle of James* (Columbus: Wartburg, 1946), p. 568.

Verse 7

Those people who hold the highest office in the land and are entitled to command great respect lose esteem among Christians when they misuse the name of Jesus. By misusing that noble name, they dishonor Jesus, offend his followers, and sin against God.

Greek Words, Phrases, and Constructions in 2:5–7

Verse 5

ἀκούσατε—the aorist active imperative stands first in the sentence for emphasis (compare 1:16, 19). James tactfully tempers the command with the verbal adjective ἀγαπητοί (beloved).

τῷ κόσμῳ—the use of the dative is understood as the dative of reference: "poor in the eyes of the world" (NAB, NEB, NIV).

ἧς—a genitive of attraction because of the preceding noun βασιλείας (kingdom).

Verse 6

ὑμεῖς—the emphatic use of the personal pronoun with the adversative particle δέ is designed to show contrast with the preceding verse, which says that God has chosen the poor to be rich.

οὐχ—this negative adverb introduces the rhetorical questions that expect a positive answer (see οὐκ in v. 7).

---

3. Keep the Royal Law
2:8–11

What does the Bible say about favoritism and discrimination? Perhaps a Jewish Christian asked James this question and then suggested that Scripture should be the measure of all things. Apparently James anticipates this type of question, which was commonly asked in Jewish circles. With the Old Testament in hand, James answers the reader who questions him and thus proves his point.

8. If you really keep the royal law found in Scripture, "Love your neighbor as yourself," you are doing right. 9. But if you show favoritism, you sin and are convicted by the law as lawbreakers.

James goes to the heart of the matter and avoids details. That is, he is not interested in searching the Scriptures to find a particular command on the sin of favoritism. Rather, he states the fundamental principle of God's law to which Jesus referred when he was questioned by an expert in the law. The expert asked Jesus, "Teacher, which is the greatest commandment in the Law?" (Matt. 22:36). Instead of listing a specific command, Jesus summarized the law for him and said, "Love the Lord your God . . . and . . . love your neighbor as yourself" (vv. 37–39; and see Deut. 6:5; Lev. 19:18).

a. *Condition*. James calls attention to only the second part of the summary, "Love your neighbor as yourself." He stresses this part, just as Paul does in his epistles (Rom. 13:9; Gal. 5:14; and compare Matt. 19:19). But the implication is the same: the entire law is summarized in expressing love for one's neighbor. Keeping the second part of the summary means fulfilling the first part as well. The two parts are inseparably connected (I John 4:20–21).[18]

James calls the summary of the law "royal." He does not elaborate and he refrains from explaining the word in context. He puts the sum and substance of the law in a conditional sentence that states a simple fact. He says, "If you really keep the royal law . . . you are doing right." The believer who fulfills the supreme law of God, given in the Scriptures, is doing God's will and keeps himself from falling into the sin of favoritism.

b. *Charge*. God shows no favoritism (Rom. 2:11), but shows his love to the poor as well as to the rich. If God is impartial, then the believers also should show love to all people without discrimination.

Perhaps James has in mind the broader context of the Old Testament teaching, "Love your neighbor as yourself" (Lev. 19:18). In this context Moses tells the Israelites, "Do not pervert justice; do not show partiality to the poor or favoritism to the great, but judge your neighbor fairly" (Lev. 19:15).

James, however, refers to the sin of favoritism that the readers are committing. Therefore, he adds that by being partial (Deut. 1:17) they stand convicted by the law of love. The summary of the law condemns them as lawbreakers. The readers are actually working at sin, says James. And they do so by stepping across the boundary that has been given to keep them from sin, namely, the law. No one is able to say that he stepped across the line in ignorance, because the law specifically forbids showing partiality (Lev. 19:15). Transgressing the law of God is a serious offense to God that makes the sinner stand before him as a lawbreaker.[19] The charge is leveled against the transgressor. When the law convicts him, no one can claim to be a partial transgressor. He is guilty.

10. For whoever keeps the whole law and yet stumbles at just one point is guilty of breaking all of it. 11. For he who said, "Do not commit adultery," also said, "Do not murder." If you do not commit adultery but do commit murder, you have become a lawbreaker.

Consider the following issues:

a. "The whole law." James uses a sentence that states a condition. He says, "If anyone of you tries to keep the entire law of God, but stumbles in regard to one of the commandments, he is guilty because the whole law condemns him."

---

18. Refer to William Hendriksen, *Galatians*, New Testament Commentary series (Grand Rapids: Baker, 1968), p. 211.
19. "To the rabbis such transgression was 'rebellion,' " writes Adamson, *James*, p. 116. Consult Johannes Schneider, *TDNT*, vol. 5, p. 741.

The Jews in the time of James made a distinction between the more important laws and those that were less significant. For example, they considered the law on sabbath observance most pressing.[20] But other commandments, like the one against swearing, they did not consider very important (see Matt. 5:33–37; James 5:12).

Even though James initially wrote his epistle to Christians with a Jewish background, he excludes no one from the obligation to observe and keep the law of God. Every reader of his letter ought to take note of the unity of God's law. We cannot maintain that keeping the commandment, "You shall not kill," is more important than the one that says, "You shall not covet." Scripture does not allow us to add value judgments to the commandments. In fact, in the Sermon on the Mount Jesus teaches that nothing from the law will disappear "until everything is accomplished" (Matt. 5:17–19). And Paul refers to the obligation of obeying the whole law (Gal. 5:3). Thus, in his discussion on the law, James, too, stresses that God's law is not made up of individual commandments but that it displays unity.[21]

b. *The unity of the law.* Certainly, the law consists of numerous commandments, but transgressing one of them means breaking the law of God. If I stub my toe, not only my toe but also my whole body hurts. Every part of my body is integrally related to the whole. "If one part suffers, every part suffers with it" (I Cor. 12:26). If I break one of God's commandments, I sin against the entire law of God.

God himself has originated and formulated his law. He also enacts and enforces it, because through the law he expresses his will. God said, "Do not commit adultery." He also said, "Do not murder." These two commandments are part of the law, that is, the Decalogue (Exod. 20:13, 14; Deut. 5:17, 18), and bear the same divine authority as the rest of God's law.

The order of the two commandments is the reverse of the grouping given in the Hebrew Bible and the modern translations. But in the Septuagint the order is the one which not only James has adopted. Luke in his Gospel (18:20) and Paul in his letter to the Romans (13:9) have this same sequence.[22]

James has selected the two commandments that are mentioned first in the section of the law that pertains to the neighbor (see Matt. 19:18–19 and parallels). The simple logic is that if a person keeps the one commandment but violates the other, he is nonetheless a lawbreaker and God declares him guilty.

---

20. See *Talmud*, Shabbat 70b. Also consult SB, vol. 3, p. 755; Adamson, *James*, p. 117; and Laws, *James*, p. 111.

21. Davids, *James*, pp. 116–17.

22. Septuagint Codex A, however, follows the order of the Masoretic Text in Exod. 20:13, 14 and Deut. 5:17, 18. So does Matthew in recording the Sermon on the Mount (5:21, 27). Also see Matt. 19:18; Mark 10:19. However, Philo in *The Decalogue* 12. 24–32 and in *Special Laws* 3. 2 stays with the Septuagintal sequence.

Doctrinal Considerations in 2:8-11

Too often we look at the commandments from a negative point of view. We do so because most of them are cast in a negative form: for example, do not murder, do not commit adultery, do not steal. But the Ten Commandments have a positive side, too. They teach us that within the boundaries of God's protective laws we have perfect freedom. As fish thrive in water because water is their natural habitat, so the child of God flourishes in the setting of the law. He realizes that God has graciously given him these laws for his protection and safety. He knows that "the law of the LORD is perfect" and that "the precepts of the LORD are right" (Ps. 19:7, 8). He experiences the love of God in these commandments, so that he in turn can express his love to God and his neighbor.

Why does the believer keep the law of God? He keeps the law because in this way he is able to show his gratitude to God. The law of God, then, is a rule of gratitude for the believer.

Greek Words, Phrases, and Constructions in 2:8-11

Verse 8

εἰ μέντοι—the particle εἰ introduces a simple fact condition that depicts reality. The particle μέντοι is a particle of affirmation and means "really." In this verse, the particle should not be taken as the adversative *however*.

νόμον τελεῖτε βασιλικόν—both the noun and the adjective lack the definite article. Therefore the adjective may be seen as an attributive adjective. "Consequently, the most probable rendering seems to be 'fulfill the royal law' (especially in view of Christ's reference to his law in Matt. 7:12 and 22:40)."[23]

ἀγαπήσεις—grammarians call this verb form a volitive future.[24] The form, however, is equivalent to an imperative.

Verse 9

ἐργάζεσθε—this present middle indicative in the apodosis with the present active indicative in the protasis of a simple fact condition (εἰ; also see v. 8) portrays the actual setting. Note the Greek idiom *to work sin*.

ἐλεγχόμενοι—as a present passive participle, this form stands in apposition to the verb ἐργάζεσθε. The prepositional phrase ὑπὸ τοῦ νόμου denotes agency to the degree that νόμος has a personal quality.

Verse 10

τηρήσῃ, πταίσῃ—introduced by the indefinite relative pronoun ὅστις (whoever), these two verbs form the protasis of an indefinite relative clause that is

23. Robert Hanna, *A Grammatical Aid to the Greek New Testament* (Grand Rapids: Baker, 1983), p. 418. However, C. F. D. Moule demurs: "The strictly correct alternative, *you fulfill the law* **as** *supreme*, is rendered less likely by the context." *An Idiom-Book of New Testament Greek*, 2d ed. (Cambridge: At the University Press, 1960), p. 108.

24. For instance, Robertson, *Grammar*, p. 874; E. D. Burton, *Moods and Tenses of New Testament Greek* (Edinburgh: Clark, 1898), p. 67.

equivalent to a conditional sentence. The particle ἄν is lacking, but the aorist active subjunctives τηρήσῃ (from τηρέω, I keep) and πταίσῃ (from πταίω, I stumble) imply possibility and probability.

γέγονεν—the perfect active indicative from the verb γίνομαι (I become) is a timeless present perfect that projects to the future.[25]

Verse 11

ὁ γὰρ εἰπών—this is a typical Jewish way to avoid using the name of God.

οὐ—the negative adverb οὐ in the place of the normal form μή in a simple fact condition shows emphasis.

---

4. Show Mercy
2:12–13

In a brief summary, James eloquently defines what he already has written at the end of the preceding chapter (1:26–27): words without accompanying action are worthless. He exhorts the readers to speak and to act within the freedom that the law of love provides.

12. Speak and act as those who are going to be judged by the law that gives freedom, 13. because judgment without mercy will be shown to anyone who has not been merciful. Mercy triumphs over judgment!

Throughout his epistle James uses direct speech in the form of commands. At times these are softened somewhat by a word of endearment, for instance, "dear brothers." This is not the case here.

a. "Speak and act." A more literal translation is "so speak and so act." James is not interested in the content of the spoken word but rather in the act of speaking. He tells the readers to put word and deed together. As Christians they ought to look at their lives from the perspective of being judged. God's eye is constantly upon them. "Nothing in all creation is hidden from God's sight. Everything is uncovered and laid bare before the eyes of him to whom we must give account" (Heb. 4:13).

b. "As those who are going to be judged." Christians must always look ahead, because their words and deeds testify either for or against them. If you keep the royal law, says James, you are doing right (v. 8). Moreover, Scripture teaches that every person will have to stand before the Judge of all the earth (compare Gen. 18:25; Ps. 7:8; 75:7; 96:10, 13; Matt. 16:27; Acts 10:42; II Cor. 5:10). All the words man speaks and all the deeds he performs are going to be judged by the law of God. Judgment is going to come and is inescapable.

c. "By the law that gives freedom." The measure God employs is his law. James repeats an earlier statement (see 1:25) when he says, "the law that gives freedom." He implies that the law should not be understood as a legislative list of rules and regulations.[26]

---

25. Robertson, *Grammar*, pp. 897, 898.
26. Curtis Vaughan, *James: A Study Guide* (Grand Rapids: Zondervan, 1969), p. 53.

The law is perfect and complete. It comes to expression in the "perfect love" that flows from God to man and from man to God and fellow man. In the freedom of the law of love the child of God flourishes.

Therefore, the Christian lives not in fear of the law but in the joy of God's precepts. As long as he stays within the boundaries of the law of God he enjoys complete freedom. But the moment he crosses one of these boundaries, he becomes a slave to sin and loses his freedom. The Christian, then, assesses every word he speaks and every deed he performs by the measure of God's law. His entire life is governed by the law of love.

d. "Because judgment without mercy will be shown." In these verses James develops the sequence of law, transgression, judgment, and mercy. No one is able to keep the law perfectly, for everyone transgresses that law and falls into sin. The inevitable consequence for the sinner is that he will have to appear before God's judgment seat. And the one who stands guilty before the Judge pleads for mercy. As Thomas Raffles put this plea in verse:

> Lord, like the publican I stand,
> And lift my heart to thee;
> Thy pardoning grace, O God, command,
> Be merciful to me.

In response to Peter's question about forgiving a brother who sinned against him, Jesus told the parable of the servant who received mercy from the king but withheld mercy from his fellow man. When the king heard that the man who had been forgiven had not shown mercy to a fellow servant, he said, "You wicked servant, . . . I canceled all that debt of yours because you begged me to. Shouldn't you have had mercy on your fellow servant just as I had on you?" (Matt. 18:32–33).

God freely grants us mercy when we ask him, but he expects us to imitate him. When we refuse or neglect to extend mercy to our fellow man, God withholds it from us and instead gives us judgment without mercy.

e. "To anyone who has not been merciful." In the parable of the unforgiving servant (Matt. 18:21–35), Jesus teaches us that exercising mercy is not an occasional setting aside of justice to demonstrate kindness. Rather, Jesus intimates that we must apply both mercy and justice. Often when we show mercy by abandoning justice, we receive the praise of God and man.[27] To be sure, we receive God's blessing in the words of the well-known beatitude, "Blessed are the merciful, for they will be shown mercy" (Matt. 5:7). But mercy ought to be practiced together with justice. We must regard mercy and justice as equal norms and apply both of them.

---

27. Simon J. Kistemaker, *The Parables of Jesus* (Grand Rapids: Baker, 1980), p. 68. "Too often we perceive justice as the norm which must be applied rigorously, and mercy as an occasional abandonment of that norm."

Mercy does not rule out justice and justice does not nullify mercy. However, if justice triumphs at the expense of mercy, God metes out justice without mercy.

f. "Mercy triumphs over judgment!" How is mercy extended to those who need it? In the last part of the second chapter, James provides an example when he refers to Rahab. When the Israelite spies came to her door, she received them, welcomed them into her home, protected them from danger, and showed them mercy. When the Israelite army destroyed Jericho, the family of Rahab, in turn, obtained mercy. More than that, Rahab, who was a Gentile, a woman, and a prostitute experienced the truth that mercy triumphs over justice.[28]

Doctrinal Considerations in 2:12–13

From biblical history we learn the sad story that God's people failed to keep the law of love by neglecting mercy. In the days of the prophets, for example, God told the unrepentant Israelites that he required mercy and not sacrifice (Hos. 6:6). Next, Micah asked and answered the question: "And what does the LORD require of you? To act justly and to love mercy and to walk humbly with your God" (6:8). And last, God spoke through the prophet Zechariah: "Administer true justice; show mercy and compassion to one another" (7:9). But the Jews turned a deaf ear to God's instruction and hardened their hearts instead. The person who refuses to extend mercy will experience God's justice without mercy.

Man can never claim God's mercy, however, by performing deeds of mercy. Mercy is never earned but is always granted when it is sought. If we were able to earn it, mercy would no longer be mercy. We must look to the One who grants it to us. "Mercy does not triumph at the expense of justice; the triumph of mercy is based on the atonement wrought at Calvary."[29] The Christian knows that in the judgment day, mercy triumphs over justice because of Christ's meritorious work.

Greek Words, Phrases, and Constructions in 2:12–13

Verse 12

λαλεῖτε—the present active imperative preceded by the adverb οὕτως (so) has a forward, not a backward, look. The same construction occurs in οὕτως ποιεῖτε (so act) for emphasis.

Verse 13

κρίσις—the sentence begins and ends with the noun *judgment*. The two Greek sentences of this verse are proverbial in form. Note that the negative appears twice in the first sentence: ἀνέλεος (without mercy) is followed by μὴ ποιήσαντι ἔλεος (not doing mercy).

---

28. William Dyrness, "Mercy triumphs over justice: James 2:13 and the theology of faith and works," *Themelios* 6 (3, 1981): 14.

29. D. Edmond Hiebert, *The Epistle of James: Tests of a Living Faith* (Chicago: Moody, 1979), p. 172. Also consult Calvin, *James*, p. 308; Vaughan, *James*, p. 54.

14 What good is it, my brothers, if a man claims to have faith but has no deeds? Can such faith save him? 15 Suppose a brother or sister is without clothes and daily food. 16 If one of you says to him, "Go, I wish you well; keep warm and well fed," but does nothing about his physical needs, what good is it? 17 In the same way, faith by itself, if it is not accompanied by action, is dead.

18 But someone will say, "You have faith; I have deeds."

Show me your faith without deeds, and I will show you my faith by what I do. 19 You believe that there is one God. Good! Even the demons believe that—and shudder.

20 You foolish man, do you want evidence that faith without deeds is useless? 21 Was not our ancestor Abraham considered righteous for what he did when he offered his son Isaac on the altar? 22 You see that his faith and his actions were working together, and his faith was made complete by what he did. 23 And the scripture was fulfilled that says, "Abraham believed God, and it was credited to him as righteousness," and he was called God's friend. 24 You see that a person is justified by what he does and not by faith alone.

25 In the same way, was not even Rahab the prostitute considered righteous for what she did when she gave lodging to the spies and sent them off in a different direction? 26 As the body without the spirit is dead, so faith without deeds is dead.

B. Faith and Deeds
2:14–26

1. Faith Without Deeds
2:14–17

The letter James has written is alive. James relates to any reader, regardless of time, culture, age, and race. When the writer involves the reader of his epistle in the discussion and asks him questions, the reader has a genuine part in a relevant subject. That subject is faith.

14. What good is it, my brothers, if a man claims to have faith but has no deeds? Can such faith save him?

James begins by posing two direct questions which the reader can answer only with a negative reply. Faith without works is useless to man, for it cannot bring him salvation. Does this mean that faith does not save man? Paul writes, "However, to the man who does not work but trusts God who justifies the wicked, his faith is credited as righteousness" (Rom. 4:5).

Is Paul saying one thing and James another? Not at all. Rather, James looks at the one side of the coin called faith and Paul at the other. To put the matter in different words, James explains the active side of faith and Paul the passive side.[30] In a sense, the writers say the same thing even though they view faith from different perspectives. Paul addresses the

---

30. Refer to Donald Guthrie, *New Testament Theology* (Downers Grove: Inter-Varsity, 1981), p. 599. Says Guthrie, "It may well be that James is correcting a misunderstanding of Paul or vice versa, but it cannot be said that James and Paul are contradicting each other." Spiros Zodhiates depicts the situation graphically: "Paul and James do not stand face to face fighting against each other, but back to back fighting opposite foes." See *The Epistle of James and the Life of Faith*, vol. 4, *The Behavior of Belief* (Grand Rapids: Eerdmans, 1966), pt. 2, p. 11.

Jew who seeks to obtain salvation by keeping the law of God. To him Paul says, "Not the works of the law but faith in Christ brings salvation." By contrast, James directs his remarks to the person who says that he has faith but fails to put it into practice.

Consider these points:

a. *Faith without deeds.* What does James mean by faith? Certainly he is not referring to a doctrinal statement that is called a confession of faith, for example, the testimony *Jesus is Lord* (I Cor. 12:3). The difference between expressing faith in a confession—reciting the Apostles' Creed—and actively confessing our faith in word and deed is that faith expressed in a confession can result in mere intellectual assent without deeds to confirm it. This is what James has in mind when he asks, "What good is it, my brothers, if a man claims to have faith but has no deeds?"

James is specific. He says, "if a man claims to have faith." He does not write, "if a man has faith." James intimates that the faith of this particular person is not a genuine trust in Jesus Christ. In fact, that man's claim to faith is hollow. If he only nods his head in assent to the words of a doctrinal statement, his faith is intellectual, barren, and worthless.[31]

Faith in God through Jesus Christ is a certainty that flows from our hearts, emanates from our minds, and translates into deeds. Vibrant faith of word and deed, spoken and performed out of love for God and our neighbor, saves us.

15. Suppose a brother or sister is without clothes and daily food. 16. If one of you says to him, "Go, I wish you well; keep warm and well fed," but does nothing about his physical needs, what good is it?

b. *Words without deeds.* For James, faith and love go together. He uses a vivid illustration to portray not a stranger or a neighbor but a "brother or sister."

This brother and sister in the Lord "belong to the family of believers" (Gal. 6:10) who look with eager expectation to the members of the church for help in time of need. James writes that the brother and sister are without clothes, that is, they are poorly clad, and they are in need of daily food. The situation is desperate, especially when the weather is cold.

What is the response to this need? "If one of you," says James, "who acts as spokesman utters only empty words but refuses to help, what good does it do when he says that he has faith?" The words are lofty: "Go, I wish you well." This is a typical Hebrew farewell that occurs numerous times in Scripture and the Apocrypha (Judg. 18:6; I Sam. 1:17; 20:42; 29:7; II Sam. 15:9; II Kings 5:19; Mark 5:34; Luke 7:50; Acts 16:36; Jth. 8:35). The greeting is more or less equivalent to our "good-bye" (God be with you).

---

31. Both James and Paul assert that intellectual assent alone without any involvement in the truth cannot save, because such faith is dead. See A. E. Travis, "James and Paul. A Comparative Study," *SWJournTheol* 12 (1969): 57–70.

I see the remark *Go, I wish you well* summarized in the popular saying *God helps those who help themselves.* That is, let the shivering, hungry brother and sister pull themselves up by their own bootstraps. "Keep warm and well fed." If the poverty-stricken brother and sister would only exert themselves, they would have plenty to eat and sufficient clothing to wear. And God would bless them.

The irony of the whole situation is that the speaker reasons from his own point of view, for he himself has sufficient clothing to protect his body from the cold and sufficient food to keep himself well fed. He is the one, however, who speaks empty words that do not cost him anything and that are meaningless to the hearer.

If this person does not do anything about the physical needs of his brother and sister, of what value is his faith? James provides the answer in the next verse.

17. In the same way, faith by itself, if it is not accompanied by action, is dead.

c. Faith that is dead. At times, Christians proclaim the gospel of the Lord without any regard for the physical needs of their hearers. They tell the people about salvation, but they seem to forget that poverty-stricken people need clothes and food to make the gospel relevant. Unless word and deed go together, unless preaching of the gospel is accompanied by a program of social action, unless faith is demonstrated in loving care and concern, faith is dead.

In teaching the parable of the sower, Jesus distinguishes between temporary faith and true faith. Temporary faith is like the seed sown on rocky soil; it has no root and lasts only a short time (Matt. 13:21). Such faith dies an unavoidable death.

By contrast, true faith is like the grain that falls into the good soil and produces an abundant harvest. True faith is firmly rooted in the heart of the believer.

In this particular verse the writer contrasts faith that is alive with faith that is dead.[32] He depicts vibrant faith by calling to mind the example of Abraham offering his son Isaac (v. 21). And he uses a synonym to represent the term *dead.* Thus, he writes that "faith without deeds is *useless*" (v. 20, italics added). Faith that is dead, then, is still faith, but it is useless, worthless.

One example of faith that has no value is the faith of King Agrippa in the prophets. Because of his background, Agrippa knew the contents of the prophetical books of the Old Testament. Paul asserts that Agrippa believed the prophets (Acts 26:27). Intellectual faith in itself, however, is dead.

Doctrinal Considerations in 2:14–17

For James, faith and deeds belong together and cannot be separated. True faith results in works that show a distinctive Christian lifestyle, and demonstrates that

---

32. Consult Ropes, *James*, p. 207.

the believer stands in a saving relationship to God. A faith that is void of deeds is not genuine and is therefore completely different from faith that is committed to Christ.

James directs his teaching against those persons who are of the opinion that only faith matters, and that faith is actually an intellectual confession (2:19). Such objective faith expressed in a confessional statement is dead. It differs from a subjective faith that exhibits a personal relationship to Jesus Christ. True faith has subjective and objective characteristics. Subjectively, the Christian places his faith in God because he knows that God rewards the person who diligently seeks him (Heb. 11:6). He has learned that "everything that does not come from faith is sin" (Rom. 14:23). His faith is expressed in love for God and for his fellow man, so that objectively his deeds are eloquent testimony to his faith in God.

For Paul and for James deeds are the natural consequence of true faith (see Phil. 1:27; I Thess. 1:3; James 2:20–24). Of course, man cannot use his works to gain favor with God. Man obtains salvation by grace through faith as a gift of God (Eph. 2:8), "not by works," says Paul, "so that no one can boast" (v. 9). By themselves, then, works have no saving power. Nevertheless, in the setting in which James writes his epistle, he "proclaims the necessity of works for salvation."[33] James is not suggesting to his readers that through their deeds they can obtain peace with God. Instead, he teaches that deeds flow forth from a heart that is at peace with God.

Greek Words, Phrases, and Constructions in 2:14–17

Verse 14

ἐὰν πίστιν λέγῃ—the word order in this sentence is somewhat irregular for the purpose of emphasis. The conditional clause with the subjunctive in the present tense stresses probability. The adversative particle δέ is strong.

ἡ πίστις—the use of the definite article is "practically equivalent to a demonstrative pronoun."[34] The definite article, then, means "such." "Can such faith save him?"[35]

Verse 15

γυμνοί—the adjective is the masculine nominative plural even though the immediate antecedent is ἀδελφή (sister), which is the feminine nominative singular. The combination *brother or sister* serves as a plural, and the masculine gender predominates.

ὑπάρχωσιν—the present active subjunctive expresses probability. The verb is generally used as a substitute for εἶναι (to be).[36]

ἐφημέρου—the adjective modifies τροφῆς (food). We have the derivative *ephemeral.*

---

33. Refer to Thorwald Lorenzen, "Faith without works does not count before God! James 2:14–26," *ExpT* 89 (1978): 234. "While for *Paul* works are the necessary *consequence* of faith and a necessary *part of salvation*, for *James* works are the necessary *presupposition* for salvation and the decisive soteriological element without which faith is dead and cannot save."

34. Hanna, *Grammatical Aid*, p. 418.

35. Moule in his *Idiom-Book*, p. 111, disputes the use of the demonstrative pronoun. He suggests that the word *him*, not the definite article, receives stress. He translates, "Can his faith save **him**?"

36. Bauer, p. 838.

Verse 16

τις αὐτοῖς ἐξ ὑμῶν—the word order reveals emphasis.

θερμαίνεσθε—the present *middle* imperative, rather than the passive, expresses the intended idea, "Keep warm."

χορτάζεσθε—the present imperative can be either middle or passive. The middle in this verb and the preceding one indicates that the hearers had to rely on their own resources to meet their needs. The verb χορτάζω (I feed, fill) has the connotation *eat your fill.*

Verse 17

καθ' ἑαυτήν—this idiomatic expression, translated "by itself," ought to be taken with πίστις.

---

2. Faith, Deeds, and Creed
2:18–19

James carefully builds his presentation of faith and deeds. He begins with an illustration of a needy brother or sister (vv. 15–17). Next, he interacts with a person who says that he has deeds and holds to the creed (vv. 18–19). And last, James presents proof that historically faith and actions always go together (vv. 20–26).[37]

18. But someone will say, "You have faith; I have deeds."
Show me your faith without deeds, and I will show you my faith by what I do. 19. You believe that there is one God. Good! Even the demons believe that—and shudder.

We divide this section into three parts:

a. *Contention.* Whether James debates a real or an imaginary person need not concern us at the moment. James develops his argument as follows:

Someone says, "You have faith; I have deeds." He does not mean to say that James has faith and he himself has deeds. The speaker refers to one person who claims to have faith but does not have deeds, and to another person who insists that he possesses deeds but lacks faith. He separates faith from works.

Suppose that one person has only faith and another only deeds. Then, possibly, the one who claims to have faith comes to God more readily than the one whose record shows only deeds. And because of his faith he considers himself to be superior to the person who lacks faith but has deeds.

b. *Challenge.* James refuses to accept a division between faith and works. True faith cannot exist separately from works, and works acceptable in the sight of God cannot be performed without true faith.

---

37. W. Nicols, "Faith and works in the Letter of James," *Neotestamentica* 9 (1975): 7–24.

James challenges the speaker: "Show me your faith without deeds, and I will show you my faith by what I do." That is, James wants to see what kind of faith the speaker possesses. If faith is not rooted in a believing heart, then that faith amounts to nothing more than empty words—it is worthless. Its opposite is true faith which is inseparably joined to deeds of love. Paul summarizes this point succinctly when he says, "The only thing that counts is faith expressing itself through love" (Gal. 5:6).

Presenting an additional argument, the speaker claims that faith is not necessary. He champions the cause of practical Christianity. He argues that doing good deeds is more important than believing a particular doctrine. He does not realize that his so-called works of charity have nothing in common with deeds of gratitude that originate in the thankful heart of a believer.

c. *Correction.* James addresses all those who wish to separate faith from works. He challenges them to show him true faith without deeds or works apart from faith. And James tells them that he will show them his faith by his conduct. That is, in everything he does, faith is the main ingredient. Just as a motor produces power because an electrical current flows into it, so a Christian produces good deeds because true faith empowers him.

We hear the echo of Jesus' teaching that we know a tree by its fruit; a tree without "good fruit is cut down and thrown into the fire" (Matt. 7:19). Those who speak but fail to act will hear Jesus say, "I never knew you. Away from me, you evildoers!" (v. 23). Faith without works is dead.

In this chapter James refers to two kinds of faith: true faith and pretense. The first kind is characteristic of the true believer who shows faith "by deeds done in the humility that comes from wisdom" (James 3:13). The second kind is a demonstration of dead orthodoxy that is nothing more than a series of doctrinal statements accurately reflecting the teachings of Scripture. For instance, the Jews recite their creed: "Hear, O Israel: The LORD our God, the LORD is one" (Deut. 6:4). But if faith is merely a reciting of the familiar words of this creed—although the words are thoroughly scriptural—it has become a cold intellectual exercise that has nothing to do with a faith flowing from the heart.

James gets to the point of his illustration. He says, "You believe that there is one God. Good! Even the demons believe that—and shudder." However, no fallen angel can claim salvation because of that factual faith. In a similar fashion, the man who gives only his intellectual assent to a scriptural truth, without displaying adherence to the God he professes, is devoid of true faith. His faith, which is nothing more than make-believe, is dead. If a person has only knowledge that God is one and has no living faith in God through Jesus Christ, he is worse than demons. Demons, says James, believe and shudder.

The implication is that even among the demons doctrinal truth prevails. They confessed the name of Christ during Jesus' ministry (see Mark 1:24; 5:7; Luke 4:34). Their knowledge of the Son of God made them shudder, but that knowledge could not save them. Knowledge without faith is worthless.

Additional Remarks

The quotation. Translators differ on the length of the statement in quotation marks in verse 18. The translators of the New American Standard Bible, for instance, take all of verse 18 as the word spoken by the opponent of James: "You have faith, and I have works; show me your faith without the works, and I will show you my faith by my works." The question, of course, relates to interpreting the pronouns *you* and *I* in this verse. Unfortunately, ancient manuscripts have no punctuation or quotation marks, and therefore, every translator and interpreter has to make his own decision.

Consider the remark, "You have faith; I have deeds." Is the person who makes the remark saying, "You, James, have faith; but I, by contrast, have deeds"? Does he continue the remark with the challenge, "Show me your faith without deeds, and I will show you my faith by what I do"? Hardly. The two remarks contradict each other if they come from the same person. Apparently, the contrast in verse 18a—"You have faith; I have deeds"—is not so much between James and the speaker as between the concepts *faith* and *deeds* exemplified in one or another person. Martin Dibelius concludes, "The main point of the opponent in [verse] 18a is not the *distribution* of faith and works to 'you' and 'me,' but rather the *total separation* of faith and works in general."[38]

For this reason, many translators and commentators have adopted a reading exemplified in the Good News Bible, "But someone will say, 'One person has faith, another has actions.' " This translation removes the ambiguity of the pronouns *I* and *you*. The objection, however, is that if James had wished to say so, he could have expressed himself much more clearly by using the terms *one* and *another*.[39] Instead James employs the personal pronouns in verses 18 and 19.

Although difficulties cling to any interpretation of this passage, the suggestion to understand verse 18a in terms of "one" and "another" meets general approval. Verses 18b and 19 are the response James makes to the speaker.

The speaker. Who is the speaker? Some interpreters see the person who speaks the words of verse 18a as a Christian who is favorably disposed toward James. He is the person who wants to mediate between two parties, one of whom stresses faith and the other works. "This kindly person, who does not wish to be too harsh on anyone, suggests that there is room for both the man who emphasizes faith and the one who insists on

---

38. Dibelius, *James*, p. 155.
39. Davids, *James*, pp. 123-24.

works."[40] This means that the first word in verse 18 cannot be *but,* which is too adversative. Many interpreters prefer the term *yes.*[41]

However, considering the characteristics of the Epistle of James, we have difficulty accepting the argument that not James but another speaker is addressing parties who are at odds with one another over the question of faith and works. Throughout his epistle James is the one who enters into a debate with his readers. He addresses them, corrects them, and encourages them.[42] And in view of his reference to the creed, "Hear, O Israel: The LORD our God, the LORD is one" (Deut. 6:4), the speaker whom James addresses must be a Jewish Christian.

Finally, in my opinion we are well advised to refrain from dogmatism in an area where interpretations and solutions to problems abound. Therefore, as long as the last word has not been spoken or written, explanations can be only tentative.

Greek Words, Phrases, and Constructions in 2:18–19

Verse 18

ἀλλ' ἐρεῖ τις—the adverb ἀλλά is the adversative *but,* followed by the definite future of the verb ἐρῶ (I will say). For this type of dialogue, see Romans 9:19; 11:19.

ἐκ—this preposition conveys the remote meaning *by means of* (consult Rom. 1:17; 3:30; I John 4:6).[43]

Verse 19

σὺ πιστεύεις—most editors of the Greek text and most translators take this clause as a declarative statement. Others read it as an interrogative statement.

δαιμόνια—in the New Testament, a neuter plural with a personal or a collective connotation takes a plural verb.[44]

---

3. The Faith of Abraham
2:20–24

In the last part of his discussion on faith and deeds, James turns to the Scriptures to show that historically faith and works are the two sides of the same coin. He addresses his opponent directly and urges him to learn from the teachings of God's Word.

---

40. C. Leslie Mitton, *The Epistle of James* (Grand Rapids: Eerdmans, 1966), p. 109.

41. In their respective translations and commentaries Moffatt has "yes," Adamson and Zodhiates "yea."

42. "To introduce an ally who disappears as abruptly as he has appeared is an unlikely procedure for any writer, however modest," writes Laws, *James,* p. 123.

43. H. E. Dana and Julius R. Mantey, *A Manual Grammar of the Greek New Testament* (New York: Macmillan, 1967), p. 103.

44. Robertson, *Grammar,* pp. 403–4. Also see Hanna, *Grammatical Aid,* p. 418.

20. You foolish man, do you want evidence that faith without deeds is useless?

The language James uses is far from complimentary. He is blunt and forceful in his address: "You foolish man."[45] In fact, the words of James are similar to the colloquial and somewhat contemptuous remark, "You fool!" (Matt. 5:22). James is actually saying to the man, "You have no basis for your argument on faith and works. Your words lack truth; they are baseless."

If the man talks of faith, he certainly needs to go to the Scriptures to learn what God has to say about this subject. James is impatient with the man who is arguing with him. He rebukes him in much the same manner as Jesus corrected the two men on their way to Emmaus: "How foolish you are, and how slow of heart to believe all that the prophets have spoken!" (Luke 24:25).

James continues to reprove: "Do you want evidence?" He is saying, "Search the Scriptures and you will learn that faith without deeds is useless. Take Abraham, the father of believers, as an example. Go to the story about Rahab and see that she acted on faith."

21. Was not our ancestor Abraham considered righteous for what he did when he offered his son Isaac on the altar?

Whenever a Jew discussed the topic *faith,* he would invariably turn to the faith of Abraham. In the schools of the Jewish rabbis, in the literature of intertestamental times, and in the New Testament, the Jew discusses his faith in relation to Abraham.[46]

As a Jew writing to fellow Jewish Christians, James is free to say, "our ancestor Abraham." However, he is not emphasizing physical descent or pride in being part of the Jewish race. He is stressing the concept *righteousness* as the outcome of faith. Abraham was considered righteous in the sight of God, because he trusted him to the point of sacrificing Isaac the son of the promise (Gen. 22:2, 9).

The incident of Abraham sustaining the test of faith, when God told him to sacrifice his son, is one of the highlights in the life of the patriarch. Poised with knife in hand, Abraham was ready to plunge the instrument of death into his son Isaac. Just at that moment, the angel of the Lord intervened and said, "Now I know that you fear God" (Gen. 22:12). Abraham showed unreserved obedience to God.

Both James and Paul designate the result of Abraham's faith as righteousness. That is, Abraham enjoyed a right relationship with God, for

---

45. In an article on the concept *empty, vain,* Colin Brown refers to its metaphorical sense ("reckless adventurers," Judg. 9:4; "a group of adventurers," Judg. 11:3). *NIDNTT,* vol. 1, p. 546. Albrecht Oepke in *TDNT,* vol. 3, pp. 659–60, also explains the figurative use of the word *empty.*

46. For instance, Sir. 44:19–21 testifies to the faith of Abraham. Jesus in the Gospels and Paul in his epistles repeatedly mention Abraham (see John 8:37–41; Rom. 4:12; Gal. 3:6–7). Also consult *Pirke Aboth* 5.19.

he gained God's approval during his lifetime.[47] God himself declared Abraham righteous (Gen. 15:6). James alludes to what Abraham did when he obediently prepared to sacrifice his son Isaac on Mount Moriah. And Paul writes, "We have been saying that Abraham's faith was credited to him as righteousness" (Rom. 4:9). In other words, every Jew who was spiritually alert knew the story of Abraham's triumph of faith and his relationship with God.

22. You see that his faith and his actions were working together, and his faith was made complete by what he did. 23. And the scripture was fulfilled that says, "Abraham believed God, and it was credited to him as righteousness," and he was called God's friend.

a. "His faith and his actions." Here James faces his opponent and opens the Old Testament Scriptures. He points to the account of Abraham's faith at the altar of sacrifice (Gen. 22) and says, "You see, here is definitive proof that faith and works go together." Faith and action, then, are never separated. The one flows naturally from the other. Deeds originate in faith and faith supports the believer in his work. Everyone hearing or reading these words from James readily admits that in the case of Abraham, the father of believers did what he had to do on the basis of faith.

b. "His faith was made complete." Purposely James alludes to Abraham's test of faith when the patriarch was asked to sacrifice Isaac. Even though we do not know how old Abraham was, we learn from Scripture that this test of faith is the last for Abraham. When he sustained this last test, he heard the voice from heaven saying, "It is enough." Abraham's faith was made complete.

In his life Abraham had shown trust and confidence in God by traveling to the promised land, waiting decades for his promised son Isaac, and finally demonstrating his obedience by being willing to sacrifice him. The supreme test was not so much in his traveling or waiting but in preparing to sacrifice Isaac. Killing his own son meant that the promise would end. But as the writer of Hebrews sums it up, "Abraham reasoned that God could raise the dead, and figuratively speaking, he did receive Isaac back from death" (11:19).

c. "The scripture was fulfilled." With interest we note that James takes his point of departure from Abraham's moment of triumph (Gen. 22) and then goes back to the time when God made a covenant with Abraham (Gen. 15). He appears to prove Abraham's faith from his obedience and willingness to sacrifice Isaac and then declares that Scripture has been fulfilled (Gen. 15:6). He goes from the event that describes Abraham's obedience on Mount Moriah (Gen. 22) to the statement of faith, "Abram believed the LORD, and he credited it to him as righteousness" (Gen. 15:6). Perhaps we would have reversed the order and proceeded from the

---

47. Dibelius, *James*, p. 162. In the intertestamental period, Mattathias the father of Judas Maccabeus addressed his sons from his deathbed: "Was not Abraham found faithful when tested, and it was reckoned to him as righteousness?" (I Macc. 2:52, RSV).

statement to the event. But James begins with Abraham's mountaintop experience of faith and concludes that this event fulfills the scriptural statement that Abraham believed God.

James's method of argument is derived from Jewish traditions of scriptural interpretation current in his day. James looks not at a single incident of Abraham's faith (Gen. 22) as fulfillment of an earlier statement concerning that faith (Gen. 15:6). Rather, the statement includes Abraham's entire life, and the experience on Mount Moriah is part of it.[48]

d. "Abraham believed God." In this particular quotation from the Old Testament, the expression *works* does not occur. However, it is implied and James understands it as such. James maintains the inherent unity of faith and works. "His contention is that, while they do not always occur together, this is the norm."[49]

Faith and deeds are not identical. But they cannot be separated either. They are like the root and the plant, always joined together and yet different. Each has its own function and yet these two form a unit.

Abraham's faith "was credited to him as righteousness." We associate the expression *credited* with banking. The bank sends us a notice by mail to inform us that a certain amount of money has been credited to our account. How do we increase our assets? In several ways. We can earn money by working for it. We put our money in a savings account and accumulate interest. Or we can receive a monetary gift from someone.

Did Abraham work for his righteousness and thus God credited it to him? Certainly not! Although the context is entirely different, Paul in his epistle to the Romans asserts that "if, in fact, Abraham was justified by works, he had something to boast about—but not before God" (4:2). The believer cannot earn his own righteousness, because his works, even those performed in love for God, are imperfect and incomplete.

How, then, is Scripture fulfilled, as James asserts? God does not credit righteousness to man because of man's intellectual knowledge of God. God justifies man when he fully trusts God, demonstrates his love for God, obediently listens to the Word of God, and acts accordingly. Abraham did that when in faith and obedience he prepared to sacrifice Isaac.[50] Note that God called Abraham his friend (II Chron. 20:7; Isa. 41:8).

24. You see that a person is justified by what he does and not by faith alone.

Here is the conclusion. James addresses all his readers when he says, "You see." With his reference to Abraham he has convincingly shown that anyone who appeals to Scripture will find that Abraham acted on the

---

48. Ibid., p. 164.

49. Nicols, "Faith and works," p. 17.

50. Calvin, *James*, p. 316. "Man is not justified by faith alone, that is, by a bare and empty knowledge of God; he is justified by works, that is, his righteousness is known and proved by its fruits."

basis of faith. James does not say that Abraham was justified because of his faith and works.

God justifies the sinner. That is, the sinner can never justify himself by his own deeds. Nor can man rely on faith alone, for faith without works is dead. James is saying that faith and works go together, that they ought not to be separated, and that faith divorced from deeds does not justify a person. God justifies a sinner who is spiritually alive and who shows trust and obedience.

Doctrinal Considerations in 2:20–24

Especially in the last half of chapter 2, James uses the term *faith* rather frequently—eleven times in the original. The question is whether James communicates the same meaning every time he employs that word. Does he always convey the sense of true faith or does the expression *faith* at times denote faith that is not true? James appears to give only one meaning to the word: true faith. From the context even verse 14 falls in this category; "a man claims to have [true] faith." In reality, however, this man does not have true faith because he had no deeds to prove it.

Does this true faith save a person? Yes, for true faith is always alive and expresses itself in deeds. James does not imply that a person who has true faith can earn salvation, for he rules this out in verse 24: "You see that a person is justified [by God] by what he does and not by faith alone." God justifies man not on the basis of merit but by grace (Eph. 2:8).

James's use of the word *justify* is different from Paul's usage. Paul interprets the term in a legal context—as if man is in a court of law. James takes a much more practical approach and says that a person who expresses his faith in deeds is justified by God.[51] In this respect, James echoes those teachings of Jesus recorded in the Sermon on the Mount: true faith must result in deeds (Matt. 7:24–27).[52]

Greek Words, Phrases, and Constructions in 2:20–24

Verse 20

θέλεις γνῶναι—this construction is a periphrastic substitute for the future tense and expresses volition.[53]

ἀργή—a number of texts feature the word νεκρά (dead), probably due to verses 17 and 26. The term ἀργή (useless) "not only is strongly supported . . . , but may also involve a subtle play on words (ἔργων ἀργή [ἀ + ἐργή])."[54]

---

51. Guthrie, *New Testament Theology*, p. 506.

52. Davids, *James*, p. 132. The concept *faith and works* in the light of Jesus' teachings predates Paul's elaborate discussion recorded in his epistle to the Romans.

53. Robertson, *Grammar*, p. 878. Also consult Hanna, *Grammatical Aid*, p. 418.

54. Bruce M. Metzger, *A Textual Commentary on the Greek New Testament*, corrected ed. (London and New York: United Bible Societies, 1975), p. 681.

Verse 22

συνήργει—the imperfect active indicative of συνεργέω (I work together) denotes continued action in the past.

ἐκ—this preposition is translated "by means of" (see v. 18).

Verse 24

ὁρᾶτε—with the present active imperative the writer turns from the use of the singular verb (see βλέπεις, v. 22) to the plural form.

μόνον—at the end of the sentence, this adverb is emphatic.

---

4. Faith and Righteousness
2:25–26

The second name James selects is that of Rahab. The contrast between Abraham, the father of believers, and Rahab, the prostitute from ancient Jericho, is telling. Precisely for this reason James introduces Rahab as the next example of faith and works.

25. In the same way, was not even Rahab the prostitute considered righteous for what she did when she gave lodging to the spies and sent them off in a different direction? 26. As the body without the spirit is dead, so faith without deeds is dead.

Here are some points we need to discuss:

a. *Contrast.* Abraham, the father of believers, serves as a striking example of faith and works. But, we object, all of us are not like Abraham. True, James answers, Abraham demonstrated both faith and works, but so did Rahab—and she was a prostitute.

Together with other writers, James links the names of Abraham and Rahab to show contrast.[55] Abraham is a Hebrew, called by God to become the father of believers. Rahab is a Gentile, an inhabitant of ancient Jericho destined for destruction by the Israelite army. As a man, Abraham is the representative head of God's covenant people (Gen. 15; 17). Rahab is a woman, known in Scripture as "the prostitute."[56] After Abraham was called by God in Ur of the Chaldees, he gave proof of his obedience to God for at least three decades. His obedience reached its climax when he showed his willingness to sacrifice his son Isaac. Rahab knew about Israel's God only by hearsay; yet she displayed her faith by identifying herself with God's people.

Abraham and Rahab have much in common: Abraham showed hospitality to the three heavenly visitors who came to him at Mamre (Gen. 18:1) and Rahab to the two Hebrew spies who came to her in Jericho (Josh.

---

55. Matthew mentions both Abraham and Rahab in the genealogy of Jesus (1:2, 5). The writer of Hebrews lists the two as heroes of faith (11:8–19, 31). Citing examples of obedience, Clement of Rome discusses the lives of Abraham and Rahab (I Clem. 10:1–7; 12:1–8).
56. Josephus writes that the Hebrew spies came to Rahab's inn (*Antiquities* 5.8). The Palestinian Targum on Josh. 2:1 describes Rahab as an innkeeper. Consult D. J. Wiseman, "Rahab of Jericho," *Tyn H Bul* 14 (1964): 8–11.

2:1). Both were foreigners among other people: Abraham dwelled among the Canaanites and Rahab with the Israelites. And last, both are listed as ancestors of Jesus (Matt. 1:2, 5).

b. *Consider.* James asks a rhetorical question that receives a positive reply: "Was not even Rahab the prostitute considered righteous for what she did?" Certainly. At the bottom of the social ladder stands the Gentile woman Rahab, candidly referred to as "the prostitute" (Josh. 2:1; 6:17, 22, 25; Heb. 11:31; James 2:25). This woman puts her faith in Israel's God and openly confesses it to the two spies:

> I know that the LORD has given this land to you and that a great fear of you has fallen on us, so that all who live in this country are melting in fear because of you. We have heard how the LORD dried up the water of the Red Sea for you when you came out of Egypt, and what you did to Sihon and Og, the two kings of the Amorites east of the Jordan, whom you completely destroyed. When we heard of it, our hearts melted and everyone's courage failed because of you, for the LORD your God is God in heaven above and on the earth below. [Josh. 2:9–11]

Rahab's faith is matched by her deeds. She protects the spies by hiding them on the roof of her house and she sends the king's messengers out of the city. She makes the spies swear by the Lord to spare her family when the Israelites come to destroy the city of Jericho (Josh. 2:12–13). And when on oath the men agree to this, she shows them the way to safety. She lowers them by a rope through the window of her house situated on the city wall.

Faith and works are prominent in the life of Rahab and are of such a nature that James asks, "Was not even Rahab . . . considered righteous for what she did?" Yes, Rahab is permitted to take a place next to Abraham, for she, too, displays her faith in Israel's God and acts in faith. For this reason she is considered righteous. Rahab, like Abraham, is putting her faith to work in daily life and under precarious conditions. God justifies her because of her faith that comes to life in her deeds.

c. *Cover.* James places emphasis on what Rahab did. He assumes that his readers are acquainted with her faith. Her deeds need to be stressed: "She gave lodging to the spies and sent them off in a different direction." The writer of the Epistle to the Hebrews expresses the same idea in different words: "By faith the prostitute Rahab, because she welcomed the spies, was not killed with those who were disobedient" (11:31). He, too, links faith and works.

Neither the writer of the Book of Joshua, nor the author of Hebrews, nor James dwells on Rahab's immoral past or on the inaccurate information she deliberately gave the messengers of the king of Jericho. Of importance is her faith in Israel's God. Because of her faith in God her sins are covered.

d. *Conclusion.* James concludes his argument by using a simple illustration. "As the body without the spirit is dead, so faith without deeds is dead." Perhaps we are inclined to turn this around and identify deeds with the body and faith with the spirit. However, we ought not to press the details of this comparison.[57]

What we have in this comparison is not a contrast of faith over against works. The point is that faith *by itself* is dead, much the same as the body without the spirit is dead. The readers of the epistle know that they ought not to touch a dead body but to avoid it whenever possible. By implication they need to avoid faith that is dead because it is like a corpse.[58]

Faith that is alive expresses itself in works that are performed in obedience to the Word of God. James eloquently illustrates this point with the examples from the lives of Abraham and Rahab. For him faith and works form an inseparable unit that can be compared to man's body and soul. These two belong together and constitute a living being.

Greek Words, Phrases, and Constructions in 2:25–26

Verse 25

ὑποδεξαμένη—derived from ὑποδέχομαι (I receive as a guest), this aorist middle participle is causal and provides the reason for considering Rahab righteous.

ἑτέρᾳ ὁδῷ—the use of the dative denotes place rather than instrument or means. The choice of ἑτέρᾳ, instead of ἄλλη (another), distinguishes the road to the hills from the highway to the Jordan River.

ἐκβαλοῦσα—the compound participle from ἐκβάλλω (I cast out, send out) indicates that Rahab sent the spies *out of* her house. The aorist is causal.

Verse 26

πνεύματος—the opposites are body and spirit. Whether the writer intends to convey the meaning *spirit* or *breath* (NAB, NEB) makes little difference, for the contrast is between a living body and one that is dead.

Summary of Chapter 2

The theme of this chapter is faith. The first part of the chapter was occasioned perhaps by an incident that took place in a local church gathering. There the rich visitor received the people's attention and courtesy while the poor man was told to stand or sit here or there (vv. 1–4). The members of the church were guilty of favoring the rich and despising the poor.

James notes that those who are materially poor in this world are spiritually rich because God has chosen them to be heirs of his kingdom. Those who are rich in faith belong to Jesus (vv. 5–7).

---

57. Adamson, *James*, p. 134.
58. Colin Brown, *NIDNTT*, vol. 3, p. 370.

The summary of the Ten Commandments consists of few words, "Love your neighbor as yourself." James calls this summary the "royal law" (v. 8) and implies that faith in Jesus means keeping the law. He links faith inseparably to God's law that sets the believer free. Next, he teaches the readers to exercise mercy because "mercy triumphs over judgment" (v. 13).

In the second part of the chapter James develops the subject *faith*. He asserts that faith that is alive comes to expression in fulfilling the law of love. If this is not the case, faith is dead (v. 17). Faith of the heart expresses itself through the deed of the hand. Religion that is spiritual ministers to the need that is physical.

Someone wishes to debate James and makes a distinction between faith and works. If faith is only an intellectual virtue, contends James, then be aware that even the demons believe that there is one God, and they shudder (v. 19).

James opens the Scriptures to prove that historically faith and deeds go together. He takes the incident of Abraham preparing to offer his son Isaac on the altar to show that faith and works form a unit. God justifies a believer who puts his faith to work in obedience to his Word (vv. 20–24). The second example comes from the Book of Joshua. Rahab displays faith in God by hiding the Hebrew spies, sparing their lives, and sending them to safety (v. 25). In his concluding remark James employs the imagery of a lifeless body from which the spirit has departed. So is faith that lacks deeds—it is dead (v. 26).

3

Restraint

3:1–18

Outline

3 1 Not many of you should presume to be teachers, my brothers, because you know that we who teach will be judged more strictly. 2 We all stumble in many ways. If anyone is never at fault in what he says, he is a perfect man, able to keep his whole body in check.

3 When we put bits into the mouths of horses to make them obey us, we can turn the whole animal. 4 Or take ships as an example. Although they are so large and are driven by strong winds, they are steered by a very small rudder wherever the pilot wants to go. 5 Likewise the tongue is a small part of the body, but it makes great boasts. Consider what a great forest is set on fire by a small spark. 6 The tongue also is a fire, a world of evil among the parts of the body. It corrupts the whole person, sets the whole course of his life on fire, and is itself set on fire by hell.

7 All kinds of animals, birds, reptiles and creatures of the sea are being tamed and have been tamed by man, 8 but no man can tame the tongue. It is a restless evil, full of deadly poison.

9 With the tongue we praise our Lord and Father, and with it we curse men, who have been made in God's likeness. 10 Out of the same mouth come praise and cursing. My brothers, this should not be. 11 Can both fresh water and salt water flow from the same spring? 12 My brothers, can a fig tree bear olives, or a grapevine bear figs? Neither can a salt spring produce fresh water.

A. Use of the Tongue
3:1–12

1. Discipline of Speech
3:1–2

What effect have our words on those who hear us? Are we speaking the truth in love? Do we control our anger and especially our tongues? David knew that alone he could not restrain his tongue. Therefore, he asked God to help him as he earnestly prayed, "Set a guard over my mouth, O LORD; keep watch over the door of my lips" (Ps. 141:3).

1. Not many of you should presume to be teachers, my brothers, because you know that we who teach will be judged more strictly. 2. We all stumble in many ways. If anyone is never at fault in what he says, he is a perfect man, able to keep his whole body in check.

At first glance James appears to introduce a subject (teachers, v. 1) that has little in common with the next verse (v. 2). Yet upon second thought we realize that those who teach do so verbally, and that their failures often relate to the words they speak. Teaching and the use of the tongue go together.

105

Already in the first chapter of his epistle James introduces the topic of use of the tongue:

> My dear brothers, take note of this: Everyone should be quick to listen, slow to speak and slow to become angry. [1:19]
>
> If anyone considers himself religious and yet does not keep a tight rein on his tongue, he deceives himself and his religion is worthless. [1:26]

This subject is extremely important to James. More than any other writer of the Scriptures, James clearly warns against the dangers of an unruly tongue. In most of chapter 3 he speaks of taming the tongue (3:1–12). And in the following chapters he tells his readers to avoid slandering one another (4:11–12) but to speak the truth (5:12).

Talk is cheap, we say. But we express ourselves in words that reflect our thoughts, intentions, and personalities. The words we speak influence those who listen to us, and with these words we teach others. Therefore, we who teach must know what to say, for Jesus said that "men will have to give account on the day of judgment for every careless word they have spoken" (Matt. 12:36).

"Not many of you should presume to be teachers, my brothers," James admonishes his readers. The New International Version provides a somewhat interpretive translation to avoid the impression that James is discouraging people from becoming teachers.[1] The New Testament encourages believers to become teachers of the good news. For example, Jesus commands us to make disciples of all nations and to teach them (Matt. 28:19–20). And the writer of Hebrews rebukes his readers for not being teachers after a period of training (5:12).

Not only the Jews of Jesus' day (see Matt. 23:7), but also the early church gave great prominence to the office of teacher. A teacher had authority and influence and many people sought to gain this position.[2] James warns his readers not to fill the role of a teacher unless they are fully qualified. He includes himself in the discussion and calls attention to the eventual outcome: "we who teach will be judged more strictly." Says Jesus, "Anyone who breaks one of the least of these commandments and teaches others to do the same will be called least in the kingdom of heaven, but whoever practices and teaches these commands will be called great in the kingdom of heaven" (Matt. 5:19; and see 18:6). Teaching,

---

1. A literal translation (with variations) is, "let not many of you become teachers" (NKJV, NASB, NEB, NAB, MLB, RSV, GNB). The JB has, "Only a few of you, my brothers, should be teachers."

2. The title *rabbi* actually means "my great [teacher]" and in the New Testament it commands honor and respect. See SB, vol. 1, pp. 916–17. Also consult Karl Heinrich Rengstorf, *TDNT*, vol. 2, pp. 152–59, and Klaus Wegenast, *NIDNTT*, vol. 3, pp. 766–68. For the role of teacher in the early church, see Acts 13:1; Rom. 12:7; I Cor. 12:28–29; Eph. 4:11; I Tim. 3:2; Titus 1:9; and *Didache* 11:1–2.

then, is a great responsibility with lasting consequences, for on the day of judgment God will pronounce the verdict (Rom. 14:10–12).

James speaks sympathetically as a thoughtful pastor. He does not elevate himself because of his teaching position. He identifies with his readers when he writes, "We all stumble in many ways." That is, we all make mistakes, err, and come to grief. In a sense, we are like a one-year-old child who stumbles repeatedly, gets up, and continues to walk. But our stumbling, although not immediately fatal, is serious. All of us fall into sin and cannot escape its power.[3] Sin robs us of our maturity, and the sin we most often commit is that of speaking carelessly.

"If anyone is never at fault in what he says, he is a perfect man, able to keep his whole body in check." Does James mean that man is able to achieve perfection by controlling his tongue? If that were true, a deaf and mute person would achieve this status. No, in the first part of his epistle James indicates what he means by "a perfect man." He writes that faith during testing leads to perseverance. "Perseverance must finish its work so that you may be mature and complete, not lacking anything" (1:4).[4] A perfect man, then, is not a sinless man but one who has reached spiritual maturity, speaks the truth in love, is filled with wisdom and understanding, and is able to keep his body in check.

Practical Considerations in 3:1–2

Numerous colleges and universities were founded for the purpose of training ministers of the gospel. In more recent times the emphasis in education has shifted to the sciences; yet theological seminaries still provide thorough training for the pastoral ministry. A theologically schooled pastor, then, need not be ashamed of himself when he is able to handle correctly the word of truth (II Tim. 2:15).

A pastor should always go to the pulpit with a carefully prepared sermon. He has been given the task of feeding the people of God spiritual food; he is the teacher of the Word of God. If he fails in this task because of inadequate training or indolence, God will hold him accountable on the day of judgment. The pastor and teacher of the Word cannot afford to take his task lightly; he handles holy things!

Perhaps under the influence of interpreters of another age,[5] some scholars have understood the first verse of James 3 to be the equivalent of Jesus' admonition, "Do not judge, or you too will be judged" (Matt. 7:1). This, however, is not

---

3. Scripture teaches about universal sinfulness in numerous passages (I Kings 8:46; Ps. 143:2; Prov. 20:9; Eccl. 7:20; Rom. 3:1–12, 19–20, 23; Gal. 3:22; James 3:2; I John 1:8–10).

4. The term *perfect* actually means "whole" in the Epistle of James. Writes Reinier Schippers, "According to James, the man who does not offend in his words is whole and without fault." *NIDNTT*, vol. 2, p. 63.

5. John Calvin writes, "But I take masters [teachers] not to be those who performed a public duty in the Church, but such as took upon them the right of passing judgment upon others: for such reprovers sought to be accounted as masters of morals." *Commentaries on the Catholic Epistles: The Epistle of James*, ed. and trans. John Owen (Grand Rapids: Eerdmans, 1948), pp. 317–18.

the intent of this verse. James is speaking of teachers of the Word—and he includes himself in that category. James points to the weighty responsibility entrusted to the teacher of Scripture. Therefore, "not many of you should presume to be teachers."

Greek Words, Phrases, and Constructions in 3:1–2

Verse 1

γίνεσθε—the present middle imperative is separated from the negative particle μή (not) for emphasis; "generally the negative occurs directly before the word negated."[6]

Verse 2

εἰ—the simple fact conditional sentence states a self-evident truth: no one is able to keep his tongue in check. The adjective δυνατός is followed by a complementary infinitive.

---

2. Examples
3:3–8

Let no one ever say that words are insignificant. Martin Luther's hymn "A Mighty Fortress Is Our God" mentions the prince of darkness, whose

> Rage we can endure,
> For lo! his doom is sure,
> One little Word shall fell him.

One word can alter the course of human history. For example, Jesus spoke the words *It is finished*, which in the Greek is only one word.

James compares man's tongue to bits in the mouths of horses, to a very small rudder of a ship, and to a small spark that devastates a great forest.[7]

3. When we put bits into the mouths of horses to make them obey us, we can turn the whole animal. 4. Or take ships as an example. Although they are so large and are driven by strong winds, they are steered by a very small rudder wherever the pilot wants to go. 5. Likewise the tongue is a small part of the body, but it makes great boasts. Consider what a great forest is set on fire by a small spark.

a. "Bits into the mouths of horses."[8] The connection between this verse

---

6. Robert Hanna, *A Grammatical Aid to the Greek New Testament* (Grand Rapids: Baker, 1983), p. 418. Consult A. T. Robertson, *A Grammar of the Greek New Testament in the Light of Historical Research* (Nashville: Broadman, 1934), p. 423.

7. The NIV follows Nestle-Aland's 26th edition of the Greek New Testament in starting a paragraph division at verse 3. The paragraph, with examples and a conclusion, continues through verse 6.

8. Textual variants at the beginning of verse 3 are responsible for differing translations. Here are a few representative versions: "Behold, we put bits in the horses' mouths" (KJV); "Indeed, we put bits in horses' mouths" (NKJV); "Now if we put the bits into the horses' mouths" (NASB); "When we put bits into the mouths of horses" (NAB).

and the preceding one is obvious. The perfect man, who is never at fault in speech, is "able to keep his whole body in check" (3:2; also see 1:26). Illustrations taken from daily life reveal James to be a person who lived close to nature. On the other hand, the illustrations are rather common; no doubt they circulated in proverbial form, handed down from generation to generation.[9]

The point of the comparison, however, is that a relatively small bit controls a large animal. If, then, man controls powerful horses with small bits placed in their mouths, he certainly should be able to control his own tongue. The points of comparison are mouth and body.

b. "A very small rudder." The second example is even more instructive, especially when we consider the awe and wonder with which the Jew regarded the innate power of the sea. Although Israel borders the Mediterranean Sea, the Jews were never a seafaring people. For the Jew of that time some of the ships were impressive indeed. Large ships carried extensive cargo and numerous people, as is evident from Luke's description of the vessel which was shipwrecked (Acts 27).

"Or take ships as an example," James writes. These large sailing vessels, driven by strong winds, are governed by very small rudders. Who determines the direction of these ships? Man controls their direction by utilizing the force of the wind to his advantage and by turning the rudder of the ship. That rudder is a very small part of the ship's structure and yet it is instrumental in setting the course the pilot has in mind. Note that not the strong wind but the pilot determines the direction of the ship. The contrast is between the smallness of the rudder and the immense size of the ship. If, then, man is able to direct the course of ocean vessels with a rudder, he certainly should be able to control his own tongue.

c. "Likewise the tongue." Before James introduces the third example of the small spark and the great forest, he makes a brief comment about the smallness of the tongue: "Likewise the tongue is a small part of the body, but it makes great boasts." The comparison should not be taken too strictly because the smallness of the tongue is compared with "great boasts" and not with the largeness of the body. The bit, rudder, and tongue have the same characteristic: they are small, yet they achieve great things. The tongue is able to boast of great things. Curtis Vaughan eloquently sums this up:

> It can sway men to violence, or it can move them to the noblest actions. It can instruct the ignorant, encourage the dejected, comfort the sorrowing, and soothe the dying. Or, it can crush the human spirit, destroy reputations, spread distrust and hate, and bring nations to the brink of war.[10]

---

9. Greek writers of ancient times frequently refer to the bits of horses and the rudders of ships; often they mention them together.

10. Curtis Vaughan, *James: A Study Guide* (Grand Rapids: Zondervan, 1969), p. 69.

"Consider what a great forest is set on fire by a small spark." This is the third example and in a sense it is the best of the three. One spark is sufficient to set a whole forest ablaze: stately oaks, majestic cedars, and tall pine trees are reduced to unsightly stumps of blackened wood. And that one spark usually can be attributed to human carelessness and neglect.

When we calculate the annual damage done to our forests by devastating fires, the amount runs into the millions in addition to the untold suffering and death inflicted on the wildlife of the stricken areas. However, the reference to the spark and forest is only an illustration. Therefore, James writes:

6. The tongue also is a fire, a world of evil among the parts of the body. It corrupts the whole person, sets the whole course of his life on fire, and is itself set on fire by hell.

Here is the application of the three illustrations of the horse's bit, the ship's rudder, and the spark in the forest. The text itself, however, is not the easiest to explain. In fact, verse 6 is one of the most difficult passages in the Epistle of James. Some scholars have attempted to explain the text by deleting a few words, for example, the phrase *a world of evil*.[11] Others wish to add a word to ease the reading of the text. For instance, in the Syriac translation of this verse, the sentence shows a balance in harmony with the preceding verse: "The tongue is fire, the sinful world like a forest."[12] Although the text presents numerous problems, we believe that one of Luther's sayings is applicable: "Let the word stand as is." That is, before we delete from or add to the wording of the text, let us see whether we can understand the message itself. For this reason we wish to stay with the wording of the text.

Note the following points:

a. *The tongue is a fire.* James writes, "The tongue also is a fire, a world of evil among the parts of the body." James compares the tongue with a fire that, by implication, is out of control and destroys everything that is combustible in its path (compare Ps. 120:3–4; Prov. 16:27). He clarifies this comparison with the remark that the tongue is a world of evil.

Perhaps James intends to continue the contrast of small versus great: the reference to a small spark and a great forest is then followed by one about the tongue and a world of evil. John Albert Bengel observes, "As

---

11. James Hardy Ropes suggests the possibility of omitting the phrase *a world of evil*, but then candidly concludes, "Exegesis by leaving out hard phrases is an intoxicating experience." See *A Critical and Exegetical Commentary on the Epistle of James*, International Critical Commentary series (1916; reprint ed., Edinburgh: Clark, 1961), p. 234. Martin Dibelius regards as a gloss the clause "a world of evil among the parts of the body." *James: A Commentary on the Epistle of James*, rev. Heinrich Greeven, trans. Michael A. Williams, ed. Helmut Köster, Hermeneia: A Critical and Historical Commentary on the Bible (Philadelphia: Fortress, 1976), p. 195. Also consult Franz Mussner, *Der Jakobusbrief*, Herder Theologischer Kommentar zum Neuen Testament series (Freiburg: Herder, 1967), p. 162.

12. Refer to James B. Adamson, *The Epistle of James*, New International Commentary on the New Testament series (Grand Rapids: Eerdmans, 1976), pp. 143, 158.

the little world of man is an image of the universe, so the tongue is an image of the little world of man."[13] The tongue as the "small part of the body" is as a world of iniquity "among the parts of the body." The tongue, then, is identified with—and in a sense is the vehicle of—a complete world of evil that resides among the members of man's body. It tells lies, slanders someone's name, kindles hate, creates discord, incites lust, and, in brief, gives rise to numerous sins. "There are few sins people commit in which the tongue is not involved."[14] Because of this inclination to evil, the tongue corrupts man's total being.

b. *The tongue corrupts.* If the phrase *a world of evil* is the first description of the tongue, the clause *it corrupts the whole person* is the second. The word *corrupts* actually means "stains" but must be taken symbolically. An evil tongue blemishes one's personality. "What comes out of a man is what makes him 'unclean.' For from within, out of men's hearts, come evil thoughts, sexual immorality, theft, murder, adultery, greed, malice, deceit, lewdness, envy, slander, arrogance and folly. All these evils come from inside and make a man 'unclean' " (Mark 7:20–23).

c. *The tongue sets on fire.* The next clause appears to be a saying that circulated in the countries bordering the Mediterranean Sea. James says, "The tongue . . . sets the whole course of [a person's] life on fire."

What does James mean when he uses the phrase *the whole course of his life?*[15] This proverbial expression probably originated in ancient Greece; the phrase in Jewish circles referred to the general course of life.[16] That is, fire consumes the entire course of man's life. Moreover, the tongue not only sets fire to man's existence, but is itself "set on fire by hell."

d. *The tongue is set on fire.* James employs the word *hell* with a Hebrew connotation: Gehenna, the valley of the son of Hinnom, outside Jerusalem (Josh. 15:8; II Kings 23:10; II Chron. 28:3; 33:6; Jer. 19:2; 32:35). Initially, Gehenna was the site of sacrifices to Molech; later, refuse was burned there. In time the name acquired another meaning: "In the gospels it is the place of punishment in the next life."[17] Symbolically, the word refers to the place where the devil resides and to which the doomed

---

13. John Albert Bengel, *Gnomon of the New Testament,* ed. Andrew R. Fausset, 5 vols., 7th ed. (Edinburgh: Clark, 1877), vol. 5, p. 24. Also consult Joseph B. Mayor, *The Epistle of St. James* (reprint ed., Grand Rapids: Zondervan, 1946), p. 115. Bauer interprets the term *kosmos* (world) as "totality, sum total," p. 447.

14. Donald W. Burdick, *James,* vol. 12, the *Expositor's Bible Commentary,* ed. Frank E. Gaebelein, 12 vols. (Grand Rapids: Eerdmans, 1981), p. 187.

15. Here are some representative translations of this phrase: "the course of nature" (KJV), "the cycle of nature" (RSV), "the wheel of our existence" (NEB), "our course from birth" (NAB), and "the whole wheel of creation" (JB).

16. Many commentators have written extensively on this question, for example, Ropes, *James,* pp. 235–39. Also read the comments of Joachim Guhrt in *NIDNTT,* vol. 1, p. 182.

17. Bauer, p. 153. The term *Gehenna* in the Greek occurs only twelve times in the New Testament; eleven of them are in the synoptic Gospels (Matt. 5:22, 29, 30; 10:28; 18:9; 23:15, 33; Mark 9:43, 45, 47; Luke 12:5).

are banished. The implication in this verse is that Satan himself sets man's tongue on fire.

James presents a clear message in verse 6, even though a few expressions are somewhat problematic. Today these need a word of explanation, but for the original readers of the epistle James communicated "with rhetorical clarity."[18]

7. All kinds of animals, birds, reptiles and creatures of the sea are being tamed and have been tamed by man, 8. but no man can tame the tongue. It is a restless evil, full of deadly poison.

James comes to a conclusion on taming the tongue. With the examples of the horse's bit and the ship's rudder he has shown the skill and capability of man (vv. 3–4). Now he portrays man as ruler in God's creation, for man has been given power to rule over all creatures that walk, fly, crawl, and swim (Gen. 1:26, 28; Ps. 8:6–8).

"All kinds of animals." We should not expect a scientific enumeration of all the species of animals that man has been able to tame. Nevertheless, James lists them in pairs:

wild animals and birds

reptiles and sea creatures

Man has been able to subdue all these creatures, for God has given man the power to rule in his great creation. Man continues to tame animals for his benefit and pleasure. We see this displayed in a circus performance where wild animals obey their trainer who merely cracks a whip, snaps his fingers, or claps his hands. Man has been endowed with a nature that is able to subdue God's creatures.

Yet man is unable to control his own tongue. When man fell into sin, he lost his ability to govern himself.[19] He lost control of himself and is now ruled by his tongue. Man can tame fierce and powerful animals, yet he cannot tame his own tongue.

James makes no exceptions: "No man can tame the tongue." With this brief and yet emphatic remark James repeats what he said earlier: "We all stumble in many ways. If anyone is never at fault in what he says, he is a perfect man, able to keep his whole body in check" (3:2).

What is man's tongue? "It is a restless evil, full of deadly poison." The picture is that of a poisonous snake whose tongue is never at rest and whose fangs are filled with lethal venom. Man's tongue is unstable, elusive, restless. Besides, it is full of a death-bringing poison. Of all the biblical authors, James most descriptively and accurately portrays the na-

---

18. Peter H. Davids, *The Epistle of James: A Commentary on the Greek Text*, New International Greek Testament Commentary series (Grand Rapids: Eerdmans, 1982), p. 144.

19. R. V. G. Tasker, *The General Epistle of James: An Introduction and Commentary*, Tyndale New Testament Commentaries (Grand Rapids: Eerdmans, 1957), p. 77.

ture of man's tongue (compare Ps. 58:4; 140:3). It is an ugly picture that shows the destructive nature of sin.

Practical Considerations in 3:3–8

Proverbial sayings on the use of the tongue are numerous. Here are a few:

There's many a slip 'twixt cup and lip. [German proverb]

A lengthy tongue and early death. [Persian saying]

The boneless tongue, small and weak, can crush and kill.

The books of Psalms and Proverbs are replete with sound advice and pertinent observations:

Keep your tongue from evil
and your lips from speaking lies. [Ps. 34:13]

When words are many, sin is not absent,
but he who holds his tongue is wise. [Prov. 10:19]

He who guards his lips guards his life,
but he who speaks rashly will come to ruin. [Prov. 13:3]

The nineteenth-century American novelist Washington Irving remarks, "A sharp tongue is the only edged tool that grows keener with constant use." James devotes a considerable segment of his epistle to this subject. Says he, "Everyone should be quick to listen, slow to speak and slow to become angry" (1:19). All of us may learn a cultural lesson from the Chinese people. They have the custom of not answering a speaker until he is completely finished speaking. They think that it is discourteous to reply immediately, for a rash reply indicates a lack of thinking and poor judgment.

Greek Words, Phrases, and Constructions in 3:3–8

Verse 3

εἰ δέ—faulty hearing of a copyist may have caused the variant ἴδε (see) or vice versa. Some weaker manuscripts have ἰδού (behold), perhaps influenced by verses 4 and 5. In context, the reading εἰ δέ seems to be more difficult to explain and therefore is preferred.[20]

τῶν ἵππων—in the structure of the sentence, the position of these two words is most emphatic. Normally they should follow either the noun *bits* or more likely the noun *mouths*.

---

20. Refer to Bruce M. Metzger, *A Textual Commentary on the Greek New Testament*, corrected ed. (London and New York: United Bible Societies, 1975), pp. 681–82.

Verse 4

ὄντα—this present active participle of the verb *to be* has a concessive connotation: "although they are so large."[21]

ὁρμή—from the verb ὁρμάω (I set out, rush) the noun occurs twice in the New Testament (Acts 14:5; James 3:4). Here it means "impulse."

Verse 6

ἡ γλῶσσα πῦρ—perhaps this clause should end with a colon to indicate that James clarifies his statement *the tongue also is a fire.* The first description of the tongue is ὁ κόσμος τῆς ἀδικίας (the world of evil) and the second ἡ σπιλοῦσα (the one that corrupts).

τὸν τροχόν—this noun occurs only here in the entire New Testament. It derives from the verb τρέχω (I run) and means "wheel." With other scholars, Bauer asks whether the noun should have the accent on the penult τρόχος and be translated "*course* or *round* of existence."[22]

Verse 7

φύσις—James repeats the noun, in the dative (of means), to show human superiority over animal species.

δαμάζεται—a present passive from the verb δαμάζω (I tame). The present tense and the following perfect tense draw a clear distinction in a progressive activity.

Verse 8

μεστή—the adjective has its antecedent in γλῶσσαν, governs the genitive case ἰοῦ (poison), and is an independent clause with the verb *to be* understood.

θανατηφόρου—the compound adjective is a combination of the noun θάνατος (death) and the verb φέρω (I bring).

---

3. Praise and Cursing
3:9–12

After such a lengthy exposition about the nature of the tongue, we can expect members of the church to object. They believe that those whom the grace of God has touched are able to control their tongues. But do Christians who praise the name of God the Father act differently from persons who refuse to praise his name? Do Christians speak with the tongues of angels? Hardly.

In my childhood I learned some stanzas of a song that expresses a longing for perfection but recognizes man's inability to achieve it.

> I wish to be like Jesus,
> So humble and so kind.
> His words were always tender,
> His voice was e'er divine.

---

21. Robertson, *Grammar*, p. 1129. See also Hanna, *Grammatical Aid*, p. 419.
22. Bauer, p. 828. Consult Robertson, *Grammar*, p. 233.

But no, I'm not like Jesus,
As everyone can see!
O Savior, come and help me,
And make me just like Thee.
—Anonymous

James reflects on the Christian's inconsistency of praising the name of the Lord and cursing his fellow man. He writes,

9. With the tongue we praise our Lord and Father, and with it we curse men, who have been made in God's likeness. 10. Out of the same mouth come praise and cursing. My brothers, this should not be.

Note these observations:

a. *Contradiction.* The prophet Isaiah teaches the believer to praise God the Father:

But you are our Father,
though Abraham does not know us
or Israel acknowledge us;
you, O LORD, are our Father,
our Redeemer from of old is your name. [Isa. 63:16]

We would expect the believer who praises God in prayer, confession, and song to be consistent. This is not the case, however. With the same tongue the believer curses his fellow men, "who have been made in God's likeness."

James reminds his readers of the creation account: God created man in his own image and likeness (Gen. 1:26). In distinction from the rest of creation, man has a special relationship to God. Therefore, if we curse men, we indirectly curse God.[23] Moreover, if we curse men, we act contrary to the explicit command of Jesus, "Bless those who curse you" (Luke 6:28; also see Rom. 12:14).

"Out of the same mouth come praise and cursing." This saying may have originated in Jewish tradition (among people prone to pronounce curses upon their fellow men) and therefore was meaningful to the readers of James's epistle.[24] Nevertheless, every reader of this epistle ought to recognize the contradiction when praise and cursing come from the same mouth. "My brothers, this should not be."

11. Can both fresh water and salt water flow from the same spring? 12. My brothers, can a fig tree bear olives, or a grapevine bear figs? Neither can a salt spring produce fresh water.

b. *Consideration.* In his letter James shows an interest in God's creation. With examples drawn from nature he seeks to illustrate his point. First he

---

23. C. Leslie Mitton is of the opinion that cursing "probably refers primarily to angry words of abuse spoken to those whom we regard as subordinate to us." *The Epistle of James* (Grand Rapids: Eerdmans, 1966), p. 131. However, if James had wanted to tell his readers not to slander or engage in backbiting, he had words to that effect at his disposal.

24. Says Dibelius, ". . . the entire view reflected in [verses] 9, 10a comes not from the life of the early Christian community, but from the life of the Jewish community." *James*, p. 203.

calls attention to a spring of water. "Can both fresh water and salt water flow from the same spring?"[25] It is impossible to expect drinkable water and water that is not drinkable from the same source. Second, James approaches his readers with two familiar examples. Generally, a Jew had his own fig tree and his own grapevine (I Kings 4:25); olive trees were common. "Can a fig tree bear olives, or a grapevine bear figs?"

The readers know that each species of fruitbearing trees produces its own kind of fruit. Fig trees bear figs, olive trees olives, and grapevines grapes. The example is reminiscent of the question Jesus asked in the Sermon on the Mount: "Do people pick grapes from thornbushes, or figs from thistles?" (Matt. 7:16). To ask the question is to answer it.

c. *Conclusion.* James answers by repeating some of the words of his first question. "Neither can a salt spring produce fresh water." If, then, nature is unable to go against its created functions, ought not man's tongue praise the name of man's creator and redeemer?

Greek Words, Phrases, and Constructions in 3:9–12

Verse 9

κύριον—the Textus Receptus and the Majority Text have the reading θεόν.[26] On the basis of external and internal evidence, scholars favor the term κύριον.

τοὺς ἀνθρώπους—the use of the definite article relates to the human race as a class. The second occurrence of the definite article introduces the explanatory clause that ends in the perfect active participle γεγονότας, derived from the verb γίνομαι (I become). The perfect tense is significant because it refers to an act in the past that has lasting effect on the present.

Verse 11

μήτι—this particle introduces a rhetorical question that expects a negative answer. The same is true for the rhetorical questions in verse 12.

ὀπῆς βρύει—James employs these two words that appear infrequently in the New Testament: the first one occurs here and in Hebrews 11:38; the other only here. The first one describes a fissure in rock or ground and the second means "to gush forth."

---

13 Who is wise and understanding among you? Let him show it by his good life, by deeds done in the humility that comes from wisdom. 14 But if you harbor bitter envy and selfish ambition in your hearts, do not boast about it or deny the truth. 15 Such "wisdom" does not come down from heaven but is earthly, unspiritual, of the devil. 16 For where you have envy and selfish ambition, there you find disorder and every evil practice.

---

25. Some versions have the translation *bitter* (KJV, NKJV); others have the word *brackish* (RSV, NEB).

26. Arthur L. Farstad and Zane C. Hodges, *The Greek New Testament According to the Majority Text* (Nashville and New York: Nelson, 1982), p. 682. Also, some translations have the word *God* instead of "Lord" (Vulgate, KJV, NKJV).

17 But the wisdom that comes from heaven is first of all pure; then peace loving, considerate, submissive, full of mercy and good fruit, impartial and sincere. 18 Peacemakers who sow in peace raise a harvest of righteousness.

B. Two Kinds of Wisdom
3:13–18

1. Earthly Wisdom
3:13–16

The Christian lives not in isolation but in fellowship with the community in which God has placed him. That community is first of all the church of Jesus Christ. True to her calling, the church stands in the midst of the world to let the light of the gospel shine forth.

To function properly in their respective places, the Christian and the church need wisdom and understanding. In the introductory part of his epistle James tells the reader how to obtain wisdom: "Ask God, who gives generously to all without finding fault" (1:5).

No one can live without wisdom, for no one wishes to be called stupid. Therefore, wisdom is treasured by those who have it and sought by those who lack it. James, then, asks a rather direct question:

13. Who is wise and understanding among you? Let him show it by his good life, by deeds done in the humility that comes from wisdom.

James addresses the members of the church. He assumes that they pray to God for wisdom, that they possess this virtue, and that the world looks to them for leadership. Knowing, however, that these things are not always true of Christians, James wants his readers to examine themselves.

a. *Examination.* "Who is wise and understanding among you?" A wise and understanding person demonstrates in what he says and by what he does that he possesses wisdom. Whether James wants to designate the teachers of his day wise men is not quite clear.[27] If this is the case, we see a direct connection between the beginning of this chapter ("Not many of you should presume to be teachers," v. 1) and the rhetorical question here (v. 13).

James qualifies the term *wise* with the word *understanding*. This means that a wise person also has experience, knowledge, and ability.[28] Wisdom consists of having insight and expertise to draw conclusions that are correct. An old proverb sums this up: "Foresight is better than hindsight, but insight is best."

Countless instances prove that knowledgeable people are not necessarily wise. But when a knowledgeable person has insight, he indeed is wise. If

---

27. Ulrich Wilckens writes, "The wise man is the finished and recognised scribe, the ordained rabbi." *TDNT,* vol. 7, p. 505.

28. Translators interpret the expression *understanding* in numerous ways: "endued with knowledge" (kjv), "clever" (neb), and "learned" (jb). The terms *wise* and *understanding* appear together only in this particular New Testament text (see also Deut. 1:13; 4:6 in the LXX).

there is a wise and understanding person among you, says James, let him demonstrate this in his life.

b. *Demonstration.* James encourages the wise man to show by his conduct that he has received the gift of wisdom. "Let him show it by his good life." James seems to indicate that among Christians wise and understanding men are in the minority, for not everyone who belongs to the Christian community acquires wisdom. But those who have it are exhorted to demonstrate by word and deed that they indeed are wise. James uses the verb *to show* in the sense of "to prove." Let a man provide actual proof that he possesses wisdom and understanding. Let him confirm this by means of his daily conduct.[29]

What does James mean by the expression *good life*? He refers to noble, praiseworthy behavior. True, James stresses "deeds done in the humility that comes from wisdom." But a wise man affirms his noble conduct in words and deeds.

c. *Affirmation.* "Actions speak louder than words." This proverbial truth underscores the necessity of looking at a person's deeds to see whether his actions match his words. What are these deeds? They are performed in a humble, gentle spirit that is controlled by a spirit of heavenly wisdom.[30]

The emphasis in this verse falls on that characteristic of wisdom described as humility. This quality can also be described as meekness or gentleness. Gentleness comes to expression in the person who is endowed with wisdom and who affirms this in all his deeds.

In Ecclesiasticus, also known as the Wisdom of Jesus the Son of Sirach, the writer lists a few precepts on humility and says, "My son, perform your tasks in meekness; then you will be loved by those whom God accepts" (Sir. 3:17, RSV).

14. But if you harbor bitter envy and selfish ambition in your hearts, do not boast about it or deny the truth.

The opposite of a gentle spirit controlled by wisdom is a heart filled "with bitter envy and selfish ambition." The contrast in this verse and the preceding one has a direct parallel in Paul's epistle to the Galatians, where he mentions among the fruits of the Spirit "gentleness and self-control" (5:23). Among the acts of the sinful nature are "selfish ambition . . . and envy" (5:20–21).

As an experienced pastor, James knows that among the members of the church are some persons whose spirit is characterized by bitter envy and selfishness. James uses the plural form *you* and indicates with a conditional sentence that the evidence is true to fact. In other words, he is well aware of the spiritual condition of the readers. If they continue to harbor envy and selfishness, they will be consumed.

---

29. In the original the word *conduct* appears thirteen times. Compare Gal. 1:13; Eph. 4:22; I Tim. 4:12; Heb. 13:7; James 3:13; I Peter 1:15, 18; 2:12; 3:1, 2, 16; II Peter 2:7; 3:11.
30. Wolfgang Bauder notes that humility is "the work of the Holy Spirit (Gal. 5:23). . . . It comes about when men are linked with Christ and are conformed to his image." *NIDNTT,* vol. 2, p. 259.

James describes envy with the adjective *bitter*. He does not explain what caused this bitter envy. His description, however, points to a transgression of the tenth commandment, "You shall not covet." Harboring bitter envy is sin. And being filled with selfish ambition goes contrary to the teaching of the royal law, "Love your neighbor as yourself" (James 2:8).

"Do not boast about [your bitter envy and selfish ambition] or deny the truth." Persons who are consumed by envy and selfishness usually talk about this to anyone who lends a listening ear. They ought to realize, however, that everything they say is contradicted by the truth. Every time they open their mouths to give vent to their feelings, they deceive themselves. When Paul admonishes the Ephesians not to grieve the Holy Spirit, he tells them to "get rid of all bitterness" (4:31). A heart that nurtures "bitter envy and selfish ambition" is devoid of heavenly wisdom.

15. Such "wisdom" does not come down from heaven but is earthly, unspiritual, of the devil. 16. For where you have envy and selfish ambition, there you find disorder and every evil practice.

The New International Version correctly puts the word *wisdom* in quotation marks to indicate that this wisdom is not genuine. The text itself explains the source and the characteristics of this so-called wisdom. Its origin is not heavenly but earthly; its peculiarities are unspiritual and devilish. James uses strong language to portray the absolute contrast between wisdom that originates in man and that which comes from God.

The believer who is truly wise prays continually to God in the name of Jesus. In prayer he is in communion with the source of wisdom, for God himself will give generously to anyone who asks him (James 1:5).

The opposite is equally true. Without faith and prayer a person can never obtain true wisdom. His words spoken out of envy and selfish ambition show a make-believe wisdom that originates with man, not with God. This type of wisdom "does not come down from heaven but is earthly."

In this verse James lists a series of three adjectives that have a descending order:

earthly
>   unspiritual
>   devilish

a. "Earthly." What the writer means to say is that which is earthly stands in contrast to what God originates in heaven. For example, the beast coming up out of the earth (Rev. 13:11) defies that which is holy and heavenly. And if God's Spirit is absent from earthly matters, sin is present.

b. "Unspiritual." In his first epistle to the church at Corinth, Paul discusses the wisdom that is taught by the Spirit of God. But, writes Paul, "the man without the Spirit does not accept the things that come from the Spirit of God, for they are foolishness to him, and he cannot understand them, because they are spiritually discerned" (I Cor. 2:14; also compare Jude 19). To be unspiritual, however, should not be understood as being without a spirit.[31]

Moreover, someone who abandons the faith follows "deceiving spirits and things taught by demons" (I Tim. 4:1).

c. "Devilish." In the preceding verse (v. 14) James tells the person whose heart is filled with "bitter envy and selfish ambition" not to deny the truth. If he denies the truth, however, this person lives a lie that finds its origin with the father of the lie, the devil. James calls a spade a spade: "such 'wisdom' . . . is . . . of the devil."

When the devil speaks the lie, it is bad. When he uses the world to perpetrate the lie, it is worse. But when the members of the church become his instruments to spread devilish wisdom, it is the worst of all situations. The letter of James leaves the impression that the devil employed some of the members of the church.

James proves this point by observing a common truth: "For where you have envy and selfish ambition, there you find disorder and every evil practice." Note the distinct correlation that, graphically put, runs as follows:

where	there
you have	you find
envy	disorder
selfish ambition	every evil practice

The one thing leads inevitably to the next in a sequence of cause and effect. If you have envy, then you will find disorder.

What is envy? Here is one explanation: "Envy is the resentful and even hateful dislike of the good fortune or blessing of another."[32] James calls envy "bitter" (3:14). Envy destroys mutual confidence, demolishes unity, and is devilish in design. As James points out, envy develops into disorder. The expression *disorder* "seems to have something of the bad associations of our word 'anarchy.'"[33]

Furthermore, selfish ambition invariably leads to evil practices because egoistic motives overshadow and eventually eliminate love for God and one's neighbor. In itself, ambition is a beneficial force that seeks to promote the welfare of others. But when it becomes self-centered, ambition degenerates into evil practices. Noting jealousy and quarreling among the Corinthians, Paul rebukes them for being worldly (I Cor. 3:3). Instead, believers ought to be God's fellow workers.

---

31. Dibelius elaborates on the Gnostic meaning of the expression *unspiritual* but concludes that James is not directing his epistle against the Gnostics. See *James*, p. 212.

32. Paul Benjamin, "Envy," in *Baker's Dictionary of Christian Ethics*, ed. Carl F. H. Henry (Grand Rapids: Baker, 1973), p. 213. Albrecht Stumpff asserts that envy is "the kind of zeal which does not try to help others but rather to harm them, the predominant concern being for personal advancement." *TDNT*, vol. 2, p. 882.

33. Ropes, *James*, p. 248.

Practical Considerations in 3:13–16

Verse 15

James mentions two types of wisdom: one from heaven and the other from the earth. He first tells us something about wisdom that is earthly before explaining the meaning of heavenly wisdom.

Earthly wisdom is not true wisdom at all because it puts one's ego before everyone and everything else. When one stridently insists upon being first, serious conflicts are unavoidable.

When we permit envy and selfishness to enter the family circle, we soon find that the stability of the home is seriously threatened. Then the home is filled with tension. It causes father, mother, and children to become uneasy, diminishes their witness for Christ, and weakens their spiritual well-being.

Take Miriam, for example. She created untold friction in the family circle of Moses when she insisted upon being first in Israel (Num. 12:1–2). The friction she caused in the family and in the community is not unlike that created by personality conflicts we encounter among church members today. These problems seriously hinder the effectiveness of many congregations in their ministry.

To find peace in the family and in the church we must bring about reconciliation by confessing sin, by giving up selfish ambition, and by praying for the spirit of God's mercy, love, and peace.

Greek Words, Phrases, and Constructions in 3:13–16

Verse 13

τίς—this is the interrogative pronoun *who*, not the indefinite pronoun *anyone*, preceded by the particle εἰ. The reading εἰ τις is relatively weak in textual support, yet some translators favor it (see JB, NAB).

ἀναστροφῆς—from the compound verb ἀναστρέφομαι (I conduct myself) this noun expresses "*life* in so far as it is comprised in conduct."[34]

Verse 14

ἔχετε—note the switch from the impersonal singular *who* (v. 13) to the second person plural *you* (v. 14).

μὴ κατακαυχᾶσθε καὶ ψεύδεσθε—the negative μή with the present imperative in both verbs implies that the action which is already in progress must be stopped.

The sentence is a mixture composed of the protasis of a simple fact condition followed by prohibitions with imperatives. Writes C. F. D. Moule, "Logically, the imperative clauses should be Future Indicative."[35] But this construction is not necessary, for James is actually saying, "If you harbor bitter envy and selfish ambition in your hearts [and I know you do], stop boasting about it and stop denying the truth."

---

34. Thayer, p. 42.

35. C. F. D. Moule, *An Idiom-Book of New Testament Greek*, 2d ed. (Cambridge: At the University Press, 1960), p. 152. Also see Hanna, *Grammatical Aid*, p. 419.

Verse 15

ἔστιν—although the verbal distance between the verb and the present participle κατερχομένη (coming down) is somewhat extensive, the construction nevertheless is the periphrastic present.[36]

---

2. Heavenly Wisdom
3:17–18

True wisdom has its origin in Jesus Christ and therefore it displays the characteristics of Christ in the believer who has received heavenly wisdom. Moreover, the believer reveals this wisdom to everyone who comes in contact with him—to believers and to unbelievers.

17. But the wisdom that comes from heaven is first of all pure; then peace loving, considerate, submissive, full of mercy and good fruit, impartial and sincere.

True wisdom comes down from heaven as a gift of God to the believer who asks for it (James 1:5, 17). This wisdom becomes evident when man makes decisions that are dependent on and in harmony with the will of God. Heavenly wisdom has its own characteristic: it is "pure."

In this text, purity is the first of seven words or phrases James uses to describe wisdom. It represents wisdom as immaculate, undefiled, innocent, just as Christ himself is pure (I John 3:3).

Why is purity mentioned as the first characteristic of wisdom? Wisdom that finds its origin in God is pure because God himself is pure, that is, holy. Therefore, the expression *pure* is a synonym of "holy." We compare purity with light that dispels the darkness, illumines everything, but is not influenced by anything.[37] Heavenly wisdom enters this sinful world, then, but is not affected by it.

The six characteristics that follow form three categories, of which the first includes the adjectives *peace-loving, considerate,* and *submissive.* These adjectives depict the attitude of a wise man.

a. *Attitude.* The believer who exercises the gift of heavenly wisdom possesses a self-controlled temperament that expresses peace. By his attitude toward others he shows that he loves peace. The peace of God dominates his thinking so that all who meet him see him as a tower of strength. Indeed, all his ways are pleasing and all his "paths are peace" (Prov. 3:17).

Another attribute of wisdom is consideration. The person who is "considerate" is fair, reasonable, gentle in all his deliberations. He quietly gathers all the facts before he gives his opinion. He refrains from placing himself first and always considers others better than himself (Phil. 2:3; 4:5).

---

36. Robertson, *Grammar,* p. 881; Moule, *Idiom-Book,* p. 17.
37. Consult E. M. Sidebottom, *James, Jude, and 2 Peter,* Century Bible series (London: Nelson; Greenwood, S. C.: Attic, 1967), p. 51.

The third characteristic in this category is that of being "submissive." That is, a wise man is open to suggestions, always ready to listen to the opinions of others, and willing to accept admonitions and corrections.

b. *Action*. The next category describes wisdom as "full of mercy and good fruits." These attributes involve the wise man in reaching out to people around him. The person filled with heavenly wisdom puts the word of Jesus into practice: "Blessed are the merciful, for they will be shown mercy" (Matt. 5:7; also see James 2:13). We show mercy to needy people who do not deserve it; otherwise it would not be mercy. We grant mercy because God sets the example and expects us to follow him (see, for instance, Mic. 6:8). The wise man is *full* of mercy. Also, he is full of good fruits. James does not specify what these fruits are, but the consequences of religion exemplify them (James 1:26–27).

c. *Judgment*. The last category of characteristics relates to the discerning judgment of a wise man. James writes that wisdom is "impartial and sincere." A wise person does not take sides in a dispute when he serves as arbitrator. He listens carefully and objectively to the arguments presented to him and then renders judgment that is first impartial and then sincere. The wise man is able to avoid being personally involved and refrain from showing favoritism, yet act sincerely (Rom. 12:9, II Cor. 6:6; I Peter 1:22). Such a man receives the respect of the community in which he lives and works.

18. Peacemakers who sow in peace raise a harvest of righteousness.
At the conclusion of this presentation, James seems to resort to a popular proverb of his day. This saying has a familiar sound. It reminds us of similar phrases in the prophetical books of the Old Testament, the words of Jesus, and the epistles of the New Testament. Here are a few texts:

> The fruit of righteousness will be peace;
>   the effect of righteousness will be quietness and confidence forever.
>   [Isa. 32:17]

> But you have turned justice into poison
>   and the fruit of righteousness into bitterness. [Amos 6:12]

> "Blessed are the peacemakers,
>   for they will be called sons of God." [Matt. 5:9]

> Now he who supplies seed to the sower and bread for food will also supply and increase your store of seed and will enlarge the harvest of your righteousness. [II Cor. 9:10]

> No discipline seems pleasant at the time, but painful. Later on, however, it produces a harvest of righteousness and peace for those who have been trained by it. [Heb. 12:11]

What is the work of peacemakers? Simply put, they are the ones who seek to bring quarreling parties together to achieve harmony and peace.

But, I hasten to add, they also practice peace by striving to live in peace with all people (Rom. 12:18). In short, they will do everything in their power to avoid strife and promote peace.

A harvest of righteousness is sown in peace by those who make peace. Translations and many commentaries provide variations in wording. Some translators understand the phrase *a harvest of righteousness* to mean "a harvest consisting of righteousness."[38] The terms *harvest* and *righteousness,* then, are synonymous. Others see it differently and say that the phrase means "a harvest produced by righteousness." Here is a representative translation: "And the harvest, which righteousness yields to the peacemakers, comes from a sowing in peace."[39]

We would expect the writer to say that peacemakers sow peace and reap a harvest of righteousness. But he says the exact opposite: righteousness sown in peace yields a harvest of righteousness. In other words, what is sown is also reaped. We ought not to fault James for inaccuracies when in common parlance we do exactly the same. In the spring of the year a gardener may say, "I planted watermelons last week." He means to say that he sowed the seed in springtime but hopes to harvest the fruit in summer.

Peacemakers sow and harvest righteousness in peace. In the context of James's discussions on heavenly versus earthly wisdom this means that "righteousness cannot be produced in the climate of bitterness and self-seeking. Righteousness will grow only in a climate of peace."[40]

Practical Considerations in 3:17–18

Although we wholeheartedly affirm our desire for peace in the context of family, church, society, and nation, we have reservations when we are told to seek peace at any price. We do not wish to compromise truth, for such a compromise is equivalent to promoting falsehood. We cannot set aside the rules of conduct we derive from Scripture. Thus we stand firm in our defense of our Christian heritage.

Within the context of church and society, however, Christians have often preached the love of God and have quoted verses of Scripture to prove their point, but in practice have shown the least love toward their neighbor. In fact, the liberal in the church or the humanist in society often demonstrates a greater degree of love for his fellow man than does the person who cites chapter and verse from the pages of the Bible. Unfortunately, Christians frequently give the world the impression that they are more interested in strife and confrontation than in peace and love.

---

38. For instance, the NASB has, "And the seed whose fruit is righteousness is sown in peace by those who make peace." Also see Davids, *James,* p. 155.

39. The MLB (also see GNB). Ropes, *James,* p. 250, explains that the harvest of righteousness is "the reward which righteous conduct brings." D. Edmond Hiebert writes, "The fruit that righteousness produces contains in itself seed that, when planted, produces a harvest of a similar kind." *The Epistle of James: Tests of a Living Faith* (Chicago: Moody, 1979), p. 237.

40. Burdick, *James,* vol. 12, the *Expositor's Bible Commentary,* pp. 191–92.

During his earthly ministry, Jesus opposed sin and publicly rebuked the spiritual leaders of Israel. Yet the moral and social outcasts (prostitutes and tax collectors) experienced the love of the Lord Jesus. They knew that he was "peace loving, considerate, submissive, full of mercy and good fruit, impartial and sincere."

Greek Words, Phrases, and Constructions in 3:17–18

Verse 17

ἀγνή—this adjective derived from the verb ἅζομαι (I stand in awe) means "morally pure, upright, sincere." The use of assonance is evident in this verse: the initial ἁ and ἐ predominate.

Verse 18

καρπὸς δὲ δικαιοσύνης—the case of δικαιοσύνης (righteousness) can be either a genitive of apposition (definition) or a genitive of origin.

τοῖς ποιοῦσιν—the dative case in the present active participle is the dative of advantage.

Summary of Chapter 3

James warns his readers against the danger of the unruly tongue that leads them to sin and shame. Teachers, he says, "will be judged more strictly" in relation to their teaching. He himself, however, is not judgmental. He realizes that at one time or other every person is at fault in what he says, and therefore no one is perfect. The person who keeps his tongue in check controls his entire body.

We rein in horses with relatively small bits that are placed in their mouths. We steer a large ship with "a very small rudder." On the other hand, a tongue that is not kept in check is a fire that affects the whole course of life. We have much greater difficulty restraining our tongue than taming any creature in the animal world. And last, we experience the restlessness of the tongue as it praises God and curses men, for this is contradictory.

After a discussion about the tongue, James describes the wise man who demonstrates wisdom by the deeds he performs. A person filled with envy and selfishness denies the truth; he possesses earthly wisdom that is unspiritual and of the devil. Heavenly wisdom, however, is pure, promotes peace, and produces a harvest of righteousness.

4

Submission

4:1–17

Outline

4 1 What causes fights and quarrels among you? Don't they come from your desires that battle within you? 2 You want something but don't get it. You kill and covet, but you cannot have what you want. You quarrel and fight. You do not have, because you do not ask God. 3 When you ask, you do not receive, because you ask with the wrong motives, that you may spend what you get on your pleasures.

4 You adulterous people, don't you know that friendship with the world is hatred toward God? Anyone who chooses to be a friend of the world becomes an enemy of God. 5 Or do you think Scripture says without reason that the spirit he caused to live in us tends toward envy, 6 but he gives us more grace? That is why Scripture says:

> "God opposes the proud
>   but gives grace to the humble."

7 Submit yourselves, then, to God. Resist the devil, and he will flee from you. 8 Come near to God and he will come near to you. Wash your hands, you sinners, and purify your hearts, you double-minded. 9 Grieve, mourn and wail. Change your laughter to mourning and your joy to gloom. 10 Humble yourselves before the Lord, and he will lift you up.

11 Brothers, do not slander one another. Anyone who speaks against his brother or judges him, speaks against the law and judges it. When you judge the law, you are not keeping it, but sitting in judgment on it. 12 There is only one Lawgiver and Judge, the one who is able to save and destroy. But you—who are you to judge your neighbor?

A. Submission in Life and Spirit
4:1–12

1. Asking with Wrong Motives
4:1–3

The connection between the last part of the preceding chapter and the first three verses of this chapter is clear. If bitter envy and selfish ambition have filled man's heart (3:14, 16), if his guiding principle is earthly wisdom that is unspiritual and devilish (3:15), if he has alienated himself from God, then he promotes "disorder and every evil practice" (3:16). When that happens, fights and quarrels are the order of the day.

1. What causes fights and quarrels among you? Don't they come from your desires that battle within you?

We have the impression that the early Christian church was marked by peace and harmony. Think of the time after Pentecost when "all the believers were one in heart and mind" (Acts 4:32). This picture of the church, however, fades within the span of a decade or more. The recipients of the Epistle of James fight, quarrel, and are filled with selfish desires that drive them into sin, as the writer puts it in the first verse of the fourth chapter.

A word-for-word translation of the text is this: "Where do wars and fights come from among you? Do they not come from your desires for pleasure that war in your members?"(NKJV). We do well to interpret this passage figuratively, in the "sense of strife, conflict, quarrel."[1]

Many translators refrain from giving a literal version of the Greek text. They think that the expression *war* points to an area of conflict outside the Christian community. James, however, is not describing international conflicts. As a pastor who is interested in the spiritual welfare of his people, he addresses "the twelve tribes scattered among the nations" (1:1).

Note that James asks the penetrating question, "What causes fights and quarrels among you?" He wants to know the origin of these fights and quarrels—the use of the plural indicates that they were not confined to an occasional disagreement. Thus, he looks beyond the symptoms to the cause of all these conflicts.

James answers his own question with a rhetorical question that elicits an affirmative reply: "Don't they come from your desires that battle within you?" The term *desires* (note the plural) is the key word. It signifies that in his life, man chooses worldly pleasures that are contrary to the expressed will of God.[2] As Jesus says in the parable of the sower, "the desires for other things come in and choke the word [of God], making it unfruitful" (Mark 4:19; also see Luke 8:14). In time, man becomes a slave to the desires of his heart and separates himself from God (Rom. 1:24; II Tim. 4:3; James 1:14; II Peter 3:3; Jude 16, 18).

When God no longer rules man's life, the pursuit of pleasure takes over, and peace is disrupted because of frequent fights and quarrels.

The New International Version gives the reading *your desires that battle within you*. Other translations have "in your members" instead of "within you."[3] Is the conflict a personal matter (within yourselves) or a congregational dispute (among the members of your church)? We find an answer to this question when we study the word *member* in its scriptural context.

In a few places, Paul uses the expression *members* to describe the church as the body of Christ (Rom. 12:4–5; I Cor. 12:12, 27; Eph. 4:16; 5:30). But more strictly, this expression refers not to a theological or sociological context but to the human body.[4] In the absence of a clear indication that James is thinking of the church, we interpret the term *members* to mean the physical bodies of the persons he addresses.

---

1. Refer to Colin Brown, *NIDNTT*, vol. 3, p. 962.

2. Gustav Stählin, *TDNT*, vol. 2, p. 921. Also consult Erich Beyreuther, *NIDNTT*, vol. 1, p. 459.

3. For example, see KJV, NKJV, ASV, NASB, RSV, NAB, MLB.

4. Consult Matt. 5:29–30; Rom. 6:13, 19; 7:5, 23; 12:4; I Cor. 6:15; 12:14, 18, 19, 20, 22, 25, 26; Col. 3:5 [nature]; James 3:5, 6. Also see Peter H. Davids, *The Epistle of James: A Commentary on the Greek Text*, New International Greek Testament Commentary series (Grand Rapids: Eerdmans, 1982), p. 157.

2. You want something but don't get it. You kill and covet, but you cannot have what you want. You quarrel and fight. You do not have, because you do not ask God.

The sentence structure reveals a degree of parallelism. The numerous verbs in these short clauses add force to the author's assertion that the readers fail to pray to God. Their desire for possessions remains unfulfilled—they "don't get" what they want.

Interpreting the words *you kill* is problematic. Is James implying that the readers are actually guilty of murder? Is the original text incorrect? Is James speaking figuratively? Or does the sentence need proper punctuation? These are some of the questions interpreters face.

a. *Conjecture.* In the sixteenth century, Erasmus suggested a change of only two letters in the Greek verb now translated "you kill." With the change in the spelling of that verb the translation becomes "you envy." This reading, then, balances the rest of the clause: "you envy and covet." It makes much more sense than the somewhat illogical sequence *you kill and covet*. Since the time Erasmus made the conjecture, his supporters have been numerous: Martin Luther, William Tyndale, John Calvin, Theodore Beza, Joseph B. Mayor, Martin Dibelius, James Moffatt, James B. Adamson, Sophie Laws, and many others.[5]

The difficulty this conjecture meets is its lack of support in the ancient manuscripts. No document exists that has this reading. Moreover, those who favor the conjecture overlook an important rule of textual criticism: only when a questionable word has no meaningful interpretation at all is a conjecture admissible.[6] And indeed meaningful interpretations of the text exist.

b. *Punctuation.* Ancient manuscripts of the Greek text lack punctuation marks. The task of the translator, then, is to add these at the appropriate places so they reflect the meaning the author wishes to convey. Some translators place a period after the word *kill* and thus seek to create balance and rhythm in the sequence of short clauses:

> You desire and do not have; so you kill.
> And you covet and cannot obtain; so you fight and wage war.
> You do not have, because you do not ask. [RSV][7]

Although the word *and* before "you covet" raises some questions, the placing of a period after the verb *kill* seems to be a feasible solution to this

---

5. The translators of the Dutch *Staten Vertaling* of 1637 took the conjecture seriously and made it their translation: "gij benijdt" (you envy). Also see *Moffatt*, who puts "you envy" in his version.

6. C. Leslie Mitton, *The Epistle of James* (Grand Rapids: Eerdmans, 1966), pp. 149–50.

7. A number of other English translations (NAB, NEB, JB, GNB, NASB) follow this punctuation.

textual problem.[8] Admittedly, a literal interpretation of this verb implies that the readers indeed had committed murder. If we interpret the verb figuratively, however, we evade the objection that the context fails to support a literal interpretation.

c. *Metaphor.* Other interpreters understand the term *kill* in the sense of hate.[9] They refer to passages of Scripture that equate murder and anger (see Matt. 5:21–22; I John 3:15). The general context provides ample evidence that the verb *to kill* should be understood figuratively, not literally (just as, in the preceding verse [4:1], for instance, the expression *fights* is a less literal, symbolic translation of the noun *wars*). In view of the context, then, we accept the figurative sense. Whatever interpretation we adopt, difficulties of one kind or another remain.

"You covet, but you cannot have what you want." When man gives free reign to his desires, he no longer obeys the command *you shall not covet.* Covetousness controls his life and this evil power may even induce him to commit murder (I Kings 21:1–14). In short, when man breaks the command not to covet, he still lacks the ability to fulfill his desires; as a consequence, his life is filled with quarrels and fights. What is wrong? James supplies the answer.

"You do not have, because you do not ask God." In these verses James echoes the teachings of Jesus given in the Sermon on the Mount. Jesus said, "Ask and it will be given to you; . . . for everyone who asks receives" (Matt. 7:7–8). Failure to ask God in prayer results in failure to receive. We may think that unbelievers refuse to pray, but believers, too, often fail to carry "everything to God in prayer." Fitting are the words Hugh Stowell prayed:

> O may my hand forget her skill,
> My tongue be silent, cold, and still,
> This bounding heart forget to beat,
> If I forget the mercy-seat.

3. When you ask, you do not receive, because you ask with wrong motives, that you may spend what you get on your pleasures.

James teaches a lesson on prayer. He asserts that even when we pray, we fail to receive an answer. The cause for this failure lies not in God but in man. When the believer asks Jesus anything in his name, Jesus will honor that request (John 14:13–14). The context in which Jesus makes

---

8. James Hardy Ropes, *A Critical and Exegetical Commentary on the Epistle of James,* International Critical Commentary series (1916; reprint ed., Edinburgh: Clark, 1961), p. 254. Also consult Sophie Laws, *A Commentary on the Epistle of James,* Harper's New Testament Commentaries (San Francisco: Harper and Row, 1980), p. 169; Mitton, *James,* p. 147; Franz Mussner, *Der Jakobusbrief,* 2d ed., Herder Theologischer Kommentar zum Neuen Testament series (Freiburg: Herder, 1967), p. 178.

9. Martin Luther's *Die Heilige Schrift* has "ihr hasset" (you hate). Donald W. Burdick takes the verb *to kill* as "hyperbole for hatred." *James,* vol. 12, the *Expositor's Bible Commentary,* ed. Frank E. Gaebelein, 12 vols. (Grand Rapids: Eerdmans, 1981), p. 193. Also see D. Edmond Hiebert, *The Epistle of James: Tests of a Living Faith* (Chicago: Moody, 1979), p. 246.

this promise, however, speaks of faith in Jesus on the one hand and of glory to God the Father on the other. That is, when the believer prays to God in the name of Jesus, he must not only believe that God will hear and answer his prayer. He must also ask himself whether his request will hallow God's name, further the cause of God's kingdom, and be in harmony with God's will (Matt. 6:9–10). If these are the believer's motives when he prays, God will prosper him by granting his request.

Many people do not even bother to pray. If they do pray, they come to God with wrong motives. They lack faith. Says Paul, "Everything that does not come from faith is sin" (Rom. 14:23). The writer of Hebrews is even more to the point: "And without faith it is impossible to please God, because anyone who comes to him must believe that he exists and that he rewards those who earnestly seek him" (Heb. 11:6). How can a person be sure that he has faith in God if he never prays to God? How can he expect God to answer his prayers if he refuses to heed the apostolic injunction to "pray continually" (I Thess. 5:17)?

God refuses to listen to men who eagerly pursue selfish pleasures. Greed is idolatry and that is an abomination in the sight of God. God does not listen to prayers that come from a heart filled with selfish motives. Covetousness and selfishness are insults to God.

Greek Words, Phrases, and Constructions in 4:1–3

Verse 1

πόθεν—James repeats this adverb of place which means "from what place." The suffix -θεν shows motion away from a particular place: ἐντεῦθεν, from this place.

πόλεμοι καὶ . . . μάχαι—the literal meaning is "wars and battles," but as a description of interpersonal relationships the words mean "fights and quarrels." Notice the inverted order of the verbs μάχεσθε καὶ πολεμεῖτε in the next verse.

Verse 2

διὰ τὸ μὴ αἰτεῖσθαι ὑμᾶς—the preposition διά expresses cause. In the articular infinitive construction the pronoun ὑμᾶς serves as the subject of αἰτεῖσθαι. The use of the middle voice is summed up in the translation *ye ask for yourselves amiss* in the next verse.[10]

---

2. Being Friends with the World
4:4–6

Straddling the line is dangerous, as every driver knows, for he has been taught to stay on his own side of the road. That is a fundamental traffic rule for safe driving.

---

10. A. T. Robertson, *A Grammar of the Greek New Testament in the Light of Historical Research* (Nashville: Broadman, 1934), p. 805. Also see Robert Hanna, *A Grammatical Aid to the Greek New Testament* (Grand Rapids: Baker, 1983), p. 419.

Nor can a Christian straddle the line. He cannot be a friend of God and a friend of the world, because "no one can serve two masters. Either he will hate the one and love the other, or he will be devoted to the one and despise the other" (Matt. 6:24). A Christian cannot pursue his selfish ambitions and still remain loyal to God. In fact, when he looks toward the pleasures of this world, he turns his back to God.

4. You adulterous people, don't you know that friendship with the world is hatred toward God? Anyone who chooses to be a friend of the world becomes an enemy of God.

Note the following points:

a. "You adulterous people." The New International Version makes the text direct and personal with the pronoun *you*. In the original the first word is an address and means "adulteresses."[11] This is difficult to interpret literally, especially when the context indicates that James is not introducing a moral issue. As in the preceding verses (4:1–3), we need to understand the phrase *you adulterous people* figuratively or, more precisely, spiritually.

James is writing to Jewish Christians who are familiar with the term *adulteress* applied to the marriage relationship of God as husband and Israel as the unfaithful wife. For example, God told the prophet Hosea, "Go, take to yourself an adulterous wife and children of unfaithfulness, because the land is guilty of the vilest adultery in departing from the LORD" (Hos. 1:2).

Jesus calls the Pharisees, Sadducees, and teachers of the law "a wicked and *adulterous* generation" (Matt. 12:39; 16:4; and see Mark 8:38; italics added). Moreover, indirectly Jesus refers to himself as the bridegroom (Matt. 9:15 and parallels) and Paul says that Christ is the husband of the church (II Cor. 11:2; Eph. 5:22–25; also consult Rev. 19:7; 21:9).

b. "Friendship with the world is hatred toward God." James puts this statement in the form of a question and appeals to the intuitive knowledge of his readers. What husband permits his wife to have an illicit affair with another man? And what do you think of a wife who forsakes marital love by engaging in adulterous relations? What do you think is God's reaction when a believer becomes enamored with the world? God is a jealous God (Exod. 20:5; Deut. 5:9). He tolerates no friendship with the world.

What does the word *world* mean? It represents "the whole system of humanity (its institutions, structures, values, and mores) as organized without God."[12] It is the meaning Paul conveyed when he wrote his sec-

---

11. At least two English-language translations (KJV, NKJV) have the reading *adulterers and adulteresses*. Bruce M. Metzger writes, "When copyists, however, understood the word [adulteresses] here in its literal sense, they were puzzled why only women were mentioned and therefore considered it right to add a reference to men as well." *A Textual Commentary on the Greek New Testament*, corrected ed. (London and New York: United Bible Societies, 1975), p. 683.

12. Davids, *James*, p. 161.

ond letter addressed to Timothy: "For Demas, because he loved this present world, has deserted me and has gone to Thessalonica" (II Tim. 4:10).

James is forceful in saying that a person cannot be friendly with the world and with God at the same time. The world does not tolerate friends of God, for they are considered enemies. The reverse is also true. God regards "a friend of the world" an enemy.

c. "An enemy of God." What a terrifying expression! A friend of God who endures the enmity of the world can always take comfort in the words of the sixteenth-century reformer John Knox, who said, "A man with God on his side is always in the majority." But the person who meets God as his enemy stands alone, for the world cannot help him. The author of Hebrews concludes, "It is a dreadful thing to fall into the hands of the living God" (Heb. 10:31).

Who is an enemy of God? The Christian has been placed in the world, even though he is not of the world (John 17:16, 18). The apostle John warns, "Do not love the world or anything in the world. If anyone loves the world, the love of the Father is not in him" (I John 2:15). When a person purposely turns to the world to become part of it, he has made a conscious choice of rejecting God and the teaching of his Word.[13] Therefore, anyone who deliberately chooses for the world and against God meets God as his enemy.

5. Or do you think Scripture says without reason that the spirit he caused to live in us tends toward envy, 6. but he gives us more grace? That is why Scripture says:

> **"God opposes the proud**
> **but gives grace to the humble."**

James turns to the Scripture to prove his point. He lets God speak to establish the truth of the matter. The difficulty, however, is that of the two references James quotes, we are able to identify only the second one (Prov. 3:34). We have no clear biblical reference for the quotation in the fifth verse. Indeed this particular text is one of the most puzzling in the entire epistle and takes a place among the most difficult passages in the New Testament. This passage puzzles the reader not only because it refers to a Scripture passage we cannot locate in the Old Testament. It also lends itself to numerous translations of the text. And last, but certainly not least, we are interested in the exact meaning of the quotation.

a. *Origin.* The fact that we are not able to locate the origin of this quotation need not surprise us at all. In other passages of the New Testament we encounter similar quotations that have no precise provenance in Scripture. To mention only one text, Matthew writes about the return of Joseph, Mary, and Jesus to Nazareth and says, "So was fulfilled what was said through the prophets: 'He will be called a Nazarene'" (2:23). The

---

13. Joseph B. Mayor writes that the person who is an enemy of God "makes it his aim" to be a friend of the world. *The Epistle of St. James* (reprint ed., Grand Rapids: Zondervan, 1946), p. 140.

Old Testament, however, provides no leads for finding the origin of this prophecy.[14]

Scholars have made numerous suggestions about the source of the quotation in verse 5. One suggests that the words come from a combination of texts (Gen. 6:3; 8:21; Exod. 20:3, 5) that had taken on a distinct form. Another thinks that the quotation has been taken from a Septuagint passage that is no longer extant. A third is of the opinion that the quoted words derive from an apocryphal book.[15] And a fourth holds that the expression *Scripture says* in verse 5 actually applies to the Old Testament quotation in verse 6.

No matter where we look for an answer to the question of source, the result remains the same: we do not know.

b. *Translations.* Because the ancient manuscripts lack punctuation marks, translators have to determine whether a sentence is a statement or a question. Here is one translation that phrases the passage as a question: "Or do you suppose the Scripture speaks to no purpose? The Spirit, who took up His abode in us, yearns jealously over us. But He affords the more grace, for He says, 'God opposes the haughty, but He grants grace to the humble-minded.'"[16] However, this translation raises more questions than it answers. First, to which scriptural passage does James refer when he says "Scripture speaks"? Second, how does the affirmative statement *the Spirit . . . yearns jealously over us* relate to the preceding question? And third, what are the reasons for not adopting the standard formula *Scripture says* that is normally used for introducing quotations?

Another problem is the translation of the word *spirit*. Does the word refer to the human spirit or the Holy Spirit? If we understand the word to mean the Holy Spirit, we meet "the added difficulty that nowhere else in the epistle does James refer to this Spirit."[17] If James had been thinking of the Holy Spirit, we would expect him to refer to the Holy Spirit in the preceding and succeeding verses, too. He does not do this. Most versions, therefore, provide the translation *spirit*.

There is one more problem. Should the last part of verse 5 be translated "that the spirit he caused to live in us tends toward envy" or "that God jealously longs for the spirit that he made to live in us" (NIV foot-

---

14. Quotations from unknown sources, even those introduced as Scripture, occur in other texts (John 7:38; I Cor. 2:9; Eph. 5:14; also consult I Clem. 23:3; 46:2).

15. Martin Dibelius writes that in James 4:5 "we have some sort of 'prophetic word,' i.e., an apocryphal book which is considered holy." *James: A Commentary on the Epistle of James,* rev. Heinrich Greeven, trans. Michael A. Williams, ed. Helmut Köster, Hermeneia: A Critical and Historical Commentary on the Bible (Philadelphia: Fortress, 1976), p. 223. John Albert Bengel infers that the quotation is from the New Testament, because "the words of James are near enough to Gal. 5:17, and following verses." *Gnomon of the New Testament,* ed. Andrew R. Fausset, 5 vols., 7th ed. (Edinburgh: Clark, 1877), vol. 5, p. 31.

16. The MLB follows the translation and the marginal notes of the RV and the ASV.

17. Sophie Laws, "Does Scripture speak in vain?" *NTS* 20 (1974): 213. Also see Laws, *James,* p. 176. And refer to Mussner, *Der Jakobusbrief,* p. 182.

note)? That is, do we take the term *spirit* as the subject or as the object of the main verb? It is either the subject ("the spirit tends toward envy") or the object ("God longs for the spirit").

The key to understanding the quotation lies in the term *envy* (NIV). In Greek, this particular word appears in "catalogues of vices."[18] In the New Testament it describes life associated with the unredeemed world (Rom. 1:29; Gal. 5:21; I Tim. 6:4; Titus 3:3; I Peter 2:1).[19] This word, then, always has a bad connotation in Greek literature and in the New Testament. Because man's spirit tends toward corruption, we conclude that the term *spirit* is the subject, not the object, of the main verb ("the spirit [God] caused to live in us tends toward envy"). The thought of verse 5 is therefore a continuation of the preceding text that warns against friendship with the world.

c. *Meaning.* Sixteenth-century German theologian Zacharias Ursinus considered whether he was able to comply with what God required of him. He concluded, "No. I have a natural tendency to hate God and my neighbor."[20] The spirit of man longs for the pleasures of this world and perversely seeks its friendship.

Is there no hope, then? Certainly! Note the contrast with the adversative *but* in the next sentence (v. 6). "But [God] gives us more grace." God comes to us in the redeeming love of his Son, who is full of grace. "From the fullness of his grace we have all received one blessing after another," writes John in the prologue of his Gospel (1:16).

James establishes his point with another quotation. This time we know the words are derived from the Book of Proverbs. "He [God] mocks proud mockers but gives grace to the humble" (3:34). Perhaps these words circulated in the early church in the form of a proverbial saying, because the apostle Peter also cites this text (I Peter 5:5). That one quotation sums up the difference between the person whose heart is filled with pride and the person who humbly lives in full dependence upon God.

God hates "haughty eyes" (Prov. 6:17) and detests those who have a proud heart (Prov. 16:5). Pride causes quarrels (Prov. 13:10) and leads to destruction (Prov. 16:18). "Since God resists the proud, the believer must learn to hate pride and to clothe himself with humility."[21] God, however, will esteem the person "who is humble and contrite in spirit" (Isa. 66:2).

Practical Considerations in 4:4–6

Verse 4

A worldly person loves himself and the pleasures of this world. His heart is filled with pride that makes him indifferent to God and his Word. Even though

---

18. Bauer, p. 857.
19. David H. Field, *NIDNTT*, vol. 1, pp. 557–58. And consult R. C. Trench, *Synonyms of the New Testament* (1854; reprint ed., Grand Rapids: Eerdmans, 1953), pp. 89–90.
20. Heidelberg Catechism, question and answer 5.
21. Gerald Barry Stanton, "Pride," *EDT,* p. 874.

he attends the worship services at a local church and participates in family devotions, he refuses to come close to God, because he knows that God condemns his pride.

Verse 6

Proud people tend to be friends of the world, for they know that not God but the world satisfies their pride. By contrast, humble people realize that they are completely dependent upon God. They are thankful to him for the rich grace he provides to fill their lives to overflowing.

Pride shuts out grace. If a patient refuses to take the medicine prescribed by the physician, he will never recover. If a son rejects the wise counsel of his parents, he can expect trouble. Pride enters the human heart because man measures himself by human standards, not God's standards.

The believer who lives in constant fellowship with God, who desires to do God's will in all things, and who demonstrates the love of the Lord Jesus is the recipient of God's abundant grace.

> Marvelous grace of our loving Lord,
> Grace that exceeds our sin and our guilt,
> Yonder on Calvary's mount outpoured,
> There where the blood of the Lamb was spilt.
> Grace, grace, God's grace,
> Grace that will pardon and cleanse within,
> Grace, grace, God's grace,
> Grace that is greater than all our sin.
> —Julia H. Johnston

Greek Words, Phrases, and Constructions in 4:4–6

Verse 4

ἡ φιλία τοῦ κόσμου—note the definite article preceding the noun φιλία (friendship). The noun is followed by the objective genitive—"friendship with the world." The next phrase, ἔχθρα τοῦ θεοῦ, also has an objective genitive—"enmity toward God."

ἐὰν βουληθῇ—the use of the aorist subjunctive in this conditional sentence introduces probability. The ingressive aorist tense of the verb expresses the deliberate choice of a person who loves the world and becomes God's enemy.

καθίσταται—this present indicative from καθίστημι (I conduct, appoint) is in the passive voice and means "he is made," that is, "he becomes."

Verse 6

μείζονα δέ—the comparative adjective in the accusative singular modifies χάριν. The particle δέ is adversative with distinct contrast.

ὑπερηφάνοις—adjectivally the word occurs "in our lit[erature] only in an unfavorable sense."[22] It describes the attitude of someone who places himself on a level equal to or higher than that of God.

---

22. Bauer, p. 841.

3. Coming Near to God
4:7–10

Road signs along the highway instruct the traveler how to reach his destination safely. Of necessity, these signs are short, descriptive, and pointed. James provides us with a number of signs that aid us as we travel along life's highway. Suited to the hurried pace of life, the sentences are concise, colorful, and direct.

7. Submit yourselves, then, to God. Resist the devil, and he will flee from you. 8. Come near to God and he will come near to you. Wash your hands, you sinners, and purify your hearts, you double-minded. 9. Grieve, mourn and wail. Change your laughter to mourning and your joy to gloom. 10. Humble yourselves before the Lord, and he will lift you up.

Like highway signs that instruct the motorist to obey traffic rules for safe driving, these clauses tell the reader how to come to God. Note that the first summons (v. 7a) and the last (v. 10a) are parallels; between them lies the message to the reader: come near to God. Moreover, the word *humble* in verse 10 forms a verbal link with the last word of the Old Testament quotation in verse 6. The sequence of these commands is:

a. *Submission.* James speaks directly to those readers who are blinded by harmful pride and indirectly, of course, to the entire church. He is pointed in his counsel and tells them how to divest themselves of pride: "submit yourselves . . . to God." He urges his readers to do it once for all, so that they may always be subject to God.

When James says "submit," he actually means "obey." In the Greek Luke uses the same verb when he describes the twelve-year-old Jesus who "was obedient" to Mary and Joseph (Luke 2:51). The wording *submit yourselves* describes a voluntary act of placing oneself under the authority of someone else to show him respect and obedience. Thus, citizens are to obey governing authorities (Rom. 13:1–7; I Peter 2:13), Corinthian believers are urged to obey their leaders (I Cor. 16:16), young men must be submissive to older people (I Peter 5:5), and wives are exhorted to submit to their husbands (Eph. 5:22; Col. 3:18; Titus 2:5; I Peter 3:1) and servants to their masters (Titus 2:9; I Peter 2:18).

When we pray "Your will be done," we have dismissed pride, are submissive to God, and are obeying his commands. When we keep God's law, Satan seeks to interfere by leading us into temptation. Therefore, James adds the injunction *resist the devil.* As we stand firm "against the devil's schemes" (Eph. 6:11; I Peter 5:9), we also pray the petition "but deliver us from the evil one" (Matt. 6:13). The biblical assurance we receive is that "he will flee from" us (James 4:7). This is a fact, for the Gospels and Acts are filled with examples of Satan and his cohorts fleeing before divine authority. When we obediently do God's will, Satan cannot lead us astray

139

but must depart. Luther aptly remarked that if we sing psalms and hymns or read Scripture, Satan will flee from us lest he scorch his wings.

b. *Preparation.* Here is the heart of the message which James introduced with the exhortation to be submissive to God and to resist the devil: "come near to God." In our struggle against sin and Satan we do not stand alone when we come in prayer to God. God surrounds us with his care and grace, so that we have no reason to fear the power of Satan.

God wants us to come to him in true repentance, faith, obedience, and prayer (see the contexts of Lam. 3:57; Hos. 12:6; Zech. 1:3; Mal. 3:7). He will fill us with his grace and crown us with his blessings. When God calls us to come near to him, he already shows us his love and grace. The initiative, then, belongs to God, not to us. For this reason we can never claim that because we first approached God, he had to come to us. God always acts first in the work of salvation.[23]

How do we approach a holy God? James uses terminology from the Old Testament when he writes, "Wash your hands, you sinners, and purify your hearts. . . ." The first admonition recalls God's instructions about ceremonial cleansing (see Exod. 30:20–21).[24] The second brings to mind David's words:

> Who may ascend the hill of the LORD?
>   Who may stand in his holy place?
> He who has clean hands and a pure heart. . . . [Ps. 24:3–4]

By linking these concepts, James clearly implies that he is speaking not of being ceremonially clean but of being spiritually pure.[25]

James calls the readers "sinners" and "double-minded." Every human being is a sinner, but James is using a term that fits the Jewish context of his people. In the Gospels, the name *sinner* was given to someone who disregarded the law of God and flouted standards of morality (see Matt. 9:10; Luke 7:37, 39).[26] The expression *double-minded* (compare James 1:8) connotes instability, fickleness, and vacillation. The terms fit the person who loves God and the world. Such persons, James says, must repent.

c. *Repentance.* The next commands are at variance with the apostolic injunction to rejoice always (I Thess. 5:16; and see James 1:2). James tells

---

23. John Calvin comments, "But if anyone concludes from this passage, that the first part of the work belongs to us, and that afterwards the grace of God follows, the Apostle meant no such thing; . . . but the very thing [the Spirit of God] bids us do, he himself fulfils in us." *Commentaries on the Catholic Epistles: The Epistle of James,* ed. and trans. John Owen (Grand Rapids: Eerdmans, 1948), p. 334. Also consult C. Leslie Mitton, *The Epistle of James* (Grand Rapids: Eerdmans, 1966), p. 158; and D. Edmond Hiebert, *The Epistle of James: Tests of a Living Faith* (Chicago: Moody, 1979), p. 262.

24. The Old and the New Testaments have many references to the ritual of washing hands. Among them are Ps. 26:6; 73:13; Isa. 1:15–16; Matt. 27:24.

25. Hans-Georg Link and Johannes Schattenmann, *NIDNTT,* vol. 3, p. 106. And consult Friedrich Hauck, *TDNT,* vol. 3, p. 425.

26. Karl Heinrich Rengstorf, *TDNT,* vol. 1, p. 327, observes that the term "partly means those who live a flagrantly immoral life, and partly those who follow a dishonourable vocation."

his readers to "grieve, mourn and wail." He is like an Old Testament prophet who calls the people to repentance by having them grieve over their sins and, so to speak, sit in sackcloth and ashes.

We experience grief when someone who is near and dear to us dies. That is one aspect of the concept *grief*. The other aspect of grief is spiritual. Scripture teaches us that repentance and grief go together. In his epistles, Paul states that those who belong to Jesus put to death their sinful nature when they repent of their sins (Rom. 6:6; Gal. 2:20; 5:24; 6:14). Repentance, then, means that a death has occurred in our own lives. We grieve because of sins we have committed against God and our fellow man.

Here are two examples—one from the Old Testament and one from the New—of saints who grieve because of their sins. David portrays his grief for sin in many of his psalms. In one of them he pleads for God's mercy and cries out,

> I am worn out from groaning;
> all night long I flood my bed with weeping
> and drench my couch with tears. [Ps. 6:6]

That is godly sorrow! Paul, describing his struggle with sin, exclaims, "What a wretched man I am! Who will rescue me from this body of death?" He himself gives the answer: "Thanks be to God—through Jesus Christ our Lord!" (Rom. 7:24–25).

"Change your laughter to mourning and your joy to gloom." The similarity to a word of Jesus is unmistakable: "Woe to you who laugh now, for you will mourn and weep" (Luke 6:25). James is not saying that a Christian should dress in black clothing, walk around with a somber face, and preach gloom and doom. A Christian ought to be happy in the Lord, thankful for the gift of salvation, and obedient in doing the will of God. When he has fallen into sin and responds to God's call for repentance, a change must occur in his life. Laughter and joy are silenced. When he reflects on his sin, the penitent is filled with mourning and gloom. Peter said that he did not know Jesus, but after he had asserted this three times, Jesus looked straight at him. Peter repented, went outside, and wept bitterly (Luke 22:60–62). "Godly sorrow brings repentance that leads to salvation and leaves no regret, but worldly sorrow brings death" (II Cor. 7:10).

d. *Humility.* James returns to the subject he introduced in the Old Testament quotation: "God . . . gives grace to the humble" (v. 6). He writes, "Humble yourselves before the Lord, and he will lift you up." This particular theme is prominent throughout Scripture:

in the psalms, "For the LORD . . . crowns the humble with salvation" (Ps. 149:4)

141

in Proverbs, "[The Lord] . . . gives grace to the humble" (Prov. 3:34)

in the prophetical books, "The lowly will be exalted and the exalted will be brought low" (Ezek. 21:26)

in the Gospels, "For whoever exalts himself will be humbled, and whoever humbles himself will be exalted" (Matt. 23:12)

in the Epistles, "Humble yourselves, therefore, under God's mighty hand, that he may lift you up" (I Peter 5:6)[27]

And last, Scripture teaches that humility has a vertical and a horizontal aspect. The believer who shows humility toward God shows it also toward others (Rom. 12:3; Phil. 2:3).

Practical Considerations in 4:7–10

Verse 8

The Gospel writers record that two people wanted to follow Jesus and were willing to relinquish everything except that which was dear to them. For the one this was his family; for the other it was money. Jesus refused to accept these would-be followers, for they could not give him their undivided devotion. In effect, they were double-minded.

This is Calvin's motto: "To you, O Lord, I offer my heart promptly and sincerely." When we present our heart to the Lord, he wants it completely. If we give part of it to the world, God cannot be our Lord and master. He demands that we approach him with singleness of heart in true humility. God will lift us up when we humble ourselves before him.

Verse 10

If God exalts us, are we not inclined to become proud? No, because in our humility we give him the praise and the glory. "Let him who boasts boast in the Lord" (I Cor. 1:31; Jer. 9:24; II Cor. 10:17).

Greek Words, Phrases, and Constructions in 4:7–10

Verse 7

ὑποτάγητε—from the verb ὑποτάσσω (I subject, submit), this aorist passive imperative exhibits some interesting characteristics: the aorist—like all the other aorists in this section—is ingressive; the passive has become the middle, "submit yourselves"; and the imperative together with the future φεύξεται (he will flee) constitutes an implied condition.

---

27. Augustine writes, "If you ask me what is the first precept of the Christian religion, I will answer, first, second, and third, Humility." And see R. E. O. White, "Humility," *EDT*, p. 537.

Verse 9

ταλαιπωρήσατε—presumably this is derived from the combination ταλάω (I bear) and περάω (I endure troubles).[28] As a verb in the aorist active imperative it occurs only once in the New Testament; as the noun ταλαιπωρία (misery, trouble), twice (Rom. 3:16; James 5:1). The adjective ταλαίπωρος (wretched) also appears twice (Rom. 7:24; Rev. 3:17).

---

4. Judging a Brother
4:11–12

James echoes the teaching about judging others that Jesus gave in the Sermon on the Mount. "Do not judge, or you too will be judged. For in the same way you judge others, you will be judged" (Matt. 7:1–2). Judging is a most difficult task because it involves not only other people but also the law itself. This is how James puts it:

11. Brothers, do not slander one another. Anyone who speaks against his brother or judges him, speaks against the law and judges it. When you judge the law, you are not keeping it, but sitting in judgment on it.

a. The author's tone changes markedly. In verse 8 he calls the readers "sinners" and "double-minded"; now he addresses them as "brothers" and tells them not to slander each other (see also I Peter 2:1). Nevertheless, verses 11 and 12 are closely tied to the preceding passage.

In one of his psalms, David links slander to a lack of humility. He says,

> Whoever slanders his neighbor in secret,
>   him will I put to silence;
> whoever has haughty eyes and a proud heart,
>   him will I not endure. [Ps. 101:5]

Slander issues from the heart of the person who fails to consider others above himself. The humble Christian, however, opposes slander and says,

> No wicked thing or slanderous accusation
> Shall stand before mine eyes with approbation;
> No hateful doings of apostasy
> Shall cleave to me.
>   —Dewey Westra

The link between verses 7 and 11 lies in the word *devil* (v. 7) and the verb *slander*. In the original, the noun *diabolos* (devil) means "slanderer." James, then, is exhorting his readers not to slander one another, for this is the work of the devil. He is telling them to stop this evil practice to which they have resorted. If they continue to slander each other in the church, they will eventually destroy the fellowship of the Christian community.

---

28. Thayer, p. 614.

b. James delves deeper into the subject and tells his readers that slandering a brother involves the law (Lev. 19:16). Note the parallel James develops in the next sentence:

Anyone who
speaks against—speaks against
his brother—the law
or—and
judges him—judges it

The emphasis in this verse is on the word *brother,* which denotes the close bond of fellowship believers have in the church. If you speak evil of your brother behind his back, you are setting aside the royal law, "Love your neighbor as yourself" (2:8; Lev. 19:18; Matt. 22:39; Rom. 13:9; Gal. 5:14). And if you set aside the law, you have become a judge of that law. Then you have placed yourself on the level of the Lawgiver.

In court a judge must be impartial in evaluating the evidence, and be just in applying the law and passing sentence. The slanderer, by contrast, generally neglects to learn the facts, avoids speaking in the presence of the accused, sets aside the law of love, and as a self-appointed judge hands down the verdict.[29]

c. James exposes the true nature of the sin of slandering when he instructs the recipients of his epistle in these words: "When you judge the law [as you are doing], you are not keeping it [because you have placed yourself above the law], but sitting in judgment on it [as a judge]."

The slanderer puts aside the law God made and thus places himself on the same level as God. Only God has the authority to abrogate a law. Blinded by sin, the backbiter often is unaware of the seriousness of his doings. The fact remains, however, that slander is a sin against the person who is accused and against God who forbids this sin by divine law.[30]

12. There is only one Lawgiver and Judge, the one who is able to save and destroy. But you—who are you to judge your neighbor?

Ultimately God is the only Lawgiver who delegates power to man to serve as lawmaker and judge. God, therefore, receives the honor of being the final authority in establishing the law and judging man. He alone is the divine judge. He cannot allow man to assume the position that belongs to him alone.

God alone has the authority "to save and destroy." That is, God makes the law, applies it, and enforces it by carrying out the sentence. The verdict is either innocent or guilty—God is able to save and destroy. In the Song of Moses, we find a parallel when God says, "There is no god

---

29. Compare R. V. G. Tasker, *The General Epistle of James: An Introduction and Commentary,* Tyndale New Testament Commentaries (Grand Rapids: Eerdmans, 1957), p. 99.

30. "Slander is not a transgression of merely one commandment, but a transgression against the authority of the law in general, and therefore against God." Dibelius, *James,* p. 228.

besides me. I put to death and I bring to life" (Deut. 32:39; also consult I Sam. 2:6–7; II Kings 5:7). And Jesus instructs his disciples not to fear the one who is able to kill the body. "Rather, be afraid of the One who can destroy both soul and body in hell" (Matt. 10:28; and see Luke 12:5).

James becomes personal. He speaks directly and emphatically to the individual reader: "But you—who are you to judge your neighbor?" The contrast between the one and only divine Lawgiver and sinful man (to be judged by the Lawgiver) is clear (Rom. 14:4). James purposely chooses the word *neighbor* to remind the reader of the royal law of love (2:8). Instead of judging his neighbor the reader ought to love him.

Practical Considerations in 4:11–12

Verse 11

Scripture teaches that all of us will have to appear before God in the day of judgment and at that time we have to give an account of "every careless word [we] have spoken" (Matt. 12:36). God holds us responsible for the very words we speak and especially the words spoken against our fellow man.

Verse 12

All of us are guilty because of our sins. We are under the law and on the same level as our fellow man. We are the accused. Therefore, instead of placing ourselves above the law and assuming the position of a judge, we ought to encourage, comfort, and love our fellow man. In short, we are in no position to judge because we ourselves are in need of the mercy and grace of Jesus Christ. Let us help each other by directing our attention to Jesus.

Do we, then, close our eyes when we see a brother falling into sin? Certainly not! James ends his epistle with advice that is to the point: "Whoever turns a sinner away from his error will save him from death and cover a multitude of sins" (5:20).

Greek Words, Phrases, and Constructions in 4:11–12

Verse 11

μὴ καταλαλεῖτε—the negative command in the present active imperative instructs the reader to stop slandering other people. The present tense indicates an activity in progress.

The repetition of "brother" (three times) and "law" (four times) makes this verse emphatic.

Verse 12

σῶσαι καὶ ἀπολέσαι—the significance of the aorist tense in these two active infinitives lies in the finality of God's verdict on the day of judgment.

145

13 Now listen, you who say, "Today or tomorrow we will go to this or that city, spend a year there, carry on business and make money." 14 Why, you do not even know what will happen tomorrow. What is your life? You are a mist that appears for a little while and then vanishes. 15 Instead, you ought to say, "If it is the Lord's will, we will live and do this or that." 16 As it is, you boast and brag. All such boasting is evil. 17 Anyone, then, who knows the good he ought to do and doesn't do it, sins.

B. Submission to God's Will
4:13–17

1. Example
4:13–15

Pride closes man's eyes to reality, so that he does not see the ridiculousness of his deeds. Man makes plans and talks as if he were the master of his life and God does not exist. Utter foolishness! James has overheard this preposterous talk, records it, and shows his readers the senselessness of living a life of practical atheism.

The persons James addresses, however, appear to be the Jewish Christians who are living in dispersion. He writes this letter to them and not to unbelievers. Although his tone changes, James seems to indicate that the readers know how to do that which is good (v. 17), which implies that they belong to the Christian community.[31] For this reason, I take the next few verses as part of the discourse addressed to the members of the church.[32]

13. Now listen, you who say, "Today or tomorrow we will go to this or that city, spend a year there, carry on business and make money." Here we have an example of people who do their planning and work without thinking about God. By ignoring God, they show as much arrogance as does the person who slanders his neighbor. The sin of failing to come to God in prayer is one of the most common offenses a Christian commits.

James addresses a segment of the church, namely, the merchants. He gets their attention with the idiomatic "Now listen." Other translations have "Come now." Then he quotes their own words that speak of going from one place to the next, spending some time there in order to do business and make money. Actually, we cannot fault a traveling salesman for moving on and doing business. This is part of his life. There is some-

31. Mayor, in *James*, p. 153, writes, "The appeal to knowledge here, as above in 1:19, is a proof that the writer is addressing Christians."
32. Even though the introductory phrases in James 4:13 and 5:1 are identical ("Now listen"), the content of the two passages and succeeding verses is unrelated. Consult E. C. Blackman, *The Epistle of James* (London: SCM, 1957), p. 137.

what of a parallel in Jesus' discourse on the end of the age in which he refers to the days of Noah: "For in the days before the flood, people were eating and drinking, marrying and giving in marriage, up to the day Noah entered the ark; and they knew nothing about what would happen until the flood came and took them all away" (Matt. 24:38–39; also compare Luke 17:26–29). Although no one faults a person for eating, drinking, and marrying, the point is that in the life of Noah's contemporaries God had no place. These people lived as if God did not exist. And this is also true of the merchants James addresses.

Note that James has no quarrel with the merchant's occupation. Nor does he write about the ethics of buying and selling; he only states that the merchants "carry on business and make money." And that is what we expect when trade flourishes. James takes the businessmen to task for their disregard for God. To them money is much more important than serving the Lord. They make plans for the future without seeking the will of God. They live like the man portrayed in the parable of the rich fool (Luke 12:16–21). They fail to realize that they cannot add even a minute to their life.[33] They are completely dependent on God.

14. Why, you do not even know what will happen tomorrow. What is your life? You are a mist that appears for a little while and then vanishes.

If we have no idea what the immediate future will bring us, then what is the purpose of life? The writer of Ecclesiastes repeatedly mentions life's brevity and characteristically comments on the meaninglessness of man's pursuit of material possessions. Nevertheless, at the conclusion of his book he states the purpose of life: "Fear God and keep his commandments, for this is the whole duty of man" (Eccl. 12:13). Seventeenth-century British theologians asked, "What is the chief end of man?" And they answered, "Man's chief end is to glorify God, and to enjoy him forever."[34]

The merchants James addresses have not asked about the meaning and duration of life. They have neglected the counsel of Solomon: "Do not boast about tomorrow, for you do not know what a day may bring forth" (Prov. 27:1). They talk about the future with absolute certainty. Yet they have no control over it. They live their life but fail to inquire into its purpose. They are blind and ignorant.

James compares human life to a mist that quickly appears and then disappears. What is a mist? Nothing but vapor that vanishes before the rising sun. It is frail and lacks durability (compare Ps. 39:6, 11; 102:3; Hos. 13:3). Moses, who lived to be 120 years old, wrote a prayer in which he said,

---

33. Writes Calvin, "But James roused the stupidity of those who disregarded God's providence, and claimed for themselves a whole year, though they had not a single moment in their own power." *James*, p. 340.
34. Westminster Shorter Catechism, question and answer 1.

> The length of our days is seventy years—
>   or eighty, if we have the strength;
> yet their span is but trouble and sorrow,
>   for they quickly pass, and we fly away. [Ps. 90:10]

15. Instead, you ought to say, "If it is the Lord's will, we will live and do this or that."

James teaches that God is sovereign in our lives. In all our planning, deeds, and accomplishments we must acknowledge our submission to God. Thus, after a comment on the brevity of life, he returns to the subject he introduced in verse 13. He says that instead of ignoring God in our daily activities, we ought to place him first and say, "If it is the Lord's will, we will live and do this or that."

In some circles and cultures, the cliché *the Lord willing* is rather common. It is a pious formula that because of its repeated usage begins to lose its intended significance. But why does James tell the merchants to use this formula? He shows them that their lives are in the hands of a sovereign God and that they should acknowledge him in all their plans. He does not tell them when and how to use the phrase *if God wills.*

Surprisingly, this phrase does not appear in the Old Testament. In the New Testament era, however, the apostle Paul teaches the Christians its proper use. Here are a few examples:

1. When Paul left Ephesus, he said to the Jews, "I will come back if it is God's will" (Acts 18:21).
2. He told the Corinthians, "I will come to you very soon, if the Lord is willing" (I Cor. 4:19).
3. He promised the believers in Corinth to spend some time with them "if the Lord permits" (I Cor. 16:7; also compare Phil. 2:19, 24; Heb. 6:3).

The New Testament, however, gives no indication that the apostles had coined a formula that was to be used frequently. In fact, Luke fails to relate its use in the narratives of Paul's journeys recorded in Acts. Even in his epistles, Paul fails to employ this formula in places where we would have expected it. This means that we do not need to use the words *God willing* as a threadbare phrase. Rather, our entire lives ought to be that of the child of God who knows he is secure in the protective care of his heavenly Father. Every believer must live in such a way that, as Horatius Bonar put it, "no part of day or night from sacredness be free." That is joyous Christian living.[35]

---

35. Dibelius, *James,* pp. 233–34, has collected a number of instances in Greek and Latin literature to prove that the expression *if God wills* or something similar was common in the pagan world. This observation, however, in no way detracts from the purpose of the New Testament writers: to teach the believers to trust in God. Also consult Gottlob Schrenk, *TDNT,* vol. 3, p. 47.

Practical Considerations in 4:13–15

Verse 13

Increasingly the word *secularism* appears in Christian circles as if it has a legitimate place in Christianity. The expression refers to a world and life view that ignores God and flouts his Word. Secularism is a philosophy that penetrates all spheres of life, that exalts man and rejects God.[36]

Verse 15

Ever since the time of the Reformation, we have treasured the truth that this world created by God and redeemed by Christ is the Christian's workshop. Therefore, our work performed in this workshop is done to the glory of God. We joyously sing, "This is my Father's world" and acknowledge him in all our ways (Prov. 3:6).

Therefore, Christians accept the lordship of Christ in every sphere of life. They choose to live in obedience to the will of God as revealed in his Word. They know that which is good, right, honorable, just, and equitable. And they practice the golden rule, "Do to others as you would have them do to you" (Luke 6:31).

Greek Words, Phrases, and Constructions in 4:13–15

Verse 13

ἄγε—originally this form was the present imperative of ἄγω (I lead). Here it is an interjection with the meaning *now listen* (see 5:1).

τήνδε—this is a demonstrative pronoun with the definite article; it means "this or that."

ποιήσομεν—three future indicatives (ποιήσομεν, ἐμπορευσόμεθα, κερδήσομεν) express determination and purpose.

Verse 14

οἵτινες—used as an adversative expression, not as an indefinite relative pronoun, the word conveys the idea *whereas actually* and shows a concessive use.[37]

ποία—as an interrogative pronoun, this expression has a qualitative sense, "what is your life?"

Verse 15

ἀντί—in this verse the preposition ἀντί means "instead of," not "against," and governs the genitive case of the articular infinitive.

καὶ . . . καί—actually the repetition of the conjunction means "both . . . and." For stylistic reasons, the first καί need not be translated.

---

36. See David W. Gill, "Secularism, Secular Humanism," *EDT*, pp. 996–97.
37. C. F. D. Moule, *An Idiom-Book of New Testament Greek*, 2d ed. (Cambridge: At the University Press, 1960), p. 124; Robertson, *Grammar*, p. 961.

2. Good and Evil
4:16–17

16. As it is, you boast and brag. All such boasting is evil.

This verse is a reminder of the stern warning James issued when he quoted from the Old Testament, "God opposes the proud but gives grace to the humble" (v. 6; Prov. 3:34).

Some of the businessmen had ventured out; they had taken risks and made a profit. As always happens, success breeds success and along with prosperity come pride and self-sufficiency. These merchants relied on their own insights and now boasted about their accomplishments. J. B. Phillips provides this paraphrase, "As it is, you get a certain pride in yourself in planning your future with such confidence. That sort of pride is all wrong."

Human boasting is worthless, for it gives man and not God the glory. Such boasting includes bragging about accomplishments. This is not only unjustified but also totally unacceptable to God. It is evil. Through the personal experience of a thorn in his flesh, Paul is able to teach us that we can boast only in weakness; in this weakness the power of Christ becomes evident (II Cor. 11:30; 12:5, 9). A Christian, then, may boast of himself "only in so far as his life is lived in dependence on God and in responsibility to him."[38]

17. Anyone, then, who knows the good he ought to do and doesn't do it, sins.

James ends this particular section of his letter with a proverbial saying that perhaps circulated in the Jewish world of his day. The adverb *then* links the proverb to the preceding discourse; the tone of the address changes, because James no longer speaks directly to the businessmen but to every reader of his epistle.

The proverbial saying conveys a stern warning against the sin of neglect. Not the sin of commission but the sin of omission is mentioned. That particular sin raises its ugly head when man ignores God, makes plans, is successful, and brags about his achievements (James 4:13–16). Man repeats the sin of omission when he neglects to do the good he knows he must do. Jesus put this sin into focus when he portrayed the priest and the Levite in the parable of the Good Samaritan (Luke 10:30–35); the rich man who disregarded Lazarus (Luke 16:19–31); and the people who during their life on earth neglected to feed the hungry, entertain the stranger, clothe the poor, and visit the sick and the prisoner (Matt. 25:40–46).

James addresses the person who *knows* the good he must do. He is not speaking to people who commit sin in ignorance. Says Paul to the Athenian philosophers on the Areopagus, "In the past God overlooked such

---

38. Hans-Christoph Hahn, *NIDNTT,* vol. 1, p. 229.

ignorance, but now he commands all people everywhere to repent" (Acts 17:30). Sin is lawlessness, says John in one of his epistles (I John 3:4). Whether this is the sin of commission or omission, it is an affront to God, especially when the sinner knows God's commandments.

Sin ought never to be taken lightly. This is especially true of the sin of omission which is often given the innocuous appearance of oversight. But this is not so. Consider the farewell speech of Samuel. He says to the Israelites, "As for me, far be it from me that I should sin against the LORD by failing to pray for you" (I Sam. 12:23). Samuel shunned the sin of neglect. Neglect is the equivalent of ignoring God and the neighbor and is therefore a sin against the law of God.

Greek Words, Phrases, and Constructions in 4:16–17

Verse 16

ταῖς ἀλαζονείαις ὑμῶν—"your pretensions" is a literal translation of this phrase. A more idiomatic version is "brag."

τοιαύτη—this correlative adjective denotes quality ("of such a kind"), not quantity.

Verse 17

εἰδότι—the perfect active participle in the dative singular masculine from the verb οἶδα (I know how, understand how) refers to the present.

καλόν—without the definite article, this substantive adjective means "something good."[39]

Summary of Chapter 4

James admonishes his readers to submit to God. He notes that the fights and quarrels that rage among them originate in hearts that are not in harmony with the will of God. The readers pray, but with the wrong motives: their requests are selfish prayers.

The readers are developing a friendship with the world that makes them enemies of God. James proves his point by referring to the Old Testament Scriptures: "God opposes the proud but gives grace to the humble." Because God is gracious, the readers ought to submit to him. They have to resist the devil, cleanse themselves of sin, repent of their deeds, cease their slander, and stop judging others.

James concludes this section by reminding the readers, especially the merchants, to trust in God and not in financial profits. They know how to do the good; therefore they are under obligation to serve God and do his will. If they fail to do this, they sin.

39. Friedrich Blass and Albert Debrunner, *A Greek Grammar of the New Testament and Other Early Christian Literature,* trans. and rev. Robert Funk (Chicago: University of Chicago Press, 1961), sec. 264(2).

5

Patience

5:1–20

Outline

5 1 Now listen, you rich people, weep and wail because of the misery that is coming upon you. 2 Your wealth has rotted, and moths have eaten your clothes. 3 Your gold and silver are corroded. Their corrosion will testify against you and eat your flesh like fire. You have hoarded wealth in the last days. 4 Look! The wages you failed to pay the workmen who mowed your fields are crying out against you. The cries of the harvesters have reached the ears of the Lord Almighty. 5 You have lived on earth in luxury and self-indulgence. You have fattened yourselves in the day of slaughter. 6 You have condemned and murdered innocent men, who were not opposing you.

A. Impatience Toward the Rich
5:1–6

Riches are a blessing of the Lord, as Solomon testifies: "The blessing of the LORD brings wealth, and he adds no trouble to it" (Prov. 10:22). But when wealth is devoid of the Lord's blessing, trouble accompanies it in the form of envy, injustice, oppression, theft, murder, abuse, and misuse. Love for God and the neighbor becomes love for money that leads to all kinds of evil (I Tim. 6:10). When this happens, man worships and serves not God but money. Then he is a friend of the world and God is his enemy.

1. Address
5:1

1. Now listen, you rich people, weep and wail because of the misery that is coming upon you.

Like an Old Testament prophet James assails the rich people who have arrogantly disregarded God and his Word.[1] Forcefully he captures their attention and tells them to listen to what he has to say. Apparently, these rich people were not part of the Christian community but were oppressing the believers who lived in poverty (compare 2:6). If they were Jews, they had drifted away from the spiritual teachings of the Scriptures and had become people of the world. Whether the rich would hear the rebuke

---

1. The prophets in the Old Testament era denounce the rich for oppressing the poor (e.g., see Isa. 3:14–15; 10:1–2; Amos 4:1; Mic. 2:1–2).

of James remains a question.[2] But the poor and oppressed in the Christian community derived comfort and encouragement from the knowledge that God knew of their hardship.

James pronounces divine judgment upon the rich, and they cannot escape from it. They have their reward, so to speak, in the form of a curse. They have their share of "misery that is coming upon them." The words are an echo of Jesus' pronouncement: "But woe to you who are rich, for you have already received your comfort" (Luke 6:24).

"Weep and wail." The readers of the epistle are exhorted to cleanse themselves from sin, to "grieve, mourn and wail" (4:9), and to repent. James gives the rich no hope for repentance but tells them to "weep and wail." The term *wail* actually means "howl." It describes the sound a person utters when he suffers extraordinary pain or grief. What then is the difference between weeping in repentance and weeping without repentance? John Calvin observes, "Repentance has indeed its weeping, but being mixed with consolation, it does not proceed to howling."[3] The life of luxury the rich have enjoyed is about to turn into a life filled with misery that includes suffering and "pain caused by physical diseases."[4]

Greek Words, Phrases, and Constructions in 5:1

οἱ πλούσιοι—the use of the definite article indicates the generic class of rich people.

ὀλολύζοντες—this present active participle from ὀλολύζω (I cry out in joy or pain) denotes manner; that is, it describes weeping accompanied by recurring shouts of pain. The sound of the participle is an imitation of the sound associated with its meaning.

ταῖς ἐπερχομέναις—the present middle participle from the compound verb ἐπέρχομαι (I come upon) refers to the future.

---

2. Wealth
5:2–3

2. Your wealth has rotted, and moths have eaten your clothes. 3. Your gold and silver are corroded. Their corrosion will testify against you and eat your flesh like fire. You have hoarded wealth in the last days.

Note the following points:

a. "Rotted." What is wealth? Its definition depends on the culture and the times in which one lives. Job was a rich man because God had blessed him with vast numbers of animals (seven thousand sheep, three thousand camels, five hundred yoke of oxen and five hundred donkeys [Job 1:3]).

---

2. Old Testament prophets often pronounced divine judgment upon nations surrounding Israel (Isa. 13:6; 19:4; 33:1). These nations might not hear these pronouncements, but God's people did.

3. John Calvin, *Commentaries on the Catholic Epistles: The Epistle of James*, ed. and trans. John Owen (Grand Rapids: Eerdmans, 1948), p. 343.

4. Roland K. Harrison, *NIDNTT*, vol. 3, p. 858.

At the dawn of Christianity, rich people who possessed lands or homes sold them and gave the money to the poor (Acts 4:34–35). For the recipients of the Epistle of James, wealth apparently consisted of foodstuffs, clothing, gold, and silver.

James rebukes the rich because they have allowed their wealth to rot. The verb actually means "to decay" and seems to apply to food supplies.[5] God has designed nature in such a way that every growing season brings forth a new supply of food for man and animals. Supplies, then, ought not to be hoarded (Luke 12:16–20); they are subject to decay. What God has provided in nature should be used for the daily sustenance of his creatures (Matt. 6:19). With proper distribution of these supplies no one needs to be hungry, for God's bountiful earth produces sufficient food for all.

b. "Eaten." In the absence of preventive chemicals, a moth attacks clothing of both the rich and the poor. The poor, however, have no worry that their garments will be eaten by moths, for they wear the only clothes they possess. The rich store their expensive garments and in time find them ruined by devouring larvae. An insignificant nocturnal insect deposits eggs that are hatched in costly garments. The garments are then ruined and worthless (Job 13:28; Isa. 51:8).

c. "Corroded." "Your gold and silver are corroded." Of course, precious metals do not rust. Therefore, we need to explain the verb *to corrode* not literally but figuratively.[6] The hoarding of silver and gold simply for the sake of hoarding does not serve any meaningful purpose. In a sense, these metals are as useless as if they were thoroughly corroded. James speaks of corrosion to indicate the worthlessness of earthly possessions.

d. "Testify." In another sense, the corrosion of metals has negative value. In a court of law, for instance, this can be used as evidence against the rich. That is, someone can accuse the rich of having been unworthy stewards of their riches. Instead of helping the poor and alleviating their needs, these rich people hoarded wealth and used it either for their own selfish pleasures or for no purpose at all.

e. "Eat." James is rather descriptive in his denunciation of the rich. He says that "corrosion will . . . eat your flesh like fire."[7] Fire is a devastating

---

5. Consult Joseph B. Mayor, *The Epistle of St. James* (reprint ed., Grand Rapids: Zondervan, 1946), p. 154.

6. In the ancient world a reference to the rusting of precious metals was understood figuratively: "Lose your silver for the sake of a brother or a friend, and do not let it rust under a stone and be lost. Lay up your treasure according to the commandments of the Most High, and it will profit you more than gold" (Sir. 29:10–11, RSV).

7. This part of verse 3 is somewhat problematic. First, in the Greek the word *flesh* is in the plural. Second, some translators want to separate the idea of rust from that of fire. With different punctuation the word *fire*, then, becomes part of the next sentence: "It was a burning fire that you stored up as your treasure for the last days" (JB), or, "since you have stored up fire," James Hardy Ropes, *A Critical and Exegetical Commentary on the Epistle of James*, International Critical Commentary series (1916; reprint ed., Edinburgh: Clark, 1961), p. 287.

power; at sufficiently high temperatures it will consume everything in its path. James alludes to the judgment of God that is coming upon them (see Deut. 24:4; Isa. 10:16–17; 30:27; Ezek. 15:7; Amos 5:6). That judgment they cannot escape. In other words, although everyone will eventually appear before the judgment throne, God's wrath can strike the sinner even in this life, so that his physical body is destroyed. King Herod, boasting of his own power and riches, experienced God's immediate judgment when "an angel of the Lord struck him down" (Acts 12:23).

f. "Hoarded." Here is the conclusion of the matter: "You have hoarded wealth in the last days." This text lends itself to various interpretations.

First, man's life on earth is short, as James points out (4:14), and will soon come to an end. On earth, people envy the rich because of their wealth and influence, but at the moment of death those who are materially rich are spiritually bankrupt. What man ought to do is to build up his spiritual bank account by storing up treasures in heaven (Matt. 6:20).

Second, a number of translations have the reading "you have laid up treasure *for* the last days" (italics added).[8] Some interpreters assert that the rich accumulate treasures in the form of "storing up wrath against [themselves] for the day of God's wrath" (Rom. 2:5).[9]

Third, in the broader context of this verse, James twice mentions the imminent coming of the Lord (vv. 7–8) and then adds that "the Judge is standing at the door" (v. 9). The Lord and the Judge, of course, are one and the same.[10] The expression *the last days* refers to the so-called end time, which is the age of fulfillment predicted in the Old Testament (Jer. 23:20; Ezek. 38:16; Hos. 3:5; Joel 2:28) and realized in the New Testament times (John 11:24 [singular]; 12:48 [singular]; Acts 2:17; II Tim. 3:1; Heb. 1:2). Precisely, the expression includes the period from Christ's first to his second coming. Rich people, says James, have gathered material wealth in the shadow of Christ's return. But when he comes, they must face judgment.

Practical Considerations in 5:2–3

Verse 2

When reporters ask people on the last day of the calendar year what they expect from the new year, nine out of ten say that they hope to make more money. Money gives us security and the ability to acquire the necessities of life.

---

8. Consult the RSV. Also see KJV, JB, and MLB. The NAB has "against the last days."

9. Calvin, *James*, p. 344; also see E. M. Sidebottom, *James, Jude, and 2 Peter*, Century Bible series (London: Nelson; Greenwood, S.C.: Attic, 1967), p. 57; and James B. Adamson, *The Epistle of James*, New International Commentary on the New Testament series (Grand Rapids: Eerdmans, 1976), p. 185.

10. Compare Donald Guthrie, *New Testament Theology* (Downers Grove: Inter-Varsity, 1981), p. 811.

We cannot live without money. We sell our skills and time on the labor market for financial returns, and all of us have the desire to progress by making more money. We never seem to get enough, for the more we receive the more we want.

What should be our attitude toward making money? Earthly possessions are like the tides of the sea: they come and go. Therefore, we ought not to base our destiny on the instability of earthly riches. Rather, we should receive every good and perfect gift out of God's hand (James 1:17) and then wisely dispense the money God gives us. When we remember the needs of our fellow man and give generously, we reflect God's generosity toward us.

Verse 3

What is our message to those who have been endowed with earthly riches? The answer is Paul's relevant instruction to Timothy:

> Command those who are rich in this present world not to be arrogant nor to put their hope in wealth, which is so uncertain, but to put their hope in God, who richly provides us with everything for our enjoyment. . . . In this way they will lay up treasure for themselves as a firm foundation for the coming age, so that they may take hold of the life that is truly life. [I Tim. 6:17, 19]

Greek Words, Phrases, and Constructions in 5:3

εἰς—with the noun *testimony* this preposition means "with a view to" or "resulting in."[11]

τὰς σάρκας—the plural form also occurs in other passages (Rev. 17:16; 19:18, 21). The noun σάρξ represents a person's physical existence and possessions.

ἐν—this preposition refers to time, not purpose.

---

3. Theft
5:4

One sin always leads to others. The sin of greedily hoarding riches instead of sharing them with the poor prompts the sinner to rob the poor. In this instance, the rich rob the laborers who have mowed the fields in the harvest season.

4. Look! The wages you failed to pay the workmen who mowed your fields are crying out against you. The cries of the harvesters have reached the ears of the Lord Almighty.

James takes the readers out to the open fields, as it were, where no one can hide. Here they can see the injustice poor people suffer at the hands of the rich. Apparently the harvest season has come to an end, the fields

---

11. C. F. D. Moule, *An Idiom-Book of New Testament Greek,* 2d ed. (Cambridge: At the University Press, 1960), p. 70.

are empty, and the barns of the rich are filled with the bounties of the earth. Although we cannot be certain, the readers of the epistle may have been among those who harvested the fields of the rich landowners.

a. "The wages you failed to pay." The workers were day laborers who agreed with an employer on the daily wage and who expected to be paid at the end of the day (Matt. 20:8). The law of Moses stipulated that the employer ought "not [to] hold back the wages of a hired man overnight" (Lev. 19:13; Deut. 24:14–15). Their families were dependent on the daily earnings of these workers; delay in payments meant no food at the dinner table and anguish in the souls of the laborers.

b. "The workmen who mowed your fields." Cultivated fields that yielded crops belonged to prosperous landowners. Some of them had appointed managers while they themselves lived elsewhere. They hired extra farm laborers to cut the standing grain, bundle it, and to collect the sheaves into shocks. These workers were needed so that the ripened grain did not spoil because of bad weather or other reasons.

c. "The wages . . . [of] the workmen . . . are crying out against you." Instead of the joy of the harvest season (see Ps. 126:5–6), these laborers had to cope with anger because of broken promises, delays, and the prospect of not being paid at all. They cried out against the rich and demanded justice. Presumably they were acquainted with the curse God pronounced upon the rich who made their "countrymen work for nothing" (Jer. 22:13; also see Mal. 3:5). Perhaps they knew the saying of Jesus, "the worker deserves his wages" (Luke 10:7; and compare I Tim. 5:18). They had no one to defend them but God.

d. "The cries of the harvesters have reached the ears of the Lord Almighty." The mowers and the harvesters are the same people. Their cries are not heard by the rich, but the Lord hears his people. The New King James Version provides a literal translation of the Greek in the words *the Lord of Sabaoth*. The New International Version, by contrast, translates these words "Lord Almighty." This translation communicates but does not necessarily give the significance of the original expression *Lord Sabaoth*, that is, Lord of the armies in heaven and on earth.[12] God the omnipotent is on the side of the downtrodden. He puts his majestic power to work to vindicate his people and to mete out swift justice to their adversaries. Thanks to Martin Luther we have become familiar with the name *Sabaoth*.

> Dost ask who that may be?
> Christ Jesus, it is He;
> Lord Sabaoth His name,
> From age to age the same,
> And He must win the battle.

---

12. The term *Sabaoth* is a transliteration from the Hebrew into Greek and English. It occurs numerous times in the LXX (especially in Isa.). Paul uses it in Rom. 9:29 (quoting Isa. 1:9).

Greek Words, Phrases, and Constructions in 5:4

ἀμησάντων—the aorist tense of this active participle from ἀμάω (I mow) specifies that the work had ended.

ἀπεστερημένος—from ἀποστερέω (I deprive, defraud), this perfect passive participle differs not in meaning from the perfect passive participle ἀφυστερημένος (derived from ἀφυστερέω, I withdraw, defraud). The perfect tense denotes an action that began in the past and continues in the present.

---

4. Indulgence
5:5

The sin of greed causes a person to degenerate from theft to living a life of luxury and indulgence. In other words, the money taken from the poverty-stricken laborers is spent on extravagances. In scathing tones James denounces the rich.

5. You have lived on earth in luxury and self-indulgence. You have fattened yourselves in the day of slaughter.

After they have increased their wealth, the rich turn to luxuries and sinful pleasures. They are able to afford all the bodily comforts they desire and literally squander their resources on wasteful living.

Jesus portrayed the rich man "who was dressed in purple and fine linen and lived in luxury every day" (Luke 16:19) as a man deserving hellish punishment not for what he did but for what he failed to do.[13] That is, the rich man failed to love God and failed to care for his neighbor Lazarus. That was his sin.

In another parable Jesus pictures an immoral young man who "squandered his wealth in wild living" (Luke 15:13). According to the young man's brother, he wasted it on prostitutes (v. 30). This is the life those rich people whom James denounces pursued. Therefore James addresses them harshly.

"You have fattened yourselves in the day of slaughter" (compare Jer. 12:3; 25:34). In picturesque language James compares them to domestic animals that are daily gorging themselves without knowing their destined end. As cattle being fattened for the day of slaughter, so the rich are indulging themselves in luxury and licentiousness and are unaware of the impending day of judgment.[14] Yet their doom is certain and their destruction swift.

---

13. Simon J. Kistemaker, *The Parables of Jesus* (Grand Rapids: Baker, 1980), p. 239.

14. Peter H. Davids shows that the expression *day of slaughter* "is part of a long tradition of the day of God's judgment as a day of the slaughter of his enemies." *The Epistle of James: A Commentary on the Greek Text,* New International Greek Testament Commentary series (Grand Rapids: Eerdmans, 1982), p. 178. He amasses a host of references to Scripture (Ps. 22:29; 37:20; 49:14; Isa. 30:33; 34:5–8; Jer. 46:10; 50:26–27; Lam. 2:21–22; Ezek. 39:17; Rev. 19:17–21) and to apocryphal literature.

Greek Words, Phrases, and Constructions in 5:5

ἐθρέψατε—the aorist tense with that of the other two verbs in this verse is constative; that is, the aorist encompasses the entire period in which the rich fattened themselves. The noun καρδίας (hearts) need not be translated literally; with the verb it expresses the reflexive "themselves."

ἐν—this preposition means "on" or "in," not "for" (εἰς).

---

5. Murder
5:6

The last sin is that of murder. In their quest for wealth the rich have not shrunk from taking the lives of others. Their sin of greed gave birth to theft; that sin spawned self-indulgence; and eventually it caused them to commit murder.

6. You have condemned and murdered innocent men, who were not opposing you.

How do we understand the word *murdered?* We can interpret it literally or figuratively. Those rich people who perhaps brought poor people into court (2:6) now are guilty of murder.[15] Directly or indirectly they killed a human being who was unable to defend himself.

We can also take the word metaphorically. For instance, a rich man who withholds the wages of a laborer deprives him of his livelihood and thus indirectly commits an act of murder. In the second century before Christ, Joshua ben Sira said,

> The bread of the needy is the life of the poor; whoever deprives them of it is a man of blood. To take away a neighbor's living is to murder him; to deprive an employee of his wages is to shed his blood. [Sir. 34:21–22, RSV]

By taking the two verbs *condemn* and *murder* together, we understand the text to say that the rich had gone to court and had used their wealth to subvert justice. They were determined to rid themselves of the poor man, although he was righteous and had not opposed the rich.[16] With the law on their side, they had committed murder. The precise details of time, place, and circumstances, James does not reveal. He is interested only in the fact that the rich perpetrate murder of innocent men.

---

15. Donald W. Burdick, *James*, vol. 12, the *Expositor's Bible Commentary*, ed. Frank E. Gaebelein, 12 vols. (Grand Rapids: Eerdmans, 1981), p. 200.

16. The ungodly men say, "Let us oppress the righteous poor man. . . . Let us lie in wait for the righteous man, because he is inconvenient to us and opposes our actions; he reproaches us for sins against the law" (Wis. 2:10, 12).

The New International Version puts the object *innocent men* in the plural. Other versions give a literal translation of the text, for example, "You have condemned, you have killed the righteous man; he does not resist you" (RSV). Instead of attempting to explain who the righteous man is—some interpreters think of Jesus or James himself, for he bore the name *the Just*—we do well to take the words *righteous man* distributively and therefore to refer to the murdering of innocent people who refuse to resist oppression (compare Matt. 5:39).

Greek Words, Phrases, and Constructions in 5:6

τὸν δίκαιον—the definite article with the substantive (adjective) defines the generic class of righteous people.[17]

---

7 Be patient, then, until the Lord's coming. See how the farmer waits for the land to yield its valuable crop and how patient he is for the autumn and spring rains. 8 You too, be patient and stand firm, because the Lord's coming is near. 9 Don't grumble against each other, brothers, or you will be judged. The Judge is standing at the door!

10 Brothers, as an example of patience in the face of suffering, take the prophets who spoke in the name of the Lord. 11 As you know, we consider blessed those who have persevered. You have heard of Job's perseverance and have seen what the Lord finally brought about. The Lord is full of compassion and mercy.

B. Necessity of Patience
5:7–11

1. Plea for Patience
5:7–8

In this part of the epistle the author assumes the role of the pastor. He has given vent to his indignation toward the rich; now he affectionately addresses the readers by calling them "brothers" (also see vv. 7, 9, 10, 12, 19). He expresses his concern that they exercise the virtue of patience. He resorts to repetition: four times in succession he uses the term *patience* (vv. 7 [twice], 8, 10) and twice he employs the concept *persevere* (v. 11). And that is where James puts the emphasis.

7. Be patient, then, brothers, until the Lord's coming. See how the farmer waits for the land to yield its valuable crop and how patient he is for the autumn and spring rains. 8. You too, be patient and stand firm, because the Lord's coming is near.

Note these observations:

a. *Command.* Fully aware of their adversities, James tells his readers to exercise patience. The adverb *then* links the command to be patient to the

---

17. A. T. Robertson, *A Grammar of the Greek New Testament in the Light of Historical Research* (Nashville: Broadman, 1934), p. 757.

preceding verses in which James describes the oppressive conditions under which the poor live. In a sense, James takes up the theme with which he begins his epistle: "Consider it pure joy, my brothers, whenever you face trials of many kinds" (1:2).

Patience is a virtue possessed by few and sought by many. We are living in a society that champions the word *instant*. But to be patient, as James uses the word, is much more than passively waiting for the time to pass. Patience is the art of enduring someone whose conduct is incompatible with that of others and sometimes even oppressive. A patient man calms a quarrel, for he controls his anger and does not seek revenge (compare Prov. 15:18; 16:32).[18]

The old English term *long-suffering* does not mean to suffer a while but to tolerate someone for a long time. To say it differently, patience is the opposite of being short-tempered. God displays patience by being "slow to anger" when man continues in sin even after numerous admonitions (Exod. 34:6; Ps. 86:15; Rom. 2:4; 9:22; I Peter 3:20; II Peter 3:15).[19] Man ought to reflect that divine virtue in his day-to-day life.

James knows that the readers of his epistle are unable to defend themselves against their oppressors. Therefore, he urges them to exercise patience and to leave matters in the hands of God, who is coming to deliver them. Even if they were able to do so, they should not take matters into their own hands. God has said, "It is mine to avenge; I will repay" (Deut. 32:35; Rom. 12:12; Heb. 10:30).

"Be patient . . . until the Lord's coming." The readers know that the Lord is coming back in the capacity of Judge.[20] They ought to exercise self-control toward their adversaries and demonstrate patience in respect to the coming of the Lord. He will avenge his people when he returns (II Thess. 1:5–6).

b. *Example.* Throughout his epistle the writer reveals his love for God's creation. In this verse he portrays the expectations of the farmer who anticipates a bountiful harvest but must patiently wait for the arrival of "the autumn and spring rains." The farmer has learned that everything grows according to the seasons of the year. He knows how many days are needed for a plant to develop from germination to harvest. Moreover, he knows that without the proper amount of rainfall at the right moment, his labors are in vain.

---

18. "Patience is the self-restraint which does not hastily retaliate a wrong." J. B. Lightfoot, *Saint Paul's Epistles to the Colossians and to Philemon* (London: Macmillan, 1890), p. 138; Thayer, p. 387.

19. Louis Berkhof defines the patience of God as *"that aspect of the goodness or love of God in virtue of which He bears with the froward and evil in spite of their long continued disobedience."* *Systematic Theology* (Grand Rapids: Eerdmans, 1953), p. 72.

20. Johannes Horst, *TDNT,* vol. 4, p. 385; Ulrich Falkenroth and Colin Brown, *NIDNTT,* vol. 2, p. 771; Everett F. Harrison, "Patience," in *Baker's Dictionary of Christian Ethics,* ed. Carl F. H. Henry (Grand Rapids: Baker, 1973), p. 488.

Although the amounts of rainfall in Israel fluctuate, the farmer knows that he can expect the autumn rain, beginning with a number of thunderstorms, in the latter part of October. Then he can plant his seed so that germination takes place. And he eagerly hopes for a sufficient amount of rainfall in April and May when the grain is maturing and the yield increases every time the rains come down. He depends, therefore, on the autumn and the spring rains (Deut. 11:14; Jer. 5:24; Hos. 6:3; Joel 2:23).[21] He is able to predict the coming of the rain, but he cannot speak with certainty about the harvest. He waits with eager expectation.

c. *Repetition.* James applies the example of the farmer to the readers. "You too, be patient and stand firm, because the Lord's coming is near." As the farmer confidently waits for the coming of the autumn rain and the spring rain on which his harvest depends, so the believer waits patiently for the coming of the Lord. As God promised Noah that "as long as the earth endures, seedtime and harvest . . . will never cease" (Gen. 8:22), so the Lord has given the believer the promise that he will return.

James tells the readers to be patient and to stand firm ("to strengthen your hearts" in the original). They can say with confidence that the Lord is coming back, but they do not know when that will be. While they are waiting, doubt and distraction often enter their lives. For this reason, James counsels his readers to stand firm in the knowledge that the Lord in due time will fulfill his promise made to the believers. He falls into repetition, but the reminder of the Lord's imminent return is necessary so that the readers will not lose heart in difficult circumstances.

Greek Words, Phrases, and Constructions in 5:7–8

Verse 7

μακροθυμήσατε—from the combination μακρός (long) and θυμός (temper). Although the action is durative by nature, in the aorist imperative it is punctiliar.[22] In a sense, it is similar to the present tense (also see v. 8).

ἕως λάβῃ—the temporal conjunction ἕως (until) controls the aorist subjunctive of the verb λάβῃ (from λαμβάνω, I receive).

Verse 8

καὶ ὑμεῖς—the inclusion of the adjunctive use of καί and the personal pronoun ὑμεῖς are for emphasis.

ἤγγικεν—from ἐγγίζω (I approach), the perfect active indicative denotes an event that has come near and is now at hand (consider, among other verses, Matt. 21:34; 26:45; Luke 21:8; 22:1; Acts 7:17; Rom. 13:12; I Peter 4:7).

---

21. John H. Paterson, *ZPEB*, vol. 5, pp. 27–28; George Adam Smith, *The Historical Geography of the Holy Land* (London: Hodder and Stoughton, 1966), pp. 62–70; Alfred H. Joy, *ISBE*, vol. 4, pp. 2525–26. The average amount of rainfall in Jerusalem (measured over a fifty-year period) is 26.16 inches (66.44 cm). The lowest amount has been 12 inches (30.48 cm) and the highest 40 inches (101.60 cm).

22. Robertson, *Grammar*, p. 856.

2. Warning Against Impatience
5:9

James is fully aware of the oppression and hardship the recipients of his letter daily experience. He deals with them pastorally and advises them accordingly.

9. Don't grumble against each other, brothers, or you will be judged. The Judge is standing at the door!

The people James addresses live in oppressive situations that cause them to lose patience with those who deprive them of the basic necessities. In time, they become irritable toward those who share their miseries.[23] They give vent to their repressed feelings and lash out at those who are close to them. Their behavior is understandable. At this point, however, pastor James appears and admonishes them not to grumble against one another. He knows that they are grumbling against members of the Christian community. We assume that the rich who oppressed them were too far removed from them to hear their groanings.

Groaning and grumbling is the opposite of being joyful and thankful. Although at times the believer may find himself in unenviable living conditions, the fact remains that when he begins to grumble, he falls into sin. He sins because he accuses God, perhaps indirectly, for the misfortunes he receives.

Directly, the grumbler finds fault with his fellow man, blames him for the troubles both he and his fellow man have to endure, and judges him unjustly. That is contrary to the royal law of love, for the complainer then "speaks against the law and judges it" (4:11). James reminds the grumblers, whom he affectionately calls "brothers," that they fall into judgment themselves. God himself will judge them. In fact, James says, "The Judge is standing at the door!"

The sinner is only one heartbeat away from the Judge. For when death strikes, the grumbler enters the presence of God, who will judge him for every idle word he has spoken. Everyone who passes through the portals of death meets the Judge on the other side. Writes Calvin, "What, then, will be the case, but that every one who seeks to bring judgment on others, must allow the same against himself; and thus all will be given up to the same ruin."[24]

The remark of James is a word of warning for the impatient grumbler

---

23. Martin Dibelius sees "no need to find some sort of connection between the warning not to 'grumble against one another' and the preceding saying." *James: A Commentary on the Epistle of James*, rev. Heinrich Greeven, trans. Michael A. Williams, ed. Helmut Köster, Hermeneia: A Critical and Historical Commentary on the Bible (Philadelphia: Fortress, 1976), p. 244. He grants, however, that the themes of the coming of the Lord and the judgment form a link between this verse and the preceding.

24. Calvin, *James*, p. 349. "Let no one, then, ask for vengeance on others, except he wishes to bring it on his own head."

and a word of comfort for the person who keeps his eye of faith fixed on Jesus. The church of all ages utters the prayer the apostle John has recorded at the close of the New Testament, "Amen. Come, Lord Jesus" (Rev. 22:20).

Doctrinal Considerations in 5:7–9

In the middle of the first century of the Christian era, leaders in the church expected the Lord Jesus Christ to return in their lifetime. In his letters Paul tells his readers that the day of Christ is at hand (Rom. 13:11–12; I Cor. 1:8; II Cor. 1:14; Phil. 1:6, 10; 2:16; I Thess. 5:2; II Thess. 2:2). Of course, Paul's two epistles to the church at Thessalonica deal primarily with the topic of Christ's return. For Paul, the coming of Jesus was imminent.

The writer of the Epistle to the Hebrews also speaks about the end of time. Says he, "In these last days [God] has spoken to us" (1:2). He declares that "Christ . . . will appear a second time . . . to bring salvation to those who are waiting for him" (9:28). And he points to the imminence of Christ's return when he says, "Let us not give up meeting together, . . . but let us encourage one another—and all the more as you see the Day approaching" (10:25).

James also mentions the doctrine of Christ's return. In the fifth chapter of his epistle he addresses the rich who "have hoarded wealth in the last days" (v. 3). Especially in exhorting his readers to be patient, James notes that the coming of the Lord is near (vv. 7–8). Moreover, he identifies the Lord with the Judge who "is standing at the door" (v. 9). James anticipates that the return of the Lord will take place soon so that the wicked receive their just reward and the righteous be delivered from oppression.[25]

Greek Words, Phrases, and Constructions in 5:9

μὴ στενάζετε—the present tense of the imperative preceded by the negative particle μή indicates that the readers were engaged in grumbling.

κριθῆτε—the aorist passive subjunctive in this negative purpose clause implies that Christ is the Judge on the judgment day.

πρό—this preposition governs the genitive case and means "before." With the plural τῶν θυρῶν (the doors) it constitutes an idiom in New Testament Greek that is translated in current English as "at the door."

ἕστηκεν—the perfect tense from ἵστημι (I stand still) has a present connotation.

---

3. Examples
5:10–11

James takes the first example of patience from nature—the expectation of the fall and the spring rains (5:7)—and the second from Scripture. He

---

25. G. E. Ladd observes that for James the return of the Lord is a living hope. "Such a hope argues strongly for an early date." *A Theology of the New Testament* (Grand Rapids: Eerdmans, 1974), p. 590. Also see Guthrie, *New Testament Theology*, p. 811.

knows that the readers are fully acquainted with the history of the Old Testament prophets. Therefore, he writes,

10. Brothers, as an example of patience in the face of suffering, take the prophets who spoke in the name of the Lord.

Once again the pastor addresses the members of the church by tenderly calling them "brothers" (see 5:7, 9). He instructs them not by a negative command (v. 9) but by a positive example. He exhorts them to follow the scriptural model of the prophets.

The word *example* is most important. In the original it stands first in the sentence and thus receives all the emphasis. The expression has two meanings: in the bad sense, it refers to the ungodly whose conduct we are told to avoid (Heb. 4:11; II Peter 2:6); in the good sense, it describes the righteous whose conduct we are to imitate (John 13:15).

Who are the righteous who are worthy to be imitated? They are the prophets mentioned in the Old Testament. The readers were familiar with the history of the prophets, for in Jewish synagogues and Christian churches the Old Testament was read. We ought not limit the term *prophets* to describing only those who wrote prophetical books. Prominent figures of the Old Testament era are examples of patient endurance (see the list of the heroes of the faith in Heb. 11).[26] Think of the persecution Elijah endured from King Ahab, the hardship Jeremiah suffered at the hands of the kings of Judah, and the perseverance Daniel displayed when he was put in the lions' den during the time of the exile. All of these, and numerous others, suffered because they "spoke in the name of the Lord."

In his prayer of confession, Daniel addresses God and says, "We have not listened to your servants the prophets, who spoke in your name to our kings, our princes and our fathers, and to all the people of the land" (Dan. 9:6). This is what the prophets did, and James exhorts the readers of his epistle to follow their example. When they imitate the prophets, they will have to endure insult and persecution, and run the risk of losing their lives. Nevertheless, they ought to count themselves among those who are called blessed.

11a. As you know, we consider blessed those who have persevered.

In this verse we hear the echo of one of Jesus' beatitudes, "Blessed are you when people insult you, persecute you and falsely say all kinds of evil against you because of me. Rejoice and be glad, because great is your reward in heaven, for in the same way they persecuted the prophets who were before you" (Matt. 5:11–12). James intimates that the readers are familiar with this word of Jesus.

Blessed are the people who have persevered and continue to persevere. In the introduction to his epistle James writes the beatitude, "Blessed is

---

26. Mayor mentions Noah, Abraham, Jacob, Moses, Isaiah, and Jeremiah as "preeminent patterns of endurance," *James*, p. 163. New Testament references to persecuting and killing prophets are numerous (Matt. 5:12; 23:29–37; Acts 7:52; Rom. 11:3; I Thess. 2:15; Heb. 11:35–38; Rev. 11:7; 16:6; 18:24).

the man who perseveres under trial" (1:12; also see 1:3). Toward the end of his epistle, he mentions "perseverance" in the context of a discussion on patience (5:11). James seems to say that the persevering believer actively bears up under trials and temptations and remains courageous.[27] He provides a striking example by referring to Job.

11b. You have heard of Job's perseverance and have seen what the Lord finally brought about.

Perhaps because of our reliance on Bible translations, the proverbial patience of Job has become well known. But in his epistle, James uses the word *perseverance* rather than "patience."[28] He introduces the noun *perseverance* with the verb *to persevere* in the preceding sentence: "As you know, we consider blessed those who have persevered" (v. 11a; also see 1:3, 4, 12). Patience can be described as passive endurance; by contrast, perseverance is the active determination of a believer whose faith triumphs in the midst of afflictions.

What do we know about the patience of Job? The prophet Ezekiel mentions him with Noah and Daniel. However, the prophet extols not patience but righteousness as the qualifying virtue of Job (Ezek. 14:14, 20). Even in the Book of Job, patience is not one of Job's outstanding characteristics. Job betrays his impatience when he curses the day of his birth (3:1) and when he says that the "long-winded speeches" of his three friends never end (16:3).

Then, what makes Job unforgettable? He is known for his steadfastness, that is, his persevering faith that triumphed in the end. Because "Job did not sin in what he said" (2:10), God eventually blessed him with twice as many possessions as he had before (42:12–13). For this reason, James tells his readers that they "have seen what the Lord finally brought about." God blessed Job because of his persevering faith.

11c. The Lord is full of compassion and mercy.

If God permitted Satan to take everything Job possessed, if God allowed the rich people to oppress the poor in the days of James, is he at all concerned about man's lot on earth?

Yes, God is concerned about his people. James writes these assuring words, "The Lord is full of compassion and mercy." Although he does not quote the Old Testament Scriptures, he alludes to at least two passages:

> The LORD, the LORD, the compassionate and gracious God, slow to anger, abounding in love and faithfulness. [Exod. 34:6]

> The LORD is compassionate and gracious,
> slow to anger, abounding in love. [Ps. 103:8]

---

27. R. C. Trench observes that God possesses the attribute of patience, but perseverance "can find no place in Him." It is God who gives endurance to the believers (Rom. 15:5). See *Synonyms of the New Testament* (1854; reprint ed., Grand Rapids: Eerdmans, 1953), p. 198.
28. A number of translations have the reading *patience* (consult KJV, RV, ASV, JB, GNB).

But James goes one step further than these two passages. He coins a word in Greek that does not occur anywhere else in the New Testament. He says, "The Lord is *full of compassion*" (italics added).[29] God is more than compassionate; he is filled with compassion. His heart goes out to the person in need of help.

What is compassion? It is a feeling; the word is best translated "heart." Furthermore, compassion is synonymous with mercy. Mercy extends to man and is received by him. Mercy has an external aspect; it reaches out to man.

James exhorts the readers to imitate the prophets, reminds them of Job's perseverance, and teaches them about God's abounding love and mercy. His message is: God will sustain you.

Doctrinal Considerations in 5:10–11

When the governor of a state grants mercy to a criminal on death row, he acts on the basis of compassion and forbearance. Mercy is received by the convict, who experiences a mitigation of the penalty.

God grants mercy to the sinner because of the sacrificial death of Jesus Christ. Man's plea for mercy that is presented to God in the name of Christ is met in the form of remission of sin. Man's sins are erased as if he had never sinned at all.

God's mercy, however, goes beyond the pardon of sin. God extends mercy in the form of help in time of need. Whenever someone appeals to him, God sends aid because he has given his covenant promise to his people: "I will be their God, and they will be my people" (Jer. 31:33; Heb. 8:10). God keeps his Word and fulfills his promise.[30]

Greek Words, Phrases, and Constructions in 5:10–11

Verse 10

τῆς κακοπαθίας καὶ τῆς μακροθυμίας—the first noun has an active meaning and refers to the "*suffering* that a person endures, a *strenuous effort* that one makes, or *perseverance* that he practices."[31] The second noun *patience* can be taken together with the first. Because both nouns are in the genitive case, the one is dependent on the other. The translation, then, is "patience in suffering."[32]

---

29. Helmut Köster, *TDNT*, vol. 7, p. 557, is of the opinion that the term *full of compassion* "can hardly have been coined by the author of James." He bases this on its occurrence in the writings of Hermas. But the Epistle of James predates Hermas. Also consult Hans-Helmut Esser, *NIDNTT*, vol. 2, p. 600.

30. Stanley D. Walters, "Mercy," in *Baker's Dictionary of Christian Ethics*, ed. Carl F. H. Henry (Grand Rapids: Baker, 1973), pp. 418–19. Also see Peter C. Craigie, "Mercy," *EDT*, pp. 708–9.

31. Bauer, p. 397.

32. Friedrich Blass and Albert Debrunner, *A Greek Grammar of the New Testament and Other Early Christian Literature*, trans. and rev. Robert Funk (Chicago: University of Chicago Press, 1961), sec. 442(16).

τοὺς προφήτας—with ὑπόδειγμα (example) this noun is part of a double accusative, and thus it lacks the helping particle ὡς (as). The accusative is used predicatively.[33]

Verse 11

τοὺς ὑπομείναντας—the participle in the aorist tense with the definite article refers to a general class of people. The aorist is constative.

τὸ τέλος κυρίου—the context clearly indicates that this phrase is not a reference to the death of Jesus.

---

12 Above all, my brothers, do not swear—not by heaven or by earth or by anything else. Let your "Yes" be yes, and your "No," no, or you will be condemned.

C. Oaths
5:12

Once more James returns to a discussion on the use of the tongue (see 1:19, 26; 3:1–12). The connection between this verse and the preceding verses is scant. The warning not to grumble against one another to avoid falling under judgment (5:9) is somewhat parallel to the prohibition not to use an oath lightly, "or you will be condemned" (5:12).

12. Above all, my brothers, do not swear—not by heaven or by earth or by anything else. Let your "Yes" be yes, and your "No," no, or you will be condemned.

What is the significance of the phrase *above all*? If James means to say that the readers ought to pay *special* attention to the warning not to swear, we would have expected a more elaborate admonition. And if James wished to convey the importance of this verse in the light of the preceding verses, we would have expected a definite connection. As it stands now, this verse has little in common with the foregoing passage. Perhaps we must conclude that James is coming to the end of his epistle and wishes to mention a series of admonitions (compare I Peter 4:8).

a. *Similarity.* The resemblance between the words of Jesus recorded in the Sermon on the Mount and this verse is unmistakable. By placing the verses in parallel columns, we can see that James relied on the saying of Jesus.

Matthew 5:34, 35, 37	*James 5:12*
"But I tell you,—	Above all, my brothers,
Do not swear at all:—	do not swear—
either by heaven,—	not by heaven
for it is God's throne;	
or by the earth,—	or by earth
for it is his footstool;	

---

33. Moule, *Idiom-Book,* p. 35; Robertson, *Grammar,* p. 480.

or by Jerusalem,—or by anything else.
for it is the city of the
Great King. . . . Simply
let your 'Yes' be 'Yes,'—Let your "Yes" be yes,
and your 'No,' 'No';—and your "No," no,
anything beyond this —or you will be
comes from the evil one."—condemned.

Most likely James depended on memory and not on manuscript when he wrote these words. If the Epistle of James was written in the first part of the first century of the Christian era, the writer would have taken these words from the oral gospel preached by the apostles and the apostolic helpers. James, then, bases his admonition to refrain from swearing careless oaths not merely on Scripture but in this case directly on the authority of Jesus.

b. *Practice.* Like Jesus, James fulminates against the Jewish custom of strengthening statements with nonbinding oaths. The people knew the commandment, "You shall not misuse the name of the LORD your God, for the LORD will not hold anyone guiltless who misuses his name" (Exod. 20:7; Deut. 5:11). To remain guiltless, the Jews had made a distinction between binding and nonbinding oaths. Instead of using the divine name (which would be binding), they swore "by heaven or by earth or by anything else." In their opinion, that would be nonbinding and would not incur the wrath of God.[34] Both Jesus and James denounce this practice; the intention of appealing to God remains the same, even though one pretends to avoid using God's name.

c. *Implications.* Is the swearing of oaths forbidden? Both Jesus and James say "do not swear." If in a court of law defendant, plaintiff, lawyers, jury, and judge could be certain that every spoken word would be absolutely true to fact, oath taking would be superfluous. Because men shade the truth and falsify the facts at hand, the use of the oath is necessary. The person who takes the oath and breaks it faces divine wrath.

The teaching of Jesus, reiterated by James, is simple: "Let your 'Yes' be 'Yes,' and your 'No,' 'No.'" That is, be honest and speak the truth at all times. Let no flippant word come from your lips. Let everyone know that "your word is as good as gold."

d. *Application.* James concludes his admonition by saying that if you fail to speak the truth, "you will be condemned." A literal translation of this clause is, "so that you may not fall under judgment" (NASB). That is, God's judgment strikes anyone who carelessly swears an oath and fails to uphold the truth. Says Jesus to the Pharisees of his day, "But I tell you that men

---

34. Refer to SB, vol. 1, pp. 332–37, for rabbinic sources. Also see D. Edmond Hiebert, *The Epistle of James: Tests of a Living Faith* (Chicago: Moody, 1979), p. 310; D. Edmond Hiebert, "The Worldliness of Self-Serving Oaths," *Direction* 6 (1977): 39–43.

will have to give account on the day of judgment for every careless word they have spoken. For by your words you will be acquitted, and by your words you will be condemned" (Matt. 12:36–37).[35]

Practical Considerations in 5:12

Change the customs, culture, country, and nationality of people in the first century to our day and the truth of this text remains the same. True, we are not in the habit of swearing by heaven or earth to affirm the words we speak. And certainly we would not think of using the name of God in vain. But we seem to have no objection to the expression *by George* and its numerous variations. Some people cross their hearts to assert the veracity of their words. These worldly practices, however, are contrary to the teachings of Scripture. Those who resort to them incur divine condemnation.

Houses and buildings that are built on firm foundations need no supporting props. Likewise, the person whose foundation is Jesus Christ, with whom he continually communicates in prayer, has no need to strengthen his words. He speaks the truth because he himself is grounded in Christ, who said "I am . . . the truth" (John 14:6). Truth depends not on the use of expressions that approach profanity, but on the simple yes that remains yes and no that stays no.

> On Christ the solid rock I stand
> All other ground is sinking sand.
> —Edward Mote

Greek Words, Phrases, and Constructions in 5:12

πρό—this preposition means "before," and indicates preference "in the sense of superiority."[36]

μὴ ὀμνύετε—the present active imperative preceded by the negative particle is a prohibition to stop doing something that is being practiced. That is, stop the practice of swearing oaths.[37]

ἄλλον—the adjective ἄλλος refers to another of the same kind. ὅρκον (oath) is a cognate accusative with the verb ὀμνύω (I swear).

ἤτω—this is the alternate form of ἔστω (see Matt. 5:37) as the third person singular present active imperative of εἰμί (I am).

πέσητε—from πίπτω (I fall). The negative purpose clause demands the use of the subjunctive. The aorist points to single action.

---

35. The Greek text of Erasmus and the translation of William Tyndale give the reading *lest ye fall into hypocrisy*. Arthur L. Farstad and Zane C. Hodges, *The Greek New Testament According to the Majority Text* (Nashville and New York: Nelson, 1982), follow the text of Erasmus.

36. Robertson, *Grammar*, p. 622. Also consult Moule, *Idiom-Book*, p. 74, who takes it metaphorically.

37. Moule is of the opinion that "the reason for the use of the tense is difficult to detect." See his *Idiom-Book*, p. 21.

13 Is any one of you in trouble? He should pray. Is anyone happy? Let him sing songs of praise.   14 Is any one of you sick? He should call the elders of the church to pray over him and anoint him with oil in the name of the Lord.   15 And the prayer offered in faith will make the sick person well; the Lord will raise him up. If he has sinned, he will be forgiven.   16 Therefore confess your sins to each other and pray for each other so that you may be healed. The prayer of a righteous man is powerful and effective.

17 Elijah was a man just like us. He prayed earnestly that it would not rain, and it did not rain on the land for three and a half years.   18 Again he prayed, and the heavens gave rain, and the earth produced its crops.

D. Persistence in Prayer
5:13–18

James seems to have a penchant for formulating short questions and short answers for the benefit of the church. These short, pithy sentences are quite effective.

1. Prayer and Praise
5:13

13. Is any of you in trouble? He should pray. Is anyone happy? Let him sing songs of praise.

The Christian does not always live on a mountaintop of faith. Although Paul instructs the believer to rejoice always (Phil. 4:4; I Thess. 5:16), the simple facts of life are that from time to time the believer is in trouble. This trouble can be physical, mental, personal, financial, spiritual, or religious—to mention no more. When someone is mentally depressed, even with special effort he finds it difficult to be joyful. Therefore, James counsels anyone who is in trouble to pray.

James urges us to seek strength from God in prayer. As Peter puts it, "Cast all your anxiety on him because he cares for you" (I Peter 5:7). Paul exhorts us to pray continually (Eph. 6:18; Col. 4:2; I Thess. 5:17). Prayer is the vital link that keeps us in touch with "the author and perfecter of our faith" (Heb. 12:2).

"Is anyone happy?" Periods of joy follow times of sadness (Ps. 30:5). When the sunshine of God's favor rests upon us, we are filled with cheer and happiness. Then the time has come to sing for joy. "Let him sing songs of praise." The writers of the Book of Psalms instruct us how to do so. They keep their joy and happiness within proper bounds and give God the glory, honor, and praise that belong to him (e.g., consult Ps. 33:2–3; 81:1–2; 92:1–3; 98:4–6; 144:9; 149:1–5; 150; and see Eph. 5:19; Col. 3:16). In short, we ought to be prayerfully patient in adversity and thankfully happy in prosperity.

Greek Words, Phrases, and Constructions in 5:13

The two short questions and two short answers are much more effective than one single sentence that is smooth, balanced, and declarative. The use of the present imperative in προσευχέσθω (let him pray) and ψαλλέτω (let him sing) heightens the effectiveness of these sentences.

---

2. Prayer and Faith
5:14–15

The next two verses, although well known, are often misunderstood. Perhaps this is because these verses seem to raise challenging questions rather than provide conclusive answers. Nevertheless, the teachings of this section are clear and to the point.

14. Is any one of you sick? He should call the elders of the church to pray over him and anoint him with oil in the name of the Lord. 15. And the prayer offered in faith will make the sick person well; the Lord will raise him up. If he has sinned, he will be forgiven.

Note these comments:

a. "Is any one of you sick?" James spells out what he means by the word *trouble* (v. 13). It is physical sickness of one kind or another. That is, someone is bodily weakened by internal or external ailment and in urgent need of medical help. Then, what should the Christian community do?

b. "Call the elders of the church." The sick person himself or others, at his request, must call the elders of the church. The New Testament records the expression *elder* (presbyter) soon after the founding of the church at Pentecost. In the Jerusalem church, the elders were the representatives of the believers (Acts 11:30; 21:18). They were the men who exercised leadership in pastoral oversight of the congregation they represented (Acts 20:28; I Peter 5:1–4). On his first missionary journey, Paul and Barnabas appointed elders in each church (Acts 14:23) and Paul instructed Titus to appoint elders in every town in Crete (Titus 1:5).[38] Note that James uses the word *meeting* (synagogue) in 2:2 and the term *church* here. Obviously, these two terms are interchangeable in the Epistle of James.

c. "Pray over him and anoint him with oil in the name of the Lord." What does this mean? First, in the original the main emphasis is on prayer; the act of anointing with oil is secondary to prayer. This is evident from the next verse, where James affirms the power of prayer: "And the

---

38. The term *presbyteros* (elder) refers to the office of elder; the word *episcopos* (bishop) denotes the function of that office in the sense of overseeing the church. In Acts and in Paul's epistles the two expressions seem to mean the same thing (see Acts 20:17, 28; I Tim. 3:1; 5:17; Titus 1:5–9). Consult Günther Bornkamm, *TDNT*, vol. 6, pp. 664–68; Lothar Coenen, *NIDNTT*, vol. 1, pp. 199–200; Ronald S. Wallace, "Elder," *EDT*, p. 347.

prayer offered in faith will make the sick person well" (v. 15).[39] Second, in various places the Bible teaches that olive oil has medicinal qualities. Think of the Samaritan who applied oil and wine to the wounded man along the Jericho road—the oil soothed and the wine was antiseptic (Luke 10:34). When the twelve disciples went out on their first missionary journey, they "anointed many sick people with oil and healed them" (Mark 6:13).[40] In the time and culture of James, olive oil was used as common medicine. Third, oil often has a symbolic meaning in Scripture. Some interpreters take the word *oil* together with the phrase *in the name of the Lord,* and say that oil symbolizes the healing power of the Lord Jesus.[41] Fourth, the words of James must not be understood as an apostolic command to anoint the sick with oil. On the contrary, in his healing ministry Jesus did not resort to its use. In the Book of Acts, the apostles healed the sick on numerous occasions, but did not use oil (3:6; 5:15–16; 9:34; 14:8–10; 16:18; 28:8–9).[42] The emphasis is on prayer, not on oil.

d. "The prayer offered in faith will make the sick person well." Called to the bedside of the sick, the elders pour out their prayers in behalf of the sick. They depend fully on the Lord, who will grant healing and restoration. They offer their prayers in faith because they have the promise that the Lord will heal the sick and raise him from his bed.

e. "If he has sinned, he will be forgiven." The last part of this verse seems rather direct, yet seems to link sickness to sin.

The statement "if he has sinned, he will be forgiven" emphasizes the interrelatedness of body and soul. For instance, Jesus healed the paralytic spiritually when he said, "Your sins are forgiven," and physically by saying, "Get up, take your mat and go home" (Mark 2:5, 9–11). Jesus heals soul and body to make man complete.

Is illness due to sin? Not always. Let us take the life of Job as a case in point. Covered with painful boils, Job knew that his affliction had not come to him because of sin. God afflicted him to test his faith. Even though his friends urged him to confess his sin, Job maintained his innocence and integrity (see Job 6:28–30).

---

39. In the apocryphal book Sirach, the writer advises, "My son, when you are sick do not be negligent, but pray to the Lord, and he will heal you. Give up your faults and direct your hands aright, and cleanse your heart from all sin" (38:9–10).

40. In ancient times, Jewish households used oil as a common medicine to combat physical discomforts ranging from headaches to external wounds. Refer to SB, vol. 2, pp. 11–12; vol. 3, p. 759.

41. The Roman Catholic Church seeks to derive the sacrament of extreme unction from a symbolical interpretation of this text. In the middle of the sixteenth century, the Council of Trent defined this last rite to the dying as "truly and properly a Sacrament instituted by Christ our Lord and promulgated by blessed James the apostle." Consult Thomas W. Leahy, "The Epistle of James," in *The Jerome Bible Commentary,* ed. Raymond E. Brown, Joseph A. Fitzmeyer, and Roland E. Murphy, 2 vols. (Englewood Cliffs, N.J.: Prentice-Hall, 1968), vol. 2, p. 377.

42. Consult J. Wilkinson, "Healing in the Epistle of James," *ScotJT* 24 (1971): 326–45.

Nevertheless, the sick person ought to examine his spiritual life to "see if there is any offensive way in" him (Ps. 139:24). Physical ailments are often related to a guilty conscience. God often uses a period of sickness in the life of a person to have him come to self-examination and a plea for the forgiving grace of God (see Deut. 28:22, 27; Isa. 38:17; John 5:14; I Cor. 11:30). Once he recognizes his sin, uncovered for him by the Spirit of God, he must confess. God is ready to forgive sin we confess. In fact, he will never remind us of sin. When God cancels sin, he will never remember it—we stand before him as if we had never sinned at all.

Practical Considerations in 5:13–15

These well-known verses are among the most neglected and misunderstood in the church today. First, they are neglected. When someone is in trouble, he readily prays. But when someone is happy, we do not hear him sing songs of praise. Our technological age has taken over and we have become a society that listens, not a people that sings. Another point. Although pastors make regular hospital calls to visit the sick, the practice of calling the elders of the church to pray over the sick seems to belong to a bygone age. One of the tasks of the elders in the church is to pray for the sick when they are called to do so; nevertheless, this work is usually assigned to the pastor.

Second, these verses are often misunderstood. Many people have claimed the so-called gifts of healing (I Cor. 12:9, 28, 30) and therefore offer prayers in faith to make sick people well. They claim that the verses in the Epistle of James clearly state that "the prayer offered in faith will make the sick person well" (5:15). No one denies that God works healing miracles in the Christian community today in answer to the prayers of the saints. But what happens when God does not heal the sick? Is there a lack of faith? Is there unconfessed sin? Yes, but not always. Consider Paul, who had been given the gift of healing. He seems to have been unable to deliver his friend Epaphroditus from a lingering illness that almost caused his death (Phil. 2:27). Moreover, Paul writes, "I left Trophimus sick in Miletus" (II Tim. 4:20). Why did Paul not pray in faith so that his friends were healed instantaneously? Undoubtedly Paul prayed, but he learned from his own experience, when he pleaded for the removal of the thorn in his flesh, that God does not always heal us as we wish. He heard God say, "My grace is sufficient for you, for my power is made perfect in weakness" (II Cor. 12:9).

Greek Words, Phrases, and Constructions in 5:14–15

Verse 14

προσκαλεσάσθω—this aorist middle imperative discloses, first, that the initiative to call the elders must come from the sick person and, second, that the call is a single action.

ἀλείψαντες—from ἀλείφω (I anoint), this aorist active participle denotes either time (while anointing) or manner (by anointing).

177

Verse 15

τῆς πίστεως—this is a descriptive genitive. It refers to the prayer that is based on faith.

ἢ πεποιηκώς—a perfect active participle of ποιέω (I do) and the present subjunctive of εἰμί (I am) from the perfect periphrastic construction in the protasis of a conditional sentence. The use of the perfect expresses "broken continuity."[43]

---

3. Power of Prayer
5:16

Confession of sin and praying for one another are vital ingredients of the healing ministry in the Christian community. When sin is removed, the power of prayer becomes evident in its amazing effectiveness.

16a. Therefore confess your sins to each other and pray for each other so that you may be healed.

In this text we note three essential verbs: confess, pray, and heal.

a. "Confess." James says, "Therefore confess your sins to each other." With the adverb *therefore,* he links this sentence to the preceding verse where he writes of sickness, sin, and forgiveness. James uses the adverb to refer to the previous verse, to provide a basis for the succeeding sentence, and to stress the necessity of confessing sin.

Unconfessed sin blocks the pathway of prayer to God and at the same time is a formidable obstacle in interpersonal relations. That means, confess your sins not only to God but also to the persons who have been injured by your sins. Ask them for forgiveness!

"Confession cleanses the soul." That is a time-worn saying which does not lose its validity. Confession is a mark of repentance and a plea for forgiveness on the part of the sinner. When the sinner confesses his sin and asks for and receives remission, he experiences freedom from the burden of guilt.[44]

To whom do we confess our sins? The text says "to each other." James does not specify the church or the elders; rather, he speaks of mutual confession on a one-to-one basis within a circle of believers. He does not rule out that members of the church ought to confide in the pastor and elders (v. 14). Some sins concern all believers in the church and thus these sins ought to be confessed publicly. Other sins are private and need not be made known except to persons who are directly involved. Discretion and limitation, therefore, must guide the sinner who wishes to confess his personal sins. Curtis Vaughan makes this telling observation:

---

43. Robertson, *Grammar,* p. 908.
44. Dieter Fürst, *NIDNTT,* vol. 1, p. 346. Among other passages consult Matt. 3:6; 6:12; Mark 1:5; I John 1:9.

But whereas the Roman Catholics have interpreted confession too narrowly, many of us may be tempted to interpret it too broadly. Confession of *all* our sins to *all* the brethren is not necessarily enjoined by James' statement. Confession is "the vomit of the soul" and can, if too generally and too indiscriminately made, do more harm than good.[45]

b. "Pray." The beauty of Christian fellowship comes to expression in the practice of mutual prayer after sins have been confessed and forgiven. The offender and the offended pray on behalf of each other; together they find spiritual strength and comfort in the Lord. In their prayers they visibly and audibly demonstrate reciprocity. The forgiven sinner prays for the spiritual welfare of his fellow believer, who in turn commends him to the mercies of God.

c. "Be healed." James states the purpose for confessing sin and praying for each other by saying, "so that you may be healed." He is purposely vague in this statement; that is, he fails to mention whether he means physical or spiritual healing, actual or possible healing, individual or corporate healing. What is certain, however, is that when believers confess their sins to each other and pray for one another, a healing process takes place. And that can be applied to any situation.

16b. The prayer of a righteous man is powerful and effective.

Who is this righteous man? We are inclined to look to spiritual giants, to the heroes of the faith, and to men and women of God. In our opinion they are the people who through prayer are able to move mountains. But James mentions no names, except that of Elijah with the qualification that he is "just like us" (v. 17). He means to say that any believer whose sins have been forgiven and who prays in faith is righteous. When he prays, his prayers are "powerful and effective."

Both prayer and the answer to prayer are powerful and effective. The one does not cancel the other. That is, prayer offered in faith by a forgiven believer is a powerful and effective means to approach the throne of God. And, God "rewards those who earnestly seek him" (Heb. 11:6), for his answers to prayer are indeed powerful and effective.[46]

---

45. Curtis Vaughan, *James: A Study Guide* (Grand Rapids: Zondervan, 1969), p. 120. The *Didache* (also known as the *Teaching of the Twelve Apostles*), which in its original form probably dates from the first century, has this admonition: "In the congregation thou shalt confess thy transgressions, and thou shalt not betake thyself to prayer with an evil conscience. This is the way of life." *The Apostolic Fathers*, 2 vols., vol. 1, *The Didache*, 4:14 (LCL).

46. Translations of James 5:16b vary because the Greek participle *is at work* can be translated either in the passive or in the middle voice. Although the evidence for either position is impressive, on the basis of usage in a number of New Testament passages (see the constructions in Rom. 7:5; II Cor. 4:12; Eph. 3:20; II Thess. 2:7) translators seem to favor the middle voice. Consult Bauer, p. 265. Also consult Mayor, *James*, pp. 177–79; and an article by K. W. Clark on "The meaning of *energeo* and *katargeo* in the New Testament," *JBL* 54 (1935): 93–101.

Practical Considerations in 5:16

Scripture provides numerous examples of the power of prayer. Here are a few chosen at random:

Joshua prayed and the sun stood still (Josh. 10:12–13)
Elijah prayed and the widow's son came back to life (I Kings 17:19–22)
Elisha prayed and the Shunammite's son was restored to life (II Kings 4:32–35)
Hezekiah prayed and 185,000 Assyrian soldiers were slain (Isa. 37:21, 36)
The Jerusalem church prayed and Peter was released from prison (Acts 12:5–10)

Scripture portrays these people as ordinary men and women who sinned, sought forgiveness, prayed in faith, and received divine answers to prayer. In short, they are our kind of people.

Greek Words, Phrases, and Constructions in 5:16

εὔχεσθε—the present middle imperative denotes continued action. The variant reading προσεύχεσθε, which is compound but identical in meaning to the single verb εὔχεσθε, occurs eighty-seven times in the New Testament as compared to seven times for the single form. Applying the rule that the reading which is more unusual is probably the original, I accept the single verb form.

ἐνεργουμένη—the "transitive sense [of the verb] seems best" in the translation *"powerful in its effect."*[47]

4. Example
5:17–18

James brings his discussion on prayer to a conclusion by turning to Scripture. He refers to the prophet Elijah and presents his prayer life as an example to his readers.

17. Elijah was a man just like us. He prayed earnestly that it would not rain, and it did not rain on the land for three and a half years. 18. Again he prayed, and the heavens gave rain, and the earth produced its crops.

Out of numerous names of people who are known as prayer warriors (compare I Sam. 12:23), James chooses that of Elijah. In the first century he seems to have been credited with having superhuman attributes. The

47. Moule, *Idiom-Book*, p. 26.

Jews held Elijah in high esteem, as we learn from the New Testament. They regarded him as the forerunner of the Messiah, as the prophet Malachi had prophesied, and expected his return (4:5). Moreover, the name of Elijah is prominent in all four Gospels.[48]

a. James says, "Elijah was a man just like us" (compare Acts 14:15). With that remark he intimates that the Old Testament prophet was an ordinary human being like anyone else; he had to cope with fears, periods of depression, and physical limitations (I Kings 19:1–9). But James also discloses that we, like Elijah, are able to avail ourselves of the power of prayer.

b. "He prayed earnestly that it would not rain." We infer from I Kings 18:42 that Elijah prayed for rain, but we find no indications anywhere that relate to Elijah's prayer for drought. We assume that for this information James relied on a Jewish oral tradition.

c. "And it did not rain in the land for three and a half years." We encounter the same thought in the sermon Jesus delivered in his hometown synagogue in Nazareth: "I assure you that there were many widows in Israel in Elijah's time, when the sky was shut for three and a half years and there was a severe famine throughout the land" (Luke 4:25).

From what source did Jesus and James receive the information on the duration of the drought? The Old Testament record shows only that "in the third year" of the drought God told Elijah to go to Ahab (I Kings 18:1). That is not the same as three years and a half. From Jewish sources we learn that the expression *three and a half years* is an idiom which, because of frequent usage, came to mean "for quite some time."[49] Therefore, we ought to take the expression figuratively, not literally.

Furthermore, the Jewish custom of counting part of a unit of time as a full unit sheds additional light on our understanding of the text. A striking example, of course, is the duration of Jesus' death and burial (from late afternoon on Friday until early Sunday morning). Yet this period is counted as three days and three nights (Matt. 12:40). Similarly, the time of the famine during the days of Elijah may not have been exactly three and a half years.[50]

d. "Again he prayed, and the heavens gave rain, and the earth produced its crops." Man is able to do amazing things but he cannot change the weather. Nevertheless, James presents the prophet Elijah as a man

---

48. The name occurs nine times in Matthew, nine times in Mark, eight times in Luke, twice in John's Gospel, once each in Romans and James. The writer of Sirach furnishes an insight into the thinking of the people during intertestamental times. He extols the virtues and accomplishments of the prophet Elijah by depicting him as a superhuman being (Sir. 48:1–11).

49. Refer to SB, vol. 3, pp. 760–61. For additional information consult Mayor, *James*, pp. 180–81; and Ropes, *James*, p. 311.

50. Refer to F. W. Grosheide, *De Brief aan de Hebreeën en de Brief van Jakobus* (Kampen: Kok, 1955), p. 415.

who, through prayer, influenced the weather. The prophet assumed a posture that indicates he prayed earnestly and presumably for some time (I Kings 18:42–44). As a result of Elijah's prayer the drought ended. God listened to the prayer of his servant, ended the dry spell, and gave abundant rain to produce an eventual harvest sufficient for man and beast.

Greek Words, Phrases, and Constructions in 5:17–18

Verse 17

προσευχῇ προσηύξατο—literally "he prayed in prayer," this verb in the aorist middle indicative is preceded by a noun in the dative—a dative of manner. The construction is "like the Hebrew infinitive absolute which is reproduced by the Greek instrumental" (dative).[51] The translation of this particular dative is adverbial to express the intensity of the verb: "he prayed earnestly."

τοῦ μὴ βρέξαι—this is the articular infinitive construction with the negative particle as a request (an indirect command) after the verb *to pray*. The infinitive in the aorist tense indicates single action.

ἐπὶ τῆς γῆς—that is, on the land of Israel.

Verse 18

ἡ γῆ—the earth (ground) as the complementary part of heaven (sky) brings forth its fruit.

---

19 My brothers, if one of you should wander from the truth and someone should bring him back, 20 remember this: Whoever turns a sinner from the error of his way will save him from death and cover over a multitude of sins.

E. Rescuing the Wayward
5:19–20

James continues the theme of patience in these last two verses of his epistle. The conclusion lacks the anticipated greetings and benediction, so that the ending is not that of a letter but of a book. Nevertheless, the address remains personal and intimate.

19. My brothers, if one of you should wander from the truth and someone should bring him back, 20. remember this: Whoever turns a sinner from the error of his way will save him from death and cover over a multitude of sins.

In these last two verses of his epistle James stresses the corporate responsibility Christians have toward one another. They not only should confess their sins and pray together; they also should exercise spiritual care that is mutual and beneficial. This care should be administered to the

---

51. Robertson, *Grammar*, p. 531.

individual believer through private counseling and to the church through the preaching of the Word.

a. *Condition.* After the final address "my brothers,"[52] James writes a conditional sentence that has a lengthy first part with two different subjects ("one of you" and "someone"), followed by a short second part that consists of an imperative ("remember this").

"If one of you should wander." James singles out the individual in the community when he refers to one or any one (vv. 13, 14). If someone belonging to the church happens to wander from the truth either on his own volition or under the influence of others (see 1:16), the believers ought to know that they are responsible for the spiritual welfare of this wandering brother or sister. In a sense, James proclaims the same message of urgency that the writer of the Epistle to the Hebrews communicates:

> See to it, brothers, that none of you has a sinful, unbelieving heart that turns away from the living God. But encourage one another daily, as long as it is called Today, so that none of you may be hardened by sin's deceitfulness. [3:12–13]

The readers ought to practice mutual care (Gal. 6:1), so that the believers continue to adhere to the truth.

"Wander from the truth." In effect James admonishes the people not to wander from God's revelation. Truth, then, is the fullness of the gospel. Already he has informed them that they received their spiritual birth "through the word of truth" (1:18) and has counseled them not to deny the truth (3:14).

"If . . . someone should bring him back." Erring members of the church are not necessarily passively waiting to be brought back to the truth. They are not like sheep that have gone astray and are waiting patiently for the shepherd to rescue them. Tactfully reproving a person who is wandering from the truth is one of the most difficult tasks in the work of the church. Numerous pastors, elders, deacons, and church leaders have yielded to the temptation of placing erring members on the inactive list of the church rolls. Yet with loving concern, the church must seek out those who are wandering from the truth and urge them to come back.

"Remember this." Actually, the Greek puts it this way: "Someone who is bringing the sinner back to the truth *must know* that he who turns a sinner away from his error will save him from death and cover over a multitude of sins." This rule of conduct is so well known that James considers it sufficient to state it as a simple reminder.

b. *Rule.* The writer of the Epistle to the Hebrews appeals to the readers to exercise their corporate responsibility toward the individual church member who drifts away from the truth. James, however, is even more

---

52. The address *brothers* or *my brothers* appears fifteen times in the Epistle of James. In 2:1 and 5:19 the expression *my brothers* stands first in the original sentence and thus receives emphasis.

direct; he addresses the members of the church individually and shows them their responsibility.

"Whoever turns a sinner away from his error." Any member of the congregation knows that he or she must care for the spiritual needs of a fellow member. If someone of the church wanders from the truth and falls into one of Satan's traps, the other members must be prepared to rescue the wayward. If we fail to warn or speak out, we ourselves are guilty, for God holds us responsible (Ezek. 3:17–19). We are our brother's keeper. Wisely and tactfully, therefore, we must point out to our brother the error of his conduct and restore him gently.

"Will save him." Outside the church are countless people trapped in sin and unable to turn from the error of their way. These, too, must hear the gospel of salvation. At the beginning of the twentieth century, in 1912 to be precise, A. T. Robertson wrote these remarkable words that have not lost their significance:

> It is enough to discourage any social worker in the slums or in the tenement districts of our cities to see the hopeless condition in which the victims live. Drugs have fastened some with clamps of steel; drink has fired the blood of others; cigarettes have deadened the will of others; and immorality has hurled still others into the pit. They stumble into the rescue halls, "cities of refuge" in our cities. Happy are those who know how to save souls like these who have known better days and who have gone down into the valley of sin and sorrow.[53]

"From death." When we reach out to rescue the one who is perishing in sin, we seek to save his soul. We see a sinner in danger of dying an eternal death and about to be excluded from eternal life.[54] We must remember, however, that God uses us as instruments to restore the spiritual relationship between God and man. Salvation, then, is and remains God's work. We are only fellow workers for God (I Cor. 3:9).

"And cover over a multitude of sins." This last statement of this verse ought not to be taken literally, for man is unable to cover sin. Scripture teaches that not man but God has the authority to forgive. The expression *cover over* implicitly refers to God's act of forgiving sin (see for example Ps. 32:1; 85:2).

A line in the Book of Proverbs reveals a parallel: "Love covers over all wrongs" (10:12; and compare I Peter 4:8). What is James trying to convey with this allusion to Proverbs? Why does he say that the believer covers "a multitude of sins"? Says Calvin, "James teaches here something higher, that is, that sins are blotted out before God; as though he had said, Solomon has declared this as the fruit of love, that it covers sins; but

---

53. A. T. Robertson, *Studies in the Epistle of James,* rev. and ed. Heber F. Peacock (Nashville: Broadman, 1959), p. 197.

54. Günther Harder, *NIDNTT,* vol. 3, p. 685.

there is no better or more excellent way of covering them than when they are wholly abolished before God."[55]

When God forgives sin, he accepts the sinner as if he had never sinned. He removes sin as far as the east is from the west (Ps. 103:12) and covers the sinner with the pristine mantle of righteousness.[56] Of course, God forgives the sinner on the basis of the sacrifice of Jesus Christ. In this last verse of his epistle, however, James refers not to the meritorious work of Jesus but to God's gracious act of forgiving sinners. His intention is to show that forgiven Christians ought to work together for the mutual well-being of the church.

Greek Words, Phrases, and Constructions in 5:19–20

Verse 19

πλανηθῇ—the aorist passive subjunctive of the verb πλανάω (I wander, go astray) is part of the protasis in a conditional sentence. The subjunctive denotes probability. This verb form is open to two interpretations: as a true passive, "to be led astray," or a deponent (middle), "to go astray on one's own accord." Both explanations are possible and acceptable at the same time.

τις . . . τις—these two indefinite pronouns represent two different subjects. The first one relates to the sinner, the second one to the believer who turns the sinner away from his error.

Verse 20

γινωσκέτω—this is the present active imperative in the third person singular. Some ancient manuscripts have the reading γινώσκετε (the second person plural present active imperative). This reading "appears to be an amelioration, having been introduced either in order to conform to the address (ἀδελφοί μου, v. 19), or in order to avoid ambiguity of who is to be regarded (the converted or the converter) as the subject of the verb."[57]

αὐτοῦ ἐκ θανάτου—the reading which has the possessive pronoun following ψυχήν (soul) is preferred. The transfer of αὐτοῦ in some manuscripts to the position after θανάτου seems to have been caused by uncertainty over the identity of ψυχήν.

---

55. Calvin, *James*, p. 362.

56. Some interpreters say that the sins of the *converter*, not those of the *converted*, are forgiven as a reward for his evangelistic work. Among others, consult Ropes, *James*, pp. 315–16; Mayor, *James*, p. 185; C. Leslie Mitton, *The Epistle of James* (Grand Rapids: Eerdmans, 1966), p. 216. Eduard Schweizer, however, understands the phrases *save him from death* and *cover over a multitude of sins* to refer to the *converted*. He bases this on the apparent quotation (Prov. 10:12) which points to the sinner, and the words *multitude of sins* that "could hardly be spoken of in relation to the monitor" (*converter*). *TDNT*, vol. 9, p. 652. Also Davids notes that these two phrases relate to the same person. See his *James*, p. 201.

57. Bruce M. Metzger, *A Textual Commentary on the Greek New Testament*, corrected ed. (London and New York: United Bible Societies, 1975), pp. 685–86.

Summary of Chapter 5

In the first few verses of this chapter, James rebukes the rich who have hoarded wealth in their spiritual blindness and who find that their wealth has become useless. They have gained their wealth by neglecting to pay the harvesters who mowed their fields; they squandered it by living in luxury and self-indulgence; and they brutally oppressed the innocent, even to the point of killing them.

Next, James exhorts the readers of his epistle to exercise patience and to stand firm in expectation of the Lord's coming. He resorts to the use of examples (the farmer, the prophets, and Job) to accentuate his exhortation. Knowing the characteristics of his people, he admonishes them not to use oaths but to speak the truth at all times.

In the last section of the chapter, the writer presents a few instructions pertaining to wholesome Christian living in times of adversity, happiness, sickness, and sin. He stresses prayer as a source of power and illustrates this by citing an example from the life of the prophet Elijah.

In his final remark, James reminds the readers of their corporate responsibility toward the person who wanders from the truth. The members of the church must administer spiritual care to the wayward and bring him to repentance, so that he may live and his sins be forgiven. William Walsham How gave poetic expression to this truth when he said,

> The captive to release,
> To God the lost to bring,
> To teach the way of life and peace—
> It is a Christ-like thing.

Select Bibliography

Commentaries

Adamson, James B. *The Epistle of James.* New International Commentary on the New Testament series. Grand Rapids: Eerdmans, 1976.

Bengel, John Albert. *Gnomon of the New Testament.* Edited by Andrew R. Fausset. 4 vols. 7th ed. Vol. 4. Edinburgh: T. and T. Clark, 1877.

Blackman, E. C. *The Epistle of James.* London: SCM, 1957.

Burdick, Donald W. *James.* Vol. 12, the *Expositor's Bible Commentary,* edited by Frank E. Gaebelein. 12 vols. Grand Rapids: Eerdmans, 1981.

Calvin, John. *Commentaries on the Catholic Epistles: The Epistle of James.* Edited and translated by John Owen. Grand Rapids: Eerdmans, 1948.

Davids, Peter H. *The Epistle of James: A Commentary on the Greek Text.* New International Greek Testament Commentary series. Grand Rapids: Eerdmans, 1982.

Deissmann, Adolf. *Bible Studies.* Translated by Alexander Grieve. Edinburgh: T. and T. Clark, 1923. Reprint. Winona Lake, Ind.: Alpha, 1979.

Dibelius, Martin. *James: A Commentary on the Epistle of James.* Revised by Heinrich Greeven, translated by Michael A. Williams, edited by Helmut Köster. Hermeneia: A Critical and Historical Commentary on the Bible. Philadelphia: Fortress, 1976.

Grosheide, F. W. *De Brief aan de Hebreeën en de Brief van Jakobus.* Kampen: Kok, 1955.

Hiebert, D. Edmond. *The Epistle of James: Tests of a Living Faith.* Chicago: Moody, 1979.

Johnstone, Robert. *A Commentary on James.* 1871. Reprint. Edinburgh: Banner of Truth Trust, 1977.

Laws, Sophie. *A Commentary on the Epistle of James.* Harper's New Testament Commentaries. San Francisco: Harper and Row, 1980.

Lenski, R. C. H. *The Interpretation of the Epistle to the Hebrews and of the Epistle of James.* Columbus: Wartburg, 1946.

Mayor, Joseph B. *The Epistle of St. James.* 1913. Reprint. Grand Rapids: Zondervan, 1946.

Mitton, C. Leslie. *The Epistle of James.* Grand Rapids: Eerdmans, 1966.

Moffatt, James. *The General Epistles: James, Peter, and Judas.* New York and London: Harper and Brothers, n.d.

Mussner, Franz. *Der Jakobusbrief.* 2d ed. Herder Theologischer Kommentar zum Neuen Testament series. Freiburg: Herder, 1967.

187

Plummer, Alfred. *The General Epistles of St. James and St. Jude.* New York: A. C. Armstrong and Son, n.d.

Reicke, Bo. *The Epistles of James, Peter, and Jude.* Garden City, N.Y.: Doubleday, 1964.

Roberts, J. W. *The Letter of James.* Austin, Tex.: Sweet, 1977.

Robertson, A. T. *Practical and Social Aspects of Christianity: The Wisdom of James.* New York: Hodder and Stoughton, 1915.

————. *Studies in the Epistle of James.* Revised and edited by Heber F. Peacock. Nashville: Broadman, 1959. Reprint of *Practical and Social Aspects of Christianity: The Wisdom of James.*

Robinson, J. A. T. *Redating the New Testament.* Philadelphia: Westminster, 1976.

Ropes, James Hardy. *A Critical and Exegetical Commentary on the Epistle of James.* International Critical Commentary series. 1916. Reprint. Edinburgh: T. and T. Clark, 1961.

Ross, Alexander. *The Epistles of James and John.* New International Commentary on the New Testament series. Grand Rapids: Eerdmans, 1954.

Sevenster, J. N. *Do You Know Greek?* Leiden: Brill, 1968.

Sidebottom, E. M. *James, Jude, and 2 Peter.* Century Bible series. London: Nelson; Greenwood, S.C.: Attic, 1967.

Stevenson, Herbert F. *James Speaks for Today.* London: Marshall, Morgan and Scott, 1966.

Stringfellow, William. *Count It All Joy: Reflections on Faith, Doubt, and Temptation Seen Through the Letter of James.* Grand Rapids: Eerdmans, 1967.

Sweeting, George. *How to Solve Conflicts.* Chicago: Moody, 1973.

Tasker, R. V. G. *The General Epistle of James: An Introduction and Commentary.* Tyndale New Testament Commentaries. Grand Rapids: Eerdmans, 1957.

Vaughan, Curtis. *James: A Study Guide.* Grand Rapids: Zondervan, 1969.

Warfield, B. B. *The Lord of Glory.* London: Hodder and Stoughton, 1907. Reprint. Grand Rapids: Zondervan, n.d.

Williams, R. R. *The Letters of John and James.* The Cambridge Bible Commentary series. Cambridge: At the University Press, 1965.

Zodhiates, Spiros. *The Epistle of James and the Life of Faith.* vol. 1, *The Work of Faith;* vol. 2, *The Labor of Love;* vol. 3, *The Patience of Hope;* vol. 4, *The Behavior of Belief.* Grand Rapids: Eerdmans, 1959–66.

Related Books and Articles

Bird, John L. *Faith That Works: A Study Guide on the Book of James.* Grand Rapids: Zondervan, 1965.

Cranfield, C. E. B. "The Message of James." *Scottish Journal of Theology* 18 (1965): 182–93, 338–45.

Forbes, P. B. R. "The Structure of the Epistle of James." *Evangelical Quarterly* 44 (1972): 147–53.

Gaebelein, Frank E. *The Practical Epistle of James: Studies in Applied Christianity.* Great Neck, N.Y.: Doniger and Raughley, 1955.

Gwinn, Ralph A. *The Epistle of James: A Study Manual.* Grand Rapids: Baker, 1967.

Ironside, H. A. *Expository Notes on the Epistle of James.* Neptune, N.J.: Loizeaux, 1947.

Kelly, Earl. *James: A Practical Primer for Christian Living.* Nutley, N.J.: Craig, 1969.

Krutza, William J., and Philip P. DiCicco. *Living That Counts: A Study Guide to the Book of James.* Grand Rapids: Baker, 1972.

Longenecker, Richard N. *The Christology of Early Jewish Christianity.* Studies in Biblical Theology, no. 17, 2d series. Naperville, Ill.: Allenson, 1970.

Mussner, Franz. " 'Direkte' und 'indirekte' Christologie im Jakobusbrief." *Catholica* [Münster] 24 (1970): 111–17.

Prins, P., and H. A. Wiersinga. *Om Het Goud Des Geloofs.* Kampen: Kok, n.d.

Tools

Bauer, Walter, W. F. Arndt, F. W. Gingrich, and F. W. Danker. *A Greek-English Lexicon of the New Testament and Other Early Christian Literature.* 2d ed. Chicago: University of Chicago Press, 1979.

Blass, Friedrich, and Albert Debrunner. *A Greek Grammar of the New Testament and Other Early Christian Literature.* Translated and revised by Robert Funk. Chicago: University of Chicago Press, 1961.

Bromiley, Geoffrey W., ed. *The International Standard Bible Encyclopedia.* Rev. ed. 4 vols. Grand Rapids: Eerdmans, 1979–.

Brown, Colin, ed. *New International Dictionary of New Testament Theology.* 3 vols. Grand Rapids: Zondervan, 1975–78.

Dana, H. E., and Julius R. Mantey. *A Manual Grammar of the Greek New Testament.* New York: Macmillan, 1967.

Elwell, Walter A., ed. *Evangelical Dictionary of Theology.* Grand Rapids: Baker, 1984.

Eusebius. *Ecclesiastical History.* 2 vols. Translated by J. E. L. Oulton. Loeb Classical Library series. Cambridge: Harvard University Press, 1980.

Farstad, Arthur L., and Zane C. Hodges. *The Greek New Testament According to the Majority Text.* Nashville and New York: Nelson, 1982.

Guthrie, Donald. *New Testament Introduction.* Downers Grove: Inter-Varsity, 1971.

———. *New Testament Theology.* Downers Grove: Inter-Varsity, 1981.

Hanna, Robert. *A Grammatical Aid to the Greek New Testament.* Grand Rapids: Baker, 1983.

Henry, Carl F. H., ed. *Baker's Dictionary of Christian Ethics.* Grand Rapids: Baker, 1973.

Josephus. *Antiquities.* Translated by Henry St. John Thackeray. Loeb Classical Library series. Cambridge: Harvard University Press, 1976–81.

Kittel, Gerhard, and Gerhard Friedrich, eds. *Theological Dictionary of the New Testament.* Translated by Geoffrey W. Bromiley. 10 vols. Grand Rapids: Eerdmans, 1964–76.

Ladd, G. E. *A Theology of the New Testament.* Grand Rapids: Eerdmans, 1974.

Metzger, Bruce M. *A Textual Commentary on the Greek New Testament.* Corrected edition. London and New York: United Bible Societies, 1975.

Moule, C. F. D. *An Idiom-Book of New Testament Greek.* 2d ed. Cambridge: At the University Press, 1960.

Nestle, Eberhard, and Kurt Aland, rev. *Novum Testamentum Graece.* 26th ed. Stuttgart: Deutsche Bibelstiftung, 1981.

Robertson, A. T. *A Grammar of the Greek New Testament in the Light of Historical Research.* Nashville: Broadman, 1934.

Soulen, Richard N. *Handbook of Biblical Criticism.* 2d ed. Atlanta: John Knox, 1981.

Strack, H. L., and P. Billerbeck. *Kommentar zum Neuen Testament aus Talmud und Midrasch.* 5 vols. München: Beck, 1922–28.

Tenney, Merrill C., ed. *The Zondervan Pictorial Encyclopedia of the Bible.* 5 vols. Grand Rapids: Zondervan, 1975.

Thayer, Joseph H. *A Greek-English Lexicon of the New Testament.* New York, Cincinnati, and Chicago: American Book Company, 1889.

Vine, W. E., Merrill F. Unger, and William White, Jr. *An Expository Dictionary of Biblical Words.* Nashville and New York: Nelson, 1984.

Wikenhauser, Alfred. *New Testament Introduction.* New York: Herder and Herder, 1963.

Zahn, Theodor. *Introduction to the New Testament.* 3 vols. Edinburgh: T. and T. Clark, 1909.

Exposition
of the
Epistles of John

Introduction

Outline

T he second and the third epistles of John display the characteristics of a letter. They include the title of the sender, the addressees, the greetings, the personal message, and the salutations at the end. Although they lack information on place and date, these letters attributed to John are comparable in form to the epistles written by Paul or Peter.

The First Epistle of John, however, is different. It is devoid of names of sender and recipients, of greetings and benediction, and of places of origin and destination. This epistle could be called a theological treatise. But this designation does not quite fit, because the letter shows the personal touch of the writer from beginning to end. He tenderly addresses the recipients as "dear friends" or "dear children," and uses the personal pronouns *we* and *I*. The tone of this document definitely indicates that it is a letter—not a treatise—from a respected and revered writer to recipients who knew him well.

A. Who Wrote the Epistles?

1. External Evidence

What do writers of the second and third centuries say about the Epistles of John? Polycarp, who reportedly was a disciple of John, wrote a letter to the church at Philippi around A.D. 110. The resemblance is plain to see in these specific references:

Philippians 7.1	*I John 4:2–3*
"For everyone who does not confess that Jesus Christ has come in the flesh is an antichrist"; and whosoever does not confess the testimony of the Cross is of the devil.[1]	Every spirit that acknowledges that Jesus Christ has come in the flesh is from God, but every spirit that does not acknowledge Jesus is not from God. This is the spirit of the antichrist [see 3:8].

Next, Papias, who was bishop of Hierapolis (near Laodicea) around A.D. 125, "used quotations from the first Epistle of John."[2] We are told by Irenaeus, who was bishop of Lyons and Vienne in southern France around A.D. 185, that Papias was "the hearer of John, [and] a companion

---

1. Polycarp, Philippians 7.1, in *The Apostolic Fathers*, 2 vols., vol. 1 (LCL).
2. Eusebius *Ecclesiastical History* 3. 29. 17 (LCL).

of Polycarp."[3] We can rely, therefore, on the voices of witnesses who personally knew John. In the beginning of the second century, these two disciples of John used his first epistle and implicitly bear witness to its authenticity. If this epistle had not originated with John, they would have been able to make this known.

Near the end of the second century, Irenaeus not only quoted from the epistle but also attributed it to John, the disciple of the Lord.[4] Next, the Muratorian Canon, which presumably originated about A.D. 175, states: "Indeed the Epistle of Jude and two of the above-mentioned John are accepted in the Catholic [church or epistles]." Because the Latin original is rather imprecise, scholars have difficulty determining the exact meaning of this saying.

In the third century, a number of writers frequently use John's Epistle and testify that it belongs to John. They are Clement of Alexandria, Origen, Tertullian, and Dionysius the disciple of Origen.

What external support is there for the second and third epistles of John? Due to their brevity and relatively minor importance in the context of the New Testament, we are not surprised that the evidence is somewhat meager. In fact, we stand amazed that in the providence of God these short letters are extant and are incorporated in the canon.

Irenaeus, who was a disciple of Polycarp, both quotes from the second epistle (vv. 10–11) and mentions the apostle John by name. In his discourse against the Marcosians he writes, "And John, the disciple of the Lord, has intensified their condemnation, when he desires us not even to address to them the salutation of 'good-speed;' for, says he, 'He that bids them be of good-speed is a partaker with their evil deeds.' "[5] At another place he quotes verses 7 and 8 of the second epistle and attributes them to the disciple of the Lord, that is, John.[6]

In the third century, Clement of Alexandria indicates that he is familiar with a second epistle, because he refers to the "longer epistle" of John.[7] Another Alexandrian of that century, Dionysius, discusses the authorship of the Epistles of John and says, "Nay, not even in the second or third extant epistles of John, although they are short, is John set forth by name."[8] And his contemporary Origen notes that he is acquainted with John's two shorter epistles, but adds, "not all say that these are genuine."[9] Also Eusebius, a century later, puts the second and third epistles among

---

3. Ibid. 3. 39. 1 (LCL).
4. Irenaeus *Against Heresies* 3. 16. 5, 8, in *The Ante-Nicean Fathers,* vol. 1.
5. Ibid. 1. 16. 3.
6. Ibid. 3. 16. 8.
7. Clement of Alexandria *Stromata* 2. 15. 66.
8. Eusebius has recorded the letters of Dionysius in *Ecclesiastical History* 7. 25. 11 (vol. 2, p. 201 [LCL]).
9. Eusebius *Ecclesiastical History* 6. 25. 10 (LCL).

the so-called disputed books.[10] But toward the end of that century the councils of Hippo Regius (393) and Carthage (397) acknowledged the canonicity of John's epistles.

2. Internal Evidence

The similarity between the Gospel of John and the epistles is striking in verbal parallels and choice of words. First, we take a few examples from John's first epistle and his Gospel:

First Epistle	Gospel
We write this to make our joy complete [1:4]	"Ask and you will receive, and your joy will be complete" [16:24]
But whoever hates his brother is in the darkness and walks around in the darkness; he does not know where he is going, because the darkness has blinded him [2:11]	"Walk while you have the light, before darkness overtakes you. The man who walks in the dark does not know where he is going" [12:35]
And this is his command:. . .to love one another as he commanded us [3:23]	"A new commandment I give you: Love one another. As I have loved you, so you must love one another" [13:34][11]

The vocabulary in both the epistle and the Gospel of John shows unmistakable similarity. Both books emphasize the same themes: love, light, truth, witness, and sonship. The expression *one and only Son* occurs in John 1:14, 18 [variant reading], 3:16, and I John 4:9. The Greek word *Paraclete* appears in John 14:16, 26; 15:26; 16:7 ("Counselor", NIV) and in I John 2:1 ("one who speaks to the Father in our defense," NIV).

Both the epistle and the Gospel reveal the literary use of contrast: life and death, light and darkness, truth and the lie, love and hate. The similarity in style and thoughts is striking indeed.

Moreover, the three epistles of John appear interrelated in thought and verbal expression. Cross-references abound among the three epistles and the Gospel, so the thought that the books have a common author becomes prominent. This thought stands out still more when we consider the greeting of the "elder" in the second and the third epistles:

II John 1	III John 1
The elder,	The elder,
To the chosen lady and her children,	To my dear friend Gaius,
whom I love in the truth.	whom I love in the truth.

---

10. Ibid. 3. 25. 3.

11. For a complete list of similarities between the first epistle and the Gospel, consult A. E. Brooke, *A Critical and Exegetical Commentary on the Johannine Epistles*, International Critical Commentary series (Edinburgh: Clark, 1964), pp. ii–iv. And see Raymond E. Brown, *The Epistles of John*, Anchor Bible, vol. 30 (Garden City, N.Y.: Doubleday, 1982), pp. 757–59.

II John 12	*III John 13–14*
I have much to write to you, but I do not want to use paper and ink. Instead, I hope to visit you and talk with you face to face.	I have much to write you, but I do not want to do so with pen and ink. I hope to see you soon, and we will talk face to face.

Since the length and format of these two epistles are the same, common authorship seems undeniable. Furthermore, the writer of the epistles speaks not merely as a local church official known as an "elder." In his address, he refers to himself as "*the* elder" (italics added). John indicates that his influence extends beyond local boundaries and is therefore universal. In short, he writes with apostolic authority.

3. Common Authorship

Did one author write the three epistles? If we approach the second and the third epistles first, we can assume that because of form, word choice, and style the same person most likely wrote these letters. In fact, the similarities in these two epistles strongly suggest that the letters come from the hand of one writer.

Next, if "the elder" composed II and III John, could the first epistle have come from his pen as well? In spite of the brevity of the second and third epistles, the verbal resemblances between them and I John and the Gospel are clearly recognizable.[12] Besides similarities, however, differences are also prominent. The writer identifies himself in the last two epistles but not in the first epistle. The author mentions the addressees of II and III John, although they are not known to us. He does not mention the recipients of his first epistle, even though he tenderly addresses them as "my dear children." The differences are of minor importance, so common authorship of the Johannine Epistles is probable. In fact, most scholars believe that one person wrote all three epistles.

4. Difficulties

If the writer of the second and third epistles is no one else than the apostle John, why does he refer to himself as "*the* elder?" He would have followed the custom of Paul and Peter if he had introduced himself as "John, an apostle of Jesus Christ." Peter, in his first epistle, calls himself "an apostle of Jesus Christ" (1:1) and appeals to the elders "as a fellow elder" (5:1). Although the contexts differ in respect to the First Epistle of

---

12. In his *Epistles of John*, Brown lists six of these resemblances for III John and fifteen for II John (see pp. 755–56).

Peter and the Second and Third Epistles of John, the fact remains that an apostle can be an elder. The term *elder* in these epistles is virtually equivalent to the expression *apostle*.

Many scholars, however, are not ready to equate the terms *elder* and *apostle* with reference to the epistles of John. They do not think it likely at all that the writer of II and III John is the apostle John, the son of Zebedee. In regard to III John, for instance, C. H. Dodd questions the author's apostolic authority. He asks, "Can we doubt that if he had possessed the apostolic dignity, he would have flung out a defiant 'John, apostle of Jesus Christ by the will of God,' and reduced Diotrephes to silence?"[13]

However, a well-known remark made by Papias in the first part of the second century is the crux of the issue. This remark Papias wrote in one of the five books on the "Interpretation of the Oracles of the Lord." Only fragments of these books have been preserved; they have been recorded by the fourth-century historian Eusebius. Here is the remark:

> And I shall not hesitate to append to the interpretations all that I ever learnt from the presbyters and remember well, for of their truth I am confident. . . . But if ever anyone came who had followed the presbyters, I inquired into the words of the presbyters, what Andrew or Peter or Philip or Thomas or James or John or Matthew or any other of the Lord's disciples, had said, and what Aristion and the presbyter John, the Lord's disciples, were saying. For I did not suppose that information from books would help me so much as the word of a living and surviving voice.[14]

In this lengthy quotation, Papias equates the terms *presbyters* and *disciples*. Note that the term *presbyter* occurs three times and refers to Jesus' disciples. That is, the names of the disciples of Jesus stand in apposition to and are an explanation of the word *presbyters*.

Papias, accordingly, informs the readers that he has gained information about the Lord directly from his disciples. He indicates that there were stages in the collecting of information. He uses the past tense when he writes, "I inquired into the words of the presbyters, what Andrew or Peter or Philip or Thomas or James or John or Matthew, or any other of the Lord's disciples, *had said*" (italics added). Then when most of them had passed away, he inquired into "what Aristion and the presbyter John, the Lord's disciples, *were saying*" (italics added).[15]

We know very little about Aristion, but we have a remark about the end

---

13. C. H. Dodd, *The Johannine Epistles*, Moffatt New Testament Commentary series (New York: Harper and Row, 1946), p. lxix.

14. Eusebius *Ecclesiastical History* 3. 39. 3–4 (LCL).

15. Refer to C. Steward Petrie, "The Authorship of 'The Gospel According to Matthew': A Reconsideration of the External Evidence," *NTS* 14 (1967): 17.

of John's life. According to Irenaeus, the apostle John lived "until the times of Trajan."[16] Trajan was emperor from A.D. 98 to 117. We conclude, then, that the apostle John was the only disciple of the Lord still alive at the end of the first century. Also, we understand Papias's remark that he sought information from "a living and surviving voice" rather than from books.

Is Papias referring to one person by the name of John or to two individuals? Does he call John a disciple and an elder, or is he introducing the apostle John and another person known as John the Elder? Eusebius comments on Papias's ambiguity:

> It is worth noting here that he twice counts the name of John, and reckons the first John with Peter and James and Matthew and the other Apostles, clearly meaning the evangelist, but by changing his statement places the second with the others outside the number of the Apostles, putting Aristion before him and clearly calling him a presbyter. This confirms the truth of the story of those who have said that there were two of the same name in Asia, and that there are two tombs at Ephesus both still called John's.[17]

In that same context, Eusebius calls Papias "a man of very little intelligence" and makes this judgment on the basis of Papias's millennial views. Eusebius disagrees with Papias's view of an earthly millennium in which Christ reigns as king. He is of the opinion that Papias received these notions "by a perverse reading of the apostolic accounts."[18] We are unable to determine the level of intelligence of Papias because his books are no longer extant. Yet we dare say that Eusebius is unusually harsh in judging Papias's intellectual capabilities in the light of doctrinal issues.

If we examine the life of John, we see that he filled the role of disciple, apostle, and elder. For three years John had been a disciple of Jesus; after Jesus' ascension he served as one of the twelve apostles; and in the church he became known as "the elder." Because John outlived all the other apostles, he is mentioned twice. Papias lists him among Jesus' disciples, whose voices were silenced by death, and he mentions John with Aristion (who was not a disciple) as a surviving voice that still witnesses for Jesus. We conclude, then, that although the wording of Papias is ambiguous, the intent is to stress that John, the disciple of the Lord and elder in the church, is the unique surviving witness for the Lord.

Is there any evidence for a person known as the elder John who was a contemporary of and successor to John? In the third century, Dionysius of Alexandria had heard that there were two tombs of John in Ephesus.

---

16. Irenaeus *Against Heresies* 2. 22. 5. Also see Eusebius, who writes, "And all the presbyters who had been associated in Asia with John, the disciple of the Lord, bear witness to his tradition, for he remained with them until the times of Trajan." *Ecclesiastical History* 3. 23. 3.

17. Eusebius *Ecclesiastical History* 3. 39. 5–6.

18. Ibid. 3. 39. 12–13.

Writing about John Mark, who left the company of Paul and Barnabas during their first missionary journey, he says, "But I think that there was a certain other [John] among those that were in Asia, since it is said both that there were two tombs at Ephesus, and that each of the two is said to be John's."[19]

Dionysius ascribes the Gospel and the epistles to John, the apostle, but he thinks that Revelation was composed by some other person with the name John. He shows that he has difficulties understanding Revelation and therefore does not believe that John, the son of Zebedee, wrote it.

Also Eusebius wants nothing to do with millennial views taken from Revelation. He sees in the wording of one of Papias's fragments the possibility of ascribing the Book of Revelation to another person known as John and thus mentions the existence of the apostle John and the presbyter John.

However, nothing is known about the so-called presbyter John, for even Polycrates, bishop at Ephesus near the end of the second century, is silent on this matter. In a letter addressed to a certain Victor and the church at Rome he mentions that John, "who lay on the Lord's breast," was buried in Ephesus.[20] But he fails to provide any information about a second tomb for a person known as the presbyter John. We hesitate, therefore, to make a distinction between the apostle John and the presbyter John as long as the evidence is insufficient to substantiate a decided difference.

Moreover, arguments that attempt to make adherence to common authorship for all three Johannine Epistles impossible are not compelling. In fact, scholars who espouse the view that John, the son of Zebedee, wrote the epistles can gain support from writers in the early Christian church. Some of these writers were disciples of John.

5. Objections

A number of scholars are not at all convinced that the apostle John is the writer of the Gospel and the epistles. They envision that John was surrounded by a group of disciples who wrote in behalf of the apostle. A school of writers, they claim, is responsible for the Johannine literature. Many of these writers were engaged in composing different parts of this literature. According to these scholars, writers in this school used the same vocabulary, diction, and style. Furthermore, the writers expressed a common theology, so that in respect to similarities and differences all their writings bore the telltale marks of belonging to the same school of thought; that is, a Johannine School.

The term *Johannine School* refers to the community in which the literature attributed to John (especially the Gospel and the epistles) was writ-

---

19. Ibid. 7. 25. 16; also see 3. 39. 6.
20. Ibid. 5. 24. 3.

ten. In this school, the apostle John functioned as leader, so that the individual writers actually composed the books in his name.[21]

This hypothesis, however, faces some objections. First, groups of writers usually compose collections of opinions on a given topic and write them in the form of short essays. They put these essays together in one book. We call such a book a symposium. But the Gospel and the epistles of John do not appear to be a collection of opinions that are held together by a common theme. Instead, the Gospel—and to a great extent the First Epistle of John—reveals progress and development, eyewitness reports, and personal details that focus attention on one author.

Next, proponents of the Johannine-school hypothesis have to demonstrate how disciples of the apostle John composed their writings that eventually became known as the Gospel and the epistles of John. That is, they have to show that John could not have written the Gospel and the epistles and that these documents had to come from the hand of his disciples. But their hypothesis merely assumes that not John but his followers wrote. For scholars who have not yet adopted this point of view but who believe that John, the son of Zebedee, is the writer of the Johannine literature, a mere assumption can hardly be called convincing evidence.[22]

6. Differences

Dodd maintains that differences between the Gospel of John and the first epistle are pronounced. These differences are, first of all, linguistic. They include style, the occurrence of certain verbs, a lack of some prepositions and particles, a simple vocabulary, and a limited use of grammatical idiom in the first epistle.

Besides, the Johannine writings display differences in religious background. For example, whereas the Gospel has many quotations from the Old Testament, the epistle has none. Semitisms that are numerous in the fourth Gospel are conspicuous by their absence in John's epistle.

And last, theological emphases are different in the Gospel and the first epistle. These differences pertain to eschatology, which in the epistle diverges from its presentation in the Gospel; interpretation of the death of Christ, which the writer of the epistle does in a form that hardly progresses beyond the elementary preaching of the gospel message; and the

---

21. Refer to R. Alan Culpepper, *The Johannine School: An Evaluation of the Johannine-School Hypothesis Based on an Investigation of the Nature of Ancient Schools*, Society of Biblical Literature Dissertation Series, no. 26 (Missoula, Mont.: Scholars Press, 1975), pp. 1–38. Also see Brown, *The Epistles of John*, pp. 108–12; Rudolf Schnackenburg, *Die Johannesbriefe*, Herder's Theologischer Kommentar zum Neuen Testament, 7th ed. (Freiburg: Herder, 1984), vol. 13, 3, p. 41; I. Howard Marshall, *The Epistles of John*, New International Commentary on the New Testament series (Grand Rapids: Eerdmans, 1978), p. 32; Stephen S. Smalley, *1, 2, 3 John*, Word Biblical Commentary (Waco: Word, 1984), vol. 51, p. xxii.

22. D. A. Carson, "Historical Tradition in the Fourth Gospel: After Dodd, What?" in *Gospel Perspectives, Studies of History and Tradition in the Four Gospels*, ed. R. T. France and David Wenham (Sheffield: JSOT Press, 1981), vol. 2, p. 134.

doctrine of the Holy Spirit, which is prominent in the Gospel but absent from the first epistle.[23]

Dodd's linguistic argument lost ground when a detailed study by W. G. Wilson on the linguistic evidence revealed that "in respect of important words there is less variation between the Fourth Gospel and I John than exists between I Corinthians and Philippians."[24] It is extremely difficult to maintain that two separate writings of a particular author must reveal the same linguistic features. It is also difficult to determine whether or not two separate writings which possess similar linguistic features come from the hand of more than one author. Especially when a writer addresses two different audiences or pursues different purposes, variations in vocabulary and idioms are unavoidable.

Thus, in another study, W. F. Howard points out that the reason for linguistic divergencies "may be found partly in the difference of subject-matter, in the class of writing, in the manner of composition and of dictation, partly also in external events and their effect upon the mind of the Christian pastor or leader and upon the needs of the Church."[25] Also, similarities in the language and thought of the Gospel and epistles provide sufficient evidence to indicate common authorship.

Dodd's differences pertaining to religious background are not consequential. Many scholars explain these differences in the light of the respective audiences of the Gospel and the epistles. The recipients of the epistles seem to have been Gentiles whose familiarity with Old Testament citations diverged from that of Jewish readers who read the Gospel.

Last, Dodd's theological emphases appear to have been overstated. For instance, although the expression *antichrist* appears three times in the first epistle (2:18, 22; 4:3) but never in the Gospel, a similar Johannine term, "prince of this world," occurs in John 12:31; 14:30; 16:11.[26] The interpretation of the death of Christ is expressed in the Gospel as "the Lamb of God, who takes away the sin of the world" (1:29) and in I John as "the atoning sacrifice for our sins, and not only for ours but also for the sins of the whole world" (2:2).[27] Finally, even though the Holy Spirit in person and work is prominent in the Gospel, the first epistle is not devoid of direct and indirect references to the Spirit (2:20, 27; 4:4; 5:8). In view of the evidence presented, be it in cursory form, the conclusion may be

---

23. Refer to Dodd, *The Johannine Epistles*, pp. xlvii–lvi; "The First Epistle of John and the Fourth Gospel," *Bulletin of the John Rylands Library* 21 (1937): 129–56.

24. W. G. Wilson, "An Examination of the Linguistic Evidence Addressed Against the Unity of Authorship of the First Epistle of John and the Fourth Gospel," *JTS* 49 (1948): 156.

25. W. F. Howard, "The Common Authorship of the Johannine Gospel and Epistles," *JTS* 48 (1947): 25. Also consult A. P. Salom, "Some Aspects of the Grammatical Style of I John," *JBL* 74 (1955): 96–102.

26. Refer to Donald Guthrie, *New Testament Introduction* (Downers Grove: Inter-Varsity, 1971), p. 880.

27. Consult Schnackenburg, *Die Johannesbriefe*, p. 37. Also refer to Donald W. Burdick, *The Letters of John the Apostle* (Chicago: Moody, 1985), p. 22.

drawn that "there hardly exists adequate reason to suppose another author for I John than for John."[28]

7. Personal References

The use of the first person plural in the opening verse of I John is striking. "That which was from the beginning, which we have heard, which we have seen with our eyes, which we have looked at and our hands have touched—this we proclaim concerning the Word of life" (1:1). In the succeeding verses (vv. 2–4), the writer continues to use the first person plural pronoun *we* to distinguish himself from his readers. When he resorts to using that pronoun in subsequent verses, he uses it comprehensively to include himself with the readers. See, for example, the verse frequently used in worship services: "If we confess our sins, he is faithful and just and will forgive us our sins and purify us from all unrighteousness" (1:9).

In the introductory verses (also see 4:14), John tells his readers that he is an eyewitness who saw Jesus, heard his voice, and touched him with his hands. His use of the words *we, us* and *our* must be understood exclusively. That is, he is communicating to his readers that he and his fellow disciples had the unique experience of seeing and hearing Jesus, but that the readers did not have this opportunity. Instead they receive the teachings of Jesus from one of the surviving disciples.[29]

What is the precise meaning of the pronoun *we* in 1:1–4? Here are a few interpretations:

1. "We" is equivalent to "I" because the writer employs the plural to indicate his authority in the church. He is the apostle John, who speaks with indisputable authority. But John's words are not dictatorial and haughty. In his writings he makes no mention of his apostolic office.

2. The author may use the pronoun *we* as an editorial "we." That is, he tries to avoid calling attention to himself alone, and therefore resorts to the general "we." But the so-called editorial "we" is too vague to be applicable here.

3. The pronoun *we* refers to a group of persons who have had the same experiences. They are the disciples of Jesus, who have been with the Lord Jesus, "beginning from John's baptism to the time when Jesus was taken up" (Acts 1:22). These persons are witnesses of Jesus' resurrection and form the distinct group that constitutes the circle of the twelve apostles. John, then, is "the last survivor of those who had heard and seen the Lord, the sole representative of His disciples, speaking in their name."[30]

---

28. Paul Feine, Johannes Behm, and Werner Georg Kümmel, *Introduction to the New Testament*, 14th rev. ed. (Nashville: Abingdon, 1965), p. 312.

29. Consult F. F. Bruce, *The Epistles of John* (1970; Grand Rapids: Eerdmans, 1979), p. 38.

30. Alfred Plummer, *The Epistles of St. John*, Cambridge Greek Testament for Schools and Colleges series (Cambridge: At the University Press, 1896), p. 14. B. F. Westcott has a similar observation: "St. John throughout this section uses the plural as speaking in the name of the apostolic body of which he was the last surviving representative." *The Epistles of St. John, The Greek Text, with Notes and Addenda* (1883; Grand Rapids: Eerdmans, 1966), p. 4.

4. Some scholars understand the "we" (vv. 1–4) to include the writer and the whole church. The writer, says Dodd, "speaks not exclusively for himself or for a restricted group, but for the whole Church to which the apostolic witness belongs," and he addresses the "you" who have no knowledge of the Father and the Son.[31] We demur. The recipients of the letter whom the author addresses repeatedly as "dear children" are not unbelievers. They are "the children of God" (3:1).

If the recipients are part of the church and part of the group Dodd mentions, then 1:3 means that this group—"We proclaim to you what we have seen and heard"—is addressing itself. Also, the addressees have not seen and heard Jesus and certainly have not touched him with their hands. Concludes Donald W. Burdick, "It is much easier to accept the more natural interpretation, which sees the author as an eyewitness, than to adopt Dodd's unnatural interpretation in order to avoid the eyewitness claim."[32]

5. Last, Raymond E. Brown understands the "we" in the introduction of I John in relation to the so-called Johannine School. They are the Johannine writers, "the tradition-bearers and interpreters who stand in a special relationship to the Beloved Disciple in their attempt to preserve his witness."[33] Brown is fully aware of the objection that Johannine writers could not say that they had touched Jesus with their own hands (1:1). He tries to remove the objection by suggesting that these people "participated in the sensation only vicariously."

The reader who accepts apostolic authorship, however, has no difficulties especially in the light of the testimony of eyewitnesses. For instance, Peter writes, "We did not follow cleverly invented stories when we told you about the power and coming of our Lord Jesus Christ, but we were eyewitnesses of his majesty" (II Peter 1:16). Only Jesus' original disciples can say and write that they touched him with their hands, as John states in the introductory verses of his first epistle. Consequently, we favor the third interpretation given.

J. R. W. Stott succinctly summarizes the explanation of the pronoun *we* in the prologue of I John (1:1–4).

> The first person plural is used not only of the verbs describing the historical experience, but also of the verbs describing the proclamation of it. The persons who make the announcement are the persons who had the experience. . . . It is they whose eyes have seen, ears heard and hands handled, whose mouths are opened to speak.[34]

---

31. Dodd, *The Johannine Epistles*, p. 16.
32. Burdick, *The Letters of John the Apostle*, p. 29.
33. Brown, *The Epistles of John*, p. 160.
34. J. R. W. Stott, *The Epistles of John: An Introduction and Commentary*, Tyndale New Testament Commentaries series (Grand Rapids: Eerdmans, 1964), pp. 31–32.

B. Who Received the Epistles?

The writer reveals himself as a man who speaks with authority and whose voice is revered. As a distinguished leader in the church, he addresses the readers without identifying himself in the first letter. That is, the recipients of the first epistle have no need to ask who sent it. They know because the writer appears to have been a long-time resident in their area; he has taught and preached in their churches.

The author addresses his readers with words of tender love. The address *my dear children* or *dear children* occurs numerous times (2:1, 12, 13, 18, 28; 3:7, 18; 4:4; 5:21) and indicates that the writer is advanced in age. As a father in the church, he considers his readers to be his spiritual offspring. He affectionately calls them "dear friends." Older translations render this term "beloved" (2:7; 3:2, 21; 4:1, 7, 11; also see III John 1, 2, 5, 11).

The author writes to the recipients in a personal manner by using the first person pronoun *I* repeatedly throughout the three epistles. The bond between writer and readers is intimate and strong. They know one another and detailed introductions are not needed.

Even though the author and the recipients were fully acquainted, the modern reader can only guess about the identity of these people when he carefully reads the internal evidence. The writer reveals himself indirectly and at the same time provides a number of details about the readers. Consequently, we rely on the written text to gain insight into the problems the author and his readers faced.

Apart from the tone of these letters which is marked by the virtues of love and truth, the writer nowhere leaves the impression that he is soft and weak.[35] On the contrary, he is unafraid to use the word *liar* (1:10; 2:4, 22; 4:20; 5:10); he labels his opponents "antichrist" (I John 2:18, 22; 4:3; II John 7); and he makes a clear distinction between the "children of God" and the "children of the devil" (3:10). According to the writer, the "false prophets" possess the "spirit of falsehood" (4:1, 6). Besides, the person who does not bring the teaching of Christ performs a "wicked work" (II John 10–11).

The author speaks with absolute authority when he commands his readers not to love the world (2:15), to remain in Christ (2:27), to believe in the name of Jesus (3:23), to love one another (4:7, 11, 21), to walk in love (II John 6), not to invite a false teacher to teach in their homes (II John 10), and to imitate that which is good (III John 11).

We are able to glean enough information from the three epistles to ascertain that the writer is an eyewitness and hearer of Jesus (1:2), a proclaimer of the Word (1:5) who can speak with authority about "the

---

35. In a sermon on Gal. 6:10, "Let us do good to all people," Jerome relates that the apostle John in his old age was too feeble to preach, that he had to be carried into the church, and that he repeated the exhortation, "Dear children, love one another." John added the explanation, "This is the Lord's command; and when only this command is kept, it is sufficient."

beginning" (1:1; 2:7, 13, 14, 24; 3:11; II John 5, 6) and function as *the* elder in the midst of the churches (II John 1; III John 1). When the writer identifies himself as "the elder," he seems to have nothing more in mind than a synonym for the word *apostle*. This eminent writer, because of his widespread influence and acclaim, has no need to identify himself. He is known as John, the son of Zebedee.

If the author implicitly reveals himself in his letters, does he provide information about the identity of his readers? In his second and third epistles he spells out the address: II John is sent to "the chosen lady and her children" and III John to his "dear friend Gaius." In I John he fails to identify the readers. Indirectly, however, he provides numerous clues about their identity.

1. Recipients of I John

The readers of the first epistle were generally not recent converts but had been Christians for some time. The writer addresses "fathers" and "young men" (2:13, 14), many of whom have heard the gospel "from the beginning" (2:7, 24; 3:11). They know the teachings of Christ (3:23), obey his commands (2:7), and confess his name (2:23; 5:10). They are fully aware of the pernicious attacks of the devil (2:13, 14, 16; 3:10; 4:3; 5:19), who appears to them in the form of the antichrist (2:18, 22; 4:3), false prophets (4:1), and liars (2:4, 22; 4:20).

Direct references to the Old Testament are few. The author mentions Cain by name and describes him as the one "who belonged to the evil one and murdered his brother" (3:12; also see Gen. 4:8). Even allusions to the teachings of the Old Testament are infrequent. The words "If we claim to be without sin, we deceive ourselves and the truth is not in us" (1:8) echo Proverbs 28:13, "He who conceals his sins does not prosper, but whoever confesses and renounces them finds mercy."

God is described as "faithful and just" (1:9). This phrase is a repetition and summary of a line from the Song of Moses, "A faithful God who does no wrong, upright and just is he" (Deut. 32:4). And the words "there is nothing in him to make him stumble" (2:10) relate to Psalm 119:165, "Great peace have they who love your law, and nothing can make them stumble." Last, the observation "And his commands are not burdensome" (5:3) resembles the instruction of Moses, "Now what I am commanding you today is not too difficult for you or beyond your reach" (Deut. 30:11).

The direct reference and the allusions to the Old Testament provide a description of the author, not of the readers. They indicate that the author's mind was conditioned by Jewish teaching; this cannot be said of the readers. The absence of Old Testament quotations leaves the impression that his readers were of Gentile origin. For them the Scriptures of the Old Testament were relatively new.

Tradition holds that John wrote his epistles during his ministry in Ephesus, and that his first epistle was addressed to a church or group of churches whom the author knew well.[36] Succeeding Paul and Timothy, John was a pastor in Ephesus until his death in about A.D. 98. From Ephesus he wrote his epistles, presumably to Gentile audiences rather than to readers who were Jewish Christians.

2. Recipients of II John

"The elder" sends his letter to "the chosen lady and her children" (v. 1). He greatly rejoices in the knowledge that some of the children of this elect lady are "walking in the truth" (v. 4). He uses the plural pronoun *you* when he tells them that he has much to write but that he hopes to visit them soon (v. 12). And last, he concludes his second epistle by conveying the greetings of the children of the lady's chosen sister (v. 13).

Some commentators take the words "to the chosen lady and her children" literally and understand them either as "the Chosen Lady" or "a Chosen Lady." Others even transliterate the Greek words and present them as given names: "Electa the Lady," or "the chosen Kyria," or "Electa Kyria." However, the evidence to prove common usage of these transliterated Greek names in Greek literature is nil. Therefore, only the two translations *the chosen lady* and *a chosen lady* are valid.[37]

Granted that we are able to understand the address literally—a chosen lady and her children—we can also take the words to refer to a local church. Then the phrase *and her children* designates the members of the church. Also, the last verse in the letter, "The children of your chosen sister send their greetings," represents another way of saying that the members of a sister church convey their greetings. Note that the children send their greetings, not their mother. If we take the wording literally, we have to conclude that the sister of the chosen lady is no longer living. By contrast, if we understand the expression *chosen sister* to mean the church, we have an acceptable explanation. "The elder" (v. 1) undoubtedly is a member of this particular church.[38]

Furthermore, the changes from the singular to the plural (the singular in vv. 4, 5, 12 over against the plural in vv. 6, 8, 10, 13) make it more likely that the reference is to a church rather than to an individual person. I hasten to add that these changes are not always noticeable in translation. Because of the use of the plural *you*, the writer appears to address not a single family but an entire community.

In addition, the apostles Peter and Paul personified the church with a feminine name. For example, in his first epistle Peter writes, "She who is in Babylon, chosen together with you, sends you her greetings" (I Peter 5:13). He evidently means to say, "The church in Rome . . . greets you."

---

36. Brooke, *Commentary on the Johannine Epistles*, p. xxx.
37. Refer to Burdick, *The Letters of John the Apostle*, p. 416; Plummer, *The Epistles of St. John*, pp. lxxvi, 132. Also compare Guthrie, *New Testament Introduction*, pp. 890–91.
38. Consult Westcott, *The Epistles of St. John*, p. 224. And see Dodd, *The Johannine Epistles*, pp. 144–45.

And Paul calls the church the virgin or the bride of Christ (II Cor. 11:2; Eph. 5:25–29). In conclusion, then, the feminine identification in II John for a particular congregation harmonizes with this practice elsewhere.

We simply cannot determine where the recipients of II John lived. In view of John's lengthy ministry in Ephesus, we surmise that he addressed his letter to a particular church well known to him and located in the western part of Asia Minor.

3. Recipients of III John

"The elder" writes a personal letter to his friend Gaius (v. 1) and other friends (v. 14). We know virtually nothing about Gaius, except by way of information the writer provides in his third letter. The name itself occurs five times in the New Testament (Acts 19:29; 20:4; Rom. 16:23; I Cor. 1:14; III John 1). Whether Gaius is one of those mentioned by Luke in Acts or by Paul in his epistles is difficult to say.

Gaius, the dear friend of "the elder," is a diligent worker in the church (v. 3). He has cared for traveling missionaries who needed food and lodging (v. 8). And he has had to endure malicious slander from Diotrephes (v. 10).

John mentions that he has written an earlier letter to Diotrephes, who has refused to respond to its content. Although John does not address his third epistle directly to this malcontent but to Gaius, he nevertheless writes that he is coming for a visit to "call attention to what [Diotrephes] is doing" (v. 10).

"The elder" refers to Demetrius last of all. This person is the opposite of Diotrephes in Christian conduct. He receives praise and commendation (v. 12). As in the case of Gaius, we know next to nothing about Demetrius. Any effort to link him with Demetrius the silversmith (Acts 19:24) or to Demas (II Tim. 4:10), whose name may be an abbreviated form of Demetrius, is futile.

We cannot ascertain where Gaius, Diotrephes, and Demetrius resided. Their place of residence was within traveling distance from Ephesus, so that John in his old age was still able to visit them. Perhaps all we can say is that these people lived in Asia Minor.

C. Why Were the Epistles Written?

What were the problems facing the church in the second half of the first century? What caused John to write three epistles to churches and individuals? What were the motives that occasioned the composition of these epistles? These are some of the questions we wish to consider in this section of the Introduction.

1. Heresies

We already are able to detect problems in the churches from a cursory reading of the epistle. For instance, we read that the antichrist is coming and that "even now many antichrists have come." Who are they? John writes, "They went out from us, but they did not really belong to us. For if they had belonged to us, they would have remained with us; but their going showed that none of them belonged to us" (2:19). And the author warns the readers not to believe every spirit, "but [to] test the spirits to see whether they are from God, because many false prophets have gone out into the world" (4:1).

From these passages we learn first that the antichrists were at one time members of the church who left on their own accord. And second, they departed for doctrinal reasons and appeared subsequently as false prophets who were trying to lead the members of the church astray (2:26; II John 7).

And last, we learn that the church faces direct opposition from those who formerly belonged to the Christian community. These opponents now teach doctrines that are at variance with the Christian faith. To strengthen the members of the church and to warn them against false teachings the author composed his epistles.

Christology

Throughout I and II John the doctrine of Christ is central. The writer affirms the teaching that Jesus Christ is human and divine, and is the Son of God. Already in the introduction of his first epistle he teaches the humanity and divinity of Jesus Christ. John writes that he, with others, heard Jesus, saw him, and also touched him with his hands (1:1). That is, Jesus is truly human. John concludes the introduction by inviting the readers to have fellowship "with the Father and with his Son, Jesus Christ" (1:3). Thus he clearly indicates that Jesus Christ is divine.[39]

The false prophets refused to confess that Jesus Christ has come in the flesh (4:2–3; II John 7). They denied that Jesus is the Christ (2:22) and that he is the Son (2:23; 4:15; II John 9). They taught that Jesus Christ could not have come in human form.

John affirms the teaching concerning the humanity and divinity of Jesus Christ by asking, "Who is it that overcomes the world? Only he who believes that Jesus is the Son of God. This is the one who came by water and blood—Jesus Christ. He did not come by water only, but by water and blood" (5:5–6). And he states, "Every spirit that acknowledges that Jesus Christ has come in the flesh is from God" (4:2). Therefore, John exhorts the believers to remain firm in the truth which they have heard from the beginning, for then they "will remain in the Son and in the Father" (2:24).

Morality

The false prophets who deny the central doctrine concerning the person of Christ also develop a warped view of sin and the law. For instance, they claim that they are without sin (1:8) and make it known that they

---

39. Here are additional references to the phrase *Son of God*: 1:7; 3:8, 23; 4:9, 10, 15; 5:5, 9, 10, 11, 12, 13, 20.

have not sinned (1:10). They deny that fellowship with God demands that they must "live by the truth" (1:6). They refuse to follow the example Jesus set during his earthly ministry (2:6). They claim to be in fellowship with God but continue to "walk in the darkness" (1:6); and they profess to know God but are unwilling to obey his commands (2:4).

These deceivers ignore the commands of God by refusing to love their spiritual brother. In fact, John writes, "Whoever hates his brother is in the darkness and walks around in the darkness; he does not know where he is going, because the darkness has blinded him" (2:11). John is not afraid to call these people "children of the devil" (3:10); they hate their spiritual brother (2:9; 3:15; 4:20) and deny him the necessities of life when it is in their power to give (3:17).

Affirming God's demands for a life that demonstrates obedience, John states that the person who lives in Christ imitates the life of Jesus (2:6), seeks the purity that is in Christ (3:3), does not continue in sin (3:6; 5:18), and loves his fellow man (4:11).

Claims

With his "if we claim" statements, John succinctly delineates the teaching of the false prophets. In his refutation, he purposely falls into repetition. Notice, first, the false teachers claim to have fellowship with God (1:6), but the truth is that they walk in darkness. If they know God as the God of light (1:5), then fellowship with him excludes darkness. Now they live in darkness, deceive one another, and are devoid of truth.

Next, they claim to be without sin (1:8), but they deceive themselves by not telling the truth. Third, they claim that they have not sinned (1:10), but as they make that claim they designate God a liar.

Moreover, the false prophets claim to know God (2:4), but refuse to obey God's commands and therefore live outside the sphere of truth. And last, they claim to be in the light (2:9), but are in the darkness because they hate their brothers. Their claims and John's refutations are repetitious in their simplicity. Nevertheless, John's purpose is clear: he exposes the lie and proclaims the truth.

2. Heretics

Who are the adversaries John addresses in his epistles?[40] Granted that evidence from the first century is meager, we have sufficient testimony from writers in the second century. And although we must be careful in our evaluation of this testimony, we can readily see that the roots of heresy in the second century go back into the first century.

---

40. Stephen S. Smalley thinks that the author has more than one group of adversaries in mind: one group with a "low" Christology and another group with a "high" Christology. See his *1, 2, 3 John*, p. xxiii. Also see his article, "What about 1 John?" *Studia Biblica 1978*, vol. 3, *Papers on Paul and Other New Testament Authors*, ed. E. A. Livingstone (Sheffield: Journal for the Study of the New Testament Supplement Series, 1980), pp. 337–43.

Gnostics

The term *gnostic* derives from the Greek word *gnosis* (knowledge) and is broad in meaning. Gnostics of the second century promoted various teachings, but a survey of these teachings falls outside the scope of this study. Gnostic teachings in Syria, Palestine, and Egypt, however, basically relate to our study. Therefore, I will briefly summarize these views.

First, Gnostics exalted the acquisition of knowledge, for in their view knowledge was the end of all things. Because of their knowledge, they had a different understanding of the Scriptures. And because of this understanding they separated themselves from the uninitiated Christian.

Second, Gnostics declared that matter is evil. They based this doctrine on the many imperfections we observe in nature. Accordingly, they taught the following points:

1. The world is evil. This evil causes a separation, in the form of an unbridgeable gulf, between the world and the supreme God. Therefore, the supreme God cannot have created the world.
2. The God of the Old Testament created the world. He is not the supreme God, but an inferior and evil power.
3. Any teaching of the incarnation is unacceptable. It is impossible for the divine Word to live in an impure body.
4. There can be no resurrection of the body. They who are set free experience liberation from the shackles of an impure body.[41]

In respect to point 3, some Gnostics championed the cause of Docetism (from the Greek verb *dokein*, to appear). These Gnostic teachers denied that a sinless Christ could have a human (and thus sinful) body. They, then, made a distinction between the human body of Jesus and the Christ who came from heaven. Christ only descended upon the body of Jesus. In this manner, the Docetists sought to maintain that the heavenly Christ had no contact with a body that was evil. They actually taught that Christ did not really come in the flesh (compare I John 4:3; II John 7).

From the epistles of John, however, we cannot ascertain whether the author directs his letters against strict Docetists. Even though John stresses the humanity of Jesus Christ, he does not indicate that his opponents regarded the body of Christ a mere phantom.[42] In the introduction of I John and throughout the first and second epistles, John affirms the unity of the two natures (human and divine) of Jesus Christ.

Brown has compiled a list of similarities between verses in I and II John and teachings in Gnostic literature. Here are a few examples:

---

41. Consult Plummer, *The Epistles of St. John*, p. xxiii; Gerald L. Borchert, "Gnosticism," *EDT*, pp. 445–46.

42. However, consult Brown, who thinks that the author's adversaries (secessionists) "drifted into the type of docetism opposed by Ignatius of Antioch wherein the humanity of Jesus was only apparent." *The Epistles of John*, p. 105.

1. The contrast of light and darkness, truth and falsehood (compare I John 2:9; 4:6) is a theme in the *Gospel of Truth.*
2. The claim to sinlessness because of a special union with God (see I John 1:6, 8, 10; 2:4, 6) has an echo in the *Gospel of Mary,* in which the Savior says, "There is no sin."
3. John teaches the biblical truth that "God is light" (I John 1:5) and thus the believer is in the light (2:9). In *Corpus Hermeticum* (I. 29) we read, "God the Father from whom the Man came is light and life."[43]

These Gnostic references are from a period that is removed a century or more from that in which John wrote his epistles. Also, these references, as they stand, are rather innocuous and seem to be no threat to the Christian community. Therefore, we need to look at a source that is contemporaneous with John, and which is regarded as Gnostic by Christian writers of the second century.

Cerinthians

The church fathers tell us about a certain Cerinthus who lived in Ephesus. Irenaeus reports a story that Polycarp used to tell about Cerinthus and the apostle John:

> There are also those who heard from him that John, the disciple of the Lord, going to bathe at Ephesus, and perceiving Cerinthus within, rushed out of the bath-house without bathing, exclaiming, "Let us fly, lest even the bath-house fall down, because Cerinthus, the enemy of the truth, is within."[44]

When more than a century later Eusebius writes his history of the church, he twice includes this account in virtually the same wording.[45] In his first epistle John writes, "No lie comes from the truth. Who is the liar? It is the man who denies that Jesus is the Christ. Such a man is the antichrist—he denies the Father and the Son" (2:21–22). Did John write these words in reaction to the teaching of Cerinthus?

What was the teaching of Cerinthus? Again Irenaeus provides the information when he writes at length,

> Cerinthus, again, a man who was educated in the wisdom of the Egyptians, taught that the world was not made by the primary God, but by a certain Power far separated from him, and at a distance from that Principality who is supreme over the universe, and ignorant of him who is above all. He represented Jesus as having not been born of a virgin, but as being the son of Joseph and Mary according to the ordinary course of human generation, while he nevertheless was more righteous, prudent, and wise than other men. Moreover, after his

---

43. Ibid., pp. 60–61.
44. Irenaeus *Against Heresies* 3. 3. 4.
45. Consult Eusebius *Ecclesiastical History* 3. 28. 6; 4. 14. 6.

baptism, Christ descended upon him in the form of a dove from the Supreme Ruler, and that then he proclaimed the unknown Father, and performed miracles. But at last Christ departed from Jesus, and that then Jesus suffered and rose again, while Christ remained impassible, inasmuch as he was a spiritual being.[46]

Cerinthus reveals that he is a Gnostic who attributes creation not to God but to a certain power that is separate from God. His crucial teaching pertains to the humanity and divinity of Jesus Christ. He distinguishes between the human Jesus born "according to the ordinary course of human generation" of Joseph and Mary and the divine Christ. In the form of a dove, Christ descended upon Jesus, so that the Christ is actually the equivalent of the Spirit.

Cerinthus wants to separate the divine Christ from the sinful Jesus, who suffers and rises from the dead. According to Cerinthus, the divine Christ cannot suffer because he is a spiritual being. Christ returns, or flies back, to the Pleroma (the fullness).[47]

In his epistles John reacts to this type of teaching. He calls the one who does "not acknowledge Jesus Christ as coming in the flesh" a deceiver and antichrist (II John 7). He teaches that Jesus Christ, the Son of God, "came by water and blood" (I John 5:6). And he affirms the unity of the Father and the Son by declaring, "No one who denies the Son has the Father; whoever acknowledges the Son has the Father also" (I John 2:23). Thus he seems to write against the Cerinthian doctrine of "the unknown Father." For John, the Son Jesus Christ and God the Father are one.

We rely only on the writings of the church fathers of the first few centuries, because we have no documents from the Cerinthians themselves. In the fourth century, Epiphanius mentions that a *Gospel According to Cerinthus* was in circulation. Whatever the truth of that information may be, we have the distinct impression from all that has been written that Cerinthus was a formidable Gnostic opponent of the early Christian church, and that Irenaeus gives an acceptable description of the teaching of Cerinthus.[48] If, then, Irenaeus has received his information from Polycarp, who was a disciple of the apostle John, we have a fairly reliable account about the person and teaching of Cerinthus.

Already in the closing years of the first century, leaders in the church vigorously opposed the threat of false doctrines that Cerinthus and others tried to propagate among the members of the Christian community. John saw that false doctrine led to false practice and to a disregard for the law

---

46. Irenaeus *Against Heresies* 1. 26. 1.

47. In three other passages, Irenaeus describes Gnostic doctrine when he says, first, that "the Christ from above [was] another, who also continued impassible, descending upon Jesus and flew back again into His Pleroma" (*Against Heresies* 3. 11. 1); next, "the Christ from above descended upon him, being without flesh, and impassible" (ibid. 3. 11. 3); and last, "that Christ remained impassible, but that it was Jesus who suffered" (ibid. 3. 11. 7).

48. Consult Brown, *The Epistles of John*, pp. 766–71.

of God. The Nicolaitans (see Rev. 2:6, 15), who were contemporaries of Cerinthus, had made their presence known in Asia Minor. Irenaeus writes, "The Nicolaitans . . . lead lives of unrestrained indulgence."[49]

John composed his letters not only to counteract the aberrations in doctrine and life that opponents taught and modeled. He also wrote his epistles to strengthen the believers in their understanding of the nature and person of Jesus Christ and their faith in him.

3. Detractors

What were the reasons for the composition of the second and third epistles? In spite of their brevity, these two letters show a difference in purpose. The second letter addresses the same problems as the first one: the emergence of many deceivers (v. 7) whom John calls false prophets in I John 4:1. The third epistle, however, is a personal letter to the writer's dear friend Gaius and contains advice on a matter that relates to local congregations.

Deceivers

The heart of the matter in II John is identical to that of the preceding letter. John warns the readers about the false doctrine taught by many deceivers who say Jesus Christ did not come in the flesh (v. 7). The parallel to this warning is John's repeated admonition to the readers of I John not to be led astray by deceivers (2:26; 3:7; 4:1–6).

John tells the readers that such a deceiver is the antichrist, that they should watch out not to lose their spiritual heritage, not to invite a deceiver into their houses or house churches, and never to support him in his wicked work (vv. 7–11).

On the surface, we see a contradiction in terms between the second and the third epistles. In the second, the readers are forbidden to extend hospitality to the false teachers, but in the next letter they are told "to show hospitality" to those who preach the Name of Jesus Christ (III John 8). And yet upon reflection, we notice that the contradiction vanishes when we see the purposes of these two parties: the one group wished to enter Christian homes to spread pernicious doctrine contrary to the teaching of Christ (II John 9–10); the other group refused to accept help and hospitality from pagans, but instead accepted food, lodging, and aid from Christians so that they together might work for the truth (III John 7–8).

John's exhortation to welcome preachers of the gospel and his admonition not to extend hospitality to false teachers has an echo in the *Didache*, the so-called Teaching of the Twelve Apostles. We read,

Whosoever then comes and teaches you all these things aforesaid, receive him. But if the teacher himself be perverted and teach another doctrine to destroy these things, do not listen to him, but if his teach-

---

49. Irenaeus *Against Heresies* 1. 26. 3. Also consult Eusebius *Ecclesiastical History* 3. 29. 1–2.

ing be for the increase of righteousness and knowledge of the Lord, receive him as the Lord.[50]

John vehemently attacked these false teachers by calling them antichrists. He realized that their set purpose was to destroy the foundation of Christianity; they denied the humanity of Jesus Christ and induced the believers to disobey the law of God.

Diotrephes

The composition of John's last epistle was occasioned by traveling missionaries. They gave a report about the faithfulness of Gaius and the harshness of Diotrephes. The one opened his home to missionaries of the gospel, the other wanted to have nothing to do with them.

Consequently, John writes a letter in which he praises his friend Gaius and mentions that he plans to come to "call attention to what [Diotrephes] is doing" (v. 10). In his selfishness, Diotrephes wishes to be the undisputed ruler in the church. He makes some malicious remarks about John and members of the church, and rejects the authority of the elder John.

In his first and second epistles, John expresses his opposition to heretical teachings. In his last epistle, however, John gives no indication that he is opposing heretics. He writes his third epistle because of a personality conflict that eventually comes to a head when the author and Diotrephes meet. The letter, then, serves as a notice to Gaius, to the church, and indirectly to Diotrephes that the visit is forthcoming.

The word *church* occurs three times in this short epistle (vv. 6, 9, 10). From the context, the writer seems to apply this term to more than one congregation—first to the church to which John himself belongs (v. 6), and then to the church in which Diotrephes functions as leader (vv. 9 and 10). However, the church to which John addressed his letter ("I wrote to the church," v. 9) need not be the congregation of which Gaius is a member. We may conclude that Diotrephes had not excommunicated Gaius. In itself, this point may indicate that Gaius belongs to another church.

Last, John wrote his third epistle to commend Demetrius. We know nothing more of this faithful believer than what the writer reveals. Demetrius receives a word of commendation.

D. When Were the Epistles Written?

In addition to putting a date to the composition of the epistles, we have to address the question whether the epistles precede or succeed the Gospel of John. Even though a study of the fourth Gospel falls outside the scope of an introduction to the letters of John, we must consider the matter of temporal priority.[51] Also, we ought to be careful not to construct

---

50. *The Didache* 11: 1–2 (LCL). This document probably dates from the early second century or even earlier, so that it probably is contemporary with John's epistles.

51. Even the order of composition of the epistles is debatable. Marshall is of the opinion that II and III John should precede I John. *The Epistles of John*, p. 2.

an edifice to substantiate a claim when the author himself fails to provide the bricks for this edifice.

The epistles themselves provide no information to help us in determining a date for their composition. Scholars generally date the composition of John's epistles at about A.D. 90–95.[52] The reasoning is that the epistles were written to counteract the teachings of Gnosticism, which was becoming influential near the end of the first century. Arguments for dating the fourth Gospel before the letters of John center on the break between synagogue and church after the publication of the Gospel.[53] This break apparently indicates the reason that the epistles lack specific quotations from the Old Testament. That is, the initial recipients of the Gospel differ from those who received John's epistles. Moreover, some passages in I John appear to be direct references to the Gospel (e.g., compare 1:5 with John 8:12 ["God is light" and "I am the light"]). In general, the evidence seems to support the view that the Gospel precedes the First Epistle of John.[54]

In his second letter, John stresses the concept *truth* (vv. 1–4). He presents an elaborate exposition of this concept in his first epistle (1:6, 8; 2:4, 21; 3:18, 19; 4:6; 5:6). False teachers who wish to enter the homes of believers do not present this truth but the lie (II John 7–11). For this reason, scholars favor the view that John wrote his letters in the sequence in which they have come to us.

We are unable to detect references to time in any of the epistles. Therefore, if we accept the usual order of I, II, and III John, we assume that this is the order which has been handed down throughout the centuries.

Does the third epistle follow the second? Even if we answer in the affirmative, we cannot prove anything about sequence. Certainly we cannot say that the remark in III John 9, "I wrote to the church," is a reference to II John. The context of III John 9 makes no reference to an epistle that has the message of II John or even I John. In short, we must confess that we lack the necessary details to speak meaningfully about the sequence of II and III John.

Furthermore, we are unable to prove that the situation in the churches had deteriorated after the composition of II John, so that John had to write another epistle.[55]

---

52. At least one scholar wants to date the three letters of John in the seventh decade of the first century: A.D. 60–65. Consult J. A. T. Robinson, *Redating the New Testament* (Philadelphia: Westminster, 1976), p. 307.

53. Consult Raymond E. Brown, *The Community of the Beloved Disciple* (New York: Paulist, 1979), pp. 82–85.

54. For a detailed discussion on priority, consult Brooke, *Commentary on the Johannine Epistles*, pp. xix–xxvii.

55. Glenn W. Barker assumes that more than a year had elapsed between the composition of the second and the third epistles. *1 John*, in the *Expositor's Bible Commentary*, ed. Frank E. Gaebelein, 12 vols. (Grand Rapids: Zondervan, 1981), vol. 12, p. 301. Even though this view may be correct, it remains an assumption.

From the order in which the early church placed John's epistles, we infer that the three letters were composed in the sequence in which we have received them. And from the content of these writings, we draw the inference that I, II, and III John date from about A.D. 90 to 95.

E. What Is the Content of the Epistles?

Anyone who reads the first epistle receives the impression that the writer frequently repeats himself. Is this repetition characteristic of a writer advanced in age? Are we seeing the work of an author whose culture and time differ from our own?

Answering these questions, some commentators point out that the sequence in I John is not circular but rather spiral in form. They see a spiral structure that is similar to the construction of the prologue in the Gospel of John. In other words, they view the structure of the first epistle as something that is typical of the apostle John. Also the discourses Jesus uttered in the presence of his disciples in the upper room—recorded in John 14–17—display this same characteristic.[56]

1. Theological Themes in I John

What are recurring themes in I John? After a brief introduction (1:1–4) in which he invites the readers to fellowship with the Father and the Son Jesus Christ, the author says, "God is light" (1:5). The first theme, then, pertains to the characteristics of God.

Characteristics of God

John uses the motto *God is light* to refute the contentions of his Gnostic opponents who say that they can have fellowship with God but do not have to "live by the truth" (1:6). He tells them that they are living in darkness and are liars. He even goes a step further and asserts that they make God a liar (1:6, 8, 10). John strengthens the believers by assuring them that if they walk in the light, they have fellowship with one another. He also assures them that God forgives their sins through the blood of Jesus (1:7, 9).

The love of God is the next characteristic (2:5, 15). God's love illumines the believer when he obeys the commands of God, for then he knows that he is in God. The command to love is not new but old. Therefore, the person who obeys this old command loves his brother and lives in the light (2:10). He is the recipient of the love and the light of God. He is the one in whom the word of God lives (2:14); the one who does the will of God has eternal life (2:17).

God the Father lavishes his love upon his children (3:1); these children

---

56. Consult especially Plummer, *The Epistles of St. John,* p. liv; R. Law, "The Epistles of John," *ISBE* (1st ed. [1939]), vol. 3, pp. 1711–20; R. C. H. Lenski, *Interpretation of the Epistles of St. Peter, St. John, and St. Jude* (Columbus: Wartburg, 1945), p. 367; and Burdick, *The Letters of John the Apostle,* p. 91.

are told to love one another (3:11, 14, 23). Love originates with God (4:7), and the person who is a child of God (4:4, 6) knows him because "God is love" (4:8, 10, 16).

How does the child of God express his love for God? By obeying his commands (5:3). The person who is born of God does not live in continual sin, for God keeps him safe from the evil one (5:18). And why does God care for his child? God loves his child because of his Son Jesus Christ, who is true God and eternal life (5:20).

Son of God

Already in the introduction to his first epistle, John clearly demonstrates that Jesus Christ is human and divine. He states that Jesus Christ has a physical body, is eternal life, and is the Son of God (1:1–3). John opposes the teachings of the false prophets who deny the humanity of Christ (4:1–3; II John 7). "The denial that Christ has come in the flesh is also a denial that Jesus is the Son of God (4:15; 5:5)."[57]

The Gnostics taught that because God dwells in pure light, his Son cannot live in an impure human body among sinful men. The consequence of this teaching is that the Christ of the Gnostics cannot be God's Son as the Scriptures reveal him.

John reveals Jesus Christ as the person with whom we have fellowship (1:3), who forgives us and "purifies us from every sin" (1:7, 9). Jesus is the one who speaks in our defense before his Father. He is our defense lawyer who pleads for our acquittal and is able to set us free (2:1). He has offered himself as a sacrifice for sin (2:2).

John reveals that God commands us to believe in the name of the Son of God (3:23). Believing in Jesus Christ must come to expression in acknowledging that Jesus Christ "has come in the flesh" (4:2). The person who confesses that Jesus Christ is the Son of God has fellowship with God and is a child of God (4:15; 5:1). That person has faith in God.

Faith in God

John explicitly spells out God's command: "Believe in the name of his Son, Jesus Christ" (3:23). When we obey this command, we have fellowship with God and his Son.

The believer, however, must exercise the ability to discern whether a teaching is from God or from the evil one. He recognizes the Spirit of God when he acknowledges that Jesus Christ has come in human flesh (4:2). Faith in Christ is basic for the child of God, because that faith gives him the victory in opposing evil and overcoming the world (5:4). Jesus Christ, the Son of God, is truly human; he began his public ministry by submitting himself to baptism and he ended his earthly life when he shed

---

57. G. E. Ladd, *A Theology of the New Testament* (Grand Rapids: Eerdmans, 1974), p. 611. Donald Guthrie notes that in I John the term *Son* is mentioned twenty-one times. See *New Testament Theology* (Downers Grove: Inter-Varsity, 1981), p. 316.

his blood on Calvary's cross (5:6–7). And Jesus is truly divine, because he possesses eternal life (1:2; 5:11, 13, 20).

The difference between the believer and the unbeliever is that the one accepts the testimony God has given about his Son, and the other rejects this testimony and thus labels God a liar (5:10). What is the testimony of God? John is specific, for he writes, "And this is the testimony: God has given us eternal life, and this life is in his Son" (5:11). Everyone who believes in the name of Jesus Christ accepts him as the Son of God and through him possesses eternal life (5:13). Jesus Christ is eternal life and shares this with all who believe in him.

Also, faith and knowledge are inseparably intertwined. John teaches this truth when he says, "And so we know and rely on the love God has for us" (4:16).

Knowledge of God

The first epistle gives the reader a quiet assurance that God takes care of his children so that the power of the evil one cannot harm them. "1 John breathes an atmosphere of quiet confidence, without denying the responsibility of man."[58]

This confidence comes to expression when the believer is able to say that he knows God, has fellowship with him, and obeys his commands (2:3). How do we know that we have fellowship with God? John writes, "This is how we know we are in him: Whoever claims to live in him must walk as Jesus did" (2:5–6). John praises the fathers because they have known God from the beginning and he commends the children because they have known the Father (2:13–14).

The believer knows the truth (2:21), has received the anointing of God's Spirit living within him (2:27), and confidently awaits the return of Jesus Christ (2:28). Not only does he wait for the coming of Christ, but also he has fervent hope and an assured knowledge that believers shall be like Christ and shall be purified from sin (3:2, 3, 5).

Already the believers are able to express themselves about the present time: they have passed from death caused by sin into the life that Christ has given them. They demonstrate this life in their love for one another. They know what love is by looking to Jesus who laid down his life for them (3:16). And when they see the effect of love in their lives, they realize that they belong to the truth and that God, through his Spirit, lives within them (3:19, 24).

John teaches that the believer, because he knows God, also has the ability to distinguish between teachings that come from God and doctrines that are false (4:2). The child of God, then, knows how to recognize the Spirit of truth over against the spirit of falsehood (4:6). He is able to do so because the Spirit of God lives within him (4:13).

---

58. Guthrie, *New Testament Theology*, p. 616. Also see I. Howard Marshall, "John, Epistles of," *ISBE*, vol. 2, p. 1094.

Finally, the believer has complete confidence that God will hear his prayers and petitions. Whenever he asks anything in prayer, provided the request is in harmony with God's will, God answers that prayer. In fact, John removes every uncertainty about the future when he writes with absolute assurance, "And if we know that he hears us—whatever we ask—we know that *we have* what we asked of him" (5:15, italics added). John ends his first epistle by revealing the source of our confidence: the Son of God. Jesus Christ has come and has given us the knowledge of truth and eternal life (5:20).

Sin

Sin is a theological theme that John discusses in every chapter of his first epistle. He notes that Jesus Christ purifies us from every sin and all unrighteousness; when we confess our sins, he is willing to forgive us and cleanse us (1:7, 9). He also remarks that if we claim to be sinless or say that we have not sinned, we are in the power of deception. That is, we deceive ourselves and designate God a liar (1:8, 10).

Remission of sin, for all of us have stumbled into sin, becomes possible through Jesus Christ, the Righteous One (2:1). He is the advocate for us in court when the Father charges us with disobedience. Then the Son of God speaks in our defense. He is our atoning sacrifice for sin (2:2), and we know that our sins have been forgiven because of his name (2:12). He fulfilled the demands of God the Father, who initiated our redemption. In his love for us, God sent his Son "as an atoning sacrifice for our sins" (4:10).

If the believer receives remission of sin, what is the assurance that Christ will keep him from sin? John replies by making three statements that begin with the expression *no one*. First, "No one who lives in him keeps on sinning." Next, "No one who continues to sin has either seen him or known him" (3:6). Last, "No one who is born of God will continue to sin" (3:9). The devil and his followers continue in sin, but this can never be said of the children of God. The believer obtains forgiveness of sin through Jesus Christ, but the unbeliever continues to live in sin.[59]

How do we know that we are children of God and not of the devil? John answers, "Anyone who does not do what is right is not a child of God; nor is anyone who does not love his brother" (3:10).

In pithy language John states, "Sin is lawlessness" (3:4). He returns to this statement toward the end of his first epistle (5:16–17). There he elaborates on the meaning of sinning willfully. He realizes that "all wrongdoing is sin," but he adds that "there is sin that does not lead to death" (5:17); the sin that leads to death is a deliberate rejection of God's law.

---

59. Consult Burdick, *The Letters of John the Apostle,* who calls attention to the use of the present tense (3:9) to describe the lives of the false teachers who continue to sin. The use of the aorist tense (2:1) depicts the life of the genuine believer who "commits acts of sin that need to be confessed and forgiven" (p. 77).

"Whereas the Christian has a restraint against deliberate sinning of this nature, the world has no such restraint."[60] John exhorts the readers to pray for the brother who commits a sin that is not mortal. He emphasizes that he is not exhorting his readers to pray for the person who has committed a mortal sin (5:16). To reassure the readers, however, he reminds them that the child of God does not continue in sin, is kept safe, and is out of Satan's reach (5:18).

Eternal Life

In the literature of John, the teaching on eternal life is rather prominent. For example, in the so-called high-priestly prayer, Jesus declares, "Now this is eternal life: that they may know you, the only true God, and Jesus Christ, whom you have sent" (John 17:3). In I John, the concept *eternal life* is embodied in Jesus Christ, so that the writer of this epistle actually says, "We proclaim to you the eternal life, which was with the Father and has appeared to us" (1:2). With the other apostles John proclaimed the "Word of life" (1:1). John discloses that this Word is eternal and therefore he implies that the Son of God "has lived eternally with God for the benefit of men (Jn. 1:4; I Jn. 1:1 f.), i.e. he is the source of divine life and power both in the old and in the new creation."[61]

Jesus Christ has appeared to give man eternal life. In one sense, this gift of life is a promise (2:25); in another sense, it is a possession, for we already have passed from death into life (3:14). Perhaps we ought to think in terms of promise and fulfillment. In principle we already possess eternal life because of our union with Christ. But at the moment of death when we leave this earthly scene and enter eternity, we receive eternal life in full as God promised in his Word.

When we know the Son of God as our personal Savior and believe in his name, then we *have* eternal life (5:13). John asserts that "God has given us eternal life" (5:11). He specifies that the origin of this life is in the Son of God, and that whoever has the Son has life (5:12).

Forgiveness of sin results in life. That is, if you see a brother committing a sin that is not mortal, then you should pray and ask God to forgive him, "and God will give him life" (5:16). God grants remission of sin and eternal life through his Son Jesus Christ.

Throughout his first epistle, John speaks of eternal life which God gives to the believer, and he mentions that Jesus Christ is the embodiment of eternal life. In the conclusion of his epistle he notes that the Son of God is "the true God and eternal life" (5:20) and that we are in him. The purpose of I John is to make known that we, because we are in Jesus Christ, have eternal life.

Nowhere in John's epistle do we detect any contrast between the de-

---

60. Guthrie, *New Testament Theology*, p. 196.
61. Hans-Georg Link, *NIDNTT*, vol. 2, p. 482.

scription of the present life in Jesus Christ and that of eternal life. John does not enumerate the differences of possessing life in the present and the fullness of life in the future. Instead he describes eternal life in terms of intimate fellowship with Jesus Christ. When we are in him, we possess eternal life (1:2; 2:24–25; 5:20).

The Return of Christ

What does John say about the eventual return of Jesus Christ and the life hereafter? Indirect and direct references to the event of Christ's return are few.

Here are the indirect references. John mentions that this world and its desires will come to an end; by contrast, the believer who obediently executes God's will lives forever (2:17). He informs the readers that they are now living in the last hour, which includes the entire present era. And in this particular era the antichrist has come (2:18). The spirit of the antichrist has appeared and is making its presence felt in the world in which we live (4:3; II John 7).

Another indirect reference is the word *victory*, which relates to the conclusion of conflict. John speaks about the victory of faith that has conquered the world (5:4). The child of God, more precisely the believer in the Son of God, is the victor, even though he knows that the whole world is controlled by the evil one (5:19).

The direct references to the return of Christ are more explicit. John clearly speaks about the appearance of the Lord. For instance, he exhorts us to continue in Christ, "so that when he appears we may be confident and unashamed before him at his coming" (2:28). John refers to Christ's return and not to his first coming, as is evident from the broader context. He speaks with anticipation about our future status and appearance. He exclaims, "Dear friends, now we are children of God, and what we will be has not yet been made known. But we know that when he appears, we shall be like him, for we shall see him as he is" (3:2). Here he tells us that we shall see Jesus upon his return, and he informs us that we shall be like Jesus in appearance. In another passage John puts the appearance of Jesus in the context of his earthly ministry, "But you know that he appeared so that he might take away our sins" (3:5).

Last, John introduces the thought of the judgment day. He encourages us with the teaching that love makes us complete; therefore, "we will have confidence on the day of judgment" (4:17). Because we are one with Christ in love, fear is absent. Love has banished fear, and fear is related to punishment. In short, the believer does not face punishment on the judgment day (4:18). In chapter 2, John states that the believer may rely on Jesus Christ to defend him in court (v. 1). On the day of judgment, then, Jesus will speak on behalf of the believer and say to his Father that he has atoned for all his sins (2:2).

There are other themes John expounds, including the concepts *world*, *hate,* and *evil one.* These concepts, however, are the reverse of the themes that relate to the fellowship believers have with God, the love they express toward him and toward each other, and the blessings they receive from Christ. As we trace the positive themes, we implicitly take note of the reverse themes. Therefore, we are aware of them, but consider them only in elementary form. In other words, we stress the positive at the expense of the negative and thus follow the example of the apostle John.

2. Outlines of I, II, and III John

This is a plain five-point outline of I John that can be committed to memory without difficulty.

1:1–4	Preface
1:5–2:17	Walk in the Light
2:18–3:24	Believe in Jesus
4:1–5:12	Love God
5:13–21	Epilogue

Here is a detailed outline of I John.

I. 1:1–4	Preface: The Word of Life	
	A. From the Beginning	1:1
	B. Life Appeared	1:2
	C. To Have Fellowship	1:3–4
II. 1:5–2:17	Walk in the Light	
A. 1:5–10	Fellowship and Forgiveness	
	1. God Is Light	1:5
	2. Darkness and Light	1:6–7
	3. Deception and Confession	1:8–10
B. 2:1–6	Knowledge and Obedience	
	1. Defender and Sacrifice	2:1–2
	2. Knowledge and Love	2:3–5a
	3. Christian Conduct	2:5b–6
C. 2:7–11	Love and Light	
	1. New and Old	2:7–8
	2. Light and Darkness	2:9–11
D. 2:12–14	Two Appeals	
	1. First Address	2:12–13a
	2. Second Address	2:13b–14
E. 2:15–17	The World and the Will of God	
	1. Do Not Love the World	2:15
	2. Do the Will of God	2:16–17

And here is an outline of II John.

Last, this is an outline for III John.

Commentary
The First Epistle of John

1

Preface: The Word of Life

(1:1–4)

and Walk in the Light, *part 1*

1:5–10

Outline

1   1 That which was from the beginning, which we have heard, which we have seen with our eyes, which we have looked at and our hands have touched—this we proclaim concerning the Word of life.   2 The life appeared; we have seen it and testify to it, and we proclaim to you the eternal life, which was with the Father and has appeared to us.   3 We proclaim to you what we have seen and heard, so that you also may have fellowship with us. And our fellowship is with the Father and with his Son, Jesus Christ.   4 We write this to make our joy complete.

I. Preface: The Word of Life
1:1–4

A. From the Beginning
1:1

This letter is known as the First Epistle of John. But is it an epistle? Indeed its beginning is unique, because the author's name, a reference to the addressees, and the customary greetings of a letter are absent. The writer knows the readers intimately. Repeatedly he addresses them as "dear children," "dear friends," and "my brothers."[1] And he indicates that he belongs to their own fellowship (2:19). He is a person endowed with authority who speaks as an eyewitness—one who has heard and seen the Lord Jesus Christ.

The introduction of the Epistle to the Hebrews (1:1–4) parallels that of the First Epistle of John. The writer of Hebrews, however, displays a style that is characteristic of classical Greek, whereas John writes in a style typical of Semitic Greek. Classical Greek sentences show careful structure and balance with numerous subordinate clauses (compare Luke 1:1–4). Semitic Greek has many coordinate clauses that are short and often are connected by the conjunction *and*. For instance, here is a literal translation of I John 1:2: "and the life was manifested, and we have seen and bear witness and proclaim to you the eternal life, which was with the Father and was manifested to us" (NASB).

1. That which was from the beginning, which we have heard, which we have seen with our eyes, which we have looked at and our hands have touched—this we proclaim concerning the Word of life.

---

1. These are the references: "dear children" (2:1, 12, 18; 3:7, 18; 4:4; 5:21), "dear friends" (2:7; 3:2, 21; 4:1, 7, 11), "brothers" (3:13).

Note the following clauses:

a. "That which was from the beginning." The first word in this epistle is "that" instead of "who." Instead of saying, "Jesus Christ, who was from the beginning," John writes, "That which was from the beginning." The term *that* is broader than the word *who*, for it includes the person and message of Jesus Christ. The term refers to God's revelation, namely, the gospel which, says John, "we proclaim concerning the Word of life."

The first words of this epistle echo the opening sentence of the Gospel of John, "In the beginning was the Word" (1:1), and the introductory phrase of the Old Testament, "In the beginning" (Gen. 1:1). However, John writes "from the beginning," not "in the beginning" (see 2:7, 13, 14, 24; 3:8, 11). In the clause "that which was from the beginning," John points not to the proclamation that Jesus came in the flesh but to the divine revelation—disclosed in history and recorded in the Old Testament—that teaches the eternal existence of the Son of God.[2] The message which is proclaimed is that Jesus, who "made his dwelling among us" (John 1:14), is eternal. John specifies and proceeds to inform the readers about the message he has heard.

b. "Which we have heard." John personally listened to the words coming from the lips of Jesus. He was one of the twelve disciples who accompanied the Lord from the time of Jesus' baptism to his ascension (Acts 1:21–22). He received instruction in the doctrines pertaining to the work and words of God, from the beginning of creation through the history of redemption in Jesus Christ.[3] John, then, speaks of the training he and his fellow apostles received from Jesus. He reformulates the words which he with Peter uttered before the Sanhedrin: "For we cannot help speaking about what we have seen and heard" (Acts 4:20).

c. "Which we have seen with our eyes." From the spiritual instruction he received, John turns to his instructor Jesus and focuses attention on him. John is saying, "We, apostles, are eyewitnesses who not only have heard the voice of Jesus. We also have seen him with our eyes." In a sense, these words are redundant. But John stresses that the apostles physically saw Jesus. That is, they did not see an apparition whose voice they heard but whose body they could not see. Jesus has a physical body, for "we have seen [him] with our eyes."

d. "Which we have looked at and our hands have touched." John resorts to another verb to express the act of seeing Jesus; he says, "We have

---

2. Refer to S. Greijdanus, *De Brieven van de Apostelen Petrus en Johannes, en de Brief van Judas,* Kommentaar op het Nieuwe Testament series (Amsterdam: Van Bottenburg, 1929), p. 383.
3. Consult A. E. Brooke, *A Critical and Exegetical Commentary on the Johannine Epistles,* International Critical Commentary series (Edinburgh: Clark, 1964), p. 2.

looked at [him]."[4] Purposely John informs the readers that he employed three of his physical senses to ascertain the presence of the Lord. He heard his voice, he saw him with his eyes, and he touched him with his hands.

The words *and our hands have touched* are reminiscent of the appearance of Jesus on Easter in the upper room when Jesus invited the Eleven and those with them to touch him and to see for themselves that he had a physical body. "A ghost does not have flesh and bones, as you see I have," Jesus said (Luke 24:39; also consult John 20:20, 25, 27).

John teaches the apostolic doctrine of the resurrection of Jesus. He speaks as an eyewitness, for with his natural senses he and those with him personally heard, saw, and touched Jesus and declare that the resurrected physical body of the Lord is real.[5]

e. "This we proclaim concerning the Word of life." The New International Version has added the words *this we proclaim* to summarize and complete the sentence.[6] John supplies these words in the immediate context.

What is the meaning of the phrase *the Word of life*? First, it is equivalent to the "that" of the earlier part of the verse, namely, the message of Jesus Christ. And next, this message is the Word that has become flesh, as John writes in the prologue of his Gospel (1:14).[7] The term *Word* is one of the names John uses to describe Jesus Christ (John 1:1, 14; I John 1:1; Rev. 19:13). Jesus, who is called the Word, speaks God's words with absolute authority. He reveals the will of God and "testifies [to man] to what he has seen and heard" (John 3:32) in the presence of God.[8] Furthermore, Jesus not only reveals the message of life; he also possesses life (John 1:4;

---

4. In his Gospel, John employs the verb *to look at* (in the Greek) for seeing the glory of Jesus (1:14), for observing the Spirit come down from heaven (1:32), for Jesus who notices the two disciples who follow him (1:38), for opening one's eyes to see the fields ready for the harvest (4:35), and for seeing a great crowd of people coming toward Jesus (6:5). Also note John 11:45 and I John 4:12, 14 where he uses the same verb.

5. B. F. Westcott observes, "The tacit reference is the more worthy of notice because St John does not mention the fact of the Resurrection in his Epistle; nor does he use the word in his own narrative of the Resurrection." See *The Epistles of St. John, The Greek Text, with Notes and Addenda* (1883; Grand Rapids: Eerdmans, 1966), p. 6.

6. Some translations follow the word order of the Greek text and have the reading *concerning the word of life* (RSV, NKJV, NASB, and see KJV). Others supply the verb *to write*: "We write [are writing] to you about the Word of life" (GNB, MLB). Still others borrow the verb *to proclaim* from the context and have the wording "This is what we proclaim to you" (NAB and with modification NIV). The NEB has the verb *to tell*: "it is of this we tell."

7. M. de Jonge writes, "The exegesis we prefer presupposes that the word *logos* [word] used in the Greek must be seen against the background of the Prologue of the Gospel, and, consequently, refers to Jesus Christ." "An Analysis of I John 1. 1–4," *The Bible Translator* 29 (1978): 327. Donald W. Burdick agrees that "the weight of evidence favors the personal meaning of the term." See *The Letters of John the Apostle* (Chicago: Moody, 1985), p. 100.

8. Refer to Bertold Klappert, *NIDNTT*, vol. 3, p. 1114.

11:25; 14:6) and shares it with all who listen to his Word in faith. He is the life giver.

B. Life Appeared
1:2

2. The life appeared; we have seen it and testify to it, and we proclaim to you the eternal life, which was with the Father and has appeared to us.

This verse is actually an explanatory note on the word *life*. Translators and expositors usually regard verse 2 as a parenthetical remark and indicate that it is the equivalent of a comment on the preceding text. Verses 1 and 3, then, present continuity of thought.

A literal translation of the first clause in this text is, "And the life appeared." Although most translations omit the conjunction *and,* some render it "for," "when," or even "yes." To be sure, this conjunction conveys an affirmative intent that can be translated "indeed." That is, "indeed the life appeared."

Note that John writes "the life," not "life." He wants to explain the meaning of the term *life*. Therefore, he places the definite article *the* before the noun *life* to call attention to the fullness of life in Jesus Christ. He further explains by adding the words "the eternal life, which was with the Father and has appeared to us."

First, John actually writes, "the life, the eternal life, that which was with the Father." He is emphatic in describing the extent of this life by characterizing it as eternal. It is life that never ends, for it has the mark of eternity.[9] But the life which John describes is more than a concept. It stands for Jesus Christ, as John shows in the clause "that which was with the Father." The words *with the Father* imply not only that the Son is in the presence of the Father; also the preposition *with* in the original Greek has the root meaning *near* or *facing*. Life, then, personified in the Son is near to or faces the Father (see John 1:1).

Second, John writes that "the life appeared" and "the eternal life . . . has appeared to us." John refers to the historic event of Jesus' birth, life, death, resurrection, and personal visits after his resurrection. During the first century, Christians gave expression to Jesus' appearance when they sang the hymn:

> He appeared in a body,
>> was vindicated by the Spirit,
> was seen by angels,
>> was preached among the nations,

---

9. Both in the Gospel and in his first epistle, John employs the expression *eternal life* repeatedly. In the Gospel it occurs seventeen times (3:15, 16, 36; 4:14, 36; 5:24, 39; 6:27, 40, 47 [everlasting], 54, 68; 10:28; 12:25, 50; 17:2, 3). And in I John it appears six times (1:2; 2:25; 3:15; 5:11, 13, 20).

> was believed on in the world,
> was taken up in glory.
> —I Timothy 3:16

Once again John emphasizes that he and those with him have seen Jesus. They saw him in human flesh and after his resurrection in his glorified body. As witnesses of Jesus' victory over death, the apostles testified of Jesus' life, death, resurrection, and ascension. The verb *testify* (a word John uses frequently in his vocabulary)[10] points to the following verb *proclaim*. The apostles proclaimed the Word of life. They proclaimed the word and work of Jesus.

C. To Have Fellowship
1:3–4

3. We proclaim to you what we have seen and heard, so that you also may have fellowship with us. And our fellowship is with the Father and with his Son, Jesus Christ.

These are the points John communicates:

a. *Emphasis.* After the parenthetical comment, John resumes the thought of the first verse and repeats from the second verse the verb *proclaim.* John emphasizes proclaiming the message which he and the other apostles had received from the Lord. He builds his argument by repeating clauses from verse 1. But note that he reverses the verbs, for he says, "We proclaim to you what we *have seen* and *heard*" (italics added). Also, this is the third time that he uses the verb *to see.* What is John saying?

By reiterating the same verbs, John seems to warn the readers against false doctrines that deny the human nature, physical appearance, and bodily resurrection of Jesus. John testifies that he has seen Jesus and has heard his voice. John wants his readers to know the core of the apostolic message: "Jesus Christ, the Son of God, has appeared in human flesh." As an eyewitness and earwitness, John is able to testify to the veracity of this message and proclaim what he has seen and heard.[11]

b. *Purpose.* John states the purpose of his letter in this verse. Says he, "We proclaim to you what we have seen and heard, so that you also may have fellowship with us." He states a parallel purpose near the end of his letter: "I write these things to you . . . so that you may know that you have eternal life" (5:13). The purpose is to invite the readers to the fellowship of the apostles who are eyewitnesses of the earthly life and ministry of Jesus.

The invitation serves two ends. First, John seeks to shield the readers

---

10. In the Greek the verb occurs thirty-three times in the Gospel and ten times in the epistles (I John 1:2; 4:14; 5:6, 7, 9, 10; and III John 3, 6, 12 [twice]).

11. The NIV omits the word *also* of a verbatim translation: "What we have seen and heard we proclaim to you *also*" (NASB, italics added). Although textual evidence favors including the word, translators tend to delete it because it is redundant. In the next clause, the term *also* appears once more: "so that you *also* may have fellowship with us."

from the doctrinal attacks of false teachers and to strengthen them spiritually within the fellowship of the apostles and disciples.[12] When people have
fellowship, they share their mutual gifts, goals, and goods (compare Acts
4:32–37). The apostles shared their spiritual gifts with members of the
church. And second, John invites the readers of his epistle to join the eyewitnesses in their fellowship "with the Father and with his Son, Jesus Christ."

c. *Focus.* In the last part of verse 3, John reveals the focal point of his
introduction: Jesus Christ, the Son of God. This focus is significant, because in his epistle the name *Christ* is the official title of Jesus. Except for
one instance (1:7), John always uses the combination *Jesus Christ* (rather
than the terms *Jesus* or *Christ*) or the clause *that Jesus is the Christ.*[13] He
wants his readers to know that the human Jesus is indeed the heavenly
Messiah, that is, the Christ.

John also considers the name *Son* significant. In his first epistle this is a
key word.[14] John emphasizes the basic confession of the church: "Jesus is
the Son of God." Throughout his epistle he mentions the fellowship of
the believer with the Father and the Son (1:7), the redeeming work of the
Son (1:7; 4:10), the mission of the Son (3:8), God's testimony about the
Son (5:9), the gift of the Son in terms of eternal life (5:11, 13), and last,
the coming of the Son (5:20). Especially in chapter 5, John explains the
significance of the word *Son.*[15]

4. We write this to make our joy complete.

Translations differ on the wording of this text. Some have the reading
"And these things we write to you that your joy may be full" (NKJV).
Others, among which is the New International Version, follow the Greek
manuscripts that read, "We write this to make our joy complete." Because
of emphasis on the words *we* and *our,* the evidence seems to favor the
second reading.

Why does John say "we write," when he alone is regarded as the author
of this epistle? Only here he uses the plural form *we write,* while twelve
times in this letter he says "I write" or "I am writing" (2:1, 7, 8, 12, 13
[three times], 14 [twice], 21, 26; 5:13). Is he putting himself with the
readers in one class and then using the so-called preacher's "we"?[16]
Hardly. If this were the case, we would have difficulty determining who
the people are John addresses as "you" (see vv. 2–3). Is the use of "we" an

---

12. Refer to Greijdanus, *Johannes,* pp. 392–93; Brooke, *Commentary on the Johannine Epistles,*
p. 8.
13. The combination *Jesus Christ* occurs six times (1:3; 2:1; 3:23; 4:2; 5:6, 20). The clause
that Jesus is the Christ appears twice (2:22; 5:1).
14. With variations the expression *Son of God* occurs sixteen times (1:3, 7; 3:8, 23; 4:9, 10,
15; 5:5, 9, 10 [twice]), 11, 12, 13, 20 [twice]). And the term *Son* appears six times (2:22, 23
[twice], 24; 4:14; 5:12).
15. Consult Donald Guthrie, *New Testament Theology* (Downers Grove: Inter-Varsity, 1981),
p. 316.
16. C. H. Dodd, *The Johannine Epistles,* Moffatt New Testament Commentary series (New
York: Harper and Row, 1946), pp. 9–10.

indication of John's apostolic authority? Not quite. If we understand this pronoun to refer to the authority of the apostle John, then the use of "we" throughout the introduction is strictly individualistic and excludes the other apostles.

What then is the significance of the first person plural? The pronoun *we* must be understood literally, because John, like the other apostles, preaches and writes as an eyewitness and earwitness. Thus John is not the only one to testify orally or with pen and ink. He stands next to his fellow apostles. He says, "We [all the immediate disciples of Jesus] write this to make our joy complete."

The greatest joy to fill the heart of the apostle John and those with him is to see the believers increase in the grace and knowledge of the Lord Jesus Christ. He wants them to have full fellowship with the Father and the Son, so that the believers live in full communion with God. John underscores the well-known words of John the Baptist spoken in tribute of Jesus: "He must become greater; I must become less" (John 3:30).

Doctrinal Considerations in 1:1–4

We have received an interesting comment from Papias, who around A.D. 125 was bishop of the church in Hierapolis, which was a city near Laodicea and Colosse in Asia Minor. Reportedly he was a follower of the apostle John from whom he tried to learn as much as possible about the Lord. He writes:

> If ever anyone came who had followed the presbyters, I inquired into the words of the presbyters, what Andrew or Peter or Philip or Thomas or James or John or Matthew, or any other of the Lord's disciples, had said, and what Aristion and the presbyter John, the Lord's disciples, were saying. For I did not suppose that information from books would help me so much as the word of a living and surviving voice.[17]

The generation of apostles and eyewitnesses ended near the close of the first century. And for all those who have come after that era, the words of Jesus spoken to Thomas are applicable: "Blessed are those who have not seen and yet have believed" (John 20:29).

We cannot physically see Jesus, yet we have fellowship with him (I John 1:3). We rejoice because he is always near us and is willing to listen to us. He is our brother (Heb. 2:11–12) and our friend (John 15:14–15).

How well do we know Jesus? We readily reject the liberal teaching that separates the historical Jesus from the Christ of faith, for we hold to the scriptural doctrine that Jesus is the Christ.

But how much does the humanity of Jesus mean to us today? We have no difficulty accepting the birth, life, death, resurrection, and ascension of Jesus. When we reflect on Jesus' humanity, we ask, "What is its significance for us now?"

---

17. Eusebius *Ecclesiastical History* 3. 39. Also consult Simon J. Kistemaker, ed., *Interpreting God's Word Today* (Grand Rapids: Baker, 1970), p. 82.

For one thing, his glorified human body is a guarantee that our physical bodies shall also be glorified. Jesus "will transform our lowly bodies so that they will be like his glorious body" (Phil. 3:21). Moreover, because Jesus shares our flesh and blood, he is our "merciful and faithful high priest" who has made "atonement for the sins of [his] people" (Heb. 2:17). Jesus welcomes us into the presence of God, the Father.

Greek Words, Phrases, and Constructions in 1:1–4

Verse 1

ἀκηκόαμεν . . . ἑωράκαμεν—the perfect active in this verse and the next two verses denotes lasting effect. Hearing and seeing are the two sides of the same coin. "Hearing is equally essential with seeing."[18]

ἐθεασάμεθα—note the use of the aorist tense that contrasts with the perfect tense in the preceding verbs. This verb and ἐψηλάφησαν (aorist active of ψηλαφάω, I touch, handle) point to a specific period of history in which the apostles accompanied Jesus.

Verse 2

ἡ ζωή—John employs the definite article to specify that life is eternal. He emphasizes the concept *life* with the repetitive use of the definite article and the indefinite relative pronoun ἥτις.

Verse 3

ὅ—as in the first verse, this relative neuter pronoun ultimately refers to Jesus.[19]

καὶ ἡ κοινωνία δέ—"When the copula is sufficiently represented by δέ, a καί may be rendered by some such phrase as *Yes, and* or *Moreover*."[20]

Verse 4

ἡμεῖς—manuscript support is stronger for the reading ἡμεῖς than ὑμῖν. "Copyists were more likely to alter γράφομεν ἡμεῖς to the expected γράφομεν ὑμῖν than vice versa."[21]

ἡμῶν—manuscript support favors ἡμῶν instead of ὑμῖν. Bruce M. Metzger writes, "As regards intrinsic probability, ἡμῶν seems to suit best the generous solicitude of the author, whose own joy would be incomplete unless his readers shared it."[22]

---

18. Friedrich Blass and Albert Debrunner, *A Greek Grammar of the New Testament and Other Early Christian Literature*, trans. and rev. Robert Funk (Chicago: University of Chicago Press, 1961), sec. 342(2). Also consult Robert Hanna, *A Grammatical Aid to the Greek New Testament* (Grand Rapids: Baker, 1983), p. 433.

19. Refer to A. T. Robertson, *A Grammar of the Greek New Testament in the Light of Historical Research* (Nashville: Broadman, 1934), p. 713.

20. C. F. D. Moule, *An Idiom-Book of New Testament Greek*, 2d ed. (Cambridge: At the University Press, 1960), p. 165.

21. Bruce M. Metzger, *A Textual Commentary on the Greek New Testament*, corrected ed. (London and New York: United Bible Societies, 1975), p. 708.

22. Ibid., p. 708.

ἤ πεπληρωμένη—this is a periphrastic construction with the verb *to be* in the present subjunctive and the perfect passive participle as an "extensive perfect (completed act)."[23]

---

5 This is the message we have from him and declare to you: God is light; in him there is no darkness at all. 6 If we claim to have fellowship with him yet walk in the darkness, we lie and do not live by the truth. 7 But if we walk in the light, as he is in the light, we have fellowship with one another, and the blood of Jesus, his Son, purifies us from every sin.

8 If we claim to be without sin, we deceive ourselves and the truth is not in us. 9 If we confess our sins, he is faithful and just and will forgive us our sins and purify us from all unrighteousness. 10 If we claim we have not sinned, we make him out to be a liar and his word has no place in our lives.

II. Walk in the Light
1:5–2:17

A. Fellowship and Forgiveness
1:5–10

1. God Is Light
1:5

John has introduced his letter by proclaiming the message that Jesus Christ, who is the Word of life, has appeared and that the readers may have fellowship with the Father and the Son, Jesus Christ. John continues to expand the content of that message and explains that fellowship includes light and truth.

5. This is the message we have heard from him and declare to you: God is light; in him there is no darkness at all.

a. "This is the message." John skillfully uses the order of words in the Greek to emphasize his point.[24] Although we are able to convey the emphasis in English only with the translation *this is the message,* John puts the stress on the verb *is* to convey the sense *exists*: "There exists this message." He discloses not only the importance of the message but also its timeless significance. This message, therefore, has not been subject to change and modification, because it did not originate with John or with any other apostle or writer.

b. "The message we have heard from him." John implies that God originated the message delivered by Jesus Christ. John writes, "We have heard [it] from him." This is the third time John uses the construction *we have heard* (see also vv. 1, 3). The apostles heard the message from the lips of Jesus; they also knew it from the pages of the Old Testament. Hence David writes, "In your light we see light" (Ps. 36:9). God revealed himself to his people through the prophets (compare Isa. 49:6; II Peter 1:19).

---

23. Robertson, *Grammar,* pp. 907–8.

24. John follows the regular Greek word order in other passages of this epistle, where similar constructions occur without emphasis (see 2:25; 3:11; 5:11).

c. "We . . . declare to you." What did Jesus teach the apostles during his earthly ministry? John sums it up in one sentence. "We . . . declare to you: God is light; in him is no darkness at all." John and the other apostles received this declaration from Jesus with the command to make it known. The message is not merely for information; it is a command.[25] That is, God speaks and man must listen obediently.

d. "God is light." John formulates short statements that describe God's nature. In other places he says, "God is spirit" (John 4:24) and "God is love" (I John 4:16). Here, in verse 5, he reveals God's essence in a short statement of three words: "God is light." God is not a light among many other lights; he is not a light-bearer; God does not have light as one of his characteristics, but he is light; and although he created light (Gen. 1:3), he himself is uncreated light. Moreover, the light of God is visible in Jesus, who said, "I am the light of the world" (John 8:12). In the Nicene Creed, the church confesses Jesus Christ as

God of God, Light of Light.

In Jesus we see God's eternal light. From the moment of his birth to the time of his resurrection, the life of Jesus was filled with God's light. "Jesus was completely and absolutely transparent with the Light of God."[26] And whoever has seen Jesus has seen the Father (John 14:9).

e. "In him there is no darkness at all." Light is positive, darkness is negative. In his writings, John habitually contrasts opposites, including light and darkness, truth and falsehood, love and hate, right and wrong, life and death, faith and unbelief. He writes, "In [God] there is no darkness at all." Using the emphatic negative, John stresses the positive. God and darkness are diametrically opposed. Anyone who has fellowship with God cannot be in darkness. He is in the light, glory, truth, holiness, and purity of God.

Greek Words, Phrases, and Constructions in 1:5

ἔστιν αὕτη—the emphasis falls on the verb *to be*, which conveys the meaning *to exist*.

ἀγγελία—this noun appears twice in the New Testament, both times in the First Epistle of John (1:5; 3:11). Some Greek manuscripts have the reading ἐπαγγελία (promise), which also occurs in 2:25.

ἀναγγέλλομεν—the verb *to announce* ("declare," NIV) is directed to the audience. By contrast, the verb ἀπαγγέλλομεν ("we proclaim," NIV [1:2, 3]) relates to the original source of the message.

---

25. Refer to Ulrich Becker and Dietrich Müller, *NIDNTT*, vol. 3, p. 47. They write, "The content of the proclamation is both for information, or 'reminding' of the saving event, and commandment."

26. Thomas F. Torrance, *Christian Theology and Scientific Culture* (New York: Oxford University Press, 1981), p. 96.

φῶς—the word *light* is a typical Johannine word. "In the N[ew] T[estament] φῶς occurs 72 times, of which 33 are in the Johannine writings, 14 in the Synoptic Gospels, 13 in Paul and 10 in Acts."[27]

---

2. *Darkness and Light*
1:6–7

6. If we claim to have fellowship with him yet walk in the darkness, we lie and do not live by the truth.   7. But if we walk in the light, as he is in the light, we have fellowship with one another, and the blood of Jesus, his Son, purifies us from every sin.

The next five verses of this chapter are conditional sentences that describe probability or even possibility. The first, third, and fifth verses are negative, the second and the fourth are positive.

a. *Negative.* John repeats the word *fellowship* which he first used near the end of his introduction (v. 3). Fellowship, as he said, is with the Father and the Son, Jesus Christ. But fellowship means intimately sharing in the full light of God's presence. Nothing is hidden in the brilliance of divine revelation. In God is absolutely no darkness and no need to hide anything.

The sinner who refuses to set his life in harmony with God's will cannot claim to have fellowship with God. Perhaps some of the people who opposed the Christian faith near the end of the first century and who were known as Gnostics were saying, "We have fellowship with God." Yet these people continued to walk in darkness, that is, they were taking intense satisfaction in a life of sinful pleasures. They separated word from deed. They professed to live for God, but their deeds proved to be incompatible with their confession. They lived the lie.

What are deeds that are contradictory to the assertion of living for God? They are deeds that cannot stand in the light of God's Word (John 3:19–21). Darkness can blind a person so that his heart is filled with hatred toward his brother (I John 2:11). And this blindness results in a refusal to live according to God's precepts.

John is all-inclusive in his description of people who live in darkness. He does not say "they" but "we." If we say that we are God's people but continue to live in sin, "we lie and do not live by the truth." If we lie, we sin with our mouths but also with our entire beings. Our lives are set against God because of a heart filled with hatred and a will inclined to disobedience.

Sin alienates man from God and from his fellow man.[28] It disrupts life and fosters confusion. Instead of peace, there is discord; in place of harmony, there is disorder; and in lieu of fellowship, there is enmity.

However, when we have fellowship with God, we experience the grace

---

27. Hans-Christoph Hahn, *NIDNTT*, vol. 2, p. 493.
28. Consult Walter Thomas Conner, *The Epistles of John*, 2d and rev. ed. (Nashville: Broadman, 1957), p. 21.

of Christ dispelling darkness and flooding us with the light of God.[29] To
have fellowship with God is to live a life of holiness in his sacred presence.
The Latin saying *Coram Deo* (always in the presence of God) was a motto
of the sixteenth-century reformer John Calvin. Holiness demands truth in
word and deed.

b. *Positive.* What then is characteristic of a life spent in the light of God's
truth? "If we walk in the light, as [God] is in the light, we have fellowship
with one another." Walking in the light is continuous. It means that we
live in the radiance of God's light, so that we reflect God's virtues and
glory. God himself lives in "unapproachable light," as Paul discloses
(I Tim. 6:16).

Living for God implies that we have a wholesome relationship with our
fellow man. This truth is reflected in the summary of the Decalogue:
"Love the Lord your God . . . and love your neighbor as yourself" (Matt.
22:37–38). A longing for heavenly glory in the presence of God must be
accompanied by a fervent desire to have fellowship with the church on
earth. Timothy Dwight gave expression to his desire to serve the Lord
through the fellowship of the church when he wrote:

> I love thy church, O God:
> Her walls before thee stand,
> Dear as the apple of thine eye,
> And graven on thy hand.
>
> For her my tears shall fall,
> For her my prayers ascend;
> To her my cares and toils be giv'n,
> Till toils and cares shall end.

Furthermore, if we walk in the light and have fellowship with God and
with one another, we realize that our sins have disappeared. John says,
"And the blood of Jesus, his Son, purifies us from every sin." Jesus
cleanses us and presents us to himself "as a radiant church, without stain
or wrinkle or any other blemish, but holy and blameless" (Eph. 5:27; also
see Heb. 9:14).

We stand before God as if we have never sinned at all. The Son of God
purifies us when, after we have fallen into sin, we come to him and seek
remission. Note that John writes the name *Jesus* to call attention to the
earthly life of God's Son, who shed his blood for remission of sin. Sin
belongs to the world of darkness and cannot enter the sphere of holiness.
Therefore, God gave his Son to die on earth. Through his Son's death
God removed man's sin and guilt so that man may have fellowship with
God.

---

29. John Calvin, *Commentaries on the Catholic Epistles: The First Epistle of John,* ed. and trans.
John Owen (Grand Rapids: Eerdmans, 1948), p. 164.

Greek Words, Phrases, and Constructions in 1:7

Ἰησοῦ τοῦ υἱοῦ αὐτοῦ—although a few Greek and Latin manuscripts and at least two translations (KJV, NKJV) have the reading *Jesus Christ his Son*, it is easier to explain the word *Christ* (also see 1:3; 2:1; 3:23; 4:2, 15 [variant reading]; 5:6, 20) as an insertion than to account for its omission.

---

3. Deception and Confession
1:8–10

8. If we claim to be without sin, we deceive ourselves and the truth is not in us.

Once more John states the negative and the positive in two successive verses that express conditions. Also the last verse (v. 10) is a conditional statement, which John puts in the form of a negative conclusion.

a. *Denial.* Another claim made by opponents of the Christian faith, perhaps the so-called Gnostics, is that they have advanced to a stage beyond sinfulness. They say that they have achieved their goal: perfection.[30]

John listens to these people who assert that they are without sin. But when he quotes their claim, he includes himself and the readers. He puts the assertion in a conditional sentence and says, "If we claim to be without sin, we deceive ourselves and the truth is not in us." Anyone who has no need to pray the fifth petition of the Lord's Prayer—"Forgive us our sins" (Luke 11:4)—because he thinks that he has no sin deceives himself. King Solomon wisely observed (Prov. 28:13):

> He who conceals his sins does not prosper,
> but whoever confesses and renounces them finds mercy.

The choice of words is significant: John says, "we have no sin." He does not write, "we do not sin." The noun *sin* describes the cause and the consequence of an act of disobedience; as a verb, the word describes the act itself.[31]

In the days of the apostle John, Greek philosophers taught a separation between body and spirit. The spirit is free, they said, but the body is matter that eventually dies. That is, if the body sinned, the spirit would be blameless. Sin, then, cannot affect the spirit. The First Epistle of John provides insufficient information to conclude that John was actively opposing Greek thinking. Scripture, however, teaches the universality of sin by saying that in the human race "there is no one who does good, not even one" (Ps. 14:3; 53:3; Rom. 3:12; also see Eccl. 7:20).

---

30. Refer to Neil Alexander, *The Epistles of John, Introduction and Commentary*, Torch Bible Commentaries series (London: SCM, 1962), p. 49.
31. Refer to Westcott, *The Epistles of St. John*, p. 22.

If we say that we have no sin, we are misleading ourselves. Moreover, the truth of God's Word is not in us. In our spiritual blindness, we go contrary to the plain teaching of Scripture. And God judges us by the words we have spoken, for our own words condemn us.

9. If we confess our sins, he is faithful and just and will forgive us our sins and purify us from all unrighteousness.

The writer presents typical Semitic parallelism. Verse 8 is parallel to verse 6, and verse 9 is a partial repetition and further explanation of verse 7. Because of its affirmative message, verse 9 is one of the more well-known passages of the epistle and even of the entire New Testament.

b. *Affirmation.* The text consists of three parts. The first is the condition, the second the assurance, and the third the fulfillment.

"If we confess our sins." This is the conditional part of the sentence that points to our acknowledgment of sin. We openly and honestly face sin without hiding it or finding excuses for it.[32] We confront the sins we have committed, without defending or justifying ourselves. We confess our sins to show repentance and renewal of life. We are not told when, where, and how to confess our sins, but daily repentance of sin leads us to continual confession. John actually writes, "If we keep confessing our sins." He writes the word *sins* (in the plural) to indicate the magnitude of our transgressions.

"He is faithful and just." Here is the assurance. God is faithful with respect to his promises. He is "a faithful God who does no wrong, upright and just is he" (Deut. 32:4). He does not scold or rebuke us; he does not become impatient; and he does not go back on his word. The only condition God requires for forgiveness is that we confess our sins. True to the promises made to the people of his new covenant, God declares, "I will forgive their wickedness and will remember their sins no more" (Jer. 31:34; Heb. 8:12; 10:17).[33]

"[He] will forgive us our sins and purify us from all unrighteousness." Note the fulfillment. Although translators put the verbs in the future tense as if the acts of forgiving and purifying will eventually happen, the Greek text says that God effectively forgives and purifies once for all. The first verb *to forgive* describes the act of canceling a debt and the restoration of the debtor. And the second verb *to cleanse* refers to making the forgiven sinner holy so that he is able to have fellowship with God. God takes the initiative, for he says to us, "Come now, let us reason together. . . . Though your sins are like scarlet, they shall be as white as snow; though they are red as crimson, they shall be like wool" (Isa. 1:18).

10. If we claim we have not sinned, we make him out to be a liar and his word has no place in our lives.

---

32. Consult Dieter Fürst, *NIDNTT*, vol. 1, p. 346; Dodd, *The Johannine Epistles*, p. 23.
33. Compare J. R. W. Stott, *The Epistles of John: An Introduction and Commentary*, Tyndale New Testament Commentaries series (Grand Rapids: Eerdmans, 1964), p. 77. And see Brooke, *Commentary on the Johannine Epistles*, p. 19.

This last verse is the conclusion of the series of conditional sentences. At the same time, it serves as an introduction to the next chapter.

c. *Conclusion*. The statement *we have not sinned* reveals the blatant attitude of the unrepentant, unregenerate infidel. In verse 8 the unbeliever said that he has no sin; now he asserts that he is not a sinner. If he is not a sinner, for he maintains that he has not sinned, he makes himself equal to God, the sinless One. Through his Word God convicts man of sin. But if man refuses to listen to evidence God presents, man accuses God of lying (I John 5:10). In the sequence of three verses (6, 8, and 10), the writer works toward a climax: "we lie" (v. 6), "we deceive ourselves" (v. 8), and "we make him out to be a liar" (v. 10).

Once again John includes himself and the readers when he uses the personal pronoun *we*. If we should go so far as to say that we have not sinned, in spite of all the evidence, then the Word of God has no place in our lives. And that means that we are unbelievers who have rejected the gospel of salvation. The writer of Hebrews warns his readers not to follow the example of the rebellious Israelites who perished in the desert. "For we also have had the gospel preached to us, just as they did; but the message they heard was of no value to them, because those who heard did not combine it with faith" (Heb. 4:2).

Practical Considerations in 1:5–10

Plaques on walls and bumper stickers on cars tell the world "God is love." But no one displays the sign *God is light*. Yet this is exactly what John does in his first epistle. He first says, "God is light" (1:5) and later writes, "God is love" (4:16). Light comes before love, for light uncovers that which is hidden. When we have fellowship with God (1:3, 6), we cannot hide our sins. Sins, like darkness, have no place in God's light. They must be removed.

How does God remove sins? This is God's method: First, he cleanses us from sin with "the blood of Jesus, his Son, [that] purifies us from every sin" (v. 7). And second, he specifies our part in the remission of sin: "If we confess our sins, he is faithful and just and will forgive us our sins and purify us from all unrighteousness" (1:9). The blood of Jesus is sufficient to cleanse us from sin, but we must be willing to confess our sins. God's provision and man's responsibility go hand in hand.

To confess means that I say the same thing God says about sin.[34] God applies his law and says, "You are the sinner." And like the publican in the temple court I acknowledge my sin and pray, "God, have mercy on me, *the* sinner" (Luke 18:13, italics added—the original Greek has "*the* sinner," not "*a* sinner"). When God and man say the same thing about sin, the blood of Christ dissolves the stain of sin. God will remember sin no more. He forgives and forgets! Indeed, God is love.

---

34. J. D. Pentecost, *The Joy of Fellowship* (Grand Rapids: Zondervan, 1977), p. 31.

Greek Words, Phrases, and Constructions in 1:9–10

Verse 9

τὰς ἁμαρτίας—John writes the plural form of the noun to express the multitude of sin.

ἵνα—the conjunction introduces not so much purpose as "conceived result."[35]

Verse 10

ἡμαρτήκαμεν—the perfect active tense denotes completed action in the past—although negated by οὐχ (not)—that continues into the present.[36]

ψεύστης—this noun appears ten times in the New Testament; half of the references occur in I John (1:10; 2:4, 22; 4:20; 5:10).

Summary of Chapter 1

The first four verses of the epistle are introductory. They are a summary that tells the reader about the content of the letter. But the introduction also reminds him of the first verse of Genesis and the first verse of the Gospel of John to show him the continuity of God's message. The writer informs the reader that the message he and other eyewitnesses proclaim is true to fact. This message concerns the Word of life, namely, Jesus Christ, the Son of God. John invites the reader to have fellowship with God.

John seems to oppose religious teachers who make bold and unfounded statements. But before he alludes to some of their remarks, he states the heart of God's message to man: "God is light; in him there is no darkness at all." The statements of these erring teachers simply are unacceptable in view of God's revelation. Their remarks are contradictory to the message of God and reveal the unrepentant heart of the sinner who claims to have no sin.

John encourages the reader. He says that if we walk in the light, and confess our sins, God will forgive us our sins and purify us through the blood of Jesus, his Son. Therefore, we must walk in God's light.

---

35. Robertson, *Grammar,* p. 998; and see Blass and Debrunner, *Greek Grammar,* sec. 391(5).
36. Consult Burdick, *The Letters of John the Apostle,* p. 128.

2

Walk in the Light, *part 2*

2:1–17

and Believe in Jesus, *part 1*

2:18–29

Outline (continued)

2 1 My dear children, I write this to you so that you will not sin. But if anybody does sin, we have one who speaks to the Father in our defense—Jesus Christ, the Righteous One. 2 He is the atoning sacrifice for our sins, and not only for ours but also for the sins of the whole world.

3 We know that we have come to know him if we obey his commands. 4 The man who says, "I know him," but does not do what he commands is a liar, and the truth is not in him. 5 But if anyone obeys his word, God's love is truly made complete in him. This is how we know we are in him: 6 Whoever claims to live in him must walk as Jesus did.

B. Knowledge and Obedience
2:1–6

1. Defender and Sacrifice
2:1–2

Except for Jesus, there is no one who is sinless. Even if we know God's law and precepts, we still stumble and sin from time to time. What remedy is there for the person who has fallen into sin? John provides the answer by pointing to Jesus Christ, who is our helper.

1. My dear children, I write this to you so that you will not sin. But if anybody does sin, we have one who speaks to the Father in our defense—Jesus Christ, the Righteous One.

John addresses his readers with a term of endearment which can best be translated "dear children." He is their spiritual father, so to speak, and they are his offspring. The term occurs rather frequently in this epistle; therefore, we conclude that the term reflects John's authority as an apostle in the church and at the same time reveals his advanced age.[1] He is the person who is able to relate to fathers and young men and address them with a term of endearment.

a. *Comfort.* John writes in the singular ("I write this") as a loving pastor who admonishes his readers not to fall into sin. Note that he is not saying that they are living in sin, for their fellowship with God precludes this. John is fully aware of human frailty and Satan's seductive power. He

---

1. The diminutive term *dear children* belongs almost exclusively to John. Outside of John's writings, it appears only in Paul's epistle to the Galatians (4:19). The term occurs seven times in I John (2:1, 12, 28; 3:7, 18; 4:4; 5:21). Also see John 13:33, where Jesus addresses his disciples as "children." And last, using a different Greek word, John conveys a similar sentiment when he addresses his readers as "dear children" in I John 2:13, 18.

refers to the matters he stressed in the preceding chapter and says, "I write [these things] to you so that you will not sin." He stands next to his readers and encourages them in their struggle against sin. He knows that they wish to live a holy life, but occasionally they sin. Sin separates and alienates the sinner from God. John hears the plea of the believer who has fallen into sin: "Pastor, what must I do?"

John speaks words of comfort. "But if anybody does sin, we have one who speaks to the Father." If a believer commits a sin, he still remains a child of God. The fellowship between the Father and his son or daughter is disrupted because of sin, but the Father-child relationship continues unless the child refuses to acknowledge his sin. How, then, is the fellowship restored?

b. *Counselor.* "We have one who speaks to the Father in our defense," writes John, "Jesus Christ, the Righteous One." We have an Advocate. The New International Version broadens the concept *advocate* and circumscribes it with the phrase "one who speaks . . . in our defense." Picture a court of law in which the guilty party is summoned to appear. The sinner needs a court-appointed lawyer to represent him. God, who is the plaintiff, appoints his Son to be the intercessor for and the helper of the defendant.

Our defender is Jesus Christ, whom John describes as "the Righteous One" (compare Acts 3:14). As sinners, we have the best possible helper because he is righteous. That is, in his human nature Jesus is our brother (Heb. 2:11), is acquainted with our frailties (Heb. 4:15), saves us (Heb. 7:25), and is our intercessor. He is also God's Messiah, the Christ, who has fulfilled the demands of the law for us and therefore has been given the title *Righteous One.* As a sinless lawyer he represents us in court.

2. He is the atoning sacrifice for our sins, and not only for ours but also for the sins of the whole world.

John develops two thoughts in this verse: Jesus' sacrifice and the extent of this sacrifice. We shall consider the *sacrifice* of Jesus first.

a. "He is the atoning sacrifice for our sins." Translations of this particular clause differ. Here are some representative versions:

1. "And he is the propitiation for our sins" (KJV, NKJV, RV, ASV, NASB, *Moffatt*).
2. "And he is the expiation for our sins" (RSV)
3. "He is himself an atoning sacrifice for our sins" (MLB, NIV)
4. "He is himself the remedy for the defilement of our sins" (NEB)

What is the meaning of this text? The expressions *propitiation* and *expiation* are theological terms that belong to earlier times.[2] For this reason, today

---

2. To propitiate means to appease. To expiate is to remove the guilt incurred in an offense. To atone is to make amends or supply satisfaction for sin. For study and literature refer to Herwart Vorländer and Colin Brown, "Reconciliation, Restoration, Propitiation, Atonement," *NIDNTT,* vol. 3, pp. 145–76. And consult J. R. W. Stott, *The Epistles of John: An Introduction and Commentary,* Tyndale New Testament Commentaries series (Grand Rapids: Eerdmans, 1964), pp. 81–88.

translators have tried to find modern equivalents for these terms. Some have provided a paraphrase of the text; they attempt to clarify its meaning with the words *atoning sacrifice* as substitutes for both "propitiation" and "expiation."

Before we look closely at the wording, we must consider a parallel passage. In this passage, John uses the same wording, but the context emphasizes the love of God. "This is love: not that we loved God, but that he loved us and sent his Son as an atoning sacrifice for our sins" (I John 4:10; also consult Rom. 3:25; Heb. 2:17). Therefore we should note that in his love God gave his Son as an atoning sacrifice for our sins.

God initiated his love to a sinful world by giving his Son to cover sin and remove guilt. This gift resulted in the death of Jesus on the cross. Jesus became the acceptable sacrifice for making amends and redeeming man from the curse God had pronounced upon him. With respect to the broken relationship between God and man, Jesus brought peace (Rom. 5:1) and reconciliation (II Cor. 5:20–21). And with reference to man's sin before God, Jesus removed it by paying the debt (I John 1:7, 9). With his atoning sacrifice, Christ removes sin and guilt, demands a confession of sin from the believer, and intercedes before God in behalf of the sinner.[3]

b. "And not only for ours but also for the sins of the whole world." Here John refers to the *extent* of Christ's atoning sacrifice. Scholars usually comment that the extent of Christ's death is universal but the intent is for believers. Or in different words, Christ's death is sufficient for the whole world but efficient for the elect. John Calvin, however, observes that although these comments are true, they do not pertain to this passage.[4] The phrase *the whole world* relates not to every creature God has made, for then the fallen angels also would share in Christ's redemption. The word *whole* describes the world in its totality, not necessarily in its individuality.

In another context, John distinguishes between the "children of God" and "the children of the devil" (I John 3:1, 10) and then concludes, "Jesus Christ laid down his life for us" (v. 16). Jesus died for all the people who believe in him and who come "from every nation, tribe, people and language" as a "great multitude that no one [can] count" (Rev. 7:9).[5]

Practical Considerations in 2:1–2

On Sundays at worship you sing the words of hymns and psalms and in the company of fellow church members you recite the words of the Apostles' Creed. But during the week you fall into sin.

---

3. Refer to Friedrich Büchsel, *TDNT*, vol. 3, pp. 317–18.
4. John Calvin, *Commentaries on the Catholic Epistles: The First Epistle of John*, ed. and trans. John Owen (Grand Rapids: Eerdmans, 1948), p. 173.
5. Compare James Montgomery Boice, *The Epistles of John* (Grand Rapids: Zondervan, 1979), p. 52.

How, then, do you know that you are a Christian? In your weaker moments doubt and uncertainty enter your mind and you question whether you are a member of the family of believers. When you have sinned, you hear the voice of Satan accusing you before God and telling him that you cannot possibly be one of his children. Moreover, the Christian community is saddened by your sin, and the world questions your Christian sincerity. Because of your sin, you hear the words of the hymn, "Blessed assurance, Jesus is mine," but they are meaningless to you. You lack the assurance of salvation.

For Christians who lack assurance, John writes this message of comfort and confidence: "If anybody does sin, we have one who speaks to the Father in our defense—Jesus Christ, the Righteous One" (2:1). Jesus is their helper. He died for sinners and represents them as their defense lawyer before the judgment seat of God. And on the basis of his death he pleads for their acquittal.

Jesus has met God's demands, has defeated Satan and silences his accusations. When sinners come to him in prayer and ask for remission, Jesus offers them salvation full and free. The writer of Hebrews testifies, "For surely it is not angels he helps, but Abraham's [spiritual] descendants. For this reason he had to be made like his brothers in every way, in order that he might become a merciful and faithful high priest in service to God, and that he might make atonement for the sins of the people" (2:16–17).

How do I know I am a Christian? When I accept Jesus' testimony that he has died for me and has cleansed me from all my sins, then "I know whom I have believed" (II Tim. 1:12). And then in thankfulness I am ready and willing to obey his commands and do his will.

Greek Words, Phrases, and Constructions in 2:1–2

Verse 1

τεκνία—this diminutive from τέκνον (child) is a term of endearment. It reveals the advanced age of the writer and demonstrates his genuine interest in the development of his spiritual children.

γράφω—in 1:4, John uses the first person plural, present tense γράφομεν. There he writes on the testimony of fellow eyewitnesses and himself. Here he writes on his own authority.

ἁμάρτητε—with the form ἁμάρτῃ the aorist subjunctive conveys the idea of potential for sin; that is, the writer warns the reader not to fall into sin. The use of the present tense, by contrast, would have indicated continual and habitual sinning.

παράκλητος—from παρακαλέω (I comfort, beg, exhort), this noun, which in a court of law means "advocate," can best be translated "helper." In the Gospel of John the noun refers to the Holy Spirit (14:16, 26; 15:26; 16:7). Here it designates Jesus Christ.[6]

πρός—the preposition discloses that Jesus is not only *in the presence of* his Father; he presents our prayers *to* the Father.

---

6. Bauer, p. 618, comments that "in our literature the active sense *helper, intercessor* is suitable in all occurrences of the word."

Verse 2

ἱλασμός—this noun derived from ἱλάσκομαι (I appease) describes an action performed by Jesus Christ that appeases God the Father. A noun with a -μος ending denotes action; a noun with a -μα ending indicates the result of that action.[7]

περί—in Johannine literature περί is equivalent to ὑπέρ (for).

ὅλου—John chooses the adjective ὅλος (whole) instead of πᾶς (every, all) to communicate the idea of universality. The word ὅλος has "an indefinite meaning which πᾶς does not have."[8]

---

2. Knowledge and Love
2:3–5a

3. We know that we have come to know him if we obey his commands. 4. The man who says, "I know him," but does not do what he commands is a liar, and the truth is not in him.

With the conjunction *and* (omitted in the NIV), John connects verse 3 and the second half of chapter 1. Apparently the writer needs to complete his thoughts on having fellowship with God (1:3, 6, 7, 9). As he pointed out, walking in the light in fellowship with God means that we confess our sins (1:9). Now he adds that knowing God means obeying his commands. As a synonym of the term *fellowship* he introduces the concept *knowing God*.

a. "We know that we have come to know him." In this short verse the word *know* occurs twice. The first verb is in the present tense ("we know") and the second in the perfect tense ("we have come to know").[9]

Fellowship with God and knowledge of God are the two sides of the same coin. One's relationship with God can vary from casual acquaintance to intimate fellowship. But God is not interested in a relationship that is casual and meaningless. He desires that we come to know him intimately.

Knowing God implies that we learn about him, love him, and also experience his love. We gain our knowledge of God when we strive to do his will in the actual experiences of life. Knowing him, then, means that we live in perfect harmony with him by keeping his law.

b. "If we obey his commands." To know God is to keep his commands, and to keep his commands is to know God. John repeats this thought with slightly different words in another passage of his epistle: "This is how we know that we love the children of God: by loving God and carrying out his commands" (5:2).

The conditions of the new covenant which God revealed to Jeremiah

---

7. Consult Bruce M. Metzger, *Lexical Aids for Students of New Testament Greek* (Princeton: published by the author, 1969), p. 43.

8. A. T. Robertson, *A Grammar of the Greek New Testament in the Light of Historical Research* (Nashville: Broadman, 1934), p. 774.

9. In the Greek, John repeatedly uses the perfect tense of this verb (2:4, 13, 14; 3:6, 16; 4:16; II John 1).

(Jer. 31:33–34) and which the writer of Hebrews quotes (Heb. 8:10–11) combine law and knowledge of God.[10]

> "This is the covenant I will make with the house of Israel
>   after that time," declares the LORD.
> "I will put my law in their minds
>   and write it on their hearts.
> I will be their God,
>   and they will be my people.
> No longer will a man teach his neighbor,
>   or a man his brother, saying, 'Know the LORD,'
> because they will all know me,
>   from the least of them to the greatest,"
>   declares the LORD.

The distinctive characteristic of the child of God is that he obeys God's commands. When he keeps these commands, he demonstrates that he has come to know God. But this is not always the case, as John points out in the next verse.

c. "The man who says, 'I know him,' but does not do what he commands is a liar." Although this verse parallels the discussion of the last half of the preceding chapter (1:6, 8, 10), where John writes comprehensively about the claim of fellowship with God and the failure to live in the truth, here he quotes an individual. He quotes the person who claims to have come to know (perfect tense) God but who fails to keep (present tense) God's commands. John calls him a liar. That is, this person is a walking lie who says one thing and does the opposite (compare 4:20; Titus 1:16). The word *liar* describes the character of the man whose entire conduct is opposed to the truth.

d. "And the truth is not in him." Except for the last two words of this clause, this statement is identical to that in 1:8. The emphasis falls on "in him." This person, says John, is devoid of God's truth.

5a. But if anyone obeys his word, God's love is truly made complete in him.

One of the salient characteristics of this epistle is John's continual use of contrast. For example, he places the truth over against the lie, light in opposition to darkness, and love against hatred. Also in the first part of this verse, he states affirmatively that which he portrays negatively in the previous verse.

Another characteristic is John's use of various terms that express the same thought for the concept *word*: "truth" (1:8; 2:4), "word" (1:10; 2:5), and "command" (2:3–4)—all of them mean more or less the same thing. Even though there is similarity, the "word" is broader and more comprehensive than the "commands." As John Albert Bengel observes, "*The pre-*

---

10. Consult Kenneth Grayston, *The Johannine Epistles,* New Century Bible Commentary series (Grand Rapids: Eerdmans, 1984), p. 61. Also refer to C. H. Dodd, *The Johannine Epistles,* Moffatt New Testament series (New York: Harper and Row, 1946), p. 30.

cepts are many; *the word* is one."[11] The Word of God is God's revelation that culminates in Jesus Christ (Heb. 1:2). In fact, John echoes the words Jesus spoke in the discourse after he instituted the Lord's Supper: "If anyone loves me, he will obey my teaching [that is, my word]" (John 14:23).

Anyone who obeys God's word experiences the unrestricted love of God. John probably wrote these words to oppose Gnostic teachers who extolled gathering knowledge at the expense of obedience. John, however, teaches that the love of God fills completely the heart and life of the person who obeys God's word (compare 4:12, 18).

What is the meaning of the phrase *God's love*? Some commentators translate it objectively as "man's love for God."[12] Others understand it subjectively as "God's love for man."[13] And still others interpret it to be a description: love that is peculiar to God himself.

Although all three interpretations have merit, evidence from the immediate and the broader contexts seems to support the subjective interpretation. First, in the immediate context compare the parallel in verses 4 and 5—"[God's] truth is not in him" (v. 4) and "God's love is . . . in him" (v. 5).[14] Both truth and love originate in God but not in man. Next, in the broader context of the epistle John explains the origin of love: "love comes from God" (4:7), "God lives in us and his love is made complete in us" (4:12), and "we know and rely on the love God has for us" (4:16). God is the source and giver of love. In summary, then, the context is decisive in determining the meaning of the phrase *God's love*.

Greek Words, Phrases, and Constructions in 2:3–5a

Verse 3

ἐν τούτῳ—this construction is common in I John; it occurs fourteen times (2:3, 4, 5 [twice]; 3:10, 16, 19, 24; 4:2, 9, 10, 13, 17; 5:2). Here it is an instrumental dative.

ἐγνώκαμεν—the perfect active indicative of γινώσκω (I know) shows resultant state ("we have come to know"). γινώσκω refers to experiential knowledge; οἶδα (I know) connotes innate knowledge.[15]

---

11. John Albert Bengel, *Gnomon of the New Testament*, ed. Andrew R. Fausset, 7th ed., 5 vols. (Edinburgh: Clark, 1877), vol. 5, p. 116.

12. Among others refer to A. E. Brooke, *A Critical and Exegetical Commentary on the Johannine Epistles*, International Critical Commentary series (Edinburgh: Clark, 1964), p. 32.

13. On the basis of I John 4:9 B. F. Westcott accepts the subjective interpretation. See *The Epistles of St. John, The Greek Text, with Notes and Addenda* (1883; Grand Rapids: Eerdmans, 1966), p. 49. Also refer to R. C. H. Lenski, *Interpretation of the Epistles of St. Peter, St. John, and St. Jude* (Columbus: Wartburg, 1945), p. 408.

14. Also compare John's reference to God's commands and God's love (I John 2:4–5) with Jesus' discourse on love and obedience to his commands (John 15:9–11). Consult S. Greijdanus, *De Brieven van de Apostelen Petrus en Johannes, en de Brief van Judas*, Kommentaar op het Nieuwe Testament series (Amsterdam: Van Bottenburg, 1929), p. 422.

15. Refer to Donald W. Burdick, *The Letters of John the Apostle* (Chicago: Moody, 1985), p. 133.

Verse 5a

τετελείωται—from τελειόω (I complete), this verb in the perfect active indicative is timeless, for it reveals a customary truth.[16]

---

3. Christian Conduct
2:5b–6

5b. This is how we know we are in him: 6. Whoever claims to live in him must walk as Jesus did.

The word *this* refers to either the preceding or the following sentence or both. In other words, verse 5b can be either the concluding part of verse 5a, or the introduction to verse 6, or an independent statement. Translators generally take the second option and regard verse 5b as introductory to the next verse.[17]

How do we know that we are in him? John answers with a progressive succession of statements: "we are in him," "[we] live in him," and "[we] walk as Jesus did."

a. "We are in him." We know that we are in God when we have intimate fellowship with him through Jesus Christ (1:3). The phrase *in him* is a reassertion of "[to] have come to know him" (2:3).

b. "[We] live in him." Fellowship with God in Christ is not a static condition but an active relation that endures. If we say that " 'in him we live and move and have our being' " (Acts 17:28), we place ourselves under obligation to God himself. We must follow the example he has given us in the earthly life of his Son.

c. "[We] walk as Jesus did." As Jesus lived while he was on earth, so we must live in imitation of him. We can do this only by setting our lives in harmony with his revelation. James H. Sammis eloquently expresses this teaching in the words of his well-known song:

> When we walk with the Lord
> In the light of His Word,
> What a glory He sheds on our way!
> While we do His good will,
> He abides with us still,
> And with all who will trust and obey.

Greek Words, Phrases, and Constructions in 2:5b–6

Verse 5b

ἐν τούτῳ—although this phrase can look forward or backward, in this verse the direction appears to be forward.[18]

---

16. Robertson, *Grammar*, p. 897.

17. I. Howard Marshall comments that "statistical probability" supports this view. See his discussion in *The Epistles of John,* New International Commentary on the New Testament series (Grand Rapids: Eerdmans, 1978), p. 126, n. 17.

18. Burdick is of the opinion that the phrase "looks back to the preceding context." *The Letters of John the Apostle,* p. 138.

Verse 6

ἐκεῖνος—this demonstrative pronoun stands in contrast with αὐτός; the first pronoun is preceded by καθώς (just as), the second is followed by οὕτως (so).

---

7 Dear friends, I am not writing you a new command but an old one, which you have had since the beginning. This old command is the message you have heard.   8 Yet I am writing you a new command; its truth is seen in him and you, because the darkness is passing and the true light is already shining.

9 Anyone who claims to be in the light but hates his brother is still in the darkness.   10 Whoever loves his brother lives in the light, and there is nothing in him to make him stumble.   11 But whoever hates his brother is in the darkness and walks around in the darkness; he does not know where he is going, because the darkness has blinded him.

C. Love and Light
2:7–11

1. New and Old
2:7–8

John makes a smooth transition of thought from one paragraph to the next. He moves from a discussion of knowing God and obeying his commands to the topic of love. John begins this paragraph with the word *beloved,* which the New International Version translates "dear friends."[19] John favors this form of address, for he resorts to it frequently (I John 2:7; 3:2, 21; 4:1, 7, 11; III John 1, 2, 5, 11).

7. Dear friends, I am not writing you a new command but an old one, which you have had since the beginning. This old command is the message you have heard.

The parallel between John's Gospel and his first epistle is irrefutable, especially in respect to his comments about the new command of love. We hear the voice of Jesus saying, "A new commandment I give you: Love one another" (John 13:34).

Note the following points:

First, John shows that the new comes forth from the old when he says that the new command is actually old. After he has said that, he states that he is writing a new command. He is interested primarily in the concept *command* and secondarily in the words *new* and *old.* Even though he does not explicitly state what this command is, he discloses in succeeding verses that it is the well-known precept to love one another (2:9–10).

Next, John cannot call this command new. Already in Old Testament times when God's people were in the Sinai desert, God instructed the Israelite to love his neighbor as himself (Lev. 19:18). Since the time of Moses, Jewish people have recited the following words as part of their creed: "Love the LORD your God with all your heart and with all your soul

---

19. Some manuscripts have the reading *brothers* (adopted by the KJV and NKJV). However, manuscript evidence strongly supports the reading *beloved,* which translators favor.

and with all your strength" (Deut. 6:5). God commanded the Israelite to love his neighbor in addition to loving God.

And last, John observes that the readers have had the old command from the beginning. He implies that they have received God's revelation and therefore know that this command as such is not new. "This old command," writes John, "is the message [of God's revelation] you have heard."[20] That is, the readers knew this command from the time when they first heard the preaching and teaching of God's Word—the Old Testament and the New Testament—in the worship services of the local church.

8. Yet I am writing you a new command; its truth is seen in him and you, because the darkness is passing and the true light is already shining.

John appears to contradict himself when he first asserts that we have no new command (compare II John 5) and then proceeds to introduce "a new command." There is no contradiction, however, as we see by considering these aspects:

a. *Literal.* The word *new* in Greek suggests that the old has given birth to the new. The old does not cease to exist but continues along with the new. We note a good example with respect to the two testaments: the Old Testament prepared the way for the New Testament, but did not lose its validity when the New arrived. Likewise, the old command addressed the people of the Old Testament era but kept its validity when Jesus came. Jesus gave this command greater significance, in a new form, in the context of the New Testament.

b. *Theological.* "Yet I am writing you a new command." From the verses following Leviticus 19:18 ("Love your neighbor as yourself"), we learn that the concept *neighbor* included the fellow Israelite and the alien who lived with God's people in the land. "Love [the alien] as yourself," God said (v. 34).[21]

In New Testament times, however, Jesus gave new meaning to the command to love one's neighbor when he taught the Parable of the Good Samaritan (Luke 10:25–37) and when he told his listeners that the command to love one's neighbor extended even to the enemy (Matt. 5:43–44). Jesus became known as "a friend of tax collectors and 'sinners' " (Matt. 11:19). He explained the meaning of the command to love one another by removing manmade obstacles and by revealing the divine intent and purpose of this particular command. The command, then, has been continuously in force from the beginning of history to the present, for it does not grow old with time.[22]

---

20. The better manuscripts omit the phrase *from the beginning.*

21. Consult SB, vol. 1, pp. 353–68, for a lucid exposition of the Jewish understanding of the word *neighbor.*

22. Refer to Calvin, *First Epistle of John,* p. 178. Donald Guthrie comments, "[John] is more interested in the new commandment than the ancient law, but there is no suggestion that the O[ld] T[estament] has ceased to be valid." See his *New Testament Theology* (Downers Grove: Inter-Varsity, 1981), p. 979.

c. *Evidential.* "Its truth is seen in him and you." Indirectly John refers to Jesus. In the preceding context he mentioned him directly when he said, "Whoever claims to live in him must walk as Jesus did" (2:6). John commends the readers for conduct that is truly characterized by this new command to love one another. "If the Christian fellowship is marked by such love, then it will be recognized as the fellowship of Christ's followers; it will bear the unmistakable stamp of his love."[23]

John provides proof for his observation that the readers are obeying the new command. Here is the proof: "Because the darkness is passing and the true light is already shining." John's penchant for contrast is evident in this verse. He puts "darkness" over against "light" and the verb *is passing* in contrast with the phrase *is already shining.* Note that the darkness has not yet disappeared; it is being dispelled because the light of the gospel of Christ enlightens the believers. John identifies the light as true (John 1:9) to indicate that all other light is merely a reflection which leads to disappointment and despair. This true light, says John, is shining already at this moment.

Practical Considerations in 2:8

Some countries today are experiencing a phenomenal growth of the Christian church. People are being baptized by the thousands; new churches are being formed everywhere; and the flame of the gospel, spreading as in the first century, leaps from person to person and area to area. Church leaders make calculations and venture projections about the future.

This rapid growth of the Christian church warms the heart of every believer; nevertheless, observers who are on the scene comment that while the Christian faith is evident on Sundays, during the week in the workaday world it proves to be absent and meaningless. Somehow the light of the gospel has not yet penetrated society at large. In the areas of education, business, labor, and politics the light of God's Word as yet has not dispelled darkness.

When toward the end of the first century John wrote, "The darkness is passing and the true light is already shining," he seemed to voice optimism devoid of realism. Perhaps some people ridiculed his enthusiasm. The Roman emperor persecuted the Christians; the power of darkness enveloped the Christian church; and the light of Christianity seemed insignificant. Yet John wrote these words in faith. He did not look at outward appearances but at the effect of living in the light of the gospel. Thus he saw that after ages of darkness, the gospel light had dawned.

Greek Words, Phrases, and Constructions in 2:7–8

Verse 7

ἀγαπητοί—this is a verbal adjective that conveys the passive voice: "beloved [by God]."

---

23. F. F. Bruce, *The Gospel of John* (Grand Rapids: Eerdmans, 1984), p. 294.

ἐντολὴν καινήν—the adjective follows the noun so that the emphasis falls on the noun. Note the noun is in the singular, not the plural (2:3). The adjective καινή (new), not νέα (fresh), is important, for it describes the nature of newness which is superior to the old.[24]

εἴχετε—the imperfect active indicative of ἔχω (I have) is considered to be a progressive imperfect.[25]

Verse 8

πάλιν—the adverb means "yet," not "again."

ὅ—as a relative pronoun in the neuter singular, this word does not have its antecedent in ἐντολήν. It stands by itself and can be explained with the addition of two words: [τοῦτο] ὅ ἐστιν ἀληθὲς ἐν αὐτῷ καὶ ἐν ὑμῖν [ἐστιν]. "[This] which is true in him [is] also true in you."[26]

παράγεται—from παράγω (I pass by), this form is the present passive indicative ("is passing away").

---

2. Light and Darkness
2:9–11

Once again John shows his fondness for contrast; pairs of opposites are prominent in the next verses: light and darkness, love and hatred, walking and stumbling.

9. Anyone who claims to be in the light but hates his brother is still in the darkness. 10. Whoever loves his brother lives in the light, and there is nothing in him to make him stumble. 11. But whoever hates his brother is in the darkness and walks around in the darkness; he does not know where he is going, because the darkness has blinded him.

Note, first, the obvious link between verse 8, where John introduces the spiritual truth about light, and verse 9, where he refers to a claim made by a religious opponent. Also note that after John states a spiritual truth, for example in 1:5, 2:3, and here in 2:9, he quotes the words of a religious opponent who makes a claim he cannot substantiate. And last, the pattern John develops in these three verses—negative, positive, negative—resembles an earlier series of five verses in which three are negative and two are positive (1:6–10).

a. *Negative.* The religious opponent claims to be in the light. In fact, he is the same person who already said that he has fellowship with God (1:6) and that he knows God (2:4). He makes this known to everyone who lends a listening ear. But his words do not match his deeds; his claim is worth-

---

24. Bauer, p. 394. Also see R. C. Trench, *Synonyms of the New Testament* (reprint ed., Grand Rapids: Eerdmans, 1953), pp. 219–25.

25. Robertson, *Grammar*, p. 884. And refer to Robert Hanna, *A Grammatical Aid to the Greek New Testament* (Grand Rapids: Baker, 1983), p. 434.

26. Compare for other comments C. F. D. Moule, *An Idiom-Book of New Testament Greek* (Cambridge: At the University Press, 1960), pp. 130–31. And see Robertson, *Grammar*, p. 713.

less, because his conduct contradicts it; his profession of light translates into a life of darkness; and in the absence of love, he experiences the ruinous power of hatred in interpersonal relationships.

The words of this text, "Anyone who claims to be in the light but hates his brother is still in darkness," apply to any reader of John's epistle. Whoever claims to be in God's light but continues to harbor hatred toward his fellow man demonstrates a life of darkness. We prefer to look heavenward and avoid looking at ourselves.

> To dwell in love
>> with the saints above,
> O! that will be glory!
> To dwell below
>> with the saints we know—
> Ah! that's a different story!

To hate a brother is not a trifling matter. John repeats the thought of this text in each of the next two chapters when he says, "Anyone who hates his brother is a murderer" (3:15), and "If anyone says, 'I love God,' yet hates his brother, he is a liar" (4:20). Whoever hates a Christian brother breaks God's commands, is devoid of truth, and lives in spiritual darkness.

For those living in darkness, John tactfully leaves the door open so that they may repent and come to the light. John writes that they are "still" in darkness. They need not stay there. They are welcome to come to a knowledge of the truth, lead a godly life, love the members of the church, and live in the light of the gospel.

b. *Positive.* John's remarks concern the members of the church. And in this setting, John puts his statements in absolute terms that offer no middle ground. For him there is no twilight. There is either light or darkness, love or hatred. Where love is absent, hatred rules in darkness. But where love prevails, there is light.

John writes, "Whoever loves his brother lives in the light, and there is nothing in him to make him stumble." Love is not so much a matter of the word as of the deed. Whoever loves his spiritual brother as himself "lives in the light." And when a person lives in the light, he does not stumble, because he is able to see clearly.

Translators are not agreed on the exact wording of the last part of verse 10. Here are three differing translations:

1. "And so there is nothing in him that will cause someone else to sin" (GNB)
2. "And in it there is no cause for stumbling" (RSV)
3. "There is nothing in him to make him stumble" (NIV)

Interpreters who favor the first translation point out that the Greek word *stumble* literally means "trap" and symbolically, "to cast a stumbling-block

263

before one."[27] In the second translation, the pronoun *it* refers to the antecedent *light*. That is, in the light there is no cause for stumbling. In view of the context, the third translation seems to make the best transition to the next verse (v. 11), which portrays the person who hates his brother as the one who stumbles in the darkness.[28]

John implies that anyone who hates his brother causes his own downfall. And the cause for his stumbling cannot be attributed to outside factors but only to one's inner being that is filled with hatred.

c. *Conclusion.* John's concluding remarks are straightforward. First, anyone who hates his brother is in darkness, for he has separated himself from the light of the gospel. Second, he is relatively safe if he stays where he is, but as soon he begins to walk around in the darkness, literally as well as figuratively, he stumbles because of his inability to see (John 12:35). Darkness has a blinding effect on the eyes. When eyes are kept idle for sustained periods of time, blindness inevitably results.[29] When a person is in spiritual darkness, life becomes meaningless and goals are without purpose. The tragedy is that walking in darkness need not take place, for God's true light is available to everyone (John 1:9).

Greek Words, Phrases, and Constructions in 2:9–11

Verse 9

ὁ λέγων—three successive verses begin with the definite article and a participle in the present tense to indicate duration: ὁ λέγων (v. 9); ὁ ἀγαπῶν (v. 10); and ὁ μισῶν (v. 11).

καί—this conjunction has an adversative meaning: "and yet" or "but."

Verse 10

τὸν ἀδελφόν—in the context of the epistle John speaks of the believer as "the brother." The rest of the New Testament writers confirm this designation.

σκάνδαλον—a movable stick in a trap that is set to catch birds or animals; a stumbling block.

Verse 11

οἶδεν—John employs the verb οἶδα (I know), not γινώσκω (I know, learn to know), to stress the concept of innate knowledge.

ἐτύφλωσεν—from τυφλόω (I make blind), the aorist tense is constative.

---

27. Thayer, p. 577. Also see Bauer, p. 753. Lenski comments, "The one who loves his brother and remains in the light has nothing in him that will be a trigger stick in a trap to kill any of his brethren spiritually." See his *Interpretation of the Epistles,* p. 415.

28. Refer to Burdick, *The Letters of John the Apostle,* p. 147; also see Greijdanus, *Johannes,* p. 430.

29. Alfred Plummer, *The Epistles of St. John,* Cambridge Greek Testament for Schools and Colleges series (Cambridge: At the University Press, 1896), p. 44.

12 I write to you, dear children,
        because your sins have been forgiven on account of his name.
13 I write to you, fathers,
        because you have known him who is from the beginning.
    I write to you, young men,
        because you have overcome the evil one.
    I write to you, dear children,
        because you have known the Father.
14 I write to you, fathers,
        because you have known him who is from the beginning.
    I write to you, young men,
        because you are strong,
        and the word of God lives in you,
        and you have overcome the evil one.

D. Two Appeals
2:12–14

1. First Address
2:12–13a

In a separate section, John appeals to his readers and summarizes his thoughts in poetic form. He addresses his readers according to categories: first, all the believers receive his exhortation; next he appeals to the fathers and then to young men.

12. I write to you, dear children,
    because your sins have been forgiven on account of his name.
13a. I write to you, fathers,
    because you have known him who is from the beginning.
    I write to you, young men,
    because you have overcome the evil one.

We make the following observations:

All readers

a. "I write to you." John is the pastor who personally addresses the members of the church (see 2:1, 7, 8). When he says, "I write," he means that his words, being penned, are permanent. The members of the church are apt to forget the spoken word, but that which is written stays. The recipients of John's letter, therefore, ought to take notice. "I am writing to you," says the elderly pastor.

b. "Dear children." John makes a special appeal to his readers and addresses them with a term of endearment, "dear children," characteristic of his epistle.[30] On the basis of frequency, scholars understand the term to

---

30. For detailed information refer to n. 1 in this chapter.

refer to all the original readers of this letter. In other words, John is not addressing three age groups: children, fathers, and young men. That sequence is rather unnatural. If he were addressing age groups, the order should be children, young men, fathers. But if we take "children" in a general sense, then John appeals to two groups: fathers and young men.[31] John first speaks to all his readers and then to the fathers and the young men.

c. "Because your sins have been forgiven."[32] If there is good news from Jesus Christ, it is the announcement that our sins have been forgiven (compare Luke 24:47; Acts 13:38). The paralytic carried by four of his friends to the house where Jesus stayed heard him say, "Son, your sins are forgiven" (Mark 2:5). The sinful woman who entered the home of Simon the Pharisee and anointed Jesus' feet heard these words: "Your sins are forgiven" (Luke 7:48). That is, God forgives sins once for all. Sins have been, are, and remain forever forgiven.

d. "On account of his name." Sins are forgiven because of the name of Jesus. John purposely puts emphasis on the term *name*. He writes, "on account of his name," not "on account of Jesus." The term *name* is not a mere designation but the revelation of the person and work of God's Son (see 1:9; 2:1–2; 4:10). God forgives sins on the basis of his Son's atoning death on Calvary's cross. The implication is that everyone who believes in Jesus and repents receives remission of sin.

Fathers

John addresses the fathers in the church twice (vv. 13, 14) and gives them the same message: "because you have known him who is from the beginning." In the broader context of the epistle, John repeatedly writes about the Father.[33] He uses this expression to portray the close relationship between God the Father and his Son. The term *father* assumes sonship; with respect to God this fatherhood includes both the Son of God and the children adopted through him. We have natural fathers, but

---

31. Consult Calvin, *The First Epistle of John,* pp. 183–84; Brooke, *Commentary on the Johannine Epistles,* p. 43. Dodd comments, "The threefold arrangement is probably not much more than a rhetorical figure. All the privileges mentioned belong to all Christians, but emphasis and variety of expression are secured by distributing them into groups." See his *Johannine Epistles,* p. 38.

　J. L. Houlden proposes that the words *fathers* and *young men* are synonyms for "elders" and "deacons." Refer to *A Commentary on the Johannine Epistles,* Black's New Testament Commentaries series (London: Black, 1973), pp. 70–71. This suggestion, however, is speculative and unconvincing.

32. There are differing translations. For instance, the word *because* can be rendered "that" or omitted altogether. The Jerusalem Bible omits either "because" or "that" in the first three addresses and provides "because" for the next three. Also see B. Noack, "On I John 2:12–14," *NTS* 6 (1960): 236–41.

33. In I John the word *Father* occurs twelve times (1:2, 3; 2:1, 13, 15, 16, 22, 23 [twice], 24; 3:1; 4:14) and in II John four times (3 [twice], 4, 9).

earthly fatherhood is only a faint reflection of God's fatherhood. Nevertheless, John appeals to the fathers, because they have gained spiritual knowledge of and about Jesus Christ. In the course of time, they "have [come to know] him who is from the beginning." They have an intimate knowledge of God's revelation in Jesus Christ (1:1; John 1:1). The Christian community, then, looks to the spiritual fathers for leadership, and they, in turn, must care for their spiritual children. They are responsible to hand the torch of the gospel light to the next generation, namely, the young men in the church.

Young men

John is speaking to the youth in the church. He commends them for having "overcome the evil one." He repeats the same words in the next verse to indicate the significance of this truth. They have conquered the evil one, that is, Satan. They have repelled the attacks of the devil, have not joined Satan's camp, and rejoice in their salvation. They belong to Jesus and live in the light of his revelation. They have stood firm in the face of temptation, for in their God-given spiritual strength they have overcome.

Greek Words, Phrases, and Constructions in 2:12

γράφω—in three successive addresses John employs the present active first person singular. Then in verses 13b–14, he writes ἔγραψα three times in succession. The use of the aorist active tense (first person singular) is the so-called epistolary aorist; that is, the writer looks at his epistle from the recipient's point of view.[34] This use also occurs in I John 2:21, 26; 5:13. The epistolary aorist is translated in the present tense.

τεκνία—as a diminutive from τέκνον (child, son), this noun expresses endearment; because it is neuter, the noun refers to men, women, and children.

ἀφέωνται—from ἀφίημι (I forgive), the perfect tense indicates action that took place in the past with lasting effect for the present and future. The passive voice implies that God is the agent who forgives.

---

2. Second Address
2:13b–14

A number of translations present verse 13b as verse 14, so that the first and the second appeals form parallel sets.[35] Even though the Greek text shows a different word for "dear children," the symmetry between the first three addresses and these three is perfect: children, fathers, and young men.

---

34. Consult Robertson, *Grammar*, p. 845.

35. Greek New Testaments (among others, Nestle-Aland, United Bible Societies, Majority Text, British and Foreign Bible Societies) and some translations (NAB, JB, and GNB) begin verse 14 with the words *I write to you, children.*

> **13b. I write to you, dear children,**
> **because you have known the Father.**
> **14. I write to you, fathers,**
> **because you have known him who is from the beginning.**
> **I write to you, young men,**
> **because you are strong,**
> **and the word of God lives in you,**
> **and you have overcome the evil one.**

Once again John introduces each of his three appeals with the introductory clause *I write to you*. In Greek he uses the past tense of the verb *to write*, but in translation it is usually put in the present.

Dear children

John uses a Greek word, different from the one he used in verse 12, as a term of endearment to express his tender love to all his readers regardless of age. The reason that he appeals to the readers is this: "you have known the Father." Not only the fathers have come to know Jesus Christ from the beginning; all the believers have come to know the Father and, by implication, God's Son, Jesus Christ. Through Jesus, the believers have personally experienced the love of God the Father.

Fathers

Once more John appeals to the fathers: "you have known him who is from the beginning." The author repeats what he already has written in the preceding verse (v. 13). The repetition discloses the seriousness of the author's appeal; that is, the fathers cannot afford to relax the process of their spiritual growth.

Young men

Last, the youth of the church are strong, says John. Of course, young men are strong physically, but John means that they have proved their spiritual strength (Eph. 6:10). They oppose and overcome Satan, because they possess the word of God that is living in them (1:10; 2:5; John 5:38). "This possession is the secret of their strength and the source of their victory."[36] As long as they treasure, obey, and believe that word, they will be victorious and overcome the power and deceit of Satan.

Practical Considerations in 2:12–14

Christians in the last part of the first century encountered teachers who opposed the Christian faith with Gnostic doctrines. John consistently tells the readers of his epistle to walk in the light, to live by the truth, to obey God's commands, and to have fellowship with God and his people. His appeals, however, are not all

---

36. Plummer, *The Epistles of St. John*, p. 49.

in the form of warnings. As a wise pastor, he knows that a steady flow of admonitions can have an adverse effect on the members of the church. Positive words build confidence and assurance. John calls the attention of all the readers to the possessions they have in Christ:

a. They know that their sins have been forgiven.
b. They have known God the Father and his Son Jesus Christ.
c. They have overcome Satan through the Word of God.

Young and old thrive on words of praise, for they take pride in what they possess and are able to achieve. Although pastors must warn the church of dangers and pitfalls, they should set the goal of presenting their sermons in a positive frame and show the believers the riches they possess in Christ Jesus. Let God's people sing,

> How vast the benefits divine
> Which we in Christ possess!
> We are redeemed from guilt and shame,
> And called to holiness.
> —Augustus M. Toplady

Greek Words, Phrases, and Constructions in 2:13b–14

Verse 13b

παιδία—a diminutive from παῖς (boy, child), this noun is a synonym of τεκνία and is used as an endearment.

Verse 14

ἰσχυροί—note the word order in the Greek. The adjective precedes the verb and receives emphasis.

νενικήκατε—the perfect active from νικάω (I conquer, overcome). Notice the repeated use of the perfect in the three verbs ἐγνώκατε (three times), νενικήκατε (twice), and ἀφέωνται (once) in verses 12–14.

---

15 Do not love the world or anything in the world. If anyone loves the world, the love of the Father is not in him.   16 For everything in the world—the cravings of sinful man, the lust of his eyes and the boasting of what he has and does—comes not from the Father but from the world.   17 The world and its desires pass away, but the man who does the will of God lives forever.

E. The World and the Will of God
2:15–17

1. Do Not Love the World
2:15

After an appeal to the believers, the author sounds a warning not to love the world. Love for the world precludes love for the Father. We see a parallel between the words of John and those of James, "Anyone who chooses to be a friend of the world becomes an enemy of God" (James 4:4). John writes,

15. Do not love the world or anything in the world. If anyone loves the world, the love of the Father is not in him.

a. John issues a stern warning not to love the world. He says "do not love," not "do not like" the world. The word *love* that John employs is the same term he uses in verse 10 where he speaks about the person who loves his brother. The love which he has in mind is that of attachment, intimate fellowship, loyal devotion. It is the love which God demands in the summary of the law: "Love the Lord your God . . . and love your neighbor as yourself."

John directs his warning to those people who already have switched allegiance and are now giving their undivided attention to the affairs of the world. He tells them to stop loving the world and to desist from pursuing their worldly interests. He is not talking about a single incident but about a lifestyle.

b. John mentions the expression *world*—a word that is typically Johannine.[37] This word has various meanings, as John illustrates in his first epistle: the world of the believers, the world of sin, the world of the devil.

Thus John writes that Jesus is the Savior of the world (4:15) and that by faith the Christian is able to overcome the world (5:4–5). According to John, the characteristics of the world are cravings, lust, and boasting (2:16). The world passes away (2:17) and is ignorant of God (3:1). It hates the believers (3:13) and is the abode of false prophets (4:1), the antichrist (4:3), and unbelievers (4:5). And last, the whole world is controlled by the evil one (5:19). Concludes Donald Guthrie, "There is therefore in I John a strong parallel between the 'world' and the 'devil.' "[38]

c. John warns the readers against loving the world and that which belongs to it. He does not advise the Christian to abandon this world or to live in seclusion. John stresses not that a Christian separate himself from the world. Rather, he says that a believer should keep himself from a love for the world. Note that in this relatively short verse the concept *love* precedes the concept *world*. What, then, is John saying? In a sentence: "Love for the world and love for the Father cannot exist side by side." The Christian will love the one and hate the other, but he cannot love both at the same time (compare Matt. 6:24; Luke 16:13). The sinful world stands diametrically opposed to the Father. John describes this world in verse 16.

---

37. "The noun *kosmos* denotes the world. The sole exception is 1 Pet[er] 3:3, where it means adornment. Of the 185 occurrences of the word 78 come in John, 24 in the Johannine letters, 47 in the Pauline letters, 14 in the Synoptics and 22 in the rest of the N[ew] T[estament] writings." Joachim Guhrt, *NIDNTT*, vol. 1, p. 524.

38. Guthrie, *New Testament Theology*, p. 133.

Greek Words, Phrases, and Constructions in 2:15

μὴ ἀγαπᾶτε—the present active imperative preceded by the negative particle μή shows action in progress. Some people indeed loved the world (see v. 19). Notice that John chooses the verb ἀγαπάω (I love) and the noun ἀγάπη (love), not the verb φιλέω and its related noun φιλία (however, see James 4:4).

ἐάν τις ἀγαπᾷ—the protasis of this conditional sentence has the verb in the present subjunctive to express uncertainty and probability.

ἡ ἀγάπη τοῦ πατρός—the genitive can be either subjective or objective. In view of the contrast between "love for the world" and "the love for the Father" the objective genitive is preferred.

---

2. Do the Will of God
2:16–17

16. For everything in the world—the cravings of sinful man, the lust of his eyes and the boasting of what he has and does—comes not from the Father but from the world.

The main thought of verse 16 is this: "everything in the world . . . comes not from the Father but from the world." In his epistle, James provides a parallel idea. On the origin of wisdom, James writes, "Such 'wisdom' does not come down from heaven but is earthly, unspiritual, of the devil" (James 3:15). That which has its origin in the world comes not from God but from the devil.

What are the so-called things of the world? John spells them out in three categories: cravings of sinful man, lust of man's eyes, and boasting of what a person has or does. Of course, this list of tendencies is comprehensive in scope, but not necessarily exhaustive.[39]

Before we discuss these categories, we make the following observations. The first two categories (cravings and lust) are sinful desires; the last (boasting) is sinful behavior. The first two are internal and hidden sins; the last is an external and revealed sin. The first two pertain to the individual person, the last to the person who is surrounded by people.[40]

a. *Cravings.* Literally the Greek text has "the desire of the flesh." The New International Version, however, translates the text as "the cravings of sinful man." The word *desire* is used collectively and represents cravings that include sexual desire and covetousness. These cravings are evil because they cause man to disobey God's explicit command, "You shall not covet" (Exod. 20:17; Deut. 5:21).[41] Moreover, these cravings originate

---

39. Marshall discusses the comprehensiveness of evil tendencies and uses the term *total depravity.* He comments that this expression means "not that the world is as bad as it can possibly be but that its badness is universal." See *The Epistles of John,* p. 144.
40. Consult Plummer, *The Epistles of St. John,* p. 53.
41. Consult Friedrich Büchsel, *TDNT,* vol. 3, p. 171; Hans Schönweiss, *NIDNTT,* vol. 1, p. 457.

in man's nature and give birth to sin (James 1:15). Paul writes a similar account of this sinful nature (Gal. 5:16–17), which he says "is contrary to the Spirit."

b. *Lust.* John describes this desire as "the lust of [the] eyes." The eyes are the channels to man's soul. When man is enticed by lust, his eyes serve as instruments that cause him to transgress and sin. John reflects the sentiments of Jesus (recorded in the Sermon on the Mount), who categorized lustful looking as sin: "But I tell you that anyone who looks at a woman lustfully has already committed adultery with her in his heart" (Matt. 5:28).

c. *Boasting.* John lists the third tendency in words that cannot be translated easily. Translators provide a number of equally valid versions. Here are some representatives:

"The pride of life" (KJV, NKJV, RSV)

"The boastful pride of life" (NASB)

"All the glamour of its life" (NEB)

"The life of empty show" (NAB)

"Pride in possessions" (JB)

"The boasting of what [man] has and does" (NIV)

The reason for these numerous variations lies in two Greek words: "boast" and "life." The first word means the boasting of a braggart or impostor (compare James 4:16). This boasting may even approach the point of arrogant violence.[42] The second denotes life with respect to actions and possessions. The person who brags about his deeds and goods expresses "lust for advantage and status."[43]

The three vices (cravings, lust, and boasting) originate not in the Father but in the world, that is, from the devil. John writes "the Father" to indicate, first, the link with the preceding context (1:2, 3; 2:1, 13, 15) and, second, a reminder that the readers are God's adopted children. They are sons and daughters of their heavenly Father and do not belong to the world. In a different setting, Jesus voices the same thought. He tells his adversaries, "He who belongs to God hears what God says. The reason you do not hear is that you do not belong to God" (John 8:47).

17. The world and its desires pass away, but the man who does the will of God lives forever.

Man needs to look at the fleeting existence of worldly people, pleasures, and desires. If he places his interest in that which is here today and gone tomorrow, he reaps a harvest of instability, stumbles in the darkness of sin

---

42. Grayston is of the opinion that the word *boasting* contains "the threat of self-assertive violence." See his *Johannine Epistles,* p. 75.

43. Eberhard Güting and Colin Brown, *NIDNTT,* vol. 3, p. 32.

and, because he has cast his lot with the world, faces a similar end. "For this world in its present form is passing away" (I Cor. 7:31).

However, the child of God is secure, for he possesses eternal life. What a contrast! The person who loves the world soon passes away, "but the man who does the will of God lives forever." John echoes Jesus' words: "Not everyone who says to me, 'Lord, Lord,' will enter the kingdom of heaven, but only he who does the will of my Father who is in heaven" (Matt. 7:21; also I Peter 4:2). When the will of man is in harmony with the will of God, the Christian has fellowship with the Father and the Son that lasts forever (compare 2:5).

Practical Considerations in 2:15–17

In his high-priestly prayer, Jesus asks his Father not to take the believers out of the world but to protect them. He prays, "As you sent me into the world, I have sent them into the world" (John 17:18). Is John contradicting these words of Jesus? Is he advocating total separation from the world in which he lived? No, not at all.

When John wrote his epistle toward the end of the first century, pagan society was thoroughly corrupt. It was marked by immorality, greed, bribery, and disregard for human life and dignity. Within that society the church sought to be a restraining influence by exemplifying the virtues of honesty, morality, and a respect for life and property. But within the church some people had sided with the world because they did not really belong to the church (I John 2:19). They were false prophets who went out into the world (4:1). John warns the believers never to compromise with the spirit of the age and never to adopt a worldly lifestyle.

In a sense, our world differs little from that of John. Ours is filled with violence and immorality. In many sectors of society bribery, theft, and deceit are woven into the fabric of daily life. However, we who have been bought with a price, who have the baptismal mark of the Triune God on our foreheads, who are called holy, must keep ourselves unspotted by the world. We are in the world, but not of it. For if we were of the world, then we would not be of the Father.

Greek Words, Phrases, and Constructions in 2:16–17

Verse 16

ἡ ἐπιθυμία τῆς σαρκός—is this a descriptive or a subjective genitive? If the succeeding phrase is subjective (lust of the eyes), this phrase, too, is subjective: cravings that belong to sinful man.[44]

πᾶν τό—in the preceding verse the definite article in the neuter plural occurs (τά, the things). Here John uses the singular neuter adjective to stress the individual vices which he particularizes with three nouns: ἡ ἐπιθυμία (desire [twice]) and ἡ ἀλαζονεία (boast). Each noun has a definite article.[45]

---

44. Refer to Moule, *Idiom-Book*, p. 40; Hanna, *Grammatical Aid*, p. 434, says, "The genitive is subjective, 'the lust proceeding from the flesh.'"
45. Robertson, *Grammar*, p. 788.

βίος—this noun reflects the time, means, and manner of life. The noun ζωή refers to (eternal) life that has death as its opposite.[46]

Verse 17

παράγεται—this compound verb from παράγω is in the passive voice.
ὁ δὲ ποιῶν—the use of the present participle denotes continued action.

---

18 Dear children, this is the last hour; and as you have heard that the antichrist is coming, even now many antichrists have come. This is how we know it is the last hour. 19 They went out from us, but they did not really belong to us. For if they had belonged to us, they would have remained with us; but their going showed that none of them belonged to us.

III. Believe in Jesus
2:18–3:24

A. Warning Against the Antichrist
2:18–19

1. Antichrists Have Come
2:18

Notice that in this well-known passage about the antichrist John writes the plural of "antichrist." He tells the readers that many antichrists have come. In light of the immediate context, we see that persons who love the world and its pursuits have placed themselves in opposition to Christ and therefore are called antichrists.

18. Dear children, this is the last hour; and as you have heard that the antichrist is coming, even now many antichrists have come. This is how we know it is the last hour.

The familiar address *dear children* (see, for instance, v. 14) discloses that the writer is an elderly person who speaks with authority and is able to analyze the present and future spiritual scene. As a wise and perceptive pastor he warns his people of danger that lurks within the Christian community. He thoroughly understands the sinful age in which he and the readers live.

a. *Age.* In this verse John declares that we are living in the last hour. The term *hour* cannot be taken literally. Even though the phrase *the last hour* appears only here in the entire New Testament, it seems to be equivalent to the expressions *the last days* or *these last times* (see, among other passages, Acts 2:17; Heb. 1:2; James 5:3; I Peter 1:20).

What does John mean when he writes "the last hour"? If we understand the words figuratively and interpret them as a long period of time, that is, an age, we have to specify whether the term refers to the period that begins with Jesus' ascension and ends with his return or the final days

---

46. Thayer, p. 102. Also see Trench, *Synonyms of the New Testament*, p. 91.

before the return of Jesus. If we adopt the second view and say that the "last hour" is the last days before the end of time, we have to explain the delay of nearly two millennia that has taken place since John wrote his epistle.

Proponents of the first view also face that question.[47] They are able to point to the general context of this passage and say that John is not interested in giving a chronological time schedule.

These proponents view the broad context of this issue and maintain the following points: John looks at the spiritual development and the opposition of the world. He declares that "the world and its desires pass away" (2:17) to give place to the man who obeys the will of God. He notes that some people have left the church, because they denied that Jesus is the Christ. John calls them antichrists (2:18, 22); he observes that the spirit of the antichrist is already present in this world (4:3). Awaiting the return of Christ but not knowing when that will take place (Acts 1:7), John seems to indicate that the period between the first and second coming of Jesus is "the last hour."[48]

b. *Arrival.* John says, "The antichrist is coming." The readers had heard the gospel proclamation and knew that Jesus had said, "Many will come in my name, claiming, 'I am the Christ,' and will deceive many," and "False Christs and false prophets will appear and perform great signs and miracles to deceive even the elect—if that were possible" (Matt. 24:5, 24).

The word *antichrist* has a broader meaning than does the term *false Christ.* The preposition *anti* means not only "in the place of" (refer to II Thess. 2:3–4, where the man of lawlessness "sets himself up in God's temple, proclaiming himself to be God"). It also signifies "against." Thus, the antichrist comes in the place of Christ and stands in opposition to him.

c. *Affirmation.* John observes that many antichrists have come and are still alive. The antichrists, who deny that Jesus is the Christ, are temporal, not eternal. They "are probably to be regarded as at once forerunners of the Antichrist and evidence that his spirit is already at work in the world."[49] The presence of people who deny the Christ is definite proof that we are living in the last hour.

Doctrinal Considerations in 2:18

Is the antichrist a person or a principle? Is he a single individual or does he appear in many people, as John seems to indicate with the plural form *antichrists?* These and similar questions are often asked with reference to John's first epistle.

The early Christians in the latter part of the first century had heard about the

---

47. Consult Guthrie, *New Testament Theology,* p. 801.
48. Consult, for example, Plummer, *The Epistles of St. John,* pp. 55–56; Calvin, *The First Epistle of John,* p. 189; Stott, *The Epistles of John,* pp. 107–9.
49. Plummer, *The Epistles of St. John,* p. 57.

coming of the antichrist, and they knew that he would appear as a single person. For instance, Paul writes about the "man of lawlessness" who will be revealed and who will be destroyed by Jesus when he returns (II Thess. 2:3–4, 8–9).

But John is not interested in identifying a particular individual. He points to a principle that prevails in persons who deny the deity or humanity of Christ. John opposes this principle of apostasy and therefore, in his epistles, stresses the principle instead of the person of the antichrist. By saying that the antichrist is coming, he indicates that the future antichrist will be an individual who personifies this principle.[50]

Greek Words, Phrases, and Constructions in 2:18

ἐσχάτη ὥρα—John uses these words twice in this text, both times without the definite article. In the case of the adjective ἐσχάτη (last), the definite article is often lacking (see II Tim. 3:1; James 5:3; I Peter 1:5).[51] Because of the word order, the emphasis falls not on the noun *hour* but on the adjective *last*.

γεγόνασιν—the perfect active of γίνομαι (I come to be, become) reveals that these antichrists arose within the church itself.

---

2. Antichrists Went Out
2:19

19. They went out from us, but they did not really belong to us. For if they had belonged to us, they would have remained with us; but their going showed that none of them belonged to us.

Five times in this verse John uses the word *us*. In the original John writes "from us" four times and "with us" once. He wants to make sure that the reader understands that those whom he calls antichrists have left the church because they really did not belong to the church. The antichrists leave but the members of the church remain. Not those who deny the Christ are important, but the believers. And for this reason, John stresses the pronoun *us* at the end of every clause.

a. "They went out from us." John omits the details, but we assume that the original readers knew the situation and had vivid memories of the tension that eventually caused the departure of the unbelievers. The writer of Hebrews sketches the picture when he writes,

> It is impossible for those who have once been enlightened, who have tasted the heavenly gift, who have shared in the Holy Spirit, who have tasted the goodness of the word of God and the powers of the coming age, if they fall away, to be brought back to repentance, because to their loss they are crucifying the Son of God all over again and subjecting him to public disgrace. [6:4–6]

---

50. Refer to Boice, *The Epistles of John*, p. 86; David A. Hubbard, "Antichrist," *EDT*, p. 56; and J. E. H. Thomson, "Antichrist," *ISBE*, vol. 1, p. 140.
51. Robertson, *Grammar*, p. 769.

b. "But they did not really belong to us." John says that these people were not from within the Christian circle. They were not true Christians because they did not belong to the source, namely, Christ. They attended the worship services for some time, but they were never in Christ (compare John 15:1–6).

c. "For if they had belonged to us, they would have remained with us." This is a conditional statement with a negative implication. Note that in the first clause John implies that the people he designates antichrists never really belonged to the church because they deny the Christ. In the second clause John indicates that true believers remain, whereas the antichrists leave the fellowship of the church. Believers belong; deniers depart.

d. "But their going showed that none of them belonged to us." The New International Version differs from a more literal translation by giving the intent of a Semitic idiom. Here is the verbatim text: "that they might be made manifest that they were not all of us" (KJV). A literal translation of this idiom fails to convey the meaning John expresses. He is not saying that there are exceptions. On the contrary, the idiom means that "none of [the antichrists] belonged to us."[52]

Doctrinal Considerations in 2:19

This text teaches the doctrine of perseverance. The unbelievers who denied Jesus' divinity or humanity were never part of the church because they did not belong to Christ. Their presence in the visible church was temporary, for they failed in their perseverance. If they had been members of the invisible church, they would have remained with the body of believers. As F. F. Bruce observes, "The perseverance of the saints is a biblical doctrine, but it is not doctrine designed to lull the indifferent into a sense of false security; it means that perseverance is an essential token of sanctity."[53]

Greek Words, Phrases, and Constructions in 2:19

ἐξῆλθαν—the aorist active of ἐξέρχομαι (I go out) shows that at one time these people were part of the church and then left. The tense indicates that the departure had taken place. They left, presumably, on their own accord.

---

52. Westcott explains that when the verb separates the adjective *all* from the negative *not*, "the negation, according to the usage of the New Testament, is always universal (*all . . . not*), and not partial (*not all*)." See his *Epistles of St. John*, p. 72.
53. F. F. Bruce, *The Epistles of John* (1970; Grand Rapids: Eerdmans, 1979), p. 69. Also consult Marshall, who writes, "A person who makes a genuine confession [of faith] can be expected to persevere in his faith, although elsewhere [2:24; II John 8] John warns his readers against the danger of failure to persevere." *The Epistles of John*, p. 152. And see Stott, *The Epistles of John*, pp. 105–6; Glenn W. Barker, *1 John*, the *Expositor's Bible Commentary*, ed. Frank E. Gaebelein, 12 vols. (Grand Rapids: Zondervan, 1981), vol. 12, p. 324.

εἰ—this is a contrary-to-fact conditional sentence. Instead of the aorist tense, the past perfect μεμενήκεισαν (from the verb μένω, I remain) appears.

---

20 But you have anointing from the Holy One, and all of you know the truth. 21 I do not write to you because you do not know the truth, but because you do know it and because no lie comes from the truth. 22 Who is the liar? It is the man who denies that Jesus is the Christ. Such a man is the antichrist—he denies the Father and the Son. 23 No one who denies the Son has the Father; whoever acknowledges the Son has the Father also.

24 See that what you have heard from the beginning remains in you. If it does, you also will remain in the Son and in the Father. 25 And this is what he promised us—even eternal life.

26 I am writing these things to you about those who are trying to lead you astray. 27 As for you, the anointing you received from him remains in you, and you do not need anyone to teach you. But as his anointing teaches you about all things and as that anointing is real, not counterfeit—just as it has taught you, remain in him.

B. Anointing from the Holy One
2:20–27

1. Anointing and Discernment
2:20–21

What a contrast! The antichrists deny that Jesus is the Christ, whose name in translated form means "the Anointed One." But Christians look to the Christ, because from him they have received their anointing. Christians not only bear the name of Jesus Christ; they also share in his anointing. This truth is formulated lucidly in a sixteenth-century catechism. To the question, "But why are you called a Christian?" its writers answer,

> Because by faith I am a member of Christ and so share in his anointing. I am anointed to confess his name, to present myself to him as a living sacrifice of thanks, to strive with a free conscience against sin and the devil in this life, and afterwards to reign with Christ over all creation for all eternity.[54]

20. But you have an anointing from the Holy One, and all of you know the truth. 21. I do not write to you because you do not know the truth, but because you do know it and because no lie comes from the truth.

In these two verses (also see 2:27) John teaches his readers about their anointing. John comments that the readers have "an anointing from the Holy One." Who is the one that anoints? Paul asserts that God anoints the believers (II Cor. 1:21; also compare Acts 10:38). But in the broader context of his epistle, John conveys the thought that the Son anoints the believers (see the explanation of v. 27). Perhaps we should say that God the Father works through the Son.

---

54. Heidelberg Catechism, question and answer 32.

What is an anointing? In Old Testament times, priests, kings, and even prophets were anointed with oil to mark the beginning of their respective duties. The oil symbolized consecration.

The word *anointing* in this text refers not to oil but to the content of the anointing, which appears to be the Holy Spirit.[55] The Spirit testifies to the lasting significance of the act of anointing. Christians receive the gift of the Holy Spirit from the Holy One. Who is the Holy One? In the New Testament, the Holy One is Jesus Christ (see Mark 1:24; Luke 4:34; John 6:69; Acts 3:14).

"And all of you know the truth." In this clause we first note a translation problem. The better manuscripts have "and all of you know," while other manuscripts have "and you know all things." The latter reading leaves the impression that, because of the gift of the Holy Spirit, Christians are able to know everything. This cannot be John's intention, for in the next verse (v. 21) he writes, "you . . . know the truth." Therefore, on the basis of the context we conclude that the object of knowing is not "all things" but "the truth."

Next, we note that the Greek verb *oida* (to know) in this verse and the next relates not to acquired knowledge but to innate knowledge. John means to indicate he is not teaching the readers new truths but is reminding them of what they already know.

"I do not write to you because you do not know the truth." The readers are fully familiar with the truth in Jesus Christ, so that John has no need to communicate the gospel to them. We suppose that John writes these words to the readers to remind them that they are not without the truth. In fact they have the ability to use the truth in their opposition to Gnostic teachers who deny Jesus as the Christ. Does John write his epistle only to combat Gnosticism? No, he writes for the following reasons.

"But [I write] *because* you do know it and *because* no lie comes from the truth" (italics added). The readers know the truth and they are able to detect the lie by exposing it in the light of the truth. Truth and light are the opposites of the lie and darkness.

Some twenty years after John wrote this epistle, observes Bruce, John's disciple Polycarp, then bishop of the church in Smyrna, sent a letter to the Christians in Philippi and said:

> "For everyone who does not confess that Jesus Christ has come in the flesh is an anti-Christ"; and whosoever does not confess the testimony of the Cross is of the devil: and whosoever perverts the oracles of the

---

55. Although theologian Ignace de la Potterie ("L'onction du chrétien par la foi," *Bib* 40 [1959]: 12–69) suggests that the text means an anointing by faith with the oil of the Word of God rather than by the Holy Spirit, we must object because Scripture never mentions the Word of God in relation to anointing. In their respective commentaries, Dodd supports the view of de la Potterie, Marshall modifies it, and Stott and Burdick reject it.

Lord for his own lusts, and says that there is neither resurrection nor judgment—this man is the first-born of Satan.[56]

The believer anointed with the Holy Spirit is able to discern truth from error, oppose heresy, and withstand the attacks of Satan.

Practical Considerations in 2:20–21

Whenever someone comes to you with religious teachings that either add to the Bible or take the place of the Bible, beware. In his first epistle, but even more explicitly in his second epistle, John warns you to watch out for deceivers: "If anyone comes to you and does not bring this teaching [of Christ], do not take him into your house or welcome him. Anyone who welcomes him shares in his wicked work" (vv. 10–11).

When someone tries to teach you doctrines that do not originate in the Old and New Testaments, tell that person that you believe in Jesus Christ, that you know that Jesus died for your sins, that Jesus has opened the way to heaven for you and is preparing a place for you, and that you are happy and joyful in the Lord. When you confess your faith in Jesus, witness for the Lord, and show that you are able to discern truth from error, your visitor will depart.

Greek Words, Phrases, and Constructions in 2:20–21

Verse 20

καὶ ὑμεῖς—the conjunction is adversative. The pronoun is emphatic.

χρῖσμα—from the verb χρίω (I anoint), the noun with the -μα ending denotes action that results in possessing gifts of the Holy Spirit.[57]

ἀπό—"from," not ἐκ (out of).

οἴδατε—instead of γινώσκω (I know) John uses this verb to differentiate between possession and acquisition of knowledge.

πάντες—some manuscripts have the reading πάντα (accusative plural neuter) as the direct object of οἴδατε. This reading probably originated as "a correction introduced by copyists."[58]

Verse 21

ἔγραψα—the epistolary aorist. See the discussion of 2:12 and 14.

ὅτι—this conjunction can be translated "that" or "because." The intent of the verse calls for a causal interpretation in all three instances where this word is used. And this interpretation, then, states the reasons for the writing of the epistle.

---

56. Polycarp, Philippians 7. 1 (LCL). And see Bruce, *The Epistles of John*, p. 72.
57. Thayer, pp. 672–73.
58. Bruce M. Metzger, *A Textual Commentary on the Greek New Testament*, corrected ed. (London and New York: United Bible Societies, 1975), p. 707.

2. Denial and Profession
2:22–23

John takes the Gnostic heretic to task by calling him a liar and an antichrist for his blatant denial of Jesus as the Christ. John is unafraid to ascribe names to his opponent in this direct confrontation.

22. Who is the liar? It is the man who denies that Jesus is the Christ. Such a man is the antichrist—he denies the Father and the Son. 23. No one who denies the Son has the Father; whoever acknowledges the Son has the Father also.

Note the following points:

a. *The liar.* Fearlessly John asks the question *Who is the liar?* to which he himself gives the answer (see v. 5). He is looking at the person who perpetrates the lie.[59] He is not addressing a person who occasionally misrepresents the truth, but one who strikes at the heart of the gospel of Jesus Christ. John confronts the person who is bent on turning the truth of Jesus' humanity into a lie. The heart of the Christian faith is that Jesus is perfect God and perfect man. In the Athanasian Creed of the fourth century this doctrine is carefully formulated in articles 30–32:

> For the right faith is that we believe and confess that our Lord Jesus Christ, the Son of God, is God and man. God of the substance of the Father, begotten before the worlds; and man of the substance of his mother, born in the world. Perfect God and perfect man. . . .

From the general context, we cannot say that John is speaking to Jewish opponents who refused to accept Jesus of Nazareth as the Messiah. John is opposing Gnostic teachers who taught that Jesus was a man who lived and died. During Jesus' public ministry, the Gnostics said, the Christ descended upon him and gave him divine power from the time of his baptism to the time of his suffering. At the conclusion of Jesus' suffering, Christ departed.[60] To the Gnostics, then, Jesus was not the Christ.[61] And John says that the person who proclaims this teaching is a liar. More than that, says John, he is the antichrist.

b. *The antichrist.* Even though John speaks of *the* antichrist, he points not to the figure at the end of time but to the person who claims that Jesus is

---

59. "In John's view a 'liar' is one who is habitually deviating from God's truth and acting hypocritically," writes Guthrie in *New Testament Theology*, p. 933.

60. Consult Raymond E. Brown, *The Epistles of John*, Anchor Bible series (Garden City, N.Y.: Doubleday, 1982), vol. 30, pp. 65–68, 766–71.

61. Numerous modern theologians separate the so-called historical Jesus from the Christ of faith. In his comments on I John 2:22, Rudolf Bultmann reveals a measure of hesitation when he writes, "[John] adheres to the identity of the historical event (the historical figure of Jesus) and the eschatological event (Jesus the 'Christ,' the 'Son')." See *The Johannine Epistles*, ed. Robert Funk, trans. R. Philip O'Hara et al., Hermeneia: A Critical and Historical Commentary on the Bible (Philadelphia: Fortress, 1973), p. 39.

not the Christ. The one who denies that the Son of God has become man denies the Father-Son relationship, too. If there is no Son, there is no Father. In his epistle, John teaches that the Father and Son are intimately related (1:2, 3; 2:1, 23, 24; 4:3, 14, 15; 5:9, 10, 11, 12, 20). John reveals the heart of the gospel: God the Father has sent his Son Jesus Christ to redeem sinners. If a person rejects Jesus Christ, he also rejects God the Father and nullifies the message of the gospel of Christ. Such a person, writes John, is the antichrist.

In typical Semitic parallelism, John first states his point in negative terms and then restates it in positive wording. But the first sentence actually has a double negative ("no one" and "denies" [affirms not]), which is the equivalent of a positive statement.

Negative	*Positive*
no one who	whoever
denies	acknowledges
the Son	the Son
has the Father	has the Father also

What is the believer's confession of faith? Simply this: "Jesus is the Son of God." In his epistle John emphasizes that through the blood of Jesus, the Son, we are purified from sin (1:7); the Son promises us eternal life (2:25); the Son of God has appeared to destroy the work of the devil (3:8); and the Son is "an atoning sacrifice for our sins" (4:10).[62] The believer has fellowship with the Father and the Son (1:3) and openly confesses the name of Jesus before the people. Therefore he asks with Joseph Grigg,

> Lord Jesus, can it ever be,
> A mortal man ashamed of Thee?
> Ashamed of Thee, whom angels praise,
> Whose glories shine through endless days?

Doctrinal Considerations in 2:22–23

During the latter half of the first century, John exposed the heresy of Gnostic teachers, among whom was an Egyptian Jew named Cerinthus. This person denied Jesus' virgin birth and claimed that the Christ descended upon Jesus at the time of Jesus' baptism but left him before Jesus died.[63]

John wrote not merely for his contemporary readers but also for the church universal. In the second century Marcion denied the Son of God, and in the next century Arius and Sabellius did the same. In every century and every age, men refuse to acknowledge the Christ of the Scriptures. Some deny the virgin birth, the resurrection, the ascension, and the promise of Jesus' return. Others distinguish between Jesus of Nazareth and the exalted Christ. And still others reject

---

62. Refer to Guthrie, *New Testament Theology*, p. 316.
63. See Irenaeus *Against Heresies* 1. 26. 1. Also see Calvin, *The First Epistle of John*, p. 195.

either his divinity or his humanity. In short, everyone who repudiates the biblical teaching that Jesus Christ is the Son of God and the Son of man deceives himself and, according to John, is a liar.

---

3. Fellowship and Promise
2:24–25

John's writing is anything but impersonal. The second person plural *you* appears numerous times, and in verses 24 and 27 even in direct address. The New American Standard Bible translates the introductory word *you* in these two verses "as for you." John speaks directly to the readers and in effect says, "You, I want your attention!"

24. See that what you have heard from the beginning remains in you. If it does, you also will remain in the Son and in the Father. 25. And this is what he promised us—even eternal life.

By repeating words in verse 24 from a preceding section (v. 7), John stresses one basic thought:

a. *Remain.* When the readers hear the Christ-denying clamor all around them, how do they defend themselves against their opponents? John tells them exactly what to do. In a sense, he repeats what he already has told them in the first part of his epistle. "What you have heard from the beginning," that is, the gospel (see 1:1, 3, 5; 2:7), let that Word remain in you. As Jesus says to the believers in the church of Philadelphia, "Hold on to what you have" (Rev. 3:11), so John exhorts the readers of his epistle to treasure the biblical message they have heard all along. That Word must reside in their souls, so that in every decision they make they are guided by the Word of God.

The New International Version, perhaps in an attempt to avoid repetition, renders the next clause in three words, "If it does." Literally the text says, "If what you have heard from the beginning remains in you." John purposely stresses the concept *remain,* for he weaves it into this passage (vv. 24–28) six times. John expresses the same theme the psalmist voices: "I have hidden your word in my heart that I might not sin against you" (Ps. 119:11). John wants the reader to meditate on that Word and to live by it from day to day.

"If it does, you also will remain in the Son and in the Father." When the Word of God remains in you, says John, then as a consequence you will have fellowship with the Son and the Father. The Son and the Father take up their residence where the Word of God resides. Through the Word, the Son and the Father have fellowship with the believer and are able to communicate with him.

Purposely John lists the Son before the Father to indicate that the believer comes to the Father through the Son. This is in harmony with Jesus' high-priestly prayer for the believers: "I pray . . . that all of them may be one, Father, just as you are in me and I am in you. May they also be in us so that the world may believe that you have sent me" (John 17:20–21; and compare 14:6).

b. *Promise.* If the believer cherishes the Word of God and experiences intimate fellowship with the Son and the Father, then he is also the recipient of eternal life (1:2–3). To have fellowship with the Son and the Father is to have eternal life.

"This is what [the Son] promised us—even eternal life." The word *this* is equivalent to the expression *eternal life.* Christ has promised eternal life to everyone who believes in him (see John 3:15–16, 36; 5:24; 6:33, 40, 47, 54; 17:3). Eternal life is firmly anchored in Jesus Christ through God's Word and Spirit.

Greek Words, Phrases, and Constructions in 2:24–25

Verse 24

ὑμεῖς—the use of the personal pronoun can be either a "suspended subject" or a vocative.[64] In this verse, the writer's intent remains the same, whether we call the nominative vocative or independent. I prefer to call the nominative independent.

ἠκούσατε—the constative aorist can be translated as a perfect, "you have heard."

ἐάν—this particle introduces a conditional sentence; the protasis has the subjunctive to express probability and the apodosis has the future (durative) indicative.

Verse 25

αὕτη—the demonstrative pronoun has a forward look because of the feminine gender of the noun ζωήν.

ἡμῖν—a few manuscripts have the reading ὑμῖν ("and what is promised to you" [JB]). The reading *you* may be "the result of scribal confusion."[65]

τὴν ζωήν—note the emphatic use of the definite articles before the noun and the adjective. The adjective αἰώνιον stands last in the sentence.

---

4. Teaching and Anointing
2:26–27

John comes to the end of a segment in his epistle with a concluding remark that urges the readers to remain true to what they have learned. Knowing the difference between truth and error, they ought to avoid people who are trying to lead them astray.

26. I am writing these things to you about those who are trying to lead you astray. 27. As for you, the anointing you received from him remains in you, and you do not need anyone to teach you. But as his anointing teaches you about all things and as that anointing is real, not counterfeit—just as it has taught you, remain in him.

---

64. Robertson, *Grammar,* p. 437. Also see Lenski, *Interpretation of the Epistles,* p. 438, who chooses the vocative, and Burdick, *The Letters of John the Apostle,* p. 202, who favors the "independent nominative."

65. Metzger, *Textual Commentary,* p. 710.

Characteristically, John begins and ends his thoughts with the same words, so that the passage between verses 20 and 27 is a parenthetical remark.

a. "I am writing these things." The words *these things* refer to the preceding verses (vv. 21–25) where John writes that the believers are not ignorant but know the truth, acknowledge the Son, and remain in him and in the Father. They need to be fully aware of persons who are trying to lead them away from the truth of God's Word. They should heed the word of Jesus: "Watch out that no one deceives you. For many will come in my name, claiming, 'I am the Christ,' and will deceive many" (Matt. 24:4–5). They are not deceived as yet, but they should be ready to do spiritual battle with the deceivers and expose their lies.

b. "The anointing you received from him remains in you." Once again, John speaks directly to his readers when he says, "As for you" (compare v. 24). He is talking to the believers, not to the deceivers. Therefore, he wants the undivided attention of his readers.

John mentions "the anointing," a topic he introduced earlier (v. 20). He seems to imply that the readers received the gift of the Holy Spirit, that is, their anointing (see the explanation of v. 20), at the time of their conversion. This is a possession they received from Jesus Christ and which remains with them (II Cor. 1:21–22). The one who gives the Holy Spirit may be either the Father or the Son. Nevertheless, the context, especially verses 25 and 28, points to the Son and not to the Father.

c. "You do not need anyone to teach you." These words are reminiscent of Jeremiah's prophecy, "No longer will a man teach his neighbor, or a man his brother, saying, 'Know the Lord,' because they will all know me, from the least of them to the greatest,' declares the Lord" (Jer. 31:34; Heb. 8:11). Is John intimating that the anointing with the Holy Spirit makes instruction in biblical knowledge superfluous? Of course not! In the words of the Great Commission Jesus instructs the apostles (and by implication all of those who proclaim the Word) to teach learners all that Jesus has commanded (Matt. 28:20). Effective preaching of the Word, faithful teaching in Sunday school or catechism class, and daily reading of the Scriptures—all this is necessary for the spiritual growth of the Christian. Then what is John saying? The believers have no need of deceivers who try to teach false doctrine. They have the gift of the Holy Spirit who leads them in all truth (John 16:13).

d. "His anointing teaches you about all things."[66] That is, the Spirit of Christ will teach the believer everything (John 14:26) and will guide him in distinguishing truth from error. All believers receive the Holy Spirit

---

66. Two translations (KJV, NKJV) have the reading *the same anointing*. This construction, comments Metzger, "occurs nowhere else in either the Fourth Gospel or the three Johannine Epistles." See his *Textual Commentary*, p. 710.

and all of them are equally equipped to oppose those teachers who proclaim the lie instead of the truth.

This text teaches the fundamental equality of all believers. That is, believers do not have to consult learned professors of theology before they can accept God's truth; in the sight of God, clergy and laity are the same; the Holy Spirit is the teacher of every believer, without distinction.[67] Within the church, believers are able to learn from each other as each is a partaker of the anointing of the Spirit.

e. "Just as it has taught you, remain in him." Apparently the word *it* refers to the anointing and is equivalent to the phrase *the Spirit's teaching* in the following translation: "Obey the Spirit's teaching, then, and remain in union with Christ" (GNB). If Christ is the subject of the verb *has taught*, the translation is, "As he taught you, then, dwell in him" (NEB). However, the expression *just as* underscores the corresponding "but as" at the beginning of the sentence. Because the subject at the beginning is "the anointing" (the Holy Spirit), there seems to be no compelling reason to change it in the second part.

The heart of the sentence, however, lies in the last three words which form a command to have fellowship with Christ. The exhortation is direct: "Remain in him." In view of John's reference to Jesus' return (v. 28), the words *in him* relate to Jesus Christ.

Doctrinal Considerations in 2:26–27

Countless individuals gain a knowledge of salvation through the reading of Scripture. Guided by the Holy Spirit, they are led to Jesus Christ and accept him in faith.[68] After they accept Christ as their Savior, they are baptized in the name of the Triune God: Father, Son, and Holy Spirit. Yet before their baptism, when they first came to conversion, they already experienced the anointing of the Spirit.

Through Christ God gives his Holy Spirit to the believer, but the believer in turn must remain in Christ. Divine providence has its counterpart in human responsibility. God provides his Spirit to teach the believer all things necessary for salvation, but God also expects the Christian to remain in Christ so that he may have constant fellowship with the Father and the Son.

Greek Words, Phrases, and Constructions in 2:26–27

Verse 26

ἔγραψα—the epistolary aorist (see vv. 14, 21).

πλανώντων—this present active participle from πλανάω (I lead astray) is the

---

67. Refer to Greijdanus, *Johannes*, p. 453. Bruce writes, "But the ministry of teaching must be exercised by men who themselves share the 'anointing' of which John speaks, men who remain in the fellowship of the Spirit." See his *Epistles of John*, p. 76.

68. Consult especially Curtis R. Vaughan, *The Gifts of the Holy Spirit to Unbelievers and Believers* (reprint ed., Edinburgh: Banner of Truth Trust, 1975), p. 41.

so-called conative present. It is translated with the verb *to try* (trying to lead astray).[69]

ἵνα—the particle "expresses a conceived result."[70] Use of this particle after a noun or demonstrative pronoun is rather common in the writings of John.

αὐτοῦ—some manuscripts have αὐτό (same) instead of αὐτοῦ (of him). However, αὐτοῦ is better attested and therefore preferred.

μένετε—this verb can be either indicative or imperative. The general context suggests the imperative. The form μενεῖτε (future) has insufficient support.

---

28 And now, dear children, continue in him, so that when he appears we may be confident and unashamed before him at his coming.
29 If you know that he is righteous, you know that everyone who does what is right has been born of him.

C. Confident Before God
2:28–29

These two verses form a bridge between two chapters.[71] Verse 28 is a brief summary of chapter 2. The next verse is a prelude to chapter 3. Both verses are short and because of their respective contents, they do not form a unit. For this reason, some scholars place a division between these two verses. For the sake of conformity to the chapter divisions, however, we include them in chapter 2.

28. And now, dear children, continue in him. Here is the conclusion to the discourse in words that are repetitious. The words *and now* introduce the summary that repeats the familiar address *dear children* used already in verse 1. John reiterates the exhortation he gave in the preceding verse: "Remain in him." With this use of repetition, John teaches that fellowship with the Son of God is imperative for every believer. In the next clause, John provides the reason for continued fellowship with Christ: **so that when he appears we may be confident.**

Having fellowship with the Son is not limited to a spiritual exercise of prayer and meditation, but finds its fulfillment in the physical return of Jesus. John mentions the first coming of Jesus in the flesh—"our hands have touched" in chapter 1 (v. 1). In chapter 2 he writes about the certainty of Jesus' second coming (v. 28). The epistle has few references to his appearing, but this verse and 3:2 are clear in presenting the truth of Christ's return. The time of his return is not known, and John omits

---

69. Robertson, *Grammar*, p. 880.

70. Hanna, *Grammatical Aid*, p. 435. Also consult E. D. Burton, *Moods and Tenses of New Testament Greek* (Edinburgh: Clark, 1898), p. 218.

71. In his *Commentary on the Johannine Epistles*, Brooke writes, "These verses are transitional, and it is doubtful whether they should be attached to the preceding or the following section" (p. 64).

details except to say that "when he appears, we shall be like him, for we shall see him as he is" (3:2).

How do believers respond to the news of Jesus' return? They obey God's commands, continue in Christ, and are confident at the prospect of Jesus' return (compare 3:21). The word *confident* actually means that believers readily, frankly, and boldly speak about their Lord and Savior Jesus Christ. They communicate their faith. Moreover, in their prayers they incorporate the request of the church universal uttered since the time of the ascension, "Maranatha," that is, "Come, O Lord" (I Cor. 16:22).

Therefore, they are **unashamed before him at his coming.** Believers do not turn in shame from Christ, for they know that their sins have been forgiven. They are free from shame. But those who have pretended to be Christians cannot stand in the revealing light of his coming. They cannot hide their shame.

The expression *coming,* which is frequently used in the New Testament to describe Christ's return,[72] occurs only here in John's writings. John writes in the knowledge that the readers are fully acquainted with the doctrine of Christ's return. Alfred Plummer concludes, "This is one of the many small indications that he writes to well-instructed believers, not to children or the recently converted."[73]

29. If you know that he is righteous, you know that everyone who does what is right has been born of him.

Note the two parts of this verse:

a. *Condition.* John is telling his readers that if they know in their hearts "that he is righteous," they also will learn to know that righteous Christians are born of him. Is John reminding the believers that Jesus is "the Righteous One" (2:1)?

Do the pronouns *he* and *him* refer to Jesus? Because verse 29 looks forward and not back, the pronouns must point to God the Father (see 3:1) and not to Christ (v. 28). Also, believers are called "children of God" (3:1–2) and never "children of Christ." The phrase *born of God* appears four times in the epistle (3:9; 4:7; 5:1, 4). Furthermore, the verb *to be born* implies the existence of a father and a son. Indirectly the verb points to God the Father. The context, therefore, unmistakably suggests that the pronouns *he* and *him* signify God the Father and not Jesus the Son.[74]

b. *Conclusion.* In a pithy comment that is straight to the point, Bengel remarks that "the righteous produces the righteous."[75] God who is righteous brings forth sons and daughters who reflect his righteousness in their

---

72. See, for example, Matt. 24:3, 27, 37, 39; I Cor. 15:23; I Thess. 2:19; 3:13; 4:15; 5:23; II Thess. 2:1, 8; James 5:7, 8; II Peter 1:16.

73. Plummer, *The Epistles of St. John,* p. 68.

74. Guided perhaps by his interpretation of the context (I John 3:7), Horst Seebass understands the pronouns *he* and *him* to refer to Christ. See *NIDNTT,* vol. 3, p. 362.

75. Bengel, *Gnomon of the New Testament,* vol. 5, p. 126.

daily lives. To be righteous is the equivalent of being holy. It implies doing the will of God, obeying his commands, and loving him and one's neighbor. In short, "righteous" is a term that stands for being free from sin.

Therefore, the sentence "everyone who does what is right is born of God" does not describe those who do an occasional good deed. Rather, the sentence reveals the lifestyle of the person who is born of God. God's children try to do that which is good and pleasing in his sight. From our point of view, the sequence ought to be reversed, that is, "everyone who is born of God does what is right."[76] But John writes a conditional sentence that has two parts: a condition ("if you know that he is righteous") and a conclusion ("you know that everyone who does what is right has been born of him"). Note that the conclusion corresponds with the condition: "righteous" with "everyone who does what is right." It also explains the reason for right conduct. Their conduct is right because believers are children of God.

Practical Considerations in 2:28–29

At the end of the Parable of the Unjust Judge, recorded in Luke 18, Jesus abruptly speaks about himself when he asks his followers, "When the Son of Man comes, will he find faith on the earth?" (v. 8). This question seems to be entirely out of place at the conclusion of this parable. However, the preceding context (Luke 17:20–37) teaches the return of Jesus. When Jesus appears at his coming will he find the believers faithful to their calling? Will they be doing that which is just?

The New Testament speaks about Christ's return on nearly every page. James Montgomery Boice remarks, "It is mentioned 318 times in the 260 chapters of the New Testament. It is mentioned in every one of the New Testament books, with the exception of Galatians . . . and the very short books such as 2 and 3 John and Philemon."[77] When John writes that Jesus is coming back, he links the coming of Jesus to doing that which is right. The believer is not passively waiting for Christ's coming, but is actively promoting God's kingdom of righteousness (Luke 17:20–21). Christians are not praying for his return so that they can shirk their responsibilities. They are praying for Christ's coming so that he may find faith on the earth.

Greek Words, Phrases, and Constructions in 2:28–29

Verse 28

νῦν—this is not an adverb of time but a conclusion.[78]

ἐάν—the particle is the equivalent of ὅταν (whenever).

σχῶμεν—the aorist active subjunctive of ἔχω (I have). The aorist is constative.

---

76. Refer to Westcott, *The Epistles of St. John*, p. 84. Also consult Marshall, *The Epistles of John*, p. 169.

77. Boice, *The Epistles of John*, p. 96.

78. Thayer, p. 430.

ἀπό—following the verb *to be ashamed of*, this preposition is an echo of a Hebrew idiom.[79]

Verse 29

ἐάν—in this instance the particle has the same intent as εἰ (if).

τὴν δικαιοσύνην—the definite article specifies the noun because it stands for αὐτοῦ (his, namely, God's).

ἐξ—the preposition denotes source.

Summary of Chapter 2

John mentions God's promise for remission of sin not as an excuse for sinning but as comfort and assurance for the believer who occasionally falls into sin. He admonishes those who know the Lord to obey his commands; they must walk as Jesus walked. John gives them not a new command but an old one: love your neighbor as yourself.

In summary John exhorts all Christians whom he tenderly addresses as "dear children." He appeals to fathers and to young men because they have known Christ and they have overcome the devil. He tells them not to love the world but to obey the will of God instead.

John warns against the coming of the antichrist and instructs the believers to recognize those people who deny the Father and the Son. These persons are antichrists. He pleads with the readers to remain in the Son and in the Father and to receive the promise of eternal life.

The apostle informs the Christians about the significance of their anointing. Their anointing is the gift of the Holy Spirit who remains in them. And last, he reminds them of the coming of Christ and encourages the believers to be confident and unashamed. As children of God they are expected to pursue righteousness.

---

79. Robertson, *Grammar*, p. 473.

3

Believe in Jesus, *part 2*

3:1–24

Outline (continued)

3 1 How great is the love the Father has lavished on us, that we should be called children of God! And that is what we are! The reason the world does not know us is that it did not know him. 2 Dear friends, now we are children of God, and what we will be has not yet been made known. But we know that when he appears, we shall be like him, for we shall see him as he is. 3 Everyone who has this hope in him purifies himself, just as he is pure.

D. Children of God
3:1–3

1. God's Love
3:1

Children of the heavenly Father
Safely in his bosom gather;
Nestling bird nor star in heaven
Such a refuge e'er was given.
—Carolina V. Sandell Berg
trans. Ernst William Olson

1. How great is the love the Father has lavished on us, that we should be called children of God! And that is what we are! The reason the world does not know us is that it did not know him.

Note the following:

a. *The love of God.* In the Greek, John begins this sentence with a command: "See." He wants the readers to observe the manifestations of the Father's love. He introduces the subject of the love of God in the preceding chapter (2:5, 15), briefly discusses it in this chapter (3:1, 16, 17), and fully explains it in the next chapter (4:7–9, 10, 12, 16–18). The readers ought to fathom the kind of love the Father gives his children. That love is great. The Greek word translated "how great" or "what kind of" occurs only six times in the New Testament and "always implies astonishment and generally admiration."[1]

John does not say "the Father loves us." Then he would describe a condition. Instead, he writes, "the Father has lavished [his love] on us"

---

1. The six references are Matt. 8:27; Mark 13:1; Luke 1:29; 7:39; II Peter 3:11; I John 3:1. Refer to Alfred Plummer, *The Epistles of St. John,* Cambridge Greek Testament for Schools and Colleges series (Cambridge: At the University Press, 1896), p. 71.

and thus portrays an action and the extent of God's love. John has chosen the word *Father* purposely. That word implies the Father-child relationship. However, God did not become Father when he adopted us as children. God's fatherhood is eternal. He is eternally the Father of Jesus Christ and through Jesus he is our Father. Through Jesus we receive the Father's love and are called "children of God."

b. *Children of God.* What an honor! God calls us his children and gives us the assurance that as his children we are heirs and co-heirs with Christ (Rom. 8:17). God gives the right to become children of God (John 1:12) to all who in faith have received Christ as Lord and Savior. God extends his love to his Son Jesus Christ and through him to all his adopted children.

John underscores the reality of our status when he writes that already, at present, we are children of God. "And that is what we are!" In other words, God does not give us a promise which he will fulfill in the future. No, in fact we are already God's children. We enjoy all the rights and privileges our adoption entails, because we have come to know God as our Father.

c. *Knowledge of God.* God's children experience the love of God. They profess him as their Father, for they have an experiential knowledge of God. They put their trust and faith in him who loves them, provides for them, and protects them.

The hostile, unbelieving world, however, does not know the children of God. Unbelievers cannot understand us, says John, because they do not know God (compare John 16:2–3). "The world does not recognize us because it never recognized him."[2] The unbelieving world lives separated from God and will never know the significance of our spiritual relationship with God. If we were to become worldly, we would forfeit our status as children of God. By rejecting us, however, the world confirms our relationship with God the Father.

Greek Words, Phrases, and Constructions in 3:1

ἴδετε—the second person plural active imperative of εἶδον (the second aorist of the verb ὁράω [I see]).

τέκνα—whereas John repeatedly employs the diminutive τεκνία (dear children) to express endearment, here he uses the noun τέκνα, not υἱοί (sons), to include sons and daughters.

καὶ ἐσμέν—manuscript evidence for the inclusion of these two words is strong. "The absence of the words in several of the latest witnesses (K L most minuscules), followed by the Textus Receptus, is due either to scribal oversight, perhaps occasioned by graphical similarity with the preceding word, or to deliberate editorial pruning of an awkward parenthetical clause."[3]

---

2. Raymond E. Brown, *The Epistles of John,* Anchor Bible series (Garden City, N.Y.: Doubleday, 1982), vol. 30, p. 392.

3. Bruce M. Metzger, *A Textual Commentary on the Greek New Testament,* corrected ed. (London and New York: United Bible Societies, 1975), pp. 710–11.

γινώσκει—this verb indicates experiential knowledge, in contrast to the verb οἶδα which usually refers to innate knowledge (see v. 2).

---

2. God's Children
3:2

2. Dear friends, now we are children of God, and what we will be has not yet been made known. But we know that when he appears, we shall be like him, for we shall see him as he is.

In Greek John writes, "Beloved." This term which expresses a passive idea may imply that God is the one who loves us: "Beloved by God." John, then, continues to stress the special relationship we have with God. The Father loves us and therefore we are *now* his children. Already in this earthly life we claim the right to be God's children and are able to procure this assurance.[4]

We are in principle children of God (v. 1) who lack perfection because of sin. But that which is principle now will become full reality in the future. John, therefore, observes, "What we will be has not yet been made known." That is, God has only begun his marvelous work in us which in time he will bring to completion.

What will we be in the future? Although the Bible is a book that relates the work of creation and redemption, it also gives us a glimpse of the future. For instance, John tells his readers about their identity with Jesus.

"But we know that when he appears, we shall be like him, for we shall see him as he is."[5] In his epistles, Paul reveals the same truths. Here are three relevant passages:

> And we, who with unveiled faces all reflect the Lord's glory, are being transformed into his likeness with ever-increasing glory. [II Cor. 3:18]
>
> [Jesus Christ] will transform our lowly bodies so that they will be like his glorious body. [Phil. 3:21]
>
> When Christ, who is your life, appears, then you also will appear with him in glory. [Col. 3:4]

Scripture discloses that at the coming of Christ we will be glorified in body and soul. "We shall be like him." The Bible nowhere states that we shall be equal to Christ. Instead it tells us that we shall be conformed to the likeness of the Son of God. We share his immortality. However, Christ has the preeminence, for the Son of God is "the firstborn among many brothers" (Rom. 8:29). Believers will surround the throne of God and the Lamb. "They will see his face, and his name will be on their foreheads" (Rev. 22:4).

---

4. For related passages, see Rom. 8:15; Gal. 3:26; 4:6 where the terms *son* and *sonship* occur.
5. Scholars take the subject *it* in the variant reading of the first clause, "But we know that when *it* is made known," to refer to the preceding phrase *what we will be*. The immediate (2:28; 3:5, 8) context, however, relates to the coming of Christ. For this reason, I prefer the reading *when* he *appears*.

Greek Words, Phrases, and Constructions in 3:2

φανερωθῇ—the aorist passive subjunctive of the verb φανερόω (I reveal) lacks the subject. It can be either personal (referring to Christ) or impersonal (relating to the phrase τί ἐσόμεθα).

---

3. Knowledge of God
3:3

3. Everyone who has this hope in him purifies himself, just as he is pure.

How does the believer face the future? He has received God's promise of complete restoration, and now he lives in hope that God will fulfill this promise.[6]

John states a fact: "Everyone who has this hope . . . purifies himself." He refrains from expressing a wish ("may he purify himself"), a possibility ("he may purify himself"), or a command ("he ought to purify himself"). John puts this stated fact in positive terms. The believer lives in the hope of becoming conformed to Jesus Christ, and the more he contemplates this truth the more he purifies himself of sin. He seeks to cleanse himself from sin that contaminates body and soul; constantly he strives for holiness in reverence to God (II Cor. 7:1).

"Just as he is pure." In the preceding chapters, John writes that if we have fellowship with Jesus, he cleanses us from sin through his blood (1:7); and if we claim to have fellowship with him, we "must walk as Jesus did" (2:6). John, accordingly, stresses moral purity which every believer must demonstrate by living a life of holiness. John points to the standard: as Christ is pure, so his followers strive for purity.[7]

Doctrinal Considerations in 3:1–3

In his first epistle, John teaches the fundamental doctrine that one of God's characteristics is love.[8] Thus, John writes the pithy statement *God is love* (4:16). John conveys the thought that God initiates love and lavishes it on his people (3:1). Love, then, does not originate with man but with God (4:7). When man is the recipient of God's love, he in turn ought to reflect this love toward God and his neighbor. But the person who fails to show love to his neighbor does not

---

6. In the writings of John, the concept *hope* expressed in verb or noun is rather scarce. The verb appears only three times (John 5:45; II John 12; III John 14) and the noun once (I John 3:3).

7. Refer to Heinrich Baltensweiler, *NIDNTT*, vol. 3, p. 102. And consult Friedrich Hauck, *TDNT*, vol. 1, p. 123.

8. See Donald Guthrie, *New Testament Theology* (Downers Grove: Inter-Varsity, 1981), p. 105. And consult Harold W. Hoehner, "Love," *EDT*, pp. 656–59.

possess the love of God (3:17). Love is not private, passive, or abstract. Love is explicit, active, and intimate. It is the bond that unites giver and receiver. As children of God and recipients of his divine love, we confess that we are unable to comprehend the length, breadth, and depth of God's love. Horatius Bonar summed it up in these words:

> O love of God, how strong and true,
> Eternal, and yet ever new,
> Uncomprehended and unbought,
> Beyond all knowledge and all thought.

Greek Words, Phrases, and Constructions in 3:3

τὴν ἐλπίδα ταύτην ἐπ᾽ αὐτῷ—the noun ἐλπίδα receives emphasis from the preceding definite article and the succeeding demonstrative adjective. Note that the preposition ἐπί literally means "on." The pronoun αὐτῷ relates to Christ.

---

4 Everyone who sins breaks the law; in fact, sin is lawlessness. 5 But you know that he appeared so that he might take away our sins. And in him is no sin. 6 No one who lives in him keeps on sinning. No one who continues to sin has either seen him or known him.

E. The Nature of Sin
3:4–6

1. Sin and the Law
3:4

Although the believer seeks to live in obedience to the will of God, he knows that his deeds are tainted by sin. This does not mean that sin controls him. On the contrary, the Christian valiantly opposes sin, because he wants to do that which is right (2:29; 3:7). Should he stumble, then the child of God flees to Christ to plead for remission.

However, the person who continues to live in sin ought to know that sin is the same as lawlessness.

4. Everyone who sins breaks the law; in fact, sin is lawlessness.

This epistle of John is marked by contrast. John first depicts the child of God who purifies himself (3:3) and then portrays the person who continues to live in sin and practices lawlessness. The child of God, therefore, cannot continue to sin; and the unbeliever who indulges in sin cannot be a child of God.

What is sin? It is a breaking of the standard, that is, the law God has given.[9] Anyone can detect a crooked line when a perfectly straight line is

---

9. The seventeenth-century Westminster theologians who composed the Shorter Catechism ask the question (14) *What is sin?* and provide the answer: "Sin is any want of conformity unto, or transgression of, the law of God."

drawn next to it.[10] John makes sinful behavior more conspicuous by contrasting it with righteousness.

John explains what sin means. He says that committing sin is the same as a complete disregard for the law of God. For him, sin and lawlessness are two interchangeable terms. John actually provides a brief definition of sin by revealing its very nature: *Sin is lawlessness.* "[Sin] is a deliberate rejection of God's standards and a resort to one's own desires."[11] Sin has its origin in the devil and expresses itself as a willful act against God. The person who continues to do what is sinful, concludes John, "is of the devil" (3:8).

Greek Words, Phrases, and Constructions in 3:4

πᾶς ὁ ποιῶν—the construction of πᾶς followed by the definite article and the present or perfect participle occurs fourteen times in the epistle.[12] The present tense of the participle denotes continuative action.

τὴν ἀνομίαν ποιεῖ—John uses the noun ἀνομία only twice—in this verse. Both times the noun is preceded by the definite article. The verb ποιεῖ is in the present tense to indicate duration.

---

2. The Coming of Christ
3:5

5. But you know that he appeared so that he might take away our sins. And in him is no sin.

At times John does not clearly delineate between the first coming of Christ and his return. However, in this text John alludes to the earthly ministry of Jesus and reminds his readers that they are fully acquainted with the essence of the gospel: *Christ takes away our sins.* These words are a distinct reminder of John the Baptist's cry: "Look, the Lamb of God, who takes away the sin of the world" (John 1:29).[13]

The Old Testament prophets prophesy that the Messiah would come to remove the sins of his people (see Isa. 53). In the New Testament apostles and apostolic helpers teach this same doctrine as an accomplished

---

10. Refer to John Albert Bengel, *Gnomon of the New Testament*, ed. Andrew R. Fausset, 7th ed., 5 vols. (Edinburgh: Clark, 1877), vol. 5, p. 127.

11. Guthrie, *New Testament Theology*, p. 196. Numerous commentators accept John's definition as an equation of sin and lawlessness. Others understand John's words not as a definition but as a reference to the state of lawlessness at the end of time (II Thess. 2:3–8). For instance, consult Brown, *The Epistles of John*, pp. 399–400. However, the question remains whether John in his epistle means the spirit of lawlessness will be demonstrated only at the end of time. He calls the present time "the last hour" in which there are many antichrists (see 2:18).

12. Here are the verses: 2:23, 29; 3:3, 4, 6 [twice], 9, 10, 15; 4:7; 5:1 [twice], 4, 18.

13. For a thorough discussion of John 1:29 in the light of rabbinic sources see SB, vol. 2, pp. 363–70.

fact (e.g., II Cor. 5:21; I Peter 2:24). They teach that Christ takes away sins—note the plural—once for all because he himself is sinless. Only Christ who is sinless is able to do this.

"In him is no sin." John writes in the present tense to indicate that Christ always has been, is, and will be without sin. He implies that as the Son of God is sinless, so the Christian whose sins Christ has taken away should not yield to sin. The believer must oppose sin with all his might and strive for holiness.

One of the marks of being a child of God is to be free from the rule of sin. Should the Christian live a life of sin, his claim of being a son of God would be meaningless.

Greek Words, Phrases, and Constructions in 3:5

τὰς ἁμαρτίας—the plural signifies that all sins are taken away (however, see 5:16). The reason for including or excluding the pronoun ἡμῶν is difficult to determine. Many scholars omit the pronoun because they feel it is an assimilation to parallel phrases in 2:2 and 4:10.

---

3. Believer and Unbeliever
3:6

6. No one who lives in him keeps on sinning. No one who continues to sin has either seen him or known him.

Once again John presents a contrast. He places the believer, who has terminated a life of sin because he now lives in Christ, over against the unbeliever who, living in sin, has not seen or known Christ.

John begins with a description of the believer. Throughout his epistle, John repeats the same truth, namely, that the person who lives in Christ and has continuous fellowship with him obeys the Word of God.[14] John is fully aware that the believer occasionally stumbles into sin, and that if he confesses his sin, Christ forgives and cleanses him from all unrighteousness (1:9). John also knows that the believer is no longer in the grip of sin, for his life is controlled by Christ (compare Gal. 2:20). Says John, "No one who is born of God will continue to sin, because God's seed remains in him; he cannot go on sinning, because he has been born of God" (3:9).

What a difference we see when we compare the life of the believer with that of the unbeliever! The unbeliever continues to sin and demonstrates that he has no fellowship with Christ. In fact, John declares that the person who persists in sin has neither seen nor known Christ. "Anyone who does what is evil has not seen God" (III John 11). We should understand the verb *to see* (in the perfect tense) in a spiritual sense. It is the

---

14. See the following passages: 1:3, 7; 2:3, 5, 23, 29; 3:3, 4, 9, 10, 15; 4:7; 5:1, 3, 4, 18.

299

equivalent of the verb *to believe*. Anyone, then, who revels in sin has no faith in Christ and does not know him personally. He is an unbeliever.

Practical Considerations in 3:4–6

The world provides its own definition of sin. For many people, sin is a naughty deed—usually related to sex—that arouses chuckles and laughter. In their view, sin should not be taken seriously. Others view sin as a weakness or imperfection caused by a psychological defect. Still others try to explain sin in terms of a mistake that any human being is able to make. In short, according to the world, sin is nothing serious.

The Greek word translated *to sin* originally meant "to miss the mark." That is, someone taking a bow and arrow would aim for the center of a target but miss it. In the Greek world, therefore, sin was considered a miscalculation.

John, however, demurs. For him, sin is a serious offense against God. It signifies a deliberate disregard for and violation of his divine law. Sin is a direct affront to God; it is an expression of enmity and alienation that deserves God's wrath.

How can we find restoration? Man's sins are removed only through the sacrificial death of Jesus Christ. Writes Donald G. Bloesch, "Christ not only pays the penalty for sin, but he does more than the law requires: he accepts the sinner unto himself, adopting that person into his family as a brother or sister."[15]

Greek Words, Phrases, and Constructions in 3:6

ἁμαρτάνει—the present tense of this verb is iterative.

---

7 Dear children, do not let anyone lead you astray. He who does what is right is righteous, just as he is righteous. 8 He who does what is sinful is of the devil, because the devil has been sinning from the beginning. The reason the Son of God appeared was to destroy the devil's work. 9 No one who is born of God will continue to sin, because God's seed remains in him; he cannot go on sinning, because he has been born of God. 10 This is how we know who the children of God are and who the children of the devil are: Anyone who does not do what is right is not a child of God; nor is anyone who does not love his brother.

F. Born of God
3:7–10

1. The Righteous
3:7

In this section, John resorts to parallelism and repetition, especially in verses 4–10. If we put the verses graphically in sequence, we see this schema:

---

15. Donald G. Bloesch, "Sin," *EDT*, p. 1015. Also see Walther Günther, *NIDNTT*, vol. 3, p. 582.

$$vv. \quad 4 = 8a$$
$$vv. \quad 5 = 8b$$
$$vv. \ 6a = 9$$
$$vv. \ 7b = 10$$

Also note that while verse 7 opens the last paragraph of this section positively, verse 10 concludes it negatively.

7. Dear children, do not let anyone lead you astray. He who does what is right is righteous, just as he is righteous.

The pastor speaks tenderly to the members of the church: "Dear children." He wants them to know the difference between truth and falsehood, that is, between the teachings of Jesus and the teachings of the devil. He realizes the pernicious influence of teachers who seek to lead God's children astray, and he wishes to alert the church members to the lie that belief in God and a sinful life are compatible. John exposes this lie and warns his readers to watch out for these false teachers.

"Do not let anyone lead you astray" (compare 2:26). John asks his people to apply the standard of truth by which they are able to detect deception. Here is the criterion: "He who does what is right is righteous, just as he is righteous." The person who is born of God reflects his spiritual descent—like Father, like son. Because of his spiritual rebirth, the believer wants to express his gratitude to God and do that which is right (see 2:29). Moreover, because righteous living originates in a righteous heart, the believer shows by his conduct that he is one of God's children (3:10). He is righteous, just as Christ is righteous.

The comparison by the words *just as* does not mean that the Christian is identical to Christ in every respect. Of course not. Even though God forgives sin, the Christian does not continue to live without sin. When John writes that the believer is righteous just as Christ is righteous, he means that the child of God and the Son of God are righteous as members of God's family (compare 2:1).

2. The Unrighteous
3:8

8. He who does what is sinful is of the devil, because the devil has been sinning from the beginning. The reason the Son of God appeared was to destroy the devil's work.

The first part of this verse parallels verse 4, "Everyone who sins breaks the law; in fact, sin is lawlessness." To put it differently, verse 8a is the negative counterpart of verse 7b.

a. "He who does what is sinful is of the devil." John virtually repeats the words Jesus spoke to the Jews when he said, "Everyone who sins is a slave to sin" (John 8:34) and "You belong to your father, the devil, and you want to carry out your father's desire. He was a murderer from the beginning, not holding to the truth, for there is no truth in him" (John

8:44). Fifth-century church father Augustine describes the sinful man in these words:

> For the devil made no man, begat no man, created no man: but whoso imitates the devil, that person, as if begotten of him, becomes a child of the devil; by imitating him, not literally by being begotten of him.[16]

b. "Because the devil has been sinning from the beginning." Note that in this verse John points to the source of sin: the devil. All sin originates with Satan, for he sinned from the beginning. How do we understand the phrase *from the beginning?* John Albert Bengel wisely replies, *"from the beginning* [means] from the time when the devil is the devil."[17] How long Satan remained in his pristine angelic state, we do not know. When he fell into sin, he became the originator and instigator of sin. He enticed Adam and Eve and through them put the whole human race in the bondage of sin. As "the prince of this world" (John 12:31; 14:30; 16:11) he governs the man who lives in sin.

c. "The Son of God appeared . . . to destroy the devil's work." No one less than the Son of God appeared to set man free from the power of Satan (Heb. 2:14–15). The Son of God came to deliver his people from the bondage of sin and to restore them as children of God who are "eager to do what is good" (Titus 2:14).

Greek Words, Phrases, and Constructions in 3:8

ἁμαρτάνει—the present tense is iterative or customary.[18]

---

3. Free from the Power of Sin
3:9

9. No one who is born of God will continue to sin, because God's seed remains in him; he cannot go on sinning, because he has been born of God.

This verse parallels verse 6a (compare 5:18). It is a broader statement in which the emphasis falls on two items that are placed in an inverted sequence: 1. he who is [has been] born of God 2. will [can] not go on

---

16. Augustine, *Ten Homilies on the First Epistle of John*, trans. H. Browne, Homily 4. 10 in *Nicene and Post-Nicene Fathers of the Christian Church* (reprint ed., Grand Rapids: Eerdmans, 1974), 1st series, vol. 7, p. 486. Also see Plummer, *The Epistles of St. John*, p. 78; B. F. Westcott, *The Epistles of St. John, The Greek Text, with Notes and Addenda* (1883; Grand Rapids: Eerdmans, 1966), p. 106.

17. Bengel, *Gnomon of the New Testament*, p. 127. Also compare I. Howard Marshall, *The Epistles of John*, New International Commentary on the New Testament series (Grand Rapids: Eerdmans, 1978), p. 184, n. 30.

18. A. T. Robertson, *A Grammar of the Greek New Testament in the Light of Historical Research* (Nashville: Broadman, 1934), p. 880.

sinning; and it makes the clause "because God's seed remains in him" a link between the preceding and the following clause.

a. *Born again.* The phrase *born of God* is characteristic of John, for he uses it repeatedly (2:29; 3:9; 4:7; 5:1, 4, 18). It signifies that a person has been born spiritually in the past and continues in the present as God's child. That is, he finds his origin and existence in God. Whereas the person who practices sin has Satan as his father, the born-again believer knows that God is his Father. The words of Jesus are relevant: "A good tree cannot bear bad fruit, and a bad tree cannot bear good fruit" (Matt. 7:18).

"God's seed remains in him." The word *seed* has a figurative connotation: "God's nature" or "God's principle of life." God guards the new life he planted in the heart of the believer and causes it to develop. The Christian, then, will not and cannot yield to sin because of that divine principle in his heart.

b. *Inability to sin.* The translators of the New International Version have tried to reflect the Greek verb tenses by adding extra words. They write, "No one who is born of God *will continue to* sin, . . . he cannot *go on* sin*ning*" (italics added).[19] This is an acceptable interpretation of John's intention. In Greek, the verbs express continued action, not a single occurrence. Therefore, by using the present tenses of the Greek verbs, John is saying that the believer cannot practice habitual sin. "The thought being conveyed in I John 3:9 is not that one born of God will never commit a sinful act but that he will not persist in sin."[20]

Sin does not originate with God, for "in him there is no darkness at all" (I John 1:5). A person who is born of God and possesses God's nature cannot live in habitual sin. Nevertheless, the possibility of falling into occasional sin is always present, as every Christian can testify.[21]

Greek Words, Phrases, and Constructions in 3:9

γεγεννημένος—the perfect passive participle from γεννάω (I beget) denotes action that took place in the past; its influence, however, continues to the present.

οὐ δύναται ἁμαρτάνειν—note that John writes not "able *not* to sin," but "*not* able to sin." Some grammarians take the present infinitive to be durative; others understand it as a state.[22] That is, a Christian sins but he cannot be called a sinner.

---

19. Other translations provide a literal version, for instance, "Whoever has been born of God does not practice sin, . . . and he cannot sin" (NKJV).

20. V. Kerry Inman, "Distinctive Johannine Vocabulary and the Interpretation of I John 3:9," *WJT* 40 (1977): 142.

21. Consult P. P. A. Kotze, "The Meaning of I John 3:9 with Reference to I John 1:8 and 10," *Neotestamentica* 13 (1979): 68–83.

22. For example, consult H. E. Dana and Julius R. Mantey, *A Manual Grammar of the Greek New Testament* (New York: Macmillan, 1967), p. 195. Also see N. Turner, *A Grammar of New Testament Greek* (Edinburgh: Clark, 1963), pp. 150–51; Robert Hanna, *Grammatical Aid to the Greek New Testament* (Grand Rapids: Baker, 1983), pp. 435–36.

He belongs to Christ who has redeemed and sanctified him and who has destroyed the devil's work.

---

4. Righteousness and Love
3:10

10. This is how we know who the children of God are and who the children of the devil are: Anyone who does not do what is right is not a child of God; nor is anyone who does not love his brother.

In this entire letter John presents our existence in terms of two categories: you are either a child of God or you are a child of the devil. John sees only absolutes: light or darkness, truth or the lie, God or the devil, life or death. For him there is no middle ground. There are no alternatives.

How do we know to which category we belong? John says that the proof is in our conduct: the child of God does what is right and loves his brother, but the child of the devil fails to do these things. John puts the criterion in negative form—"anyone who does not do what is right is not a child of God"—so that the Christian takes note and applies himself actively to do God's will.[23]

Practical Considerations in 3:7–10

"The devil made me do it." Although some people use these words to disclaim responsibility for their evil deeds, no court of law will accept such testimony as a valid excuse. Unless insanity can be proved, a person is responsible for his own behavior.

Yet the admission that the devil is behind sinful deeds is undeniably true. A convicted killer explicitly becomes a murderer when he takes someone's life. But implicitly he already is a murderer when he receives the instigation to kill from the devil. If he were not in Satan's power, he would not perpetrate such a crime.

The child of the devil, as John puts it, continues to commit sin because he belongs to the evil one. By contrast, the child of God will not continue to sin because he has God's nature in him. He wants to do what is right and thus he demonstrates his love to God and man. Born of God, the believer seeks to reflect his Father's virtues and excellence. When he falls into sin, he realizes that Satan has led him astray. But when he turns to God in faith and repentance, he finds forgiveness. As a child of God he is never in the power of the evil one.

Additional Remarks

Literature on I John 3:7–10 is extensive. Numerous commentators express their opinion on what they deem is the correct interpretation of

---

23. Compare Westcott, *The Epistles of St. John*, p. 109.

these verses in the light of the entire epistle. They examine all aspects of this passage quite often from their own theological or philosophical bent. They discuss the apparent contradiction between 1:8, 10, "If we claim to be without sin, we deceive ourselves and the truth is not in us" . . . "If we claim we have not sinned, we make him out to be a liar," and 3:9c, "he cannot go on sinning" (also see 5:16). Remarks Raymond E. Brown, "No other N[ew] T[estament] author contradicts himself so sharply within such a short span of writing, and inevitably much scholarly energy has been devoted to proving that no contradiction exists."[24]

What are scholars saying about this problem? From numerous explanations here are three samples presented in summary form. First, John writes as a pastor to his people and calls them to confess their sins (1:8–10). But he also holds before them the ideal that all those who are born of God cannot sin.[25] This view, however, represents an ideal, not reality.

Next, we should distinguish between different kinds of sin: deliberate sin (5:16–17) and involuntary sins; mortal sins and insignificant sins; and the sin of refusing to believe in Jesus over against the believer's temporary lapse into sin. Nevertheless, in the sight of God every sin is a transgression of his law (James 2:9–11).

Last, with his characteristic twofold approach, John describes the person who persistently sins because he is in the power of the evil one and the Christian who sometimes may fall into sin, but cannot sin persistently.[26] In expressing this thought, John uses Greek verbs in the present tense that indicate continual action (for instance, "he cannot go on sinning" [3:9]). Many commentators have adopted this approach as a plausible interpretation.[27]

---

11 This is the message you heard from the beginning: We should love one another.   12 Do not be like Cain, who belonged to the evil one and murdered his brother. And why did he murder him? Because his own actions were evil and his brother's were righteous.   13 Do not be surprised, my brothers, if the world hates you.   14 We know that we have passed from death into life, because we love our brothers. Anyone who does not love remains in death.   15 Anyone who hates his brother is a murderer, and you know that no murderer has eternal life in him.

---

24. Brown, *The Epistles of John*, p. 413.
25. Consult Henry Alford, *Alford's Greek Testament, An Exegetical and Critical Commentary*, vol. 4, pt. 2, *James-Revelation* (reprint ed., Grand Rapids: Guardian, 1976), p. 465. Also see Ignace de la Potterie, "The Impeccability of the Christian According to I Jn 3, 6–9," in *The Christian Lives by the Spirit*, Ignace de la Potterie and Stanislaus Lyonet (Staten Island: Alba, 1971), p. 90.
26. Refer to J. R. W. Stott, *The Epistles of John: An Introduction and Commentary*, Tyndale New Testament Commentaries series (Grand Rapids: Eerdmans, 1964), p. 135.
27. This interpretation has received support from Inman, "Distinctive Johannine Vocabulary."

G. Hatred of the World
3:11–15

1. Love and Hate
3:11–12

John contrasts love and hate by first stating the command to love one another and then by recounting the hatred Cain displayed when he murdered his brother.

11. This is the message you heard from the beginning: We should love one another.   12. Do not be like Cain, who belonged to the evil one and murdered his brother. And why did he murder him? Because his own actions were evil and his brother's were righteous.

a. *Love.* Throughout his epistle John repeats the main themes of his teaching to ensure that his readers remember his instruction. Here he reminds them of the command he gave in the preceding chapter (2:7), that they love one another. He introduces this precept with the words "This is the message you heard from the beginning." When they first heard the gospel proclaimed, they became acquainted with the message to love one another. This command, then, is fundamental to the Christian religion (compare John 13:34; 15:12; I John 3:23). It can never be regarded as an afterthought in the teaching of God's revelation.

b. *Hate.* In contrast with love, hate destroys and kills. John mentions Cain without any details or qualifications, except that he belonged to the devil and that he murdered his brother. Note that John mentions Cain by name, not Abel. John concentrates on Cain, because he is the representative of those who are not born of God, but belong to the evil one (compare v. 10a; John 8:44). "It is not that Cain by murdering his brother became the child of the devil; but, being a child of the devil, his actions were evil and culminated in the murder of his brother."[28]

c. *Murder.* Translators avoid a literal translation when they provide the reader with the word *murdered:* "Cain murdered his brother." But the Greek actually says, "Cain . . . *cut* his brother's *throat*" (JB, italics added). Admittedly, the Genesis account (4:8) is very brief at this point. Also, the writer of Hebrews mentions Abel's death indirectly (11:4). The first act of slaughtering a human being, however, is inseparably connected with the name *Cain.*

d. *Evil and righteous.* "And why did he murder him?" Instead of saying that because of hatred Cain killed Abel, John contrasts the deeds of Cain with those of his brother. Cain's actions were evil and his brother's were righteous. These two adjectives provide the contrast. The Greek word *evil* is the same word John uses to describe Satan (2:13, 14; 3:12; 5:18, 19). In short, John intimates that Cain's deeds originated with Satan. The word

---

28. Glenn W. Barker, *1 John*, the *Expositor's Bible Commentary*, ed. Frank E. Gaebelein, 12 vols. (Grand Rapids: Zondervan, 1981), vol. 12, p. 335.

righteous, however, is a term that refers to Jesus Christ (1:9; 2:1, 29; 3:7). In other words, Cain belonged to Satan and Abel belonged to God.

Greek Words, Phrases, and Constructions in 3:12

Κἀϊν—this is the only direct reference to the Old Testament in the entire epistle.

τοῦ πονηροῦ—John applies this term to Satan, "while man is the battleground between Satan and Christ."[29] The adjective πονηρά (evil) describes the works of a person who belongs to Satan.

ἔσφαξεν—from the verb σφάζω (I slaughter), in the aorist this word refers to killing someone by violent methods.

χάριν—this noun in the accusative serves as a preposition that governs a genitive. Normally the preposition follows the genitive. The exception is in this verse.[30]

---

2. Hatred
3:13–14

Now John is ready to place hatred and death over against love. He writes:

13. Do not be surprised, my brothers, if the world hates you. 14. We know that we have passed from death to life, because we love our brothers. Anyone who does not love remains in death.

a. "Do not be surprised." The believers are astounded by the hatred they endure from the world around them. They were not expecting any hatred. As true Christians they provided and continue to provide help to the needy and love to the people around them. John says, "Stop being surprised." The world is filled with Cain's descendants who will express their hatred toward the children of God.

b. "My brothers." John, too, experiences the hatred of the world, and therefore he puts himself next to his readers. He calls them "brothers." The address John usually employs in his epistle is either "dear children" or "dear friends." But in this verse, and only here, he uses the word *brothers.* As their spiritual father he addresses his readers as children or friends; as a fellow believer he calls them brothers.

c. "If the world hates you." With the brothers, John endures the opposition a sinful world expresses toward Christians. When John writes, "If the world hates you," he is not predicting the possibility that this may occur. The word *if* in this sentence actually is equivalent to "that": "Do not be surprised that the world hates you." These words echo Jesus' warning that

---

29. Günther Harder, *TDNT,* vol. 6, p. 559. Also refer to Ernst Achilles, *NIDNTT,* vol. 1, p. 566.
30. Consult C. F. D. Moule, *An Idiom-Book of New Testament Greek,* 2d ed. (Cambridge: At the University Press, 1960), p. 86.

Christians will be hated by the world. "If the world hates you, keep in mind that it hated me first" (John 15:18).

d. "We . . . have passed from death to life." With this statement, John introduces a thought that is unrelated to the preceding verse (v. 14). The statement seems contrary to nature: all living beings (man, animal, plant) pass from life to death. Yet John introduces verse 14 with the reassuring words *we know*. He uses the verb *know* because the readers know the gospel. They have been taught that, like all other people, they were at one time dead in transgressions and sins (consult Eph. 2:1, 5) until they "passed from death to life" (see John 5:24). The fact that they were dead reveals that God had to lead them out of death into life. They can never claim superiority over those who are still in death. God saves, not man.

Note that John does not say, "Because we love our brothers, therefore we have passed from life to death." He declares the opposite. "Love for our brothers is the evidence, not the basis, for spiritual life."[31] Love for the brothers is really an expression of thankfulness to God for his gift of life.

e. "Anyone who does not love remains in death." The child of God passes from death to life but the person who belongs to the evil one remains in death. Why? Because he does not love. The mark of spiritual life is love. And when love comes to expression, life flourishes. If love is absent from a person's life, hatred with all its dire consequences fills the void.

Greek Words, Phrases, and Constructions in 3:13–14

Verse 13

καί—whether this conjunction should be deleted or included in the text remains an open question. Scholars usually include the word but place it within brackets to indicate that they doubt its authenticity.

εἰ—verbs of emotion, for instance, θαυμάζω (I am surprised), sometimes use the particle εἰ.[32]

Verse 14

ἡμεῖς—the use of the pronoun emphasizes the verb οἴδαμεν (we know) which indicates innate knowledge.

μεταβεβήκαμεν—the compound from the verb μεταβαίνω (I depart) is directive. It indicates moving from one place to another. The perfect tense reveals an action that happened in the past; its consequences have relevance for the present.

ἀγαπῶν—a number of manuscripts add τὸν ἀδελφόν (the brother). "The shorter reading is to be preferred (*a*) because it is attested by superior witnesses

---

31. Marshall, *The Epistles of John*, p. 191.
32. Refer to Robertson, *Grammar*, p. 965.

and (b) because copyists were more likely to add than to delete an object that completes the thought of the participle."[33]

---

3. Murder
3:15

Anyone who lacks love has a heart filled with hate. There is no middle ground. And hatred eventually ends in murder, as Cain proved.

15. Anyone who hates his brother is a murderer, and you know that no murderer has eternal life in him.

Without mentioning his name, John indirectly refers to Cain, the first person charged with homicide—more precisely, fratricide, because Cain killed his brother. John, however, calls anyone who hates his fellow man a murderer. But does hatred always lead to murder? John Calvin keenly observes, "If we wish an evil to happen to our brother from some one else, we are murderers."[34]

The word *murderer* applies to Satan (John 8:44). He instigated the slaying of Abel and thus Cain also became known as a murderer. The consequence of being a murderer is that the person forfeits eternal life. John reminds his readers of the Old Testament law against murder (Gen. 9:5–6; Exod. 21:12; Num. 35:16, 19–21) and the teaching of Jesus on this subject (Matt. 5:21–22).

John is explicit when he writes, "No murderer has eternal life in him." That is, a murderer has no part in the kingdom of God. Unless he repents and turns in faith to Christ, he is eternally lost. On the other hand, the Christian possesses eternal life already in principle (see, for instance, John 3:36; 17:3), and later when his glorified body and soul are reunited, he will enjoy eternal life in complete fullness.

Greek Words, Phrases, and Constructions in 3:15

μισῶν—this present participle is durative.

ἀνθρωποκτόνος—the compound derives from ἄνθρωπος (man) and κτείνω (I kill).

μένουσαν—the present active participle, feminine singular, describes the noun ζωήν (life). Because of its position at the end of the sentence, it receives emphasis.

---

16 This is how we know what love is: Jesus Christ laid down his life for us. And we ought to lay down our lives for our brothers. 17 If anyone has material possessions and sees his brother in need but has no pity on him, how can the love of God be in him? 18 Dear children, let us not love with words or tongue but with actions and in truth.

---

33. Metzger, *Textual Commentary*, p. 711.
34. John Calvin, *Commentaries on the Catholic Epistles: The First Epistle of John*, ed. and trans. John Owen (Grand Rapids: Eerdmans, 1948), p. 218.

H. Love for Each Other
3:16–18

1. Positive
3:16

The similarities between the Gospel of John and his first epistle are numerous and striking. In the Gospel John records the following words of Jesus: "Greater love has no one than this, that he lay down his life for his friends" (15:13; also see 10:11, 15, 17–18). And in his epistle John says,

16. This is how we know what love is: Jesus Christ laid down his life for us. And we ought to lay down our lives for our brothers.

John is a pastor and a teacher. As a wise pastor he places himself at the level of his readers by using the pronoun *we*. And as a teacher he reminds his readers of the message of the gospel by saying, "We know," that is, "We have learned our lesson and know it well."

But what do we know? We know what love is. John calls attention not to illustrations of love taken from daily life, but to the supreme example of love, namely, to "Jesus Christ [who] laid down his life for us." In short, we know what love is, because we have heard the gospel message.

Jesus' death on the cross is not a passive death comparable to the sacrificial death of an animal. Jesus died actively and purposefully.[35] Of his own will *he laid down* his life for his people. If, then, Jesus gave his life for us, what is our obligation to him? In the nineteenth century, Frances R. Havergal put this question in the form of a hymn:

> I gave My life for thee,
> My precious blood I shed,
> That thou might'st ransomed be,
> And quickened from the dead;
> I gave, I gave My life for thee;
> What hast thou given for Me?

John has an answer, for he writes, "And we ought to lay down our lives for our brothers." When he says *ought*, he imposes a moral obligation: as Jesus extends his love by giving his life, so the Christian ought to express his love for the believers by being willing to lay down his life for them. When the honor of God's name, the advancement of his church, and the need of his people demand that we love our brothers, we ought to show our love at all cost—even to the point of risking and losing our lives.

---

35. Guthrie in *New Testament Theology* observes, "The voluntary act was not in the interests of personal heroism, but because of the dynamic love. He knew that it was for this purpose he had come into the world" (p. 454).

Greek Words, Phrases, and Constructions in 3:16

ἐγνώκαμεν—the perfect active from γινώσκω (I know) means "we have come to know."

ὀφείλομεν—the verb is preceded by the personal pronoun ἡμεῖς to give it emphasis. "ὀφείλει denotes obligation, δεῖ necessity. The former is moral, the latter as it were, physical necessity."[36]

ὑπέρ—A. T. Robertson observes, "But one may argue from I John 3:16 that ὑπέρ in the case of death does not necessarily involve substitution. Surely the very object of such death is to save life."[37]

2. Negative
3:17

17. If anyone has material possessions and sees his brother in need but has no pity on him, how can the love of God be in him?

a. "If anyone has material possessions." In an extreme and exceptional case, the believer may be asked to show his love by dying for someone else. The Christian, however, can demonstrate his love in numerous ways.

What are these ways? John fails to be explicit. Implicitly he points to the possessions of one and the needs of another: "If someone has wealth and another has need." John does not complete the sentence by saying, "let the one with possessions share with the needy, and thus show love" (compare James 2:15–17). No, he expects the wealthy believer to show his love to his fellow man by sharing his earthly goods. John continues,

b. "But has no pity on him." When a person blessed with material goods (food, clothing, money) is unwilling to share his possessions, he has closed his heart (see Deut. 15:7–11). He is self-centered and has no regard for his spiritual brother. This person portrays a stark contrast to the love of Jesus. He denies his brother the basic necessities of life, whereas Jesus willingly laid down his life for his followers.

c. "How can the love of God be in him?" John is asking a rhetorical question. In fact, what he says is more an exclamation than a question. John intimates that it is impossible for the love of God to control this person.[38] John declares that if anyone says that he loves God but hates his brother, he is a liar (4:20). The command *love the Lord your God* can never be separated from the command *love your neighbor as yourself*. These two go together at all times.

---

36. Bengel, *Gnomon of the New Testament*, vol. 3, p. 282. Also consult R. C. Trench, *Synonyms of the New Testament* (reprint ed., Grand Rapids: Eerdmans, 1953), p. 392.

37. Robertson, *Grammar*, p. 632.

38. The phrase *the love of God* can mean God's love for man (subjective genitive), or man's love for God (objective genitive), or even the love which is characteristic of God (descriptive genitive). In view of the immediate context (God's gift of love to man, v. 16) and the broader context (2:5, 15), the evidence appears to favor the subjective genitive.

Greek Words, Phrases, and Constructions in 3:17

βίος—in the New Testament this noun occurs often in the sense of wealth, possessions (for instance, Mark 12:44; Luke 21:4).[39]

ἔχῃ—note that in the Greek John balances this verb with the present participle ἔχοντα in the next clause.

---

3. Conclusion
3:18

18. Dear children, let us not love with words or tongue but with actions and in truth.

Whereas John places his words in the context of love, James in his epistle discusses the same matter in connection with faith (see James 2:20). Love and faith have this in common: both need deeds to prove their genuineness. Words of love that are never translated into action are worthless.

In order to be genuine, love seeks the welfare of others: "it always protects, always trusts, always hopes, always perseveres" (I Cor. 13:7). Love is the act of giving of one's possessions, talents, and self to someone else.

Note that the words we speak must correspond to our actions, and the use of our tongue must agree with the truth of God's Word. Words and tongue find their counterpart in actions and truth. It is significant that John ends this verse with the word *truth* to remind us of Jesus, the supreme example of love, who said, "I am the . . . truth" (John 14:6).

Practical Considerations in 3:16–18

In many families today, divorce, desertion, and separation create untold grief and bitterness. Couples who at the time of the wedding declared that they would love each other "until death do us part" exhibit callous indifference when they contemplate divorce. Their wedding vows lie broken like pieces of porcelain on a stone floor. What went wrong?

Love has vanished because it could not flourish in an atmosphere of ever taking but never giving. Love can succeed only in an environment where it is allowed to give, for genuine love is sacrificial giving.

Look at the divine example. God loves nothing more than to be able to give. Indeed, he loved us so much that he gave his one and only Son to die for us (see John 3:16), and out of love for his people Jesus laid down his life. Says John, "We ought to lay down our lives for our brothers."

What does the Lord expect in marriage? Husband and wife should honor and love one another even to the point of being willing to lay down their life for one

---

39. Hans-Georg Link, *NIDNTT*, vol. 2, p. 475.

another. When husband and wife tenderly care for each other by imitating Christ's example of sacrificial love, they will experience that God keeps them together in marital love and blesses their home and family with years of wedded bliss.

Greek Words, Phrases, and Constructions in 3:18

τῇ γλώσσῃ—in this verse John lists four nouns (word, tongue, deed, and truth). Only the word *tongue* has the definite article.

---

19 This then is how we know that we belong to the truth, and how we set our hearts at rest in his presence   20 whenever our hearts condemn us. For God is greater than our hearts, and he knows everything.

I. Confidence Before God
3:19–20

John devotes two verses to look at love from another point of view: What is the effect of love on the believer's spiritual life? In the first verse he speaks of knowledge and assurance; in the second verse of God's greatness and knowledge.

19. This then is how we know that we belong to the truth, and how we set our hearts at rest in his presence   20. whenever our hearts condemn us. For God is greater than our hearts, and he knows everything.

Note the following points:

a. *To know.* These two verses are difficult to interpret, for the meaning of the text is not clear. The interpreter discovers that the wording is too general for him to give the reader a definitive explanation. In a sense, therefore, our interpretation only approximates the meaning of the passage.

"This then is how we know that we belong to the truth." The word *this* refers to the preceding context in which John exhorts the Christian to express genuine love for his brothers and sisters in Christ.[40] True children of God will know that they belong to the truth, because they will be sincere and genuine and live in accordance with the truth of God's Word.

The person who refuses to acknowledge his sin is a liar and the truth is not in him (1:8; 2:4; also compare 2:21–22; II John 4; III John 3–4). But the believer who actively and sincerely demonstrates his love belongs to the truth. Actually, the expression *belong to the truth* is synonymous with the term *born of God* (3:9).

b. *To reassure.* In the heart of every believer at times doubts arise. Even though the Christian might sing, "Blessed assurance, Jesus is mine," his conscience occasionally will bother him. He knows that he cannot meet

---

40. For similar constructions in which the phrase *this is how we know* refers to previous verses see 3:10 and 5:2.

the standards God has set and that sin remains an unrelenting and opposing force in his life.

"This then is . . . how we set our hearts at rest in his presence." As a reminder of how to live the Christian life, Calvin used the motto *Coram Deo* (in the presence of God). He knew that he spent every single moment in the sacred presence of the Almighty, and that God's eye was always on him. John expresses this same truth at the beginning of his epistle: "Our fellowship is with the Father and with his Son, Jesus Christ" (1:3). How can we know God's presence? When we love our brothers and sisters in word and deed, we have fellowship with God.

c. *To condemn.* The New International Version completes verse 19 with the words *whenever our hearts condemn us* (v. 20a). As Christians we subject ourselves to true self-examination.[41] We know that we are children of God (see 3:9–10) and as such we must strive to love our neighbor as ourselves.

Sometimes we fail in loving our fellow man and then a guilty conscience disturbs us. But when we fall into sin and our consciences accuse us for our lack of love toward our brother or sister, we should not despair as though we are lost.

d. *To be greater.* Even though from time to time our consciences oppress us and cause us to question our relationship with God, we can still turn to God. We must quiet our hearts with the knowledge that we belong to God (see 4:6), and that we have free access to the throne of God (Heb. 4:16).

John writes these reassuring words: "God is greater than our hearts, and he knows everything." That is, as Christians we can always go to God, who knows us better than we know ourselves. David testifies to this truth. At the conclusion of one of his psalms, he prays this fervent prayer:

> Search me, O God, and know my heart;
>   test me and know my anxious thoughts.
> See if there is any offensive way in me,
>   and lead me in the way everlasting.
> [Ps. 139:23–24]

Because God is greater than our hearts, he will show us mercy when we come to him; he will comfort us, and reassure us that we are his children.

Additional Remarks

1. *Translations.* Because of grammatical variance in the Greek text, this passage is difficult to translate. Therefore translations differ in choice of words and punctuation. From many examples, here are three:

> And by this we know that we are of the truth, and shall assure our hearts before Him. For if our heart condemns us, God is greater than our heart, and knows all things (NKJV).

---

41. Refer to Oswald Becker, *NIDNTT*, vol. 1, p. 590.

This is how we may know that we belong to the realm of truth, and convince ourselves in his sight that even if our conscience condemns us, God is greater than our conscience and knows all (NEB).

Only by this can we be certain that we are children of the truth and be able to quieten our conscience in his presence, whatever accusations it may raise against us, because God is greater than our conscience and he knows everything (JB).

Among the many variations, three items stand out: the verb *to assure* or *to convince*, the punctuation of the sentence(s), and the position of "for" or "because" in the conditional sentence in the last part of verse 20.

2. *Interpretations.* Although differences are numerous, there are two basic interpretations of this passage.[42] The first one explains these verses as "a digression about assurance."[43] John wants to reassure the readers that they know they belong to the truth and therefore can put their hearts at rest in God's presence. The second explanation, which originated with the early church fathers and was adopted by the Reformers, interprets the accusations of the heart as a warning to the believer not to fall into complacency.[44] God is greater because he is "more searching and authoritative in condemnation than the heart."[45] According to this view, John challenges the believers to initiate thorough self-examination and to be fully conscious of God's omniscience.[46]

Greek Words, Phrases, and Constructions in 3:19–20

Verse 19

καί—the inclusion or deletion of this conjunction is uncertain (compare 3:13). Nestle-Aland place it within square brackets to indicate uncertainty.

γνωσόμεθα—the better manuscripts support the future middle indicative of γινώσκω (I know). Textus Receptus and the Majority Text have the present tense.

πείσομεν—the future active indicative from πείθω (I persuade). The translation *we set . . . at rest* (NIV) compares with that of Matthew 28:14. The future tense is durative,[47] which is equivalent to the progressive present.

---

42. Rudolf Bultmann assumes that the text is corrupt because, in his opinion, it has lost the words *we know* before the phrase *that God is greater*. See *The Johannine Epistles*, ed. Robert W. Funk, trans. R. Philip O'Hara et al., Hermeneia: A Critical and Historical Commentary on the Bible (Philadelphia: Fortress, 1973), p. 57. However, C. H. Dodd demurs. He counsels the interpreter to follow the best Greek manuscripts. Refer to *The Johannine Epistles*, Moffatt New Testament Commentary series (New York: Harper and Row, 1946), p. 88.

43. Stott, *The Epistles of John*, p. 145.

44. Consult Calvin, *The First Epistle of John*, p. 222. Also see Alford, *Alford's Greek Testament*, p. 478. Marshall calls this view "quite inappropriate in the present context." See *The Epistles of John*, p. 198, n. 7.

45. Westcott, *The Epistles of St. John*, p. 118.

46. John M. Court, "Blessed Assurance?" *JTS* 33 (1982): 508–17, suggests another interpretation of this passage by linking it to Deut. 15:7–9.

47. Robertson, *Grammar*, p. 871.

Verse 20

ὅτι—because this verse has a second ὅτι, some scholars have suggested that the first one should be taken as ὅ τι with ἐάν (whatever, whenever). Compare I Corinthians 16:2 for a similar construction. If this is the correct reading, then the second ὅτι is causal (see the translations of NIV and JB). Other scholars omit the second ὅτι to eliminate the awkward grammatical syntax of the sentence. Although a few witnesses show this omission, the basic rule that the more difficult reading is probably the original one still has merit. Nevertheless, the presence of these two conjunctions remains an exegetical problem.

καταγινώσκη ἡμῶν—in Greek this verb is a play on words with γνωσόμεθα of the preceding verse. The personal pronoun is the direct object (in the genitive) of the verb καταγινώσκη.

---

21 Dear friends, if our hearts do not condemn us, we have confidence before God 22 and receive from him anything we ask, because we obey his commands and do what pleases him. 23 And this is his command; to believe in the name of his son, Jesus Christ, and to love one another as he commanded us. 24 Those who obey his commands live in him, and he in them. And this is how we know that he lives in us: We know it by the Spirit he gave us.

J. Trust and Obey
3:21–24

1. Confidence
3:21–22

Throughout his epistle John introduces contrasts: for instance, light and darkness, life and death, truth and the lie. Here he compares the heart that condemns with the heart that is free from condemnation.

21. Dear friends, if our hearts do not condemn us, we have confidence before God 22. and receive from him anything we ask, because we obey his commands and do what pleases him.

In the preceding verses, John discussed the guilty conscience of a believer. Fully realizing that this discussion would have a disturbing effect on his readers, the pastor now tenderly calls them "dear friends" (see also 2:7; 3:2) and shows them the other side of the matter. He wisely includes himself in the discussion by using the first person plural pronoun.

a. "If our hearts do not condemn us." John knows that the hearts of many believers do not always accuse them of sin. For example, although Peter's conscience accused him after he denied Jesus, John and the other disciples were free from guilt.

b. "We have confidence before God." If our conscience is free, the avenue to the throne of grace is open. The writer of Hebrews encourages the believer to approach that throne with confidence (Heb. 4:16; see also I John 2:28; 4:17; 5:14). The word *confidence* originally described the full citizen of a Greek city-state who had the democratic right to speak freely. In New Testament times Jesus and the apostles spoke with confidence when they publicly proclaimed the gospel (e.g., John 7:26; Acts 4:13).[48] We have the freedom to go to God in prayer and have fellowship with him and the Son, Jesus Christ (1:3).

c. "And receive from him anything we ask." John is repeating the words Jesus spoke to the disciples in his farewell address. Jesus said, "And I will do whatever you ask in my name, so that the Son may bring glory to the Father. You may ask me for anything in my name, and I will do it" (John 14:13–14; compare Matt. 7:7).

What a promise! Whatever we continue to ask for we receive from God. Note that John writes the present tense "we receive," not "we will receive." The promise is certain because God keeps his word (5:14). Does God answer any and every request? No, only those that are according to his will and for his glory. Therefore, John writes,

d. "Because we obey his commands and do what pleases him." Is John stating two prerequisites to answered prayer? Really not. Obeying God's commands must never be done under compulsion or for the purpose of receiving rewards. The Christian fulfills God's command with a cheerful heart that expresses gratitude. John is saying that when we obey his commands, we are doing what is pleasing to God. By adding the clause *and do what pleases him,* John rules out any notion of merit; pleasing God flows forth from love and loyalty. Implicitly John reminds his readers of Jesus. During his earthly ministry, Jesus always sought to please the Father by doing his will (John 8:29).[49]

The basis for answered prayer is not blind obedience but a desire to please God with dedicated love. And God fulfills our requests because of the bond of love and fellowship between Father and child.

Greek Words, Phrases, and Constructions in 3:21–22

Verse 21

ἡμῶν—the text is uncertain at this point. Bruce M. Metzger has collated eleven different readings from various Greek manuscripts.[50] Although the inclusion of ἡμῶν generates some doubt, as indicated by square brackets in the Greek text of Nestle-Aland, the word can serve either as a possessive pronoun of καρδία or as a direct object of καταγινώσκῃ.

ἔχομεν—some manuscripts have the singular ἔχει to correspond with the singular καρδία. The evidence, however, favors the plural verb.

Verse 22

αἰτῶμεν—the present subjunctive of the protasis in this conditional sentence is followed by the present indicative λαμβάνομεν (we receive) in the apodosis. The

---

48. Refer to Hans-Christoph Hahn, *NIDNTT*, vol. 2, pp. 735–37.
49. Hans Bietenhard, *NIDNTT*, vol. 2, p. 816.
50. Metzger, *Textual Commentary*, p. 712.

present tense in both verbs is timeless, that is, the tense refers to a generally accepted truth.[51]

2. Believe and Love
3:23–24

23. And this is his command: to believe in the name of his Son, Jesus Christ, and to love one another as he commanded us. 24. Those who obey his commands live in him, and he in them. And this is how we know that he lives in us: We know it by the Spirit he gave us.

Note the following observations:

a. *Faith.* John reduces the commands to a single command that has two parts: "to believe in the name of Jesus and to love one another." In a sense, John follows Jesus, who summarized the commandments of the Law in two commands: " 'Love the Lord your God with all your heart and with all your soul and with all your mind' " and " 'Love your neighbor as yourself' " (see Matt. 22:37, 39; and compare Rom. 13:9). John, however, places the phrases *believe in the name of Jesus* and *love one another* in the same command. Are the verbs *believe* and *love* identical? They are not the same but are integrally related.

This is the first time in the epistle that John uses the verb *to believe.* The verb serves as an introduction to the following chapters.[52] John asserts that God the Father gives the command and that God unequivocally tells us to believe in the name of his Son, Jesus Christ. The command is to begin and continue to believe in the name, that is, the full revelation, of the divine Son of God. John adds the names *Jesus* to refer to his earthly ministry and *Christ* to call attention to his exalted position (refer to 1:3). No one is able to come to the Father but through Jesus (John 14:6).

John moves from faith to love, for these two concepts are closely linked together. In his Gospel John reveals that Jesus repeatedly gave the command *love one another* (John 13:34; 15:12, 17). Believing in Jesus Christ, then, means to obey his command to love each other. John repeats this command. By using the present tense of the verb *to love,* he exhorts the readers to continue to love one another.

b. *Obedience.* John draws the conclusion, "Those who obey his commands live in him, and he in them." This is a theme John repeats in his Gospel (6:56; 17:21–23) and epistle (2:24; 4:13–16). They who keep God's word in their heart experience that God makes his home with them. As an eighth-century English theologian, the Venerable Bede, wrote, "Let

51. Consult Robertson, *Grammar,* p. 866.
52. The verb *to believe* occurs nine times in this epistle (3:23; 4:1, 16; 5:1, 5, 10 [3 times], 13), the noun *faith* only once (5:4).

God, then, be a home for you, and you be the home of God; remain in God and let God remain in you."[53]

c. *Knowledge.* John has a penchant for reiterating certain statements. For instance, in this verse he virtually repeats the same remark he wrote earlier (3:16), "And this is how we know." What do we know? "That he lives in us." When John writes the pronoun *he*, John does not distinguish carefully between God the Father and Jesus the Son. For him the Father works through the Son, and through Jesus God lives in us. Therefore a precise distinction is unnecessary. In this verse, however, John introduces the third person of the Trinity, the Holy Spirit.[54] How does God dwell in the heart of the believer? Through the work and testimony of the Holy Spirit. No believer can ever say that he does not know whether God lives within him. The Spirit of God testifies in the heart of the Christian and gives him this knowledge and assurance.

Practical Considerations in 3:21–24

Scripture reveals many marvelous statements, but this one is memorable: "We have confidence before God and receive from him anything we ask." Sons and daughters cannot even make this statement about their parents. As children of God, however, we can boldly make our requests known to God and receive from him anything we ask.

Scripture also says that our requests must be presented in the name of Jesus so that he "may bring glory to the Father" (John 14:13). Note that before we pray the fourth petition in the Lord's Prayer, "Give us today our daily bread" (Matt. 6:11), we already have asked that God's name be glorified, his kingdom come, and his will be done. God answers our requests when our objective is to glorify him, to promote his rule, and to do his will.

God answers every prayer, but many petitions receive a negative answer. In his wisdom God knows exactly what serves our spiritual welfare. For example, Paul prayed three times that his thorn in the flesh might be removed, but God said, "My grace is sufficient for you, for my power is made perfect in weakness" (II Cor. 12:9). And therefore, Paul testifies, "I delight in weaknesses. . . . For when I am weak, then I am strong" (v. 10).

Greek Words, Phrases, and Constructions in 3:23–24

Verse 23

ἵνα πιστεύσωμεν—the ἵνα particle introduces an indirect command clause with the aorist subjunctive πιστεύσωμεν (we believe). The aorist is ingressive.[55] The aorist tense relates to the moment the Christian accepted Jesus. Note the use of

53. Westcott in *The Epistles of St. John* provides the Latin text: "Sit ergo tibi domus Deus et esto domus Dei; mane in Deo, et maneat in te Deus" (p. 121).
54. Five times John refers to the Holy Spirit in subsequent passages (4:2, 6, 13; 5:6, 8).
55. Robertson, *Grammar*, p. 850.

the present tense in ἀγαπῶμεν (we love). The present implies that we must always love one another.

Verse 24

αὐτός—the pronoun in the form of the third person singular stands for Jesus. Its use is emphatic.

οὗ—the genitive of attraction takes the place of the accusative.

Summary of Chapter 3

John exalts the Christians, who are called children of God. Although we are not recognized as such by the world, we know that at the time of Christ's return we, as God's children, will be fully revealed in glory. We will be similar to Jesus Christ and we shall see him. Therefore, the person who belongs to Christ must cleanse himself from sin. John points to Christ, who as the sinless One has come to remove sin.

The children of God are distinguished from the children of the devil. They who live in fellowship with God do not continue to live in sin. Moreover, the child of God not only has God's seed in him; he also knows that he has been born of God.

The message John leaves with us is that we should love one another. We are not to follow the example of Cain, who belonged to the devil. However, we show our love to the brothers and know that we have passed from spiritual death to life. We will receive the hatred of the world. John observes that the person who hates his brother is a murderer.

John cites the example of Jesus Christ, who laid down his life for us. He encourages us to follow that example. We must show our love not merely by words but with deeds and in truth. By emulating that example, we learn that we are true Christians.

God answers our prayers, for we receive from him whatever we ask as long as we obey his commands and please him. God's command is that we believe in Jesus and that we love one another. If we do this, we have fellowship with God, and through the Holy Spirit we know that God lives in us.

4

Love God, *part 1*

4:1–21

Outline

4 1 Dear friends, do not believe every spirit, but test the spirits to see whether they are from God, because many false prophets have gone out into the world. 2 This is how you can recognize the Spirit of God: Every spirit that acknowledges that Jesus Christ has come in the flesh is from God, 3 but every spirit that does not acknowledge Jesus is not from God. This is the spirit of the antichrist, which you have heard is coming and even now is already in the world.

4 You, dear children, are from God and have overcome them, because the one who is in you is greater than the one who is in the world. 5 They are from the world and therefore speak from the viewpoint of the world, and the world listens to them. 6 We are from God, and whoever knows God listens to us; but whoever is not from God does not listen to us. This is how we recognize the Spirit of truth and the spirit of falsehood.

IV. Love God
4:1–5:12

A. Test the Spirits
4:1–6

1. A Warning
4:1

With this text John begins the third part of his epistle; the first section begins at 1:5, and the second at 2:18. There is a distinct parallel between the second part and the third. Both parts expound the following topics: A warning against the antichrist, children of God, love for God and one another.

In the first few verses of each section, John speaks of antichrists or false teachers. He exhorts the readers to put the teaching of false prophets to the test. Christians have to be able to detect false teachings and to examine the spirit that expresses them.

1. Dear friends, do not believe every spirit, but test the spirits to see whether they are from God, because many false prophets have gone out into the world.

As a wise pastor, John first addresses his readers with words of tender love. He calls them "dear friends" (compare 3:21; 4:7). After the address, John tactfully warns the readers against the work of false teachers and tells them not to believe every spirit. He wants them to realize that there are two spiritual spheres in this world: one is the domain of the Holy

Spirit; the other is the domain of the devil. The Holy Spirit dwells in the children of God (3:24), but the spirit of the devil lives in false prophets who speak in his name.

a. "Do not believe every spirit" (consult Jer. 29:8; Matt. 24:4; Eph. 5:6; I Tim. 4:1). Of course, we are unable to see a spirit, but we can hear and understand the teachings of that spirit. The word *spirit*, then, is equivalent to "teaching."[1]

Apparently some of the first readers of this epistle were beginning to believe the false prophets who said that their teaching was a revelation from the Holy Spirit. John exhorts the readers to distinguish carefully between the teachings of God's Spirit and false teachings. Not every teaching is an utterance of the Spirit of God. Therefore, John advises the Christians to "test the spirits to see whether they are from God" and to verify all teaching in the light of God's Word (compare I Thess. 2:4; 5:21).

b. "Many false prophets have gone out into the world." We know that false teachers have made the world their lecture hall. They desire to gain a hearing from a number of Christians. In his discourse on the end of time, Jesus warns us, "For false Christs and false prophets will appear and perform great signs and miracles to deceive even the elect—if that were possible" (Matt. 24:24; also consult Rev. 2:2).

Greek Words, Phrases, and Constructions in 4:1

μὴ παντὶ πνεύματι πιστεύετε—the negative particle μή is separated from the verb for emphasis.[2] The verb is in the present active imperative mood. With the negative it reveals that some Christians indeed believed the false teachers of that day. John tells them to stop doing so.

δοκιμάζετε—"test!"; the present imperative.

ἐξεληλύθασιν—from the verb ἐξέρχομαι (I come or go out), this is the perfect active indicative. As a compound verb it is followed by the preposition εἰς (into).

---

2. A Test
4:2–3

2. This is how you can recognize the Spirit of God: Every spirit that acknowledges that Jesus Christ has come in the flesh is from God, 3. but every spirit that does not acknowledge Jesus is not from God. This is the spirit of the antichrist, which you have heard is coming and even now is already in the world.

---

1. This is a figure of speech called metonymy; that is, there is a relation between two words that evoke one concept. The word *spirit* stands for "teaching." Consult Louis Berkhof, *Principles of Biblical Interpretation* (Grand Rapids: Baker, 1950), pp. 83–84.

2. A. T. Robertson, however, thinks that the particle negates the adjective *all. A Grammar of the Greek New Testament in the Light of Historical Research* (Nashville: Broadman, 1934), p. 752.

Note the following observations:

a. *Profession.* John gives his readers a formula for determining whether a spirit comes from God or from the devil: The Christian recognizes the Spirit of God in anyone who openly confesses that Jesus Christ is both human and divine, and that Jesus Christ, who is the Son of God, "has come in the flesh." Here we have the established principle for testing whether a particular teaching comes from the Holy Spirit (also see I Cor. 12:3).

In the Greek, John uses the perfect tense for the words *has come* to indicate that Jesus came in human nature and even now in heaven he has a human nature. That is, in addition to his divine nature he also has a human nature. Sixteenth-century German theologian Zacharias Ursinus asked whether these two natures are separated from each other. This is his answer:

> Certainly not. For since the divinity is not limited and is present every-where, it is evident that Christ's divinity is surely beyond the bounds of the humanity he has taken on, but at the same time his divinity is in and remains personally united to his humanity.[3]

Scripture teaches that the Christ is Jesus, who as our divine redeemer shares our human nature (Heb. 2:14–15). Any teaching that professes the divinity and humanity of Jesus Christ has its origin in God. The opposite is also true; as C. H. Dodd observes, "No utterance, however inspired, which denies the reality of the Incarnation, can be accepted by Christians as true prophecy."[4]

b. *Denial.* Jesus said, "Whoever acknowledges me before men, I will also acknowledge him before my Father in heaven. But whoever disowns me before men, I will disown him before my Father in heaven" (Matt. 10:32–33; also see John 8:47; II John 7). Anyone who separates the human nature from the divine nature of Jesus Christ speaks without God's authority. And anyone who denies either Jesus' human nature or divine nature "is not from God." Moreover, anyone who teaches that when Jesus was baptized God gave him a divine spirit, and that this spirit left Jesus when he died on the cross distorts the gospel. And last, whoever says that after Jesus' death God appointed him Son of God fails to present the truth of God's Word. All such teachers do not speak as representatives of Jesus Christ, have not been commissioned by God, and are not the mouthpieces of the Spirit of God in this world.[5]

---

3. Heidelberg Catechism, question and answer 48.

4. C. H. Dodd, *The Johannine Epistles,* Moffatt New Testament Commentary series (New York: Harper and Row, 1946), p. 103.

5. Rudolf Schnackenburg considers the wording of verses 2 and 3, because of their distinct contrast, a confession of faith that must be considered original. In short, this confession circulated in the early Christian church. *Die Johannesbriefe,* Herder's Theologischer Kommentar zum Neuen Testament series, 7th ed. (Freiburg: Herder, 1984), vol. 13, 3, p. 222.

Although John addresses the church of the first century, nothing has changed since that time. Today we have numerous teachers and preachers who deny that Jesus Christ is human and divine. They are not from God, says John. In fact, he labels the spirit of such denial "the spirit of the antichrist."

c. *Designation.* John repeats a thought he expressed earlier in the epistle: "The antichrist is coming, even now many antichrists have come" (2:18; consult also II John 7). Now he says, "The antichrist . . . is coming and even now is already in the world." He thinks of "all the principles and powers, all the essential characteristics of Antichrist: what . . . we might call 'the antichristian nature.' "[6] That antichristian spirit is here already and expresses itself insidiously and often violently against Jesus Christ and his followers (compare II Thess. 2:3–8).

Practical Considerations in 4:1–3

Without exception, liberal theologians refuse to accept the biblical doctrine that Jesus Christ always has been, is, and will be the Son of God, that he came from heaven to redeem his people, that he took upon himself our humanity yet remained truly divine, that he rose bodily from the dead and ascended in his glorified body to heaven, and that he will return at God's appointed day in the same body in which he ascended. If you compare the teaching of these theologians with God's Word, you will notice that their opinions are based on human philosophy and not on Scripture. Ask them what they think of the Christ, then go to your Bible and study the teachings of Scripture (Matt. 16:15).

Then there are the members of sects. In pairs they canvass the neighborhood, ring your doorbell, and announce that they are missionaries—even though they do not carry Bibles. When you listen to them, you soon learn that they do not bring the teaching of Christ. The apostle John advises, "If anyone comes to you and does not bring this teaching [of Christ], do not take him into your house or welcome him" (II John 10).

What does John mean? He means that you may receive the members of the sect into your home *only* when you intend to teach them about Jesus Christ. Tell them that you are happy in the Lord, because he is your Savior; and that you are pleased to introduce them to Jesus Christ. Then you will be a missionary for the Lord and you are in control of the situation. But if you do not intend to teach these visitors about the Lord, receive them not into your home!

Greek Words, Phrases, and Constructions in 4:2–3

Verse 2

γινώσκετε—the verb can be either indicative or imperative. Although the context calls for the imperative, translators and commentators favor the indicative.

---

6. Alfred Plummer, *The Epistles of St. John,* Cambridge Greek Testament for Schools and Colleges series (Cambridge: At the University Press, 1896), p. 97.

Ἰησοῦν Χριστόν—with reference to the direct object, at least two translations are given: "Jesus as the Christ incarnate" (*Moffatt*) and "Jesus Christ has come in the flesh" (NIV and other versions). The combination *Jesus Christ* occurs eight times in John's epistles (1:3; 2:1; 3:23; 4:2; 5:6, 20; II John 3, 7). In two places, John clearly separates the names by writing "Jesus is the Christ" (2:22; 5:1). Therefore, when the names appear together they need to be translated as such.

ἐληλυθότα—the perfect active participle of ἔρχομαι (I come) expresses an action accomplished in the past with lasting effect.

Verse 3

μὴ ὁμολογεῖ—Bruce M. Metzger prefers this reading to λύει "because of overwhelming external support."[7] The use of μή with an indicative instead of οὐ is not uncommon in the New Testament.[8]

τὸν Ἰησοῦν—the shortest reading is the one given here. Additions to the text are "derived from the previous verse."[9]

τό—the definite article needs to be complemented by the noun πνεῦμα.

ἔρχεται—this verb frequently refers to the coming of Christ. Here it stands for the coming of the antichrist.

---

3. A Contrast
4:4–5

In his teachings John clearly distinguishes between the work of God and the work of the evil one, between God's children and those who belong to Satan, and between knowing the truth and believing falsehood.

4. You, dear children, are from God and have overcome them, because the one who is in you is greater than the one who is in the world. 5. They are from the world and therefore speak from the viewpoint of the world, and the world listens to them.

The contrast in these two verses is obvious. As their spiritual father, John tenderly addresses the readers and says, "dear children." The pronoun *you* stands first to give it emphasis in the sentence. The writer wants to tell the Christians: "You, yes you, are from God." That is, the readers ought never to forget their divine heritage. They are not only special people, born of God and called "children of God" (2:29; 3:1, 9, 10); they are also different from those people who belong to the world.

Moreover, John makes an additional claim: "You . . . have overcome them" (compare 2:13, 14; 5:4, 5). The use of the plural *them* is a reference to the false teachers mentioned in the preceding paragraph. John writes the perfect tense, "you have overcome." In other words, they have already done so by obeying God's commands and honoring the teaching of his Word.

---

7. Bruce M. Metzger, *A Textual Commentary on the New Testament*, corrected ed. (London and New York: United Bible Societies, 1975), p. 713.

8. Refer to Robertson, *Grammar*, p. 1169. Also consult C. F. D. Moule, *An Idiom-Book of New Testament Greek*, 2d ed. (Cambridge: At the University Press, 1960), p. 155.

9. Metzger, *Textual Commentary*, p. 713.

God's children can never boast in themselves but always in the Lord (see Jer. 9:24; I Cor. 1:31). It is the Lord Jesus Christ who has overcome the world (John 16:33) and has set his people free (Heb. 2:15). "The battle has thus been decided, even if it is not yet over. By faith Christians participate in this victory and are thus placed in a position to overcome the world for themselves."[10]

Reassuringly John writes, "The one who is in you is greater than the one who is in the world." There are two forces that oppose one another: the Holy Spirit opposes the spirit of the antichrist. Through his Spirit, God lives with his children and is greater than the evil one. He keeps them in the truth of his Word and strengthens them to overcome temptations (compare 3:9).

The word *world* is significant, because it appears three times in this verse (v. 5). It differs in meaning from its use in the preceding paragraph (vv. 1, 3), where it has the broad connotation of a place of human life. Here it means a world of people who are hostile to God (see 3:1, 13).

The false prophets "are from the world." They derive their principles, zeal, goals, and existence from the world of hostility in which Satan rules as prince (John 12:31). Furthermore, their teachings, opinions, and values are atheistic and antichristian. John refrains from revealing the content of their speech; he mentions only the act of speaking. What the false prophets say, however, is persuasive, for "the world listens to them." The world agrees with the teachings of the false teachers and thus participates in opposing God.

Greek Words, Phrases, and Constructions in 4:4

ὑμεῖς—John employs personal pronouns for emphasis. He places them at the beginning of each verse: ὑμεις (v. 4), αὐτοί (v. 5), and ἡμεῖς (v. 6).

νενικήκατε—the perfect tense from νικάω (I conquer) reveals an event that happened in the past but has an effect on the present.

---

4. A Recognition
4:6

Although the forces of the evil one surround the believers, they need not despair for one moment. John reiterates the truth expressed in verses 4 and 5. He wants to reassure the readers that they are children of God.

6. We are from God, and whoever knows God listens to us; but whoever is not from God does not listen to us. This is how we recognize the Spirit of truth and the spirit of falsehood.

In these verses John voices the quiet confidence of knowing that God and his people are one. In this assurance, however, John does not mini-

---

10. Walther Günther, *NIDNTT*, vol. 1, p. 651. Also consult Otto Bauernfeind, *TDNT*, vol. 4, pp. 944–45.

mize our responsibility to do God's will.[11] We, who are from God, have received the knowledge of God's truth, have the duty to tell people about the Lord, and are his representatives. John stresses the word *we* by placing it at the beginning of the sentence. We, who are God's children, proclaim the Word, and when we do so, we receive a hearing from everyone who knows God.

John echoes the words of Jesus: "He who belongs to God hears what God says" (John 8:47; and compare 10:27). Why do God's people listen to preachers? Because preachers proclaim God's Word, and that Word has divine authority. God's people hear his voice when the preacher speaks.

Those people who are not from God do not listen to the proclamation of his Word. They refuse to believe the truth; instead they prefer "the spirit of falsehood." They also accept full responsibility when they willfully reject the call to repentance and faith in Christ.

We are able to recognize the Spirit of truth and the spirit of the lie by observing a listener's reaction to the preaching of God's Word. Says Paul,

> But thanks be to God, who always leads us in triumphal procession in Christ and through us spreads everywhere the fragrance of the knowledge of him. For we are to God the aroma of Christ among those who are being saved and those who are perishing. To the one we are the smell of death; to the other, the fragrance of life. [II Cor. 2:14–16; compare also John 14:17]

Practical Considerations in 4:4–6

In numerous parts of the world, the church experiences considerable increases in membership. Christians faithfully bear witness of their faith in Christ, preachers proclaim the gospel, and converts receive the sacrament of baptism. However, in many areas a dearth of qualified preachers is evident. There is an insistent cry for ordained ministers and missionaries. "The harvest is plentiful but the workers are few. Ask the Lord of the harvest, therefore, to send out workers into his harvest field" (Matt. 9:37; Luke 10:2; also see John 4:35).

The ministry of the church deserves the best possible talents available for preaching the gospel, teaching the Word, pastoring the church, translating the Bible, and evangelizing the world. They who are serving the Lord should present the challenge to qualified persons to prepare themselves for gospel ministry. In effect, these servants should recruit workers for the kingdom so that the work of the Lord may continue and increase.

Greek Words, Phrases, and Constructions in 4:6

ἡμεῖς—John stresses the first person plural in his use of pronouns and verbs to show (apostolic) authority.

---

11. Consult Donald Guthrie, *New Testament Theology* (Downers Grove: Inter-Varsity, 1981), p. 616.

ὁ γινώσκων—the present active participle describes the action of acquiring knowledge.

ἐκ τούτου—the preposition ἐκ (not ἐν, as in 2:3, 5; 3:16, 24; 4:13; 5:2) connotes cause or means.[12]

πνεῦμα—most translators parallel the two instances of this word; however, at least two translations capitalize the first use of πνεῦμα to refer to the Holy Spirit (GNB, NIV).

τῆς ἀληθείας—the genitive can be either possessive (belonging to the truth) or subjective (uttering the truth).[13]

---

7 Dear friends, let us love one another, for love comes from God. Everyone who loves has been born of God and knows God.   8 Whoever does not love does not know God, because God is love.   9 This is how God showed his love among us: He sent his one and only Son into the world that we might live through him.   10 This is love: not that we loved God, but that he loved us and sent his Son as an atoning sacrifice for our sins.   11 Dear friends, since God so loved us, we also ought to love one another.   12 No one has ever seen God; but if we love one another, God lives in us and his love is made complete in us.

B. Love One Another
4:7–12

1. Love and Knowledge
4:7–8

John mentioned the subject *love* in earlier passages (2:7–11; 3:11–18, 23). He now abruptly presents a full discussion of this topic. In this discussion John continues to present contrast and parallelism. Scholars are probably correct in viewing verses 7–10 as a poetic expression (compare 2:12–14).[14] For the sake of clarity, I write the next four verses in poetic form.

7. Dear friends, let us love one another,
for love comes from God.
Everyone who loves has been born of God
and knows God.
8. Whoever does not love does not know God,
because God is love.

These two verses and the following two are among the treasured passages of the entire epistle. They speak of love that originates in God and describe the believer as a person who loves and knows God. By contrast, the unbeliever does not love because he does not know God.

a. "Dear friends, let us love one another." John addresses the readers with the familiar term *dear friends* (2:7; 3:2, 21; 4:1, 7, 11) which literally

---

12. Refer to Moule, *Idiom-Book*, p. 73. Also consult H. E. Dana and Julius R. Mantey, *A Manual Grammar of the Greek New Testament* (New York: Macmillan, 1967), p. 103.

13. Consult R. C. H. Lenski, *The Interpretation of the Epistles of St. Peter, St. John, and St. Jude* (Columbus: Wartburg, 1945), p. 492.

14. In the 26th edition of Nestle-Aland, the editors have indented verses 7–11 to indicate that the words resemble poetry.

means "beloved." He includes in the sentence an exhortation to love one another. He is not discussing the affection that family members have for each other. Rather, he writes the verb *love,* which means "divine love." John indicates that God initiates love, showers it upon his people, and expects that in turn they express this same love to each other.

b. "Everyone who loves has been born of God and knows God." This, then, is the distinctive mark of the believer. The person who is born of God (2:29; 3:9; 5:1) is a window through which the love of God shines into the world. The believer expresses his love to his fellow man by doing for his neighbor what he himself wishes that others do for him. In short, he shows his love by obeying the Golden Rule (Luke 6:31). His love is genuinely unselfish.

The believer loves his neighbor as himself because, as John writes, the believer knows God. That is, he has fellowship with God the Father and his Son (1:3) and thus reflects the virtue of love.

Incidentally, when John says, "[he] knows God," he may have intended to refute the Gnostic heretics of his day who prided themselves on having knowledge of God.[15]

c. "Whoever does not love does not know God." John compares the believer with the unbeliever and observes that when love is absent, knowledge of God is nonexistent. The person who fails to commune with God in prayer and neglects to read the Bible cannot be the instrument through which God demonstrates his divine love. The unbeliever has not even begun to know God. Without knowledge of God, there is no love. Love and knowledge of God are two sides of the same coin.

d. "God is love." Children learn the words at home and in church. Adults treasure these three words, for in them John has stated one of God's characteristics: love. This means not only that God loves his creation and his people, or that God is full of love. It means that in his very being God is love. And this is the message John conveys in his epistle.

Augustine observes, "If nothing were said in praise of love throughout the pages of this Epistle, if nothing whatever throughout the pages of the Scriptures, and this one thing only were all we were told by the voice of the Spirit of God, *For God is love;* nothing more ought we require."[16]

Greek Words, Phrases, and Constructions in 4:7–8

Verse 7

ἀγαπῶμεν—this is the hortatory subjunctive (not the present active indicative, which is identical in form).

---

15. Consult M. de Jonge, "Geliefden, laten wij elkander liefhebben, want de liefde is uit God," *Nederlands Theologisch Tijdschrift* 22 (1968): 352–67; also see his article "To Love as God Loves (I John 4:7)," in *Jesus: Inspiring and Disturbing Presence,* trans. John E. Steely (Nashville: Abingdon, 1974), pp. 110–27.

16. Refer to Plummer, *The Epistles of St. John,* p. 101.

γεγέννηται—from γεννάω (I beget), this verb is the perfect passive indicative. In this epistle, John employs the perfect tense of this verb five times (2:29; 3:9; 4:7; 5:1, 4).

γινώσκει—the verb γινώσκω (I know), here in the present active indicative, denotes experiential knowledge.

Verse 8

ἔγνω—here John uses the aorist tense to contrast the present tense in the preceding verse. The aorist is constative.[17]

ἀγάπη—without the definite article the noun is the predicate nominative. The article in ὁ θεός designates the noun θεός the subject.[18]

---

2. God's Love
4:9-10

9. **This is how God showed his love among us:**
    He sent his one and only Son
    into the world that we might live through him.
10. **This is love:**
    not that we loved God,
    but that he loved us
    and sent his Son
    as an atoning sacrifice for our sins.

Consider the following points:

a. *Proof.* God's love emanates from his being and radiates to and in us who acknowledge him through Jesus Christ. The Son of God is the visible proof of God's love toward his people. Therefore John writes, "This is how God showed his love among us." God sent his Son into the world. Note the wording. John mentions not the name *Jesus* or *Christ;* instead he uses the word *Son* to call attention to the intimate Father-Son relationship. God the Father sent his Son into the world. More than that, "he sent his one and only Son" (also see John 1:14, 18; 3:16, 18). Jesus is not one Son among many others. The expression *one and only* "is used to mark out Jesus uniquely above all earthly and heavenly beings."[19]

God sent his one and only Son into our sinful world to give us life. If God the Father had given the world as a present to his Son, because he is the heir, God would have demonstrated evident proof of his love toward him. And we would have no difficulty understanding God's act of love. But the text says that God "sent his one and only Son into the world that

---

17. Refer to A. E. Brooke, *A Critical and Exegetical Commentary on the Johannine Epistles,* International Critical Commentary series (Edinburgh: Clark, 1964), p. 118. Donald W. Burdick calls the aorist ingressive. *The Letters of John the Apostle* (Chicago: Moody, 1985), p. 319.

18. Consult Robertson, *Grammar,* p. 794; Dana and Mantey, *Manual Grammar,* p. 149.

19. Of the numerous comments on this subject, see especially Karl-Heinz Bartels, *NIDNTT,* vol. 2, p. 725, and Friedrich Büchsel, *TDNT,* vol. 4, pp. 739-41.

we might live through him." God gave his Son to die on the cross so that we might have eternal life. He gave his Son to us. This message is too profound: we are unable to fathom the depth of God's love for us.

b. *Priority.* "This is love: not that we loved God, but that he loved us." John describes the matter first negatively and then positively. He expresses negatively that we did not love God. John does not say, "God loves us because we are God's loving children." No, the opposite is true, for Paul tells us that we have a sinful mind that is hostile to God (Rom. 8:7).

Positively, John states that love originates with God, not with man (refer to 4:19; II Thess. 2:16). God loves the unlovable. As an anonymous poet wrote,

> I sought the Lord, and afterward I knew
> He moved my soul to seek him, seeking me;
> It was not that I found, O Savior true,
> No, I was found, was found of thee.
>
> I find, I walk, I love; but O the whole
> Of love is but my answer, Lord, to thee!
> For thou wert long beforehand with my soul,
> Always, always thou lovedst me.

John concludes by saying that God "sent his Son as an atoning sacrifice for our sins." Earlier in his epistle, John wrote the same words (see the comments on 2:2; also compare Rom. 3:25). God's only Son covered our sins and set us free from guilt. Note that in this last part of verse 10 the contrast is between God's Son and our sins. God took the initiative in showing his love to man when he sent his Son.

Greek Words, Phrases, and Constructions in 4:9–10

Verse 9

τὸν υἱὸν αὐτοῦ τόν—the repetition of the definite article emphasizes the noun υἱόν (son) and the adjective μονογενῆ (unique).

ἀπέσταλκεν—the perfect active indicative of ἀποστέλλω (I send away). Note that John does not use the verb πέμπω (I send). The verb ἀποστέλλω means to send with a commission.[20] In the next verse, John writes the aorist tense ἀπέστειλεν, which is a culminative aorist.[21]

Verse 10

ἠγαπήκαμεν—the perfect tense of ἀγαπάω (I love) is followed by the aorist tense ἠγάπησεν. The aorist is constative.

---

20. Consult Lenski, *Interpretation of the Epistles,* p. 501. And see Bauer, p. 98.
21. Moule is of the opinion that the perfect and the aorist tenses in this verse are synonymous. *Idiom-Book,* p. 14.

3. Mutual Love
4:11–12

11. Dear friends, since God so loved us, we also ought to love one another. 12. No one has ever seen God; but if we love one another, God lives in us and his love is made complete in us.

The echo of John 3:16 reverberates through the first part of verse 11, except that here John is much more personal: "Since God so loved us." He employs the past tense *loved* to point to the historical event of Jesus' ministry and death: the supreme gift of love. Therefore, John writes the little word *so* which means "to such an extent." That is, God loved us to the extent of sending his own Son to die for us on Calvary's cross. In rapt amazement Paul expresses his thanks when he writes, "Thanks be to God for his indescribable gift!" (II Cor. 9:15).

The second part of verse 11—"we also ought to love one another"—relates to the summary of the law (Matt. 22:39). God gives us a command (Lev. 19:18) with a moral obligation (compare 3:16). We are the recipients of God's love and we, in turn, ought to love one another. John does not imply that we should neglect to love God, but rather, like Paul and James, he places the emphasis on the command to love our neighbor as ourselves (Rom. 13:9; Gal. 5:14; James 2:8). If our love for God must come to expression in our love for our fellow man, then we fulfill the command to love God and our neighbor, and our love for one another is genuine.[22]

"No one has ever seen God" (compare Exod. 33:20; Deut. 4:12; John 1:18; I Tim. 1:17; 6:16). John explains what he means, in the broader context, when he writes, "Anyone who does not love his brother, whom he has seen, cannot love God, whom he has not seen" (v. 20). We are able to see our fellow man, but we cannot see God. Although we say we love God, our words are meaningless unless we give visible expression to them by showing our love to one another. We must see and love God through our fellow man.

"If we love each other, God lives in us and his love is made complete in us." John reaffirms his earlier teaching that if we obey God's commands, he lives in us and we in him (3:24).

Doctrinal Considerations in 4:7–12

The First Epistle of John is the preeminent book on love. In this epistle the verb *love* appears twenty-eight times, and the corresponding noun *love* occurs eighteen times. Furthermore, almost all these references are in the section 3:1–5:3.[23]

---

22. John Calvin comments "that our love ought not be mercenary" because "we have been loved freely." *Commentaries on the Catholic Epistles: The First Epistle of John,* ed. and trans. John Owen (Grand Rapids: Eerdmans, 1948), p. 242.

23. By comparison, John uses the verb thirty-seven times and the noun seven times in his Gospel.

If God loved us before the creation of the world (Eph. 1:4–5), why did he send his Son to a cruel death on the cross? Was the death of Christ necessary? The answer to these questions is that God was displeased and angry with us because of our sins and could not be reconciled to us until Christ removed our guilt. God expresses his love toward those in whom his demand for righteousness has been met. Christ has met this demand for his people. Therefore, God's children, who are covered with his righteousness, may experience the fullness of God's love.[24]

Greek Words, Phrases, and Constructions in 4:12

ἡ ἀγάπη αὐτοῦ—the genitive is subjective, not objective.

τετελειωμένη—the perfect tense in the passive voice, from τελειόω (I make perfect), denotes action that occurred in the past but has lasting effect. God is the agent.

---

13 We know that we live in him and he in us, because he has given us of his Spirit.   14 And we have seen and testify that the Father has sent his Son to be the Savior of the world.   15 If anyone acknowledges that Jesus is the Son of God, God lives in him and he in God.   16 And so we know and rely on the love God has for us.

C. Abide in God
4:13–16a

1. The Spirit and the Son
4:13–14

In this passage, John returns to the theme of fellowship with God (see 2:24; 3:24). He links it to the context of the preceding discussion on love and views it from the aspect of the close relationship that exists between the Father and the Son.

13. We know that we live in him and he in us, because he has given us of his Spirit.   14. And we have seen and testify that the Father has sent his Son to be the Savior of the world.

a. The New International Version has "we know." But the Greek actually says, "By this we know." The words *by this* refer to the preceding context where John tells us that if we love one another, God lives in us. John's discussion of the subject *love*, therefore, is the backdrop for the confidence John expresses in God. What is this confidence? John says, "We know that we live in him and he in us." That is, from experiencing the presence of God in our lives we know that God lives in us and we in God.

b. How do we know that we dwell in God and he in us? "Because he has given us of his Spirit." Even though John uses many of the same words he wrote in 3:24, he makes a slightly different point. There he says, "We

---

24. Refer to Calvin, *The First Epistle of John*, p. 241.

know it *by* the Spirit he gave us." Here in verse 13 he writes, "He has given us *of* his Spirit." In 3:24 he states that divine blessings flow to us through the work of the Holy Spirit. The Spirit pours out God's love to us (Rom. 5:5) and reveals that God is living within us. But in verse 13, we read that the Holy Spirit himself is God's gift to us and we are the recipients.

c. The Spirit does not work alone. With the Father and the Son he takes part in the work of salvation. In verses 13 and 14, therefore, John mentions the work of the Father, Son, and Holy Spirit—the Trinity.

d. Together with the other apostles John is able to testify to the truth of the gospel. He writes, "We have seen and testify" (compare John 1:14, 15). Perhaps he is thinking of the scene of Jesus' baptism. At the Jordan, the Spirit descended in the form of a dove and the Father declared: "This is my Son, whom I love; with him I am well pleased" (Matt. 3:17; Luke 3:22). The disciples were eyewitnesses not only of the baptism of Jesus, but also of his entire life. They saw, heard, and with their hands touched Jesus (1:1). After the ascension, they proclaimed the truthfulness of Jesus' message.

e. John gives a brief summary of the gospel: "The Father has sent his Son to be the Savior of the world." This is a most profound statement! God the Father commissioned his Son to assume the task of saving the world. And God initiated this mission of the Son because of his love for this sinful world.

Jesus proclaimed the message of salvation most effectively. When he visited Sychar, the Samaritans said, "We know that this man really is the Savior of the world" (John 4:42). In the early church, the apostles preached that Jesus is Savior. They said, "God exalted him to his own right hand as Prince and Savior that he might give repentance and forgiveness of sins to Israel" (Acts 5:31; also see 13:23).[25]

The early church called attention to Jesus, who was appointed as Savior and given authority as Lord to save not only the Jews but also the Gentiles. The work of salvation, then, is worldwide in scope (John 3:16).

Greek Words, Phrases, and Constructions in 4:13–14

Verse 13

ἐκ—even though the partitive use of this preposition cannot be denied,[26] the idea of source has merit.[27]

δέδωκεν—the perfect active indicative from δίδωμι (I give). The perfect denotes progress, but the verb lacks the direct object.

---

25. Refer to Johannes Schneider and Colin Brown, *NIDNTT*, vol. 3, p. 219.
26. Refer to Robertson, *Grammar*, pp. 519, 599; Moule, *Idiom-Book*, p. 72.
27. Consult Lenski, *Interpretation of the Epistles*, p. 507.

Verse 14

ἡμεῖς—this personal pronoun is a reference to the apostolic circle.

τεθεάμεθα καὶ μαρτυροῦμεν—A. T. Robertson comments that "a real distinction exists" between the perfect tense of the verb θεάομαι (I observe) and the present tense of the verb μαρτυρέω (I testify, witness).[28]

σωτῆρα—in Johannine literature, this noun occurs only here and in John 4:42. B. F. Westcott observes that the verb σῴζειν (to save) and the noun σωτηρία (salvation) do not appear in John's epistles.[29]

---

2. God Lives in the Believer
4:15–16a

15. If anyone acknowledges that Jesus is the Son of God, God lives in him and he in God. 16a. And so we know and rely on the love God has for us.

Who are the people of the world Jesus has come to save? They are the ones who acknowledge the divine sonship of Jesus. In fact, only if the believer confesses that "Jesus is the Son of God" will God live in him and he in God. By themselves, these words are simple enough. But the phrase should not be seen as a mere confessional statement, even though it may have been equivalent to the statement *Jesus is Lord* (I Cor. 12:3).

When we look at this phrase from a biblical point of view, we soon realize that John causes us to look at theological truth. The word *Jesus* embodies the entire history of Jesus from his birth to his ascension and session at the right hand of God. The term *Son of God* has its roots in Old Testament prophecies (e.g., II Sam. 7:14; Ps. 2:7) that were fulfilled when Jesus came (compare Heb. 1:5). The confession *Jesus is the Son of God* gives voice to his humanity and divinity. And it excludes everyone who denies that Jesus is the Son of God (2:23; 5:10, 12) as one who has no fellowship with God.

"And so we know and rely on the love God has for us." Using the personal pronoun *we*, John includes all the readers of his epistle. By experience, he says, we have come to know the love of God and we have put our trust in it. The two verbs *know* and *believe* (rely) go together. Writes A. E. Brooke, "The growth of knowledge and the growth of faith act and react on each other."[30]

Doctrinal Considerations in 4:13–16a

"Abide with me," prays Henry F. Lyte in his evening song. And rightly so. John, however, tells the believer that if he confesses the divine sonship of Jesus, God

---

28. Robertson, *Grammar*, p. 894.

29. B. F. Westcott, *The Epistles of St. John, The Greek Text, with Notes and Addenda* (1883; Grand Rapids: Eerdmans, 1964), p. 154.

30. Brooke, *Commentary on the Johannine Epistles*, p. 122.

abides in him and he in God. Confession, of course, includes a readiness to obey God's commands (3:24). Moreover, the follower of Christ ought to walk as Jesus walked (2:6); then rightfully he can claim to live in Christ.

Throughout his epistle John assures us that we live in God and he in us. We have new life in him (2:6, 24, 27–28; 3:6, 24; 4:12–13, 15–16) and are fully conscious of our life in Christ (2:5; 5:20).[31]

Greek Words, Phrases, and Constructions in 4:15

ὅς ἐάν—"whoever, anyone." The combination is followed by the verb ὁμο-λογήσῃ (he confesses) in the aorist subjunctive. The aorist signifies single action and the subjunctive uncertainty.

Ἰησοῦς ἐστιν ὁ υἱὸς τοῦ θεοῦ—"Jesus is the Son of God." "If the subject is a proper noun, . . . it may be anarthrous while the predicate has an article."[32]

God is love. Whoever lives in love lives in God, and God in him.   17 In this way, love is made complete among us so that we will have confidence on the day of judgment, because in this world we are like him.   18 There is no fear in love. But perfect love drives out fear, because fear has to do with punishment. The one who fears is not made perfect in love.

19 We love because he first loved us.   20 If anyone says, "I love God," yet hates his brother, he is a liar. For anyone who does not love his brother, whom he has seen, cannot love God, whom he has not seen.   21 And he has given us this command: Whoever loves God must also love his brother.

D. Live in Love
4:16b–21

1. God Is Love
4:16b–17

Some translators and commentators mark a new paragraph beginning in the middle of verse 16.[33] The reason for this division of the chapter is that there is some parallelism regarding the word *love* in 4:7, 4:11, and 4:16b. These verses, and the sections they represent, develop the theme *love*. Thus, Raymond E. Brown observes: "They both begin and end with an emphasis on God's love."[34]

16b. God is love. Whoever lives in love lives in God, and God in him.
Why is John repeating the statement *God is love* (v. 8)? In the preceding section John defines what love is, where it originates, and how it develops.

---

31. Guthrie, *New Testament Theology*, pp. 642–43.

32. Dana and Mantey, *Manual Grammar*, p. 149.

33. GNB, NAB, NEB, NIV, and the following commentators see a break in this verse: Brooke, *Commentary on the Johannine Epistles*, p. 122; Westcott, *The Epistles of St. John*, p. 155; Kenneth Grayston, *The Johannine Epistles*, New Century Bible Commentary series (Grand Rapids: Eerdmans, 1984), p. 129; Raymond E. Brown, *The Epistles of John*, Anchor Bible series (Garden City, N.Y.: Doubleday, 1982), vol. 30, p. 590.

34. Brown, *The Epistles of John*, p. 545.

But in verses 16b–18, he tells the reader the purpose of love: God's love, living within a believer, ensures confidence, expels fear, and encourages him to be like Christ (2:6).

"God is love." God, whose essence is love, approaches his people in love. John reveals that anyone who lives in this divine love lives in God and God in him. This brief passage is what C. H. Dodd calls "the high-water mark of the thought of this epistle."[35] The love of God guarantees life and life reveals itself in love. Note the repetitious use of the terms *God, love,* and *lives* in this verse.

17. In this way, love is made complete among us so that we will have confidence on the day of judgment, because in this world we are like him.
We make three observations:

a. *Love made complete.* The translators of the New International Version have decided not to include the words *by this.* In the Greek, the words *by this* ("in this way," NIV) stand at the beginning of the verse. They can refer either to what precedes or to what follows. If they refer to what follows, then the rest of verse 17 is an explanation of the expression *by this.* If we understand it as such, the verse gives rise to a curious inconsistency: why is love made perfect now so that in the day of judgment we will have confidence? Perhaps it is better to link the words *by this* to the preceding verses. Because we love, we live in God and he lives in us; "by this, love is made complete among us." Elsewhere John uses similar constructions that refer to the preceding context (3:10, 19).

What is the meaning of love that is made complete? Explains James Montgomery Boice, "[Made complete] means 'whole' or 'mature,' and it refers to that state of mind and activity in which the Christian is to find himself when the love of God within him . . . has accomplished that which God fully intends it to accomplish."[36]

b. *Confidence.* When we have fellowship with God the Father and his Son Jesus Christ (1:3), when we remain in the Son and Father (2:24), when God lives in us and we in him (3:24; 4:12, 13, 15), then we are confident that we will not be condemned in the day of judgment. We are confident before God now (2:21) and will be confident when Christ appears in the day of judgment (2:28).

c. *Imitating Christ.* The reason for our confidence is our conformity to Christ. Says John, "Because in this world we are like him." A more literal translation is, "Because as [Christ] is, so also are we in this world" (NASB). As Christ has shown us his love, so we show our love to one another in the world in which we live. In the context of this epistle, the love of God in sending his Son is predominant. Also, we are obliged to show love for one another and thus fulfill God's command (3:23). When we imitate the love of Jesus, we need not fear the coming judgment.

---

35. Dodd, *The Johannine Epistles,* p. 118.
36. James Montgomery Boice, *The Epistles of John* (Grand Rapids: Zondervan, 1979), p. 147.

Greek Words, Phrases, and Constructions in 4:16b–17

Verse 16b

ὁ θεός—the definite article with the noun determines the subject of ἐστίν. The noun ἀγάπη is the predicate nominative (compare v. 8; John 1:1).[37]

Verse 17

παρρησίαν—"boldness." John uses this noun more than does any other New Testament writer. It occurs nine times in his Gospel (7:4, 13, 26; 10:24; 11:14, 54; 16:25, 29; 18:20) and four times in I John (2:28; 3:21; 4:17; 5:14). By contrast, Paul uses it eight times, Luke five times (in Acts), the author of Hebrews four times, and Mark once. The noun originally meant that "in the public assembly of the people one may speak out freely one's opinion."[38]

μεθ' ἡμῶν—the preposition μετά with the pronoun in the genitive case seems to mean "among us (*in our community*)."[39]

---

2. Love Expels Fear
4:18

18. There is no fear in love. But perfect love drives out fear, because fear has to do with punishment. The one who fears is not made perfect in love.

a. "There is no fear in love." As faith and doubt cannot exist together in the heart of the believer, so love and fear have nothing in common. Christians who, in fulfillment of God's command, demonstrate their love for God and their neighbor have no fear.

The word *fear* has two meanings: it can mean "alarm, fright" or it can signify "reverence, respect."[40] The latter meaning, of course, does not apply to this text. The believer loves and respects God, but he is not afraid of him (Rom. 8:15). Because of his love for God and the fellowship he enjoys with him, the Christian is not afraid of the day of judgment. Instead, he lives his life on earth "in reverent fear" (I Peter 1:17; also see Phil. 2:12).

b. "But perfect love drives out fear." What is the meaning of the term *perfect love?* "It is not flawless love; only God has that."[41] Rather it is the love that is complete because it instills within us the desire to keep God's

---

37. Consult Robertson, *Grammar*, p. 768.
38. Hans-Christoph Hahn, *NIDNTT*, vol. 2, p. 735.
39. Moule, *Idiom-Book*, p. 61.
40. Bauer, p. 863; Thayer, p. 656. A combination of these two meanings appears in the account of the giving of the Ten Commandments. "Moses said to the people, 'Do not be afraid. God has come to test you, so that the fear of God will be with you to keep you from sinning' " (Exod. 20:20).
41. Burdick, *The Letters of John the Apostle*, p. 336.

commands.[42] When love comes to expression in the act of loving God and our neighbor, then fear in the sense of fright has no place in our hearts.

c. "Because fear has to do with punishment." The reason that fear and love are mutually exclusive is because fear relates to punishment. In perfect love the idea of punishment is absent. But when there is disobedience, there is fear. And fear of impending punishment already is a penalty. Writes F. F. Bruce, " 'Punishment' is the portion of those who through disobedience are 'condemned already.' "[43] The believer who lives in close communion with God is free from the fear of punishment. He knows that God punished Jesus Christ in his place on Calvary's cross. Therefore, God does not punish the believer; otherwise Christ's work would be incomplete. God corrects and disciplines but does not punish his children.

d. "The one who fears is not made perfect in love." In this last part of the verse, John seeks to instill confidence in the heart of the believer. He puts his thoughts negatively to indicate that the person who fears lacks love. Unbelief leaves a person disturbed, but "the love of God, really known, tranquilizes the heart."[44]

Practical Considerations in 4:17–18

Television viewers are able to witness courtroom sessions almost on a daily basis. We have become accustomed to the judge, jury, defendant, plaintiff, and lawyers. We hear the verdict and see the innocent acquitted and the guilty sentenced. Often we witness the expressions of emotions that no longer can be controlled. These emotions depict at times anxiety and fear, at other times joy and happiness.

Every human being will have to appear before the judgment throne of Christ. Feelings of guilt and remorse will fill the hearts of all those who have refused to obey God's commands, to believe his Word, and to accept Christ as Savior. Their hearts will be filled with fear (Rev. 6:15–17), for they realize that the Judge will sentence them because of their sin.

They who have lived in fellowship with the Father and the Son have nothing to fear. Their hearts are filled with joy and love. And they will hear the word *acquitted* from the lips of Jesus. He will say to the Father, "I have paid it all."

Greek Words, Phrases, and Constructions in 4:18

φόβος—"fear." This noun occurs three times in one sentence with and without the definite article. "It is not necessary to have the article with [abstract] qualities."[45]

---

42. Wilhelm Mundle, *NIDNTT*, vol. 1, pp. 623–24. Also consult Glenn W. Barker, who says, "The experience of the holiness of God's love makes us desire to be even more obedient to his commands." *1 John*, the *Expositor's Bible Commentary*, 12 vols., ed. Frank E. Gaebelein (Grand Rapids: Zondervan, 1981), vol. 12, p. 346.

43. F. F. Bruce, *The Epistles of John* (1970; Grand Rapids: Eerdmans, 1979), p. 113. Also consult Johannes Schneider, *TDNT*, vol. 3, p. 817; Colin Brown, *NIDNTT*, vol. 3, p. 98.

44. Calvin, *The First Epistle of John*, p. 248. The JB has a revealing comment (see the notes on v. 18): "It is impossible to combine the love of a son with the fear of a slave."

45. Robertson, *Grammar*, p. 758.

κόλασιν—"punishment." The noun derives from the verb κολάζω (I punish). Note that the ending -σις denotes process. The noun "has reference to him who suffers."[46]

---

3. Love God and Neighbor
4:19–21

19. We love because he first loved us. Man can never claim that his love for God was prior to God's love for him. God always comes first in loving us, and we respond by loving him. Our love, then, is a copy of his love. He originates love and we follow his example.

The first part of the sentence is incomplete. John writes, "We love." But whom do we love? The broader context (vv. 7, 11–12) seems to favor the words *one another* or *each other*. Some ancient manuscripts, however, have the reading *him* or *God* to serve as the direct object of the verb *love*. Therefore, at least two translations have the reading *we love him* (KJV, NKJV).[47]

20. If anyone says, "I love God," yet hates his brother, he is a liar. For anyone who does not love his brother, whom he has seen, cannot love God, whom he has not seen.

Possibly John addressed the Gnostic teachers who said that they loved God but in their conduct showed hatred toward Christians. Love for God cannot remain a warm feeling in our hearts that moves vertically to heaven but horizontally fails to reach our fellow man. Genuine love for God and for our neighbor extends both ways.

God created man in his own image and likeness (e.g., Gen. 1:26–27; I Cor. 11:7; Eph. 4:24; Col. 3:10). He requires us to love man because we are made in that image.[48] In an entirely different context, which nevertheless expresses the same truth, James writes, "With the tongue we praise our Lord and Father, and with it we curse men, who have been made in God's likeness" (3:9). Such conduct certainly cannot be right.

John reverts to an earlier theme. Apart from a few verbal changes, he repeats what he wrote in a preceding chapter: "The man who says, 'I know [God], but does not do what he commands is a liar, and the truth is not in him" (2:4). John employs strong language with the term *liar* to depict the contrast between the truth and the lie.[49]

Some ancient texts present a slightly different reading which puts the last part of the verse in the form of a question. "For he who does not love

---

46. Thayer, p. 353.

47. Metzger states that some copyists added either the word *God* or the pronoun *him* to complete the sentence. *Textual Commentary,* p. 713.

48. Refer to Calvin, *The First Epistle of John,* p. 249.

49. The term *liar* occurs ten times in the New Testament, of which two are in the Gospel of John (8:44, 55), five in I John (1:10; 2:4, 22; 4:20; 5:10), and three in the epistles of Paul (Rom. 3:4; I Tim. 1:10; Titus 1:12).

his brother whom he has seen, how can he love God whom he has not seen?" (NKJV, KJV).

21. And he has given us this command: Whoever loves God must also love his brother.

John concludes his discussion on love by stating the summary of the law (compare 3:23). He provides the essence of the words Jesus spoke during the last week of his ministry: " 'Love the Lord your God with all your heart and with all your soul and with all your mind.' This is the first and greatest commandment. And the second is like it: 'Love your neighbor as yourself.' All the Law and the Prophets hang on these two commandments" (Matt. 22:37–40). Jesus brought together the "first and greatest commandment" (Deut. 6:5) and the second commandment (Lev. 19:18). God had given these commands to the people of Israel through Moses.

Jesus and the apostles repeatedly stressed the second part of the summary: "Love your neighbor as yourself."[50] Why do the writers of the New Testament accentuate love for our neighbor? The answer is twofold: First, because our neighbor bears the image of God. And second, because God gives us the command to love the neighbor.[51]

Greek Words, Phrases, and Constructions in 4:19–20

Verse 19

ἀγαπῶμεν—preceded by ἡμεῖς, for emphasis, the verb can be either indicative ("we love") or subjunctive ("let us love"). The context favors the indicative.

πρῶτος—this is an adjective, not an adverb: "God is the *first one* who loves" (compare John 20:4).[52]

Verse 20

οὐ—the Majority Text has the reading πῶς (how) instead of οὐ (not). According to this reading, the sentence is a question.[53] Metzger, however, thinks that πῶς "appears to be an improvement introduced by copyists in order to heighten the rhetorical style."[54]

Summary of Chapter 4

In the opening verses of this chapter John tells the readers to beware of false teachers and to discern the Spirit of God. He encourages the recipi-

---

50. Here are some of the references: Luke 10:27; John 13:34; 15:12; Rom. 13:8–9; Gal. 5:14; I Thess. 4:9; Heb. 13:1; James 2:8; I Peter 4:8; I John 3:23.

51. Consult Plummer, *The Epistles of St. John*, p. 109.

52. Robertson, *Grammar*, p. 549.

53. Arthur L. Farstad and Zane C. Hodges, *The Greek New Testament According to the Majority Text* (Nashville and New York: Nelson, 1982), p. 712.

54. Metzger, *Textual Commentary*, p. 714.

ents of his letter with the knowledge that they belong to God and he exhorts them to be faithful to the teachings of the apostles.

John admonishes us to cultivate mutual love, for love originates with God. Love is divine, for God is love. God sets the example by sending his Son into the world. And if we show love for one another, God has fellowship with us. Our acknowledgment that Jesus is the Son of God confirms that God lives in us. Thus we have confidence on the judgment day. Love expels fear. The person who fears does not have perfect love.

John concludes with the statement that if we love God and hate our brother, we are liars. We have received the command to love God and our neighbor.

5

Love God, *part 2*

5:1–12

and Epilogue

5:13–21

Outline (continued)

5 1 Everyone who believes that Jesus is the Christ is born of God, and everyone who loves the father loves his child as well. 2 This is how we know that we love the children of God: by loving God and carrying out his commands. 3 This is love for God: to obey his commands. And his commands are not burdensome, 4 for everyone born of God has overcome the world. This is the victory that has overcome the world, even our faith.

E. Faith in God's Son
5:1–4

1. Believe in the Son
5:1–2

John repeats the theme of Christ's sonship which he expounded earlier (2:22; 4:15). Near the end of his epistle, he wants to tell his readers that Christ's sonship secures their relation to God: "everyone who believes that Jesus is the Christ is a son or daughter of God." The recipients of the letter should know that they are children of God through faith in Jesus Christ. This faith characterizes them as Christians who express their love for him by obeying God's commands.

1. Everyone who believes that Jesus is the Christ is born of God, and everyone who loves the father loves his child as well. 2. This is how we know that we love the children of God: by loving God and carrying out his commands.

We note three points:

a. *Faith.* In this chapter John frequently uses the verb *to believe.*[1] He develops the significance of believing in Jesus Christ by declaring that "everyone who believes that Jesus is the Christ is born of God." When John says "everyone," he indicates that the Christian religion excludes no one. Anyone who sincerely puts his faith in Jesus is a child of God.

The main verb in the sentence is "born" and the phrase *everyone who believes* is its subject. This means that the believer is the child of God the Father, for God causes the spiritual birth of his child. The believer's faith in God is irrefutable evidence of his spiritual birth. He knows that Jesus is

---

1. In this epistle the verb *to believe* occurs nine times (3:23; 4:1, 16 [rely, NIV]; 5:1, 5, 10 [three times], 13). The noun *faith* appears only in 5:4. Also see p. 318, n. 52.

the Christ because the believer has been born of God.[2] Faith in Jesus Christ is inseparably bound to love for God's children.

b. *Love.* "Everyone who loves the father loves his child as well." The second part of verse 1 links faith and love. The one cannot exist without the other, and together they demonstrate the vibrant spiritual life of the child of God. John Calvin observes, "Since God regenerates us by faith, he must necessarily be loved by us as a Father; and this love embraces all his children."[3] In essence, faith and love are inseparable. In God's family, faith in God and love for him and his children are totally integrated.

What evidence is there for combining faith and love? John provides a ready answer. He writes, "This is how we know that we love the children of God: by loving God and carrying out his commands." Actually these words are almost a verbatim repetition of an earlier verse, "We know that we have come to know him if we obey his commands" (2:3; and see 3:23).

c. *Obedience.* John states that love for God's children must be coupled with love for God to be genuine.[4] And love for God can be true only if we obey his laws. Notice that John gives the reader a statement that consists of three parts: love for the children of God; love for God; and obedience to his commands. If any part of the statement is to be valid, it has to be linked to the other two parts. In effect, John reiterates the teachings of Jesus on this particular subject. Jesus said, "If you obey my commands, you will remain in my love, just as I have obeyed my Father's commands and remain in his love" (John 15:10; compare 14:15).

Greek Words, Phrases, and Constructions in 5:1–2

Verse 1

γεγέννηται—this perfect passive verb from γεννάω (I beget) is followed by the active participle γεννήσαντα (referring to God). This participle is in the aorist to express single occurrence. The verb is also followed by the passive participle γεγεννημένον (referring to the child of God), in the perfect to indicate lasting significance.

Verse 2

ἐν τούτῳ—this combination occurs frequently in this epistle. It can point either to the preceding or to the succeeding context. Here it looks forward.

---

2. James Montgomery Boice remarks, "We believe and, in fact, do everything else of a spiritual nature precisely because we have first been made alive." *The Epistles of John* (Grand Rapids: Zondervan, 1979), p. 153.

3. John Calvin, *Commentaries on the Catholic Epistles: The First Epistle of John,* ed. and trans. John Owen (Grand Rapids: Eerdmans, 1948), p. 250. Also see Alfred Plummer, *The Epistles of St. John,* Cambridge Greek Testament for Schools and Colleges series (Cambridge: At the University Press, 1896), p. 111.

4. C. H. Dodd comments, "No doubt the author holds that love to God and love to man are so inseparable that the presence of either is evidence of the other." *The Johannine Epistles,* Moffatt New Testament Commentary series (New York: Harper and Row, 1946), p. 125.

ποιῶμεν—a few manuscripts have the reading τηρῶμεν (we keep) to harmonize it with the next verse (v. 3) and other passages (2:3, 4, 5; 3:22, 24).[5] At least two translations have adopted this reading (KJV, NKJV).

---

2. Overcome the World
5:3–4

3. This is love for God: to obey his commands. And his commands are not burdensome, 4. for everyone born of God has overcome the world. This is the victory that has overcome the world, even our faith.

a. "Love for God." John is the New Testament writer who provides a number of pithy definitions. For example, in his Gospel he defines eternal life (17:3) and in his first epistle he repeatedly explains spiritual truths (consult 2:5–6; 3:10, 23, 24; 4:2, 10; 5:14). Here he states what love for God means: "to obey his commands." Love for God does not consist of spoken words, even if they are well-intentioned, but of determined action that demonstrates obedience to God's commands.

b. "His commands are not burdensome." John reiterates the words of Jesus, "For my yoke is easy and my burden is light" (Matt. 11:30). The Pharisees and scribes placed unnecessary demands upon the Jewish people of the first century. They added to the Decalogue hundreds of manmade rules that were burdensome to the people (see Matt. 23:4; Luke 11:46).[6]

For the person who refuses to acknowledge Jesus as the Son of God, the commands are a threat to man's self-proclaimed freedom. They are a hindrance to his lifestyle and a constant source of irritation.

The child of God, however, knows that God has given him laws for his own protection. As long as he stays within the area delineated by these laws he is safe, for in it he has his own spiritual environment. Therefore, the believer can do anything he pleases within the confines of God's commands (Deut. 30:11–14).

Augustine aptly remarks, "Love and do what you please." The Christian desires to obey God's precepts. With the psalmist he says, "I delight in [God's] commands because I love them" (Ps. 119:47; also see Rom. 7:22). Although John's teaching holds for all God's precepts, the context of verse 3 refers to the commands to believe in Jesus as the Son of God and to love the children of God (v. 1).[7]

c. "Everyone born of God." The Greek says, "all that is born of God."

---

5. Consult Bruce M. Metzger, *A Textual Commentary on the Greek New Testament,* corrected ed. (London and New York: United Bible Societies, 1975), p. 714.

6. Consult Wilhelm Mundle, *NIDNTT,* vol. 1, p. 262. Gottlob Schrenk comments on the phrase *his commands are not burdensome.* He writes, "[This] phrase signifies removal of the category of difficult commands viewed by men as demanding extraordinary achievement." *TDNT,* vol. 1, p. 557.

7. Compare S. Greijdanus, *De Brieven van de Apostelen Petrus en Johannes, en de Brief van Judas,* Kommentaar op het Nieuwe Testament series (Amsterdam: Van Bottenburg, 1929), p. 511.

John wants to place the emphasis not on the individual person but, in general, on all people who have experienced spiritual birth.[8]

d. "Has overcome the world." All who have their birth in God have overcome the world and therefore can claim victory already. They know that Jesus said, "Take heart! I have overcome the world" (John 16:33). Because Jesus has been victorious, we, too, are victorious with him. Jesus has overcome the evil one in this world and has set his people free from the power of Satan. "The battle has thus been decided, even if it is not yet over."[9]

e. "This is the victory." Note that John does not say, "This is the victor." He writes "the victory" to show that the concept itself is significant. Victory and faith are synonymous. John tells his readers that their faith has overcome the world. Their faith, of course, is in Jesus Christ, the Son of God. When believers place their faith in Jesus, then nothing can separate them from the love of God in Christ Jesus (Rom. 8:37–39; I Cor. 15:57). No evil forces in this world are able to overpower the person who trusts in Jesus. Instead, the believer is victorious over the world because of his faith in the Son of God.

> Faith is the victory!
> Faith is the victory!
> Oh, glorious victory,
> That overcomes the world.
> —John H. Yates

Practical Considerations in 5:4

Heroes usually are public idols. The younger generation especially adores and imitates successful men and women.

The Bible portrays its heroes, too. Think of David after he killed Goliath. At that time, the women in Israel sang songs in his honor:

> "Saul has slain his thousands,
> and David his tens of thousands."
> [I Sam. 18:7]

As he walks through the gallery which features the portraits of the heroes of faith, the writer of Hebrews points to numerous people (Heb. 11:4–32). When we look at these heroes, we tend to regard them as being superhuman. But these men and women were ordinary people who had to face trials and temptations that all of us encounter. What, then, makes them great? Their faith in God made them conquer, and their enduring faithfulness to the truth of God's Word made them victorious.

---

8. In Greek, John uses the neuter singular in the form *all* to indicate universality. For example, see John 6:37, 39; 17:2.

9. Walther Günther, *NIDNTT*, vol. 1, p. 651. Also refer to Donald Guthrie, *New Testament Theology* (Downers Grove: Inter-Varsity, 1981), p. 133.

Are we who are common people able to claim victory? Yes, here is the reason: The word *overcome* is significant in the seven letters Jesus instructed John to write to the seven churches in Asia Minor. Note that at the conclusion of each letter Jesus specifically addresses "him who overcomes" (Rev. 2:7, 11, 17, 26; 3:5, 12, 21). Jesus directs his words to common people who are members of local churches. When they are faithful to the end, they indeed are heroes of faith.

Greek Words, Phrases, and Constructions in 5:3–4

Verse 3

αὕτη—this demonstrative pronoun in the feminine singular stands first in the sentence to denote emphasis.

ἡ ἀγάπη τοῦ θεοῦ—the objective genitive. Compare the phrase with that in 2:5 (and 15); 3:17; 4:7, 9.

ἵνα—the use of the particle in this context is either equivalent to a recitative (indicated by a colon) or to the conjunction ὅτι (that).[10] Also see verse 11.

Verse 4

νικήσασα—the aorist tense of this participle from νικάω (I conquer) is timeless. That is, the aorist expresses a fact that is always true.

ἡ πίστις—this noun stands in apposition to ἡ νίκη.[11]

5 Who is it that overcomes the world? Only he who believes that Jesus is the Son of God.
6 This is the one who came by water and blood—Jesus Christ. He did not come by water only, but by water and blood. And it is the Spirit who testifies, because the Spirit is the truth.   7 For there are three that testify: 8 the Spirit, the water and the blood; and the three are in agreement.   9 We accept man's testimony, but God's testimony is greater because it is the testimony of God, which he has given about his Son.   10 Anyone who believes in the Son of God has this testimony in his heart. Anyone who does not believe God has made him out to be a liar, because he has not believed the testimony God has given about his Son.   11 And this is the testimony: God has given us eternal life, and this life is in his Son.   12 He who has the Son has life; he who does not have the Son of God does not have life.

F. Accept God's Testimony
5:5–12

1. Jesus Is the Son of God
5:5

Verse 5 serves as a bridge between the preceding and the following context. Some editors and translators perceive this verse to be part of the

10. Refer to A. T. Robertson, *A Grammar of the Greek New Testament in the Light of Historical Research* (Nashville: Broadman, 1934), p. 993. Also see H. E. Dana and Julius Mantey, *A Manual Grammar of the Greek New Testament* (New York: Macmillan, 1967), p. 249.
11. Consult Robertson, *Grammar*, p. 698.

preceding passage (vv. 1–5); others place it in the next paragraph (vv. 5–12).[12] I prefer the latter, because the theme of Jesus' divine sonship stands at the beginning, in the middle, and at the end of this paragraph (see vv. 5, 9 [his Son], 10, 12).[13]

5. Who is it that overcomes the world? Only he who believes that Jesus is the Son of God.

John begins this verse with an interrogative statement. He asks who this person is that conquers the world. John does not write, "Who is the victor over this world?" By using a participle that is translated as a verb ("overcomes"), he describes the continuing activity of conquering the world. The noun *victor* calls attention only to the function of the person.

In his answer, John states that the person who believes that *Jesus* is the Son of God conquers the world. Faith alone does not overcome the world. But faith in Jesus the Son of God enables the believer to rejoice in triumph. Often faith in Jesus is weak, but when faith reveals itself in an unbreakable bond between Jesus and the believer, Jesus' conquering power becomes visible in the believer.

2. Jesus and the Spirit
5:6–8

6. This is the one who came by water and blood—Jesus Christ. He did not come by water only, but by water and blood. And it is the Spirit who testifies, because the Spirit is the truth. 7. For there are three that testify: 8. the Spirit, the water and the blood; and the three are in agreement.

Observe the following points:

a. *Came.* The person to whom John alludes is obviously Jesus Christ, the Son of God. The terms *Christ* (v. 1) and *Son of God* (v. 5) are synonyms. John uses the past tense to indicate that the coming of Jesus is a historical event. He asserts a historical fact that is irrefutable.

How did Jesus come? Says John, "by water and blood." By themselves, the words *water and blood* are quite intelligible, but what do they mean with reference to Jesus? Although interpretations are many and varied, scholars generally agree that the phrase relates to the history of Jesus. That is, the terms *water* and *blood* refer respectively to the beginning of Jesus' ministry marked by his baptism in the Jordan River and to his death on Calvary's cross.

Two other views deserve recognition. First, some scholars link the terms

---

12. Editors of the Greek New Testament (Nestle-Aland [26th ed.] and Merk [9th ed.]), translators (JB), and commentators place verse 5 at the head of the following paragraph. Consult I. Howard Marshall, *The Epistles of John*, New International Commentary on the New Testament series (Grand Rapids: Eerdmans, 1978), pp. 230–31; Raymond E. Brown, *The Epistles of John*, Anchor Bible series (Garden City, N.Y.: Doubleday, 1982), vol. 30, p. 592.

13. Also consult the rest of the passages that call Jesus the Son of God (2:22, 23; 3:23; 4:15; 5:13).

water and blood to the two sacraments: baptism and the Lord's Supper. But whereas the word *water* literally stands for baptism, the expression *blood* has only symbolical significance in the Lord's Supper. Moreover, the term *blood* is never used to represent the sacrament of Holy Communion. And this is a serious objection.

Second, other commentators think that the phrase *water and blood* refers to the wound in Jesus' side from which blood and water flowed (John 19:34). But one of the major objections to this theory is that it does not answer the question why Jesus came through water and blood.

"He did not come by water only, but by water and blood." John may have written these words to combat the heretical movement known as Gnosticism. One representative, Cerinthus, taught that the divine Christ descended upon Jesus at the time of his baptism and left him before he died on the cross (see the comments at 2:22).[14] The Gnostics claimed that Christ did not experience death. In opposition to this Gnostic heresy, which presumably had just begun to exert itself when John wrote his epistle, John teaches the historical veracity of Jesus Christ: the Son of God began his earthly ministry when he was baptized; he completed this ministry when he shed his blood and died.

b. *Testify.* John continues, "And it is the Spirit who testifies, because the Spirit is the truth." The word *testify* is rather significant in this paragraph.[15] The Spirit is testifying as a witness to the birth (Matt. 1:20 [conception]; Luke 1:35; 2:25–32), baptism (Matt. 3:16; Luke 3:22), teaching (John 6:63), and ministry of Jesus (Luke 4:1, 18). John affirms the words of Jesus: "When the Counselor comes, whom I will send to you from the Father, the Spirit of truth who goes out from the Father, he will testify about me" (John 15:26).[16] The Spirit continues to testify to God's truth with reference to the person and work of Jesus.

John states the reason for the testifying work of the Spirit. He writes, "Because the Spirit is the truth." John identifies the Spirit with the truth and alludes to the words of Jesus, "I am . . . the truth." That is, both Jesus and the Spirit have their essence in the truth. The Spirit testifies because of his identity with the truth in Jesus.

"For there are three that testify: the Spirit, the water and the blood." Of the English-language translations, only two (KJV, NKJV) have the expanded verses (vv. 7–8). "For there are three who bear witness in heaven: the Father, the Word, and the Holy Spirit; and these three are one. And there are three that bear witness on earth" (NKJV). The translators of the New King James Version, however, state in a footnote that the Greek

---

14. Brown states that "there is little to establish a relationship between I John and Cerinthus, and that at most the author's adversaries may have been pre-Cerinthian in emphasizing baptism over death." *The Epistles of John*, p. 577. Also consult Irenaeus *Against Heresies* 3. 3. 4.

15. Either as a verb, a participle, or a noun, the word *testify* appears ten times in the Greek text of verses 6–11.

16. Refer to Lothar Coenen, *NIDNTT*, vol. 3, p. 1046.

New Testaments (Nestle-Aland, United Bible Societies, and Majority Text) "omit the words from 'in heaven' (v. 7) through 'on earth' (v. 8)." Only four or five very late Greek manuscripts contain these words.[17]

John actually writes that three (Spirit, water, and blood) are testifying. But why does John place the historical facts of Jesus' baptism (water) and death (blood), to which the Spirit testifies, on the same level as the Spirit? How can water and blood testify along with the Spirit? We need to look at the text from a Semitic point of view. Impersonal objects can testify; for example, the heap of stones Jacob and Laban put together was called a witness (Gen. 31:48). And according to the Mosaic law (Deut. 19:15), "One witness is not enough. . . . A matter must be established by the testimony of two or three witnesses."[18]

c. *Agree.* John writes that "the three are in agreement." He means that all three witnesses say the same thing; before a court of law the factual evidence of Jesus' baptism (water) and death (blood) is in complete agreement with the testimony of the Holy Spirit. A person cannot accept either one or two of the witnesses and omit the third. All three stand together.

Many scholars suggest that the terms *water* and *blood* in verse 8 refer to the sacraments of baptism and the Lord's Supper.[19] However, the difficulty with this view is that the Spirit, whom John mentions first in rank, cannot become a third sacrament. Because John gives no indication that the phrase *water and blood* has a meaning different from that in verse 6, we do well to accept the same interpretation for verses 6 and 8.

Doctrinal Considerations in 5:5–8

If we understand water and blood to represent the baptism and death of Christ, we think of the earthly ministry of Jesus Christ. Jesus identified himself with his people when he was baptized, and he redeemed them when he died on the cross. Water and blood, therefore, are redemptive symbols for the believer.

The believer accepts the truth that Jesus Christ came by water and blood. He knows that the Spirit testifies to this truth. Moreover, he believes that the Son of God came to cleanse his people from sin and to redeem them through his death. For the believer, then, these truths are basic.

---

17. For further information, refer to Bruce M. Metzger, *The Text of the New Testament: Its Transmission, Corruption, and Restoration,* 2nd ed. (New York and Oxford: Oxford University Press, 1968), pp. 101–2. And consult Henk Jan de Jonge, "Erasmus and the Comma Johanneum," *Ephemerides Theologicae Lovanienses* 56 (1980): 381–89.

18. Consult Brown, *The Epistles of John,* p. 581.

19. Brown counts at least fourteen scholars—and there are many more—who give a sacramental interpretation to verse 8. Here are a few: Rudolf Bultmann, *The Johannine Epistles,* ed. Robert W. Funk, trans. R. Philip O'Hara et al., Hermeneia: A Critical and Historical Commentary on the Bible (Philadelphia: Fortress, 1973), p. 80; Glenn W. Barker, *1 John,* the *Expositor's Bible Commentary,* ed. Frank E. Gaebelein, 12 vols. (Grand Rapids: Zondervan, 1981), vol. 12, p. 351; Dodd, *The Johannine Epistles,* p. 131.

As soon as we reduce the death of Jesus to that of a mere man, so soon do we lose the cardinal point of the New Testament doctrine of atonement, that *God* was in Christ reconciling the world to himself. . . . So-called theologies, which reduce talk of the incarnation to the status of myth, may be attractive to modern men, but they take away our assurance that God's character is sin-bearing love.[20]

Greek Words, Phrases, and Constructions in 5:6–8

Verse 6

ὁ ἐλθών—whereas the present participle ὁ ἐρχόμενος (the One who is coming) designates the Messiah, the aorist ἐλθών denotes the fulfillment of his coming and points to a historic event.

δι᾽ ὕδατος καὶ αἵματος—here the definite article is absent, but in the prepositional phrase beginning with ἐν both nouns have the definite article. The preposition διά conveys the meaning *by* or *through*,[21] and the preposition ἐν connotes "accompanying circumstance." Robert Hanna observes, "Both the idea of accompaniment and instrumentality appear to be present in the prepositional phrase here."[22]

αἵματος—influenced by John 3:5, some copyists wrote πνεύματος either as a substitution for αἵματος or as an addition. However, this substitution or addition does not have the support of the better manuscripts.

Verses 7–8

μαρτυροῦντες—after this participle, the Textus Receptus (the Received Text) adds the so-called Comma Johanneum (the Johannine passage): "in heaven: the Father, the Word, and the Holy Spirit; and these three are one. And there are three that bear witness on earth" (NKJV). Bruce M. Metzger states: "The passage is absent from every known Greek manuscript except four, and these contain the passage in what appears to be a translation from a late recension of the Latin Vulgate." And he adds, "If the passage were original, no good reason can be found to account for its omission . . . by copyists of hundreds of Greek manuscripts."[23]

3. Testimony of God
5:9–10

In verses 6–9, John indirectly introduces the Trinity. Notice that in verse 6, he states that Jesus Christ, the Son of God, has come. In the same verse and verse 8, John says that the Spirit testifies. And in verse 9, he mentions the testimony of God (the Father).

20. Marshall, *The Epistles of John*, pp. 233–34.

21. Consult Robertson, *Grammar*, p. 583. Also see C. F. D. Moule, *An Idiom-Book of New Testament Greek*, 2d ed. (Cambridge: At the University Press, 1960), p. 57.

22. Robert Hanna, *A Grammatical Aid to the Greek New Testament* (Grand Rapids: Baker, 1983), p. 438. And refer to Robertson, *Grammar*, p. 589.

23. Metzger, *Textual Commentary*, pp. 715, 716.

9. We accept man's testimony, but God's testimony is greater because it is the testimony of God, which he has given about his Son.

a. "We accept man's testimony." In Greek, this is a simple conditional sentence that is true to fact: "If we receive the witness of men, the witness of God is greater" (NASB). John expresses a timeless truth and, therefore, the conditional element in the sentence has lost its force. John is saying that customarily we accept man's testimony.

If we consider this verse in the broader context of Scripture, we see that the expression *man's testimony* is a reference to John the Baptist. Jesus said of the Baptist, "There is another who testifies in my favor, and I know that his testimony about me is valid" (John 5:32). In that same context, Jesus added, "I have testimony weightier [greater] than that of John. . . . And the Father who sent me has himself testified concerning me" (vv. 36–37). Perhaps John has these words of Jesus in mind when he compares the testimony of man with that of God.

b. "But God's testimony is greater." John focuses attention not on our acceptance of God's testimony but on the significance of that testimony. God's word is unquestionably true and thus in comparison with the testimony of man is much weightier.

What is this testimony? In light of the immediately preceding passage, I suggest that it is the testimony of the Spirit, water, and blood.

c. "The testimony of God, which he has given about his Son." This testimony includes the voice that spoke from heaven at Jesus' baptism (Matt. 3:17), at his transfiguration (Matt. 17:5), and at his triumphant entry into Jerusalem (John 12:28). John uses the perfect tense ("he has given") to indicate that God continues to testify about his son through his Word and Spirit.

10. Anyone who believes in the Son of God has this testimony in his heart. Anyone who does not believe God has made him out to be a liar, because he has not believed the testimony God has given about his Son.

Throughout the epistle John uses contrast and this text is no exception. First he states the positive and then the negative.

a. *Positive.* In verse 10, belief in the Son of God is central; it is part of the message John teaches in verses 1–12, namely, faith in Jesus as the Son of God. Believing, says John, is a continuous act. That is, faith is a lasting and active power that resides in the heart of the believer. Faith is the constant bond between the Son of God and the believer.

Note that John states specifically that faith is believing *in* the Son of God. The preposition *in* means that the believer puts full trust and confidence in Jesus Christ, the Son of God. The believer has accepted the testimony (see John 3:33; Rom. 8:16) which God, through the Spirit, has given about his Son. And this testimony which comes to him through external witnesses is now lodged in his heart and has become an integral part of his spiritual life.

b. *Negative.* The second part of verse 10 is not a parallel of the first part.

Instead of writing, "Anyone who does not believe in the Son of God," John says, "Anyone who does not believe God." He places the emphasis on God, who has given man testimony about his Son. Man, however, cannot accept this testimony merely for information. He does not have the freedom to take or leave it without obligation, for God gives him this testimony with royal authority. When man rejects God's testimony, he has made and continues to make God a liar (compare 1:10). And this is a serious offense, because rejection of God's Word constitutes deliberate unbelief.

John addressed the false teachers of his day, who said that they believed in God but rejected the birth and the death of his Son. John, however, addresses his word to anyone who rejects God's testimony. That is, the unbeliever takes full responsibility for his choice. "Unbelief is not a misfortune to be pitied; it is a sin to be deplored."[24] The unbeliever's sin lies first in his intentional refusal to believe God's testimony about his Son and second, in his arrogant denial that the Father and the Son are one. Man cannot say that he has faith in God and at the same time reject God's testimony about Jesus Christ.

Greek Words, Phrases, and Constructions in 5:9–10

Verse 9

εἰ—the particle introduces a simple fact condition. The verb λαμβάνομεν is timeless.

ὅτι—the first one is causal (*because*) and the second "an objective particle"[25] that is equivalent to the relative pronoun *which*.

μεμαρτύρηκεν—the perfect tense applies to instances that occurred in the past during Jesus' earthly ministry. And it refers to God's testimony given today.

Verse 10

πεποίηκεν and πεπίστευκεν—in the perfect active tense, these two verbs describe action that took place in the past and that continues in the present.

τῷ θεῷ—some manuscripts have τῷ υἱῷ. This reading "arose from a desire to make the negative clause correspond more exactly to the preceding positive clause."[26]

---

4. Eternal Life
5:11–12

11. And this is the testimony: God has given us eternal life, and this life is in his Son. 12. He who has the Son has life; he who does not have the Son of God does not have life.

---

24. J. R. W. Stott, *The Epistles of John: An Introduction and Commentary*, Tyndale New Testament Commentaries (Grand Rapids: Eerdmans, 1964), p. 182.

25. Robertson, *Grammar*, p. 964.

26. Metzger, *Textual Commentary*, p. 717.

John comes to the concluding thought of his discourse on the Son of God. He specifically states the content of God's testimony and eliminates any misunderstanding about God's Son.

What is the content of God's testimony? "God has given us eternal life." Notice that John is addressing believers when he uses the first person pronoun *us*. He does not say that eternal life will be given (future tense) but that God has given it (past tense) to us. We have this life now in principle (John 3:17), and when we enter the presence of God in glory, we will have it fully.

"And this life is in his Son." The way to obtain eternal life is by believing in the Son of God. Even though John does not say this here, in his Gospel he is explicit: "Whoever believes in the Son has eternal life, but whoever rejects the Son will not see life, for God's wrath remains on him" (John 3:36; also see 3:15; 20:31).

"He who has the Son has life." Parallels to this statement are in 2:23 and in II John 9. The word *has* stands for fellowship with Christ. It means that in faith the believer has accepted Jesus Christ as the Son of God, who said, "I am . . . the life" (John 14:6). Therefore, because of faith, God's Son and the believer are inseparable.

The converse is also true. "He who does not have the Son of God does not have life." The person who refuses to acknowledge Jesus as Son of God will never possess life. Instead he faces eternal death (compare 3:14).

In conclusion, by placing our faith in Jesus Christ we receive the gift of life. Because of our faith, Christ lives in us and we in him (3:24; 5:20). Therefore, at present we already possess eternal life and joyfully sing,

> Yes, in me, in me he dwelleth;
> I in him, and he in me!
> And my empty soul he filleth,
> Here and through eternity.
> —Horatius Bonar

Practical Considerations in 5:9–12

Daily we meet numerous people who advise us what we should know, do, or need. Much of this informative advice we take for granted and even ignore. Intellectually we may accept advice, but it does not become part of us until we are fully convinced of its validity.

We generally heed advice concerning our physical well-being, because it concerns the quality of our life. For example, someone informs us that the weather outside is cold and windy. We will not know how cold it is, however, until we have stepped outdoors to feel the temperature and experience the chill factor. Then we know if our clothing is adequate to keep us physically comfortable.

When John says that we believe God's testimony about his Son, we know this in our heart. That testimony becomes part of us because of our personal relationship with Jesus. We experience his nearness, his help, and his love because we have fellowship with him and the Father. Accordingly, we are able to testify that God's testimony is in our hearts.

Greek Words, Phrases, and Constructions in 5:11

ὅτι—in this text the conjunction can be translated "that" or it can be understood as a recitative, indicated by a colon (NIV).

---

13 I write these things to you who believe in the name of the Son of God so that you may know that you have eternal life.   14 This is the confidence we have in approaching God: that if we ask anything according to his will, he hears us.   15 And if we know that he hears us—whatever we ask—we know that we have what we asked of him.

V. Epilogue
5:13–21

A. Ask According to God's Will
5:13–15

1. Eternal Life
5:13

The similarity of the conclusion of John's Gospel to that of his first epistle is undeniable. Both in the Gospel and in the epistle, John states the purpose of his writings: to have eternal life (John 20:31; I John 5:13).

Some translators consider verse 13 part of the preceding paragraph or a separate concluding verse.[27] Others see the epilogue introduced by verse 13.[28]

13. I write these things to you who believe in the name of the Son of God so that you may know that you have eternal life.

John sums up what he has said throughout his epistle. The words *these things* refer to the entire letter. But note that John writes the letter to Christians "who believe in the name of the Son of God." He addresses the people who continue to put their faith in God's Son. In an earlier chapter he informed them of one of God's commands: "to believe in the name of his Son, Jesus Christ" (3:23; also see John 1:12). John repeats the term *name* to indicate the full revelation of the Son of God. That is, anyone who believes in the name of God's Son receives forgiveness of sins and eternal life.[29] In this epistle and especially in this chapter, John elucidates his theme: "believe in the name of the Son of God."

John combines the verbs *to believe* and *to know* in verse 13. By contrast, he concludes his Gospel with the words, "These [things] are written that

---

27. For example, refer to JB, NAB, NKJV.
28. Here are a few: GNB, NEB, NIV, RSV.
29. Refer to Hans Bietenhard, *NIDNTT,* vol. 2, p. 654.

you may believe that Jesus is the Christ, the Son of God" (John 20:31). In verse 13, however, he adds the concept *to know*, namely, to know with certainty.[30] When he writes, "so that you may know," he does not mean "to come to know" but "to have assurance." Believers have the assurance of eternal life and the right to be children of God (John 1:12).

Greek Words, Phrases, and Constructions in 5:13

ἔγραψα—the epistolary aorist takes the place of the present. "This idiom is merely a matter of standpoint. The writer looks at his letter as the recipient will."[31] Also see 2:14, 26.

εἰδῆτε—preceded by ἵνα, this verb in the perfect subjunctive from οἶδα (I know) is part of a purpose clause.

ἔχετε—the verb is between the noun ζωήν (life) and the adjective αἰώνιον (eternal) for reasons of emphasis and unity.

τοῖς πιστεύουσιν—Textus Receptus and the Majority Text, with the King James Version and the New King James Version, have an expanded text: "who believe in the name of the Son of God, that you may know that you have eternal life, and that you may *continue to* believe in the name of the Son of God" (NKJV). This expanded reading does not seem to be original in view of a possible "scribal assimilation to the statement in J[oh]n 20.31."[32]

---

2. Answered Prayer
5:14–15

14. This is the confidence we have in approaching God: that if we ask anything according to his will, he hears us. 15. And if we know that he hears us—whatever we ask—we know that we have what we asked of him.

These two verses repeat the words John wrote earlier: "We have confidence before God and receive from him anything we ask" (3:21–22).

Observe the following points:

a. *Confidence.* The Greek word John uses here and elsewhere is translated "assurance" or "confidence" (2:28; 3:21; 4:17). What he means is that because of the gift of eternal life (v. 13), the believer has the confidence, that is, the freedom, to approach God in prayer anywhere and anytime. As a child of God he freely comes to God with his praise and petitions.

b. *Will.* In the presence of God, we have the freedom to ask for anything because we know that God hears us. Indeed, God grants us the freedom to ask whatever we wish, but he adds one condition: "if we ask . . . according to his will." This is the biblical teaching on prayer. Even

---

30. Consult Donald W. Burdick, *The Letters of John the Apostle* (Chicago: Moody, 1985), p. 386.
31. Robertson, *Grammar,* p. 845.
32. Metzger, *Textual Commentary,* p. 717.

Jesus submits to the will of his Father. When he was in the Garden of Gethsemane he prayed, "Yet not as I will, but as you will" (Matt. 26:39). Moreover, Jesus teaches us to pray in his name, so that he may bring glory to the Father (John 14:13).[33]

c. *Promise.* At first sight, verse 15 seems to be repetitious. But upon close examination, we learn that John tells the readers that God indeed hears their prayers. John confirms this confidence which we have in approaching God when he writes that "we know that he hears us." And we, too, confirm that God answers prayer.

At times we experience that not every prayer we offer receives a positive answer. Then we should be ready to accept a negative response and know that God always gives us that which is good for our spiritual well-being. "Every good and perfect gift is from above, coming down from the Father of the heavenly lights" (James 1:17).

Twice in verse 15 John writes the verb *to know.* He insists that we possess the assurance that God indeed hears our prayers and responds to them. We know that if we ask anything according to his will, God grants us our request. But why does John write, "And *if* we know that he hears us"? Is John expressing doubt about the believer's knowledge that God hears us? Some translators change the word *if* to "because."[34] Although this is an attractive solution, the difficulty is that the previous verse (v. 14) also has the particle *if,* yet it is not translated "because." Perhaps another way to explain the text is to repeat the words of the previous sentence. The text then says, "And if we ask anything according to his will, we know that he hears us." This explanation is strengthened by John's assertion, "whatever we ask [provided it is in accord with God's will]."

John is definite when he writes, "we know that we have what we asked of him." He does not use the future tense "we will have" but the present tense "we have." That is, now already we possess what we asked. When we ask God anything in faith according to his will, we know that he hears us and will grant our petition in his time.

Practical Considerations in 5:14–15

How can we be sure that God hears and answers prayers? John gives us the answer. He says that when, in submission to his will, we ask God in faith to grant us our request, we know that he hears us. We also know that we have what we asked. What proof do we have that this is so? When we pray the Lord's Prayer, we say, "Give us today our daily bread." We actually claim that the bread which we request already belongs to us. We do not pray for bread but for *our* bread. And we ask God to supply it *today.* In short, "we have what we asked of him" (5:15).

---

33. References to prayer are numerous in Scripture. Here are a few passages: Jer. 29:12; Matt. 7:8; 21:22; Mark 11:24; John 15:7; 16:24; James 1:5.

34. For instance, refer to GNB, NAB [since], and *Phillips.* And see Brown, *The Epistles of John,* p. 610.

Greek Words, Phrases, and Constructions in 5:14–15

Verse 14

αἰτώμεθα—even though grammarians wish to see a distinction between the middle αἰτώμεθα and the active αἰτῶμεν, this differentiation "has only very limited validity" (compare John 16:24 with 26; but also see James 4:3).[35]

Verse 15

ἐὰν οἴδαμεν—the combination of the particle ἐάν and the indicative occurs frequently in the New Testament (Luke 19:40; Acts 8:31; I Thess. 3:8). Some grammarians give the particle a causal meaning.[36]

ᾐτήκαμεν—the perfect active from αἰτέω (I ask) indicates that continued prayer is offered by the believer.

---

16 If anyone sees his brother commit a sin that does not lead to death, he should pray and God will give him life. I refer to those whose sin does not lead to death. There is a sin that leads to death. I am not saying that he should pray about that. 17 All wrongdoing is sin, and there is sin that does not lead to death.

B. Pray for Remission
5:16–17

We should never limit our prayers to personal needs. Rather, as brothers and sisters in the Lord, we need to exercise our corporate responsibility to pray for each other. Especially when we notice a brother (or sister) committing a sin, we should pray to God for remission.

16. If anyone sees his brother commit a sin that does not lead to death, he should pray and God will give him life. I refer to those whose sin does not lead to death. There is a sin that leads to death. I am not saying that he should pray about that. 17. All wrongdoing is sin, and there is sin that does not lead to death.

John recapitulates his teaching on sin. He has conveyed this teaching in every chapter of his epistle (1:7–9; 2:1–2, 12; 3:4–6, 8–9; 4:10). Now he speaks of sin and death, of prayer and life, and of wrongdoing and remission.

a. *Sin.* "If anyone sees his brother commit a sin that does not lead to death." When John writes "brother" in his epistle, he means a fellow

---

35. Bauer, p. 25.

36. Refer to Friedrich Blass and Albert Debrunner, *A Greek Grammar of the New Testament and Other Early Christian Literature,* trans. and rev. by Robert Funk (Chicago: University of Chicago Press, 1961), sec. 372(1a).

believer.[37] Whenever a member of the Christian community notices that a brother is falling into sin, he should pray to God on his behalf (compare James 5:20).

John distinguishes between "a sin that does not lead to death" and "a sin that leads to death." In this passage he mentions the first kind three times and the second only once. He clearly implies that praying for the sinner who commits "a sin that does not lead to death" is the intent of his writing.[38]

What is the meaning of the word *death*? In addition to 5:16, where it occurs three times, the word appears twice in 3:14: "We know that we have passed from death to life, because we love our brothers. Anyone who does not love remains in death." John is not thinking of physical death.[39] Rather, he is referring to spiritual death. He contrasts death with eternal life (3:15) to set apart the believer, who possesses this life, from the person who denies that Jesus is the Son of God (2:22–23) and who hates the believer (3:13).

Who, then, commits the sin that leads to death? The person who rejects Jesus as the Christ and who does not love the believer commits this sin. He does not share in the fellowship of the Father and the Son (1:3), and is excluded from eternal life (4:12). He left the Christian community because he did not really belong to it (2:19). He had been a pretender.[40]

b. *Prayer*. Although a believer commits sin (2:1), he does not practice the sin that leads to death. If a brother sins, John counsels, the community ought to ask God to "give him life." That is, God will forgive his sin and restore him to fellowship. John knows that in the Christian community many believers fall into sin. He uses the plural and writes, "I refer to those whose sin does not lead to death."

Should the Christian community pray for the person who commits "a sin that leads to death"? John does not call this person a "brother."[41] Writes John, "I am not saying that [the believer] should pray about that." In these words we hear the echo of Jesus' voice when he prayed for his followers, "I pray for them. I am not praying for the world, but for those you have given me, for they are yours" (John 17:9). The false teachers whom John opposes in his epistle "have gone out into the world" (4:1), because "they are from the world" (v. 5). These teachers have directed their false doctrines against the believers, have been disruptive in the

---

37. Compare 2:9, 10, 11; 3:10, 12–17; 4:20–21.

38. Consult Paul Trudinger, "Concerning Sins, Mortal and Otherwise. A Note on 1 John 5, 16–17," *Bib* 52 (1971): 541–42.

39. S. M. Reynolds expounds the view that John means physical death. He supports his view with a reference to John 11:4. But because of its historical context, this passage can hardly be used as a parallel. "The Sin unto Death and Prayers for the Dead," *Reformation Review* 20 (1973): 133.

40. Consult David M. Scholer, "Sins Within and Sins Without: An Interpretation of I John 5:15–16," *Current Issues in Biblical and Patristic Interpretation*, ed. Gerald F. Hawthorne (Grand Rapids: Eerdmans, 1975), p. 242.

41. Compare Guthrie, *New Testament Theology*, p. 616.

Christian community, and have demonstrated their hatred against the church (compare II John 7). Therefore, John adds his personal advice not to pray for them. Note that 5:16 is the only passage in this epistle that has the personal pronoun *I*.

c. *Comfort.* "All wrongdoing is sin, and there is sin that does not lead to death." John calls attention to the seriousness of sin. "Sin is lawlessness" (3:4) and is always an affront to God. In fact, in the sight of God, sin is a transgression of his law and the person who "stumbles at just one point is guilty of breaking" the whole law (James 2:10).

But not every sin leads to death. When a believer transgresses God's law, he does not deny the sonship of Christ and hate the church. Moreover, God stands ready to forgive his sin. John teaches that "if we confess our sins, [God] is faithful and just and will forgive us our sins and purify us from all unrighteousness" (1:9). God forgives sin when the sinner confesses and fellow Christians pray for him, for "God will give him life."

Doctrinal Considerations in 5:16–17

The Old Testament makes a distinction between unintentional and intentional sin. When a person sins unintentionally, he is forgiven when the priest makes atonement for him. However, the person who sins intentionally blasphemes the Lord, despises his Word, and breaks his commands. "That person must surely be cut off," says God (Num. 15:31; also see vv. 22–31).

Even though John distinguishes between two types of sin in verses 16 and 17, allusions to similar teachings in the Old Testament are entirely absent. We should listen to what John has to say and interpret his message in the historical and theological context of his day.

The writer of the Epistle to the Hebrews, by contrast, exhorts his readers not to turn away from the living God and uses examples and precepts from the Old Testament to strengthen his admonition. Says he, "Anyone who rejected the law of Moses died without mercy on the testimony of two or three witnesses. How much more severely do you think a man deserves to be punished who has trampled the Son of God under foot, who has treated as an unholy thing the blood of the covenant that sanctified him, and who has insulted the Spirit of grace?" (Heb. 10:28–29; also consult 6:4–6).

Greek Words, Phrases, and Constructions in 5:16

ἐάν—this is a conditional sentence of the future more vivid type: the aorist subjunctive ἴδῃ (from ὁράω, I see) in the protasis and the future indicative αἰτήσει (he will ask) in the apodosis. The aorist signifies single occurrence.

ἁμαρτάνοντα—the present active participle denotes continued action. It is followed by the noun ἁμαρτίαν (sin) as the cognate accusative that repeats the content of the verb.[42]

---

42. Refer to Robertson, *Grammar*, p. 477; and to Moule, *Idiom-Book*, p. 32.

μή—the negative particle with an implied participle expresses condition or prohibition. The negative particle in verse 17 is οὐ (not).

δώσει—although grammatical syntax requires that the subject of this verb be the same as that of αἰτήσει, the meaning of the verbs demands that the one who prays is the believer and the one who gives life is God.

ἐρωτήσῃ—the aorist subjunctive from ἐρωτάω (I ask, request) is in a clause that indicates indirect command. In this verse, the verb ἐρωτάω is the same as the verb αἰτέω.

---

18 We know that anyone born of God does not continue to sin; the one who was born of God keeps him safe, and the evil one cannot harm him. 19 We know that we are children of God, and that the whole world is under the control of the evil one. 20 We know also that the Son of God has come and has given us understanding, so that we may know him who is true. And we are in him who is true—even in his Son Jesus Christ. He is the true God and eternal life.

21 Dear children, keep yourselves from idols.

C. Know the Son of God
5:18–21

1. Born of God
5:18

In the last part of his epistle, John summarizes three facts that his readers have learned. These facts relate to sin, the evil one, and the truth in Jesus Christ. John summarizes the principles he has taught and introduces each verse with the words *we know*.

18. We know that anyone born of God does not continue to sin; the one who was born of God keeps him safe, and the evil one cannot harm him.

Except for a minor variation in wording, the first part of this sentence is virtually identical to that of 3:9, "No one who is born of God will continue to sin." He repeats the thought by putting the words *we know* at the beginning. That is, he tells the readers that the person who has his origin in God does not keep on sinning without repentance (compare 3:6). "A child of God may sin; but his normal condition is one of resistance to sin."[43] This is a well-known principle.

In the next clause, John presents a message that appears to be vague. What does he mean by the words "The one who was born of God keeps him safe"? And who is kept safe? To begin with the last question, we conclude that the pronoun *him* refers to the believer whom God protects. If God keeps the believer safe, the phrase "the one who was born of God" must refer to Jesus Christ.[44] This designation for Jesus, however, is

---

43. Plummer, *The Epistles of St. John*, p. 125.

44. Most translators understand the subject of the clause to be Jesus. For example, "it is the Son of God who keeps him safe" (NEB, GNB). The JB has, "because the begotten Son of God protects him." But the NAB gives the reading "God protects the one begotten by him." And two translations have the reflexive pronoun *himself*, "but he that is begotten of God keepeth himself" (KJV, NKJV).

unique; it does not appear anywhere else in the New Testament. Because both Jesus and the believer are called "born of God," John differentiates by using the past tense "was born" for Jesus and the phrase *born of God* for the believer. Furthermore, John places Jesus "who was born of God" over against "the evil one." Jesus keeps the believers safe and asks God to protect them from the evil one (John 17:12, 15).

"And the evil one cannot harm him." Notice that John describes Satan as the evil one (2:13, 14; 3:12; 5:19). The evil one seeks to lay his hands on the believer but is unable to touch him because of God's protecting power. The word *touch* in this sentence means to harm or injure a person.[45] Satan desires to lead us into sin and to control us permanently. But we who are children of God belong not to Satan but to God.

Greek Words, Phrases, and Constructions in 5:18

ὁ γεννηθείς—this is the aorist passive participle from the verb γεννάω (I beget). The aorist is timeless.

αὐτόν—manuscript evidence for the reflexive pronoun ἑαυτόν (himself) is strong. However, internal evidence together with varied textual witnesses favors the personal pronoun αὐτόν (him).

---

2. Children of God
5:19

19. We know that we are children of God, and that the whole world is under the control of the evil one.

Once again John uses the words *we know* to reassure us of the knowledge we have. He actually repeats the thought he expressed earlier: "Dear friends, now we are children of God" (3:1). We have our origin in God and belong to him. But the whole world, says John, "is under the control of the evil one." He does not say that the world belongs to Satan, for Satan cannot lay claim to creating it. Jesus calls Satan "the prince of this world" (John 12:31; 14:30; 16:11). From the biblical account (Gen. 3:1–19), we know that by deception Satan took control of the entire world. When Satan tempted Jesus, he showed him all the kingdoms of the world and said, "I will give you all their authority and splendor, for *it has been given to me*" (Luke 4:6, italics added). The whole world lies passively in his power. Nevertheless Satan knows that Jesus has come to drive him out and that Jesus claims the world which rightfully belongs to God.

3. Son of God
5:20

20. We know also that the Son of God has come and has given us understanding, so that we may know him who is true. And we are in

---

45. Refer to Bauer, p. 103.

him who is true—even in his Son Jesus Christ. He is the true God and eternal life.

For the last time, John writes "we know" (3:2, 14; 5:18, 19, 20). This time, however, he reminds us of the coming of the Son of God and our understanding of Jesus. Even though we see corruption in every sphere and sector of the world, we know that Jesus Christ has come to give us insight into his true nature.[46] In a world of deceit and falsehood, God has revealed himself in the Son of God as the one who is true. God has not forsaken us to the powers of darkness, but has endowed us with the ability to discern truth from error.

God sent his Son "so that we may know him who is true." The verb *to know* in this clause denotes knowledge we acquire by close association. In the fellowship we have with God the Father and his Son Jesus Christ (1:3), we come to know his truth. We learn to know what belongs to God and what comes from Satan. God is true. "By *true* God [John] does not mean one who tells the truth, but him who is really God."[47] The adjective *true* is descriptive, for it reveals God's nature (see John 17:3; Rev. 3:7).

John says that in addition to learning to know God, "we are in him who is true." That is, we have intimate fellowship with him through his Son Jesus Christ, who is "the way and the truth and the life" (John 14:6). We are in the Father and the Son. In his high-priestly prayer Jesus prayed, "Just as you are in me and I am in you[,] may they also be in us" (John 17:21).

And last, having woven the golden thread of Jesus' divinity and sonship through the cloth of his epistle, John completes this verse with the following words: "Even in his Son Jesus Christ. He is the true God and eternal life." The Gnostic teachers denied that Jesus was the Christ, Son of God. Therefore, in this last verse John summarizes the basic teaching of the Christian faith: Jesus Christ is the Son of God, is truly divine, and is eternal life.

The translators of the New International Version have adopted the reading "*He* is the true God" instead of "*This* is the true God."[48] Some scholars say that the pronoun *he* refers to the nearest noun, Christ. Others vigorously dispute this view and claim that the pronoun refers to God the Father. They point to the wording in John 17:3, "the only true God," and see the parallel in 5:20. They have to admit, however, that their reading of verse 20 is redundant: "And we are in [God] who is true . . . he is the true God."

Proponents of the first view argue, quite rightly, that John ascribes eternal life to Jesus (1:2; also see John 11:25; 14:6). They also show that the entire epistle expounds the identity of Jesus, the Son of God. Therefore, a conclusive statement on the divinity of Jesus at the end of the

---

46. Consult Bauer, p. 187.

47. Calvin, *The First Epistle of John*, p. 273.

48. In at least two other translations the reading is "*He* is the true God" (NAB, MLB).

letter is most effective. I believe that the supporters of this view, namely, that the pronoun *he* or *this* is a reference to Jesus and not to God, have the stronger argument.

Greek Words, Phrases, and Constructions in 5:20

ὁ ἀληθινὸς θεός—the adjective describes God as real, true, and genuine. John chooses this word instead of the adjective ἀληθής (truthful).

---

4. An Admonition
5:21

21. Dear children, keep yourselves from idols.

This admonition comes without any explanation. That is, in the epistle John does not discuss idolatry. But from a historical perspective, we admit that John's admonition fits the context of first-century Christianity. Christians faced the pagan world and idol worship, as is evident from Acts (e.g., 15:29; 19:23–41) and the epistles of Paul (e.g., I Cor. 8:4, 7; II Cor. 6:16).

Here is another interpretation. We cannot rule out the possibility that John means that idols are "false conceptions of God."[49] Then we see that John's warning to test the teachings of false prophets (4:1) harmonizes with his final admonition.

Guard yourselves, says John, from idols. He urges the believers to abstain from any form of worship that draws them away from Jesus Christ. "He is the true God and eternal life."

Greek Words, Phrases, and Constructions in 5:21

φυλάξατε—the aorist imperative "is used for a precept which is valid until the coming of Christ."[50]

Summary of Chapter 5

The subject of this chapter is the doctrine that Jesus is the Christ, the Son of God. Throughout the chapter, John expounds this theme. He begins by stressing the unity that exists between God and the believer. Love for God must coincide with love for the child of God. Love for God is expressed when the believer obeys God's commands. Moreover, the believer who is born of God overcomes the world, for he believes that Jesus is the Son of God.

---

49. F. F. Bruce, *The Epistles of John* (1970; Grand Rapids: Eerdmans, 1979), p. 128.
50. Hanna, *Grammatical Aid*, p. 438.

Jesus came by water and blood; the Spirit testifies to the significant events that the words *water* and *blood* represent. We ought to accept God's testimony more readily than the testimony of man. Anyone who rejects the testimony of God concerning his Son makes God a liar. But the person who accepts this testimony has eternal life through the Son of God.

We have the assurance that God hears our prayers. Provided our requests are in accordance with his will, God grants whatever we ask. The Christian community also prays for the brother who falls into sin. Nonetheless, John advises that we do not need to pray for the person who commits a "sin that leads to death." Believers, however, do not commit this sin, for God keeps them safe. As believers, we know Jesus Christ. He is the Son of God and eternal life. John concludes this chapter with the admonition to guard against false teachings.

Commentary
The Second Epistle of John

Outline

1 The elder,
To the chosen lady and her children, whom I love in the truth—and not I only, but also all who know the truth—2 because of the truth, which lives in us and will be with us forever.

3 Grace, mercy and peace from God the Father and from Jesus Christ, the Father's Son, will be with us in truth and love.

I. Introduction
1–3

A. Address
1–2

The Second Epistle of John belongs to the category *general Epistles.* However, it differs significantly from the first epistle, which does not have a reference to the author and lacks an address. But II John is a personal letter with information about the writer and the recipients of the epistle.

1. The elder,

To the chosen lady and her children, whom I love in the truth—and not I only, but also all who know the truth— 2. because of the truth, which lives in us and will be with us forever.

a. "The elder." With this title the writer identifies himself. He omits his personal name, John, and he does not call himself an apostle of Jesus Christ. Therefore, the address is not like those of Peter's and Paul's letters.

What is the meaning of the word *elder?* The term means either "church leader" or "elderly person." If the writer is a church official, why does he say that he is "*the* elder"? He does not write "an elder," as does Peter when he addresses the church: "To the elders among you, I appeal as *a* fellow elder" (I Peter 5:1, italics added). He cannot be an elder in a local congregation, for his compelling influence reaches beyond the boundaries of one church. For example, we read in the third epistle that the writer, who calls himself "the elder" (v. 1), does not belong to the same local church as Diotrephes does (v. 9). Because of his authority, he cannot be an elder in one congregation. He fills a much higher position.

Why, then, does he not use the title *apostle?* In the second and third epistles apostolicity is not an issue. We assume that his readers knew that he was an apostle. Especially, in the last decades of the first century, his

373

readers knew John as the only surviving apostle. That is, the apostle John had reached advanced age and bore the honorable title *the elder*.

b. "To the chosen lady and her children." Once again, John does not provide a name. When he writes "the chosen lady," he may have in mind a particular family consisting of a woman and her offspring. The broader family, of course, includes the children of the woman's sister (v. 13).

Another explanation is that John uses this cryptic address as a veiled reference to a church. Verse 13 ("the children of your chosen sister send their greetings"), accordingly, denotes another congregation. This parallels Peter's ambiguous speech at the conclusion to his first epistle. Referring to a church, Peter writes, "She who is in Babylon, chosen together with you, sends you her greetings" (I Peter 5:13). Early Christians often endured intense persecution in the second half of the first century. For this reason, writers tried to safeguard the recipients by using innocuous names as designations for the church.[1] In the New Testament, the symbolic representation of the church is often a woman (e.g., John 3:29; Eph. 5:25–33). Many scholars favor the explanation that John employs symbolism for describing congregations to which he wrote his second epistle.

c. "Whom I love in the truth—and not I only, but also all who know the truth." The word *truth* occurs four times in these first three verses. John intimates that this term conveys an important concept. When he mentions truth in his epistles, he contrasts it with falsehood.[2] John speaks not merely for himself. He speaks for the Christian church when he declares that "all who know the truth" love the recipients of his letter (compare I John 2:3–4).

d. "Because of the truth, which lives in us and will be with us forever." The translators of the New International Version regard the last part of verse 1 as a parenthetical statement, so that verse 2 is linked to the clause "whom I love in the truth." John places the emphasis on the term *truth* and connects the expressions *love* and *truth* (I John 3:18; III John 1). Truth unites Christians because it is basic, resides within them, and remains forever.

Greek Words, Phrases, and Constructions in 1

ἐκλεκτῇ κυρίᾳ—the word κυρία (lady) occurs only in this letter (vv. 1, 5). The noun ἐκλεκτός (elect) is common in the New Testament (twenty-three occurrences). The words can represent proper names: "to the elect Kyria" or "to the lady Electa." Also, the words can refer metaphorically to a local congregation.[3]

---

1. Consult C. H. Dodd, *The Johannine Epistles*, Moffatt New Testament Commentary series (New York: Harper and Row, 1946), p. 145.

2. See Anthony C. Thistleton, *NIDNTT*, vol. 3, p. 890.

3. Consult Bruce M. Metzger, *A Textual Commentary on the Greek New Testament*, corrected ed. (London and New York: United Bible Societies, 1975), p. 719.

ἐγώ—this pronoun occurs twice: the first time for emphasis, the second time to specify.

ἐγνωκότες—from the verb γινώσκω (I know), this perfect active participle has "lost the notion of completion (punctiliar) and holds on to the linear alone in the present sense."[4]

B. Greetings
3

3. Grace, mercy and peace from God the Father and from Jesus Christ, the Father's Son, will be with us in truth and love.

Here is an apostolic greeting that compares with the salutations of Peter and Paul, who write the words *grace and peace* at the beginning of their epistles.[5] In two of the pastoral Epistles, Paul expands his greetings: "Grace, mercy and peace" (I Tim. 1:2; II Tim. 1:2).

a. "Grace, mercy and peace." The expression *grace* is not common to the literature of John (John 1:14, 16, 17; III John 4 [translated "joy"]; Rev. 1:4; 22:21). What is the meaning of this salutation? In his inimitable manner, John Albert Bengel summarizes the meaning of the phrase *grace, mercy and peace* in these words: "*Grace* removes guilt; *mercy* removes misery; *peace* expresses a continuance in grace and mercy."[6] And B. F. Westcott makes the following distinction: " 'Grace' points to the absolute freedom of God's love in relation to man's helplessness to win it; and 'mercy' to His tenderness towards man's misery."[7] Peace stands for harmony, trust, rest, safety, and freedom; it is God's gift to man.[8]

b. "From God the Father and from Jesus Christ, the Father's Son." Paul uses similar greetings (with only slight variations) in his letters to Timothy. However, John is more articulate when he places Jesus Christ on the same level as God the Father. John repeats the word *from* and notes that Jesus is the Son of God the Father. As in his first epistle, John opposes false doctrines concerning Jesus Christ and explicitly teaches Jesus' divinity (compare I John 2:22; 4:2; 5:1, 5; II John 7). Jesus is the Son of God.

c. "Will be with us in truth and love." John's greeting deviates considerably from that of the rest of the writers of New Testament epistles. Paul, Peter, and Jude convey their greeting in the form of a prayer or a wish: "Grace and peace be yours in abundance" (e.g., I Peter 1:2; II Peter

---

4. A. T. Robertson, *A Grammar of the Greek New Testament in the Light of Historical Research* (Nashville: Broadman, 1934), p. 1116.

5. These are the references: Rom. 1:7; I Cor. 1:3; II Cor. 1:2; Gal. 1:3; Eph. 1:2; Phil. 1:2; Col. 1:2; I Thess. 1:1; II Thess. 1:2; Titus 1:4; Philem. 3; I Peter 1:2; II Peter 1:2.

6. John Albert Bengel, *Gnomon of the New Testament*, ed. Andrew R. Fausset, 7th ed., 5 vols. (Edinburgh: Clark, 1877), vol. 5, p. 156.

7. B. F. Westcott, *The Epistles of St. John, The Greek Text, with Notes and Addenda* (1883; Grand Rapids: Eerdmans, 1966), pp. 225–26.

8. Refer to Hartmut Beck and Colin Brown, *NIDNTT*, vol. 2, pp. 776–83. Also consult Werner Foerster, *TDNT*, vol. 2, pp. 411–17.

1:2). But John is definite, because he does not express a wish but declares that "grace, mercy and peace . . . will be with us." He adds the words *in truth and love*. The three virtues (grace, mercy, and peace) flourish in an environment where truth and love prevail. Truth unites the Christian community when it faces the common foe of falsehood; it is evident among Christians when they demonstrate their unity in showing love toward one another. Then the Christian church prays the prayer John Greenleaf Whittier composed,

> Drop Thy still dews of quietness,
> Till all our strivings cease;
> Take from our souls the strain and stress,
> And let our ordered lives confess
> The beauty of Thy peace.

Greek Words, Phrases, and Constructions in 3

παρά—John resorts twice to the use of this preposition: before θεοῦ and again before Ἰησοῦ to show equality. In a similar greeting, Paul writes ἀπό (from; e.g., Rom. 1:7).

Ἰησοῦ—some manuscripts include the word κυρίου (Lord) before Ἰησοῦ. In John's epistles, however, the term *Lord* does not appear. Moreover, translators prefer to omit the term on the basis of manuscript evidence and the context of the passage.

---

4 It has given me great joy to find some of your children walking in the truth, just as the Father commanded us.　5 And now, dear lady, I am not writing to you a new command but one we have had from the beginning. I ask that we love one another.　6 And this is love: that we walk in obedience to his commands. As you have heard from the beginning, his command is that you walk in love.

7 Many deceivers, who do not acknowledge Jesus Christ as coming in the flesh, have gone out into the world. Any such person is the deceiver and the antichrist.　8 Watch out that you do not lose what you have worked for, but that you may be rewarded fully.　9 Anyone who runs ahead and does not continue in the teaching of Christ does not have God; whoever continues in the teaching has both the Father and the Son.　10 If anyone comes to you and does not bring this teaching, do not take him into your house or welcome him.　11 Anyone who welcomes him shares in his wicked work.

II. Instruction
4–11

A. Request and Command
4–6

John is ready to formulate the message of his epistle that begins with verse 4 and continues through verse 11. In this segment he exhorts his readers to remain in the truth, to keep God's precepts, and to watch out for false teachers who are bent on deceiving them.

1. Commendation
4

4. It has given me great joy to find some of your children walking in the truth, just as the Father commanded us.

The praise that John showers upon his readers differs little from that of a similar verse in the third epistle: "It gave me great joy to have some brothers come and tell about your faithfulness to the truth and how you continue to walk in the truth" (v. 3). In his epistles, Paul first greets his readers and then speaks words of thanks and praise (Rom. 1:8; I Cor. 1:4; II Cor. 1:3). John's style, therefore, conforms to the rules of conventional correspondence of that day.

a. "It has given me great joy." Either by visiting the readers or, more likely, by receiving a report from others, John rejoices greatly in the news that some of the readers are walking in the truth. The wording is vague because John does not explain why only some of the children are obeying God's command. John may mean that some people obey this command while others are accepting the heretical teaching of false prophets. However, this news would give John only partial joy. John can also mean that he is acquainted with some of the members of the church, and that he knows that they walk in the truth. Nevertheless, we cannot be certain of John's intention. We lack the necessary information.

b. "Walking in the truth." This expression conveys the idea of a believer who confesses the truth of God's Word and who lives in harmony with that Word. Everything he says or does portrays a life that is governed by God's law. John writes that the Father has commanded us to walk in the truth (compare I John 1:6–7; 2:6; 3:23). By his use of the word *Father,* John indirectly reminds his readers that "truth came through Jesus Christ . . . the One and Only, who is at the Father's side" (John 1:17–18).

Greek Words, Phrases, and Constructions in 4

ἐχάρην—the aorist passive from χαίρω (I rejoice) is active in meaning. The use of the aorist points to a definite moment in history.

εὕρηκα—the perfect active of the verb εὑρίσκω (I find) indicates an event that happened in the past but that has results for the present.

ἐκ τῶν τέκνων—the indefinite pronoun τινάς (some) should be supplied preceding this prepositional phrase.

---

2. Exhortation
5–6

5. And now, dear lady, I am not writing you a new command but one we have had from the beginning. I ask that we love one another.   6. And

this is love: that we walk in obedience to his commands. As you have heard from the beginning, his command is that you walk in love.

Note the following points:

a. *Command.* John has come to the main message of his letter and asks for the recipient's undivided attention. He addresses the members of the church, which he metaphorically calls "dear lady," and tells them that he is not writing a new command. John uses the term *command* three times in this passage to indicate his derived authority. The command is not new but old. That is, "we have had [it] from the beginning." God the Father gave this command through his Son to us (refer to John 13:34). We have had this command ever since Jesus preached the gospel during his earthly ministry.

The wording of this passage is almost identical to passages in the first epistle: "Dear friends, I am not writing you a new command but an old one, which you have had since the beginning" (2:7), and "This is love for God: to obey his commands" (5:3). The conclusion that the epistles of John come from the same author is inevitable.

b. *Love.* The command is that we love one another. The first time this command appears is when the nation Israel traveled through the Sinai desert. Then God told the people, "Love your neighbor as yourself" (Lev. 19:18). He also gave them the command, "Love the LORD your God with all your heart and with all your soul and with all your strength" (Deut. 6:5).

How do we love God and our neighbor? By obeying the commands God has given us. The commands to love are not two individual precepts God gave the people of Israel. Every command of God is a requirement to show love to him and to our neighbor (see Matt. 22:36–40; Rom. 13:8–10; Gal. 5:14). "Therefore love is the fulfillment of the law," says Paul (Rom. 13:10). When we obey God's commands, we demonstrate our love to him.

c. *Conduct.* John repeats what he has written earlier: "As you have heard from the beginning, his command is that you walk in love" (see I John 3:11, 23; 4:11). His repetition includes the hearing of the command "from the beginning" and the exhortation to "walk in love." Why does John fall into repetition? Because we have a tendency to hear but not to listen obediently. We hear the command but fail to obey. The old rule still holds: "Repetition is the mother of learning." Our conduct must conform to that of Jesus, for "whoever claims to live in [God] must walk as Jesus did" (I John 2:6).

John describes our daily conduct with the verb *to walk*—a verb he uses three times in this passage. As we walk about from place to place with confidence and assurance, so we ought to reflect steadfastness in obeying God's commands to love him and our neighbor.

Practical Considerations in 4–6

It is possible for someone to be a staunch defender of the truth of God's Word and not show any love toward others. He promotes Scripture's truth, its integrity and unity, and he professes its trustworthiness. But in his relations with persons who hold other views, he maintains a strict separation of truth and love. The church respects him for his love for the Word of God because he is walking in the truth (v. 4). However, no one has the boldness to question whether he is walking in love (v. 6).

Although someone's commitment to the truth may be impeccable, his love for others can be woefully inadequate. Scripture teaches that love is not afraid of the truth, for love and truth are companions (see II John 3). As Paul says, "Love always rejoices in the truth" (I Cor. 13:6). And in another place he writes that the Christians ought to speak the truth in love (Eph. 4:15).

Love is not a fleeting emotion but a lasting commitment. Love is a genuine manifestation and fulfillment of the Golden Rule, "Do to others as you would have them do to you" (Luke 6:31). John puts it pointedly when he exhorts his readers, "Dear children, let us not love with words or tongue but with actions and in truth" (I John 3:18).

Greek Words, Phrases, and Constructions in 5

ἐρωτῶ—John has chosen the verb ἐρωτάω (I request) instead of αἰτέω (I ask). The first verb occurs when persons of equal dignity request something of each other.[9]

οὐχ ὡς—"not as if." The combination of these two adverbs introduces "the concessive or conditional notion."[10]

εἴχομεν—refer to I John 2:7 for comments.

ἵνα ἀγαπῶμεν—this is the indirect command after the verb *to request.*

B. Warning
7–11

1. Description and Admonition
7–8

The purpose of John's letter is to alert the readers to the spiritual dangers they are facing. They ought to recognize false teachers who tamper with the truth of God's Word. And they should zealously guard the heritage of God's truth.

John calls the false teacher a deceiver and an antichrist. He describes him for his readers and admonishes them not to lose their spiritual possessions.

Furthermore, if the believers obey God's precepts, demonstrate their love, and guard the truth, God will bless them. Writes Alfred Plummer, "Truth no less than love is the condition of receiving the threefold blessing of grace, mercy, and peace."[11]

---

9. Refer to R. C. Trench, *Synonyms of the New Testament* (reprint ed., Grand Rapids: Eerdmans, 1953), p. 145.
10. Robertson, *Grammar*, p. 1140.
11. Alfred Plummer, *The Epistles of St. John*, Cambridge Greek Testament for Schools and Colleges series (Cambridge: At the University Press, 1896), p. 136.

7. Many deceivers, who do not acknowledge Jesus Christ as coming in the flesh, have gone out into the world. Any such person is the deceiver, and the antichrist.   8. Watch out that you do not lose what you have worked for, but that you may be rewarded fully.

a. "Many deceivers . . . have gone out into the world." The translators of the New International Version have omitted the word *because* which stands at the beginning of the sentence in Greek. Apart from minor variations, this sentence resembles I John 4:1, "Because many false prophets have gone out into the world." John calls these false prophets deceivers, for they are filled with a spirit of deception and seek the spiritual destruction of Christians. There are many deceivers. We assume that formerly they were part of the Christian community. They left the church (see I John 2:19) to make the world the domain for their pernicious doctrines. And in the world they try to persuade the Christians to accept their views.

b. "Who do not acknowledge Jesus Christ as coming in the flesh." Note that John mentions the full name of the Son of God, Jesus Christ, to remind his readers of his human and divine nature. These deceivers continue to proclaim their opposition to the teaching that Jesus Christ came in the flesh.

Already in his first epistle, John warns the readers to test the spirits: "Every spirit [teaching] that acknowledges that Jesus Christ has come in the flesh is from God, but every spirit that does not acknowledge Jesus is not from God" (4:2–3). Even though there is similarity between this passage and that of II John 7, the difference in the verb forms *has come* (I John 4:2) and *as coming* (II John 7) is obvious. The one verb is in the past tense, the other in the present. Is there a difference in meaning? Hardly. The past tense describes Jesus' earthly ministry, and the present tense is a descriptive term about Christ. In the New Testament, the expression *the one who is coming* is a messianic designation (e.g., Matt. 11:2; John 1:15, 27; 12:13; Rev. 1:4). Thus, John applies the present tense of the participle *coming* to Jesus Christ as a testimony to anyone who denies this truth.

c. "Any such person is the deceiver and the antichrist." John is not afraid to give the false teacher names. Here he calls him not only *the* deceiver, but also *the* antichrist—that is, the person who comes in the place of Christ (compare I John 2:18, 22; 4:3). At the beginning of this verse (v. 7), John refers to many deceivers; therefore we should understand the appellation *the antichrist* as a collective name.

d. "Watch out that you do not lose what you have worked for." In these words we hear an echo of Jesus' discourse on the signs of the end of the age. Jesus begins his teaching with the warning, "Watch out that no one deceives you" (Mark 13:5; also see vv. 9, 23, 33). Similarly, John tells the readers to keep their eyes on their spiritual possessions so that they will not lose them. He no longer requests them to do something. Instead he gives them a command.

We have three different translations for verse 8. Here they are with the variations in italics:

1. that *we* [do] not lose those things *we* have worked for, but that *we* receive a full reward (NKJV; and see KJV).
2. so that *you* may not lose all that *we* worked for, but receive *your* reward in full (NEB; also see NASB, ASV, RV, GNB, and JB).
3. that *you* do not lose what *you* have worked for, but that *you* may be rewarded fully (NIV; and see NAB, RSV, MLB, and *Moffatt*).

The better Greek manuscripts have the reading *you* in place of "we." Translators therefore favor either the second or the third reading. The difference between these two readings is the phrase *we worked for* over against "*you* worked for." Although translators are about equally divided on this point, the more difficult reading is "*we* worked for" and is to be preferred.[12]

What is the meaning of the phrase *rewarded fully*? It does not mean salvation which, because it is a gift, cannot be earned (Eph. 2:8–9). We merit a reward for faithfulness, obedience, and diligence. Nevertheless, a reward is also a gift of God and therefore "one further token of the free grace of God."[13] Scripture teaches that a worker in God's kingdom receives his full reward (compare Matt. 20:8; John 4:36; and see James 5:4).

Greek Words, Phrases, and Constructions in 7–8

Verse 7

ὅτι—a causal conjunction (because). See I John 3:11 for a similar construction.

μὴ ὁμολογοῦντες—this present active participle discloses the continued refusal by the deceivers to acknowledge the humanity of Jesus Christ.

ἐρχόμενον—in the form of a present participle the word serves as an appellation for Christ.

Verse 8

ἀπολέσητε—from the verb ἀπόλλυμι (I destroy, lose), the aorist subjunctive is an indirect command that follows the verb βλέπετε (watch out [second person plural, present imperative]). The aorist is ingressive.

εἰργασάμεθα—the aorist of ἐργάζομαι (I work) is comprehensive. The stress is "on the activity rather than on its product."[14]

---

12. In the interest of uniformity, scribes of the Johannine Epistles would be more likely to change the reading from "we" to "you" than vice versa. However, we should not be dogmatic, because the author himself readily changes from one pronoun to another in his epistles. Consult Metzger, *Textual Commentary*, p. 719.

13. Paul Christoph Böttger, *NIDNTT*, vol. 3, p. 144.

14. Robert Hanna, *A Grammatical Aid to the Greek New Testament* (Grand Rapids: Baker, 1983), p. 439.

2. Instruction

9

John takes his pastoral role seriously. He knows that the false teachers are making inroads in the Christian church. Therefore, he warns the readers to be on guard.

9. Anyone who runs ahead and does not continue in the teaching of Christ does not have God; whoever continues in the teaching has both the Father and the Son.

a. "Anyone who runs ahead." Although this is a literal translation of the Greek, the words imply that a church member at times ventures beyond the boundaries of established doctrine. When this person no longer stays within the sphere of the teaching of Christ, he has transgressed the limits. Of course, John is not against progress in developing doctrine. Nor is he depreciating growth in the grace and knowledge of Christ (see II Peter 3:18). Rather, he warns the readers not to progress and leave the Christian religion, and not to reject the instruction of Christ. If someone progresses and leaves the faith, he regresses and faces spiritual ruin. Genuine progress is always rooted in Christ's teaching.

b. "Teaching of Christ." This phrase means either "the teaching that originates with and belongs to Christ" (subjective genitive) or "the teaching about Christ" (objective genitive). Scholars have advanced arguments for either position, but from the writings of John the evidence favors the subjective genitive. For example, Jesus says to the Jews, "*My* teaching is not my own . . . *my* teaching comes from God" (John 7:16–17, italics added).[15]

c. "[He] has both the Father and the Son." Also in this verse, John teaches the fundamental doctrine of the divinity of Christ. Instead of writing "the teaching of Jesus," he says "the teaching of Christ." He wants to place emphasis on the word *Christ*. Notice, then, that John places the Son on the same level as the Father. That is, no one has the Father without the Son and no one can have God without Christ (see I John 2:23–24; 5:12). The Father and the Son are divine. Whoever continues in Christ's instruction has fellowship with the Father and the Son (I John 1:3).

Greek Words, Phrases, and Constructions in 9

ὁ προάγων καὶ μὴ μένων—the definite article governs two present participles. Therefore, the clause must be understood as one concept. That is, "going ahead" and "not remaining" go together.

Χριστοῦ—this is the only place in John's epistles where the term Χριστός stands

---

15. Also compare John 18:19; I John 1:5; 2:25; Rev. 2:14, 15.

382

alone and occurs without the noun Ἰησοῦς. John places it next to θεόν to stress
the divinity of Christ.

---

3. Prohibition
10–11

**10. If anyone comes to you and does not bring this teaching, do not
take him into your house or welcome him. 11. Anyone who welcomes
him shares in his wicked work.**

We have these observations:

a. *Come.* John states a fact, in a conditional sentence, and virtually says,
"This is how it is: false teachers are coming to all of you." His statement
does not convey possibility or probability, but fact. John writes about a
false teacher who denies the instruction of Christ and comes with the
primary purpose of leading believers astray. John calls such a deceiver the
antichrist (v. 7; and see I John 2:22; 4:3).

b. *Forbid.* When the deceiver comes to the believers, they are not to
open their homes to him and welcome him.[16] But is this prohibition not a
departure from the early Christian rule to entertain strangers (Heb.
13:2), that is, travelers who seek shelter and food? Some commentators,
therefore, have suggested that we may "decline to accept the Presbyter's
ruling here as a sufficient guide to Christian conduct."[17] We demur. John
is not talking about the traveler who needs lodging for the night. He is
referring to the teacher who intends to destroy the church of Jesus Christ.

As is evident from the New Testament (Rom. 16:5; I Cor. 16:19; Col.
4:15; Philem. 2), churches often met in the homes of individual persons.
In other words, the expression *house* may have a broader connotation.[18]

Should a Christian be concerned about the soul of this teacher? Yes, by
taking full control of the situation, he should instruct the teacher in the
doctrines of Christ. But he must never allow the teacher to enter the
Christian's home and permit him to teach! The word *teacher* in Jewish and
early Christian circles was a title that demanded deference and submission. "Pupils . . . were in duty bound to respect and obey their teacher."[19]
Christians, then, ought to pay homage to a teacher but never to a false
prophet.

If a Christian welcomes the false prophet into his home, he agrees to
submit to the prophet's instruction and accordingly destroys his own faith.

---

16. Raymond E. Brown suggests that the house "may be the house used for Community-
meetings: the Johannine house-church in the area addressed." *The Epistles of John,* Anchor
Bible series (Garden City, N.Y.: Doubleday, 1982), vol. 30, p. 676. This suggestion indeed
has merit. Nevertheless, we ought to be careful not to think of every house mentioned in the
New Testament as a "house-church."

17. Dodd, *The Johannine Epistles,* p. 152. Also refer to William Barclay, *The Letters of John and
Jude* (Philadelphia: Westminster, 1958), p. 169.

18. Refer to Brown, *The Epistles of John,* p. 676.

19. Klaus Wegenast, *NIDNTT,* vol. 3, p. 767.

Hence John warns the readers not to welcome a false teacher into their homes.

c. *Share.* Moreover, the Christian who welcomes the instructor into his house actually promotes the purpose of his visitor. In effect, the Christian gives his blessing to the work the false teacher performs. Note that John does not consider this an innocent and insignificant act. He calls it sharing in wicked work that originates with Satan (compare I John 3:12).

Practical Considerations in 9–11

Jesus and the apostles teach and apply the command to love one another. In fact, Jesus extends the command to love even to the enemy (Matt. 5:44). And Paul tells the Christians to feed the enemy when he is hungry and to give him something to drink when he is thirsty (Rom. 12:20; and see Prov. 25:21). Is John, then, correct in instructing the Christian not to welcome someone to his home? The answer is yes.

Let me explain by using an illustration. A navy commander who had access to military secrets sold them to the enemy. He was apprehended and subsequently sentenced. Reporters interviewed the man's father and asked him for his reaction. The father replied that his son, whom he loved, had betrayed his country and now had to be prosecuted to the full extent of the law. The father, in this case, separated himself from his son and regarded him as a fellow citizen who had transgressed the law.

John points to a person who no longer continues in the teaching of Christ, who denies that Jesus Christ has come in the flesh, and who wishes to enter the homes of Christians for the purpose of destroying their faith. This person has betrayed Jesus Christ and is now purposely antichristian. Although John affirms that Christians should love one another (I John 4:7), he warns against allowing the false teacher to lead the believers away from Christ and to hand them over to the evil one.

Greek Words, Phrases, and Constructions in 10–11

Verse 10

εἰ—the particle introduces a simple fact conditional sentence.

μὴ λαμβάνετε—the negative particle μή with the present imperative is a prohibition that tells the readers to stop what they are doing.

Verse 11

πονηροῖς—this adjective relates to Satan, who is called ὁ πονηρός (the evil one). For additional information, see the comments on I John 3:12.

---

12 I have much to write to you, but I do not want to use paper and ink. Instead, I hope to visit you and talk with you face to face, so that our joy may be complete.

13 The children of your chosen sister send their greetings.

III. Conclusion
12–13

12. I have much to write to you, but I do not want to use paper and ink. Instead, I hope to visit you and talk with you face to face, so that our joy may be complete.

John's conclusion is similar to that of the next letter (III John 13, 14). Perhaps the author has written these epistles in sequence. He prefers to talk, because writing appears "not always pleasing to a heart full of sacred love."[20] John has formulated the most important items he wanted to say and which he could not delay. These he has written. The rest of the items can wait until he meets the readers face to face (for the idiom, see Num. 12:8).

John provides no information about where the readers lived and how far he has to travel to reach them. He is physically able to make the journey and see them personally. Furthermore, he is looking forward to his visit, "so that our joy may be complete" (compare I John 1:4). That is, he has communicated his admonitions in the letter, expects the readers to heed his warnings to live in harmony with God's commands, and hopes to have pleasant fellowship with them to mutual satisfaction. Already he has experienced great joy upon learning that some of the readers are "walking in the truth" (v. 4). Now that he has written the letter, he anticipates not only compliance but, as a result, complete joy.

13. The children of your chosen sister send their greetings.

The wording of this last verse places the emphasis not on the "sister" but on "the children." If we interpret the word *sister* literally, we must assume that she is no longer living. But if we take it figuratively, then the word stands for "church"; the children, consequently, are the members of that church. Also notice that John himself was a member of the church that sent greetings to a sister church. In short, the members of one group of believers send greetings to another (compare the figurative language of I Peter 5:13).

Greek Words, Phrases, and Constructions in 12

ἐβουλήθην—from βούλομαι (I want, wish), the aorist is epistolary. That is, the author looks at the letter from the recipient's point of view (refer to I John 2:12–14).[21]

γενέσθαι—this aorist middle infinitive from γίνομαι (I become, am) may "denote change of location" and mean "come."[22]

---

20. Bengel, *Gnomon of the New Testament*, vol. 5, p. 158.
21. Consult Robertson, *Grammar*, p. 846.
22. Bauer, p. 159.

Summary of II John

The elder (John) sends greetings to a distinguished lady and her children. He expresses his joy about the obedience some of her children have shown in honoring the truth. He admonishes her to be steadfast in fulfilling the command to love one another and to obey God's precepts. He alerts her to the dangers that numerous deceivers pose to her, and encourages her to guard her spiritual possessions. He warns her not to have fellowship with these teachers who do not bring the teachings of Christ. If she welcomes them into her house, she promotes the cause of these false teachers. He concludes his letter with the remark that he hopes to visit her. He sends greetings from the children of the chosen sister of the lady he addresses.

Commentary
The Third Epistle of John

Outline

1 The elder,
To my dear friend Gaius, whom I love in the truth.
2 Dear friend, I pray that you may enjoy good health and that all may go well with you,
even as your soul is getting along well.

I. Introduction
1–2

A. Address
1

1. The elder,
To my dear friend Gaius, whom I love in the truth.

This is the address on the envelope, so to speak. The writer calls himself "the elder" (see also II John 1) and he sends his letter to his friend Gaius. The address, however, is very brief because the sender omits the names of places. That is, although we may assume that John resided in Ephesus, we have no knowledge of where Gaius lived.

The name *Gaius* is common in the New Testament. One of Paul's travel companions from Macedonia was Gaius (Acts 19:29), another Gaius was from Derbe (Acts 20:4), and still another Gaius was a Christian in Corinth (Rom. 16:23; I Cor. 1:14). Because we have no certainty that the recipient of John's epistle is one of these persons, we should not try to identify him.

John writes that he loves Gaius in the truth (compare II John 1). The relationship between the elder and Gaius was one of love and trust. John twice mentions that he loves Gaius, for a literal translation of the text says, "To Gaius the beloved, whom I love in truth." Gaius is loved by God and loved by John because of the truth which Gaius professes. This brief remark apparently takes the place of a greeting. In distinction from other personal letters, this epistle lacks the familiar salutation *grace, mercy and peace* or its equivalent. After the address, John expresses a wish.

B. Wish
2

2. Dear friend, I pray that you may enjoy good health and that all may go well with you, even as your soul is getting along well.

Four times in this relatively short epistle John calls Gaius his "dear friend" (vv. 1, 2, 5, 11). In verse 2 he voices a wish rather than an actual prayer. John adheres to the custom of his day and wishes the addressee health and prosperity. The wish is broad, for John includes everything. He says, "I wish that in all respects you may get along well and be healthy." John is interested in the material and physical well-being of Gaius. He knows that Gaius is spiritually active, but John desires that also in material aspects Gaius may succeed. He wants to see Gaius prosper in his business, employment, plans, and purposes.

John wishes physical health for Gaius, so that Gaius may function efficiently in his business. Following Jesus' practice (see, e.g., Mark 2:9–12; 6:34–44), John cares for the physical and the spiritual needs of Gaius. During previous meetings with him and from reports about him, John knows that Gaius is prospering spiritually. John writes, "even as your soul is getting along well." That is, Gaius has made more spiritual than material progress—and that is commendable. John, however, wishes that Gaius may get along well in regard to both body and soul.

---

3 It gave me great joy to have some brothers come and tell about your faithfulness to the truth and how you continue to walk in the truth.   4 I have no greater joy than to hear that my children are walking in the truth.

5 Dear friend, you are faithful in what you are doing for the brothers, even though they are strangers to you.   6 They have told the church about your love. You will do well to send them on their way in a manner worthy of God.   7 It was for the sake of the Name that they went out, receiving no help from the pagans.   8 We ought therefore to show hospitality to such men so that we may work together for the truth.

II. Tribute to Gaius
3–8

A. Cause for Joy
3–4

3. It gave me great joy to have some brothers come and tell about your faithfulness to the truth and how you continue to walk in the truth.   4. I have no greater joy than to hear that my children are walking in the truth.

a. "It gave me great joy." With this verse John repeats the thought, if not the words, of II John 4: "It has given me great joy to find some of your children walking in the truth."

In the composition of the letter, John follows the custom of his day. In most of the New Testament epistles, the writers follow the sequence of an address, greetings, and an expression of thanks. Even though John omits the greeting, he has an address and a word of praise to declare his great joy.[1]

---

1. The term *joy* occurs three times in the epistles of John (I John 1:4; II John 12; III John 4). The Greek verb translated *to rejoice* appears twice in the Johannine Epistles (II John 4; III John 3).

Notice that John uses the past tense in this sentence to indicate that for some time he has experienced joy.

b. "To have some brothers come and tell about your faithfulness to the truth." The original Greek indicates that the brothers were often coming to John to testify about the love and faithfulness of Gaius.

Who were these brothers? In verse 5, John praises Gaius, "You are faithful in what you are doing for the brothers, even though they are strangers to you." And in verse 8, he encourages Gaius "to show hospitality to such men." They were traveling missionaries who visited Gaius, at whose home they received lodging. They had also visited Diotrephes, who in contrast with Gaius had refused to welcome them (v. 9). Now they have come to John with glowing words of praise for Gaius and disapproval for Diotrephes. In the home of Gaius, they have experienced the evidence of Christian love, which the New International Version translates "faithfulness to the truth."

c. "How you continue to walk in the truth." Gaius has followed the example of Jesus (I John 2:6) and thus fulfilled the expectations John had for his friend. Hence John called him his dear friend "whom I love in the truth" (v. 1).

d. "I have no greater joy than to hear that my children are walking in the truth." John repeats the word *joy* but qualifies it with the adjective *greater*. John rejoiced to hear that Gaius walks in the truth. He has even greater joy when he learns that in addition, numerous Christians are doing the same thing.

John speaks of "children," not in the sense of physical descent but spiritual birth. Similarly, Paul writes to the believers in Corinth and says, "In Christ Jesus I became your father through the gospel" (I Cor. 4:15; also see Gal. 4:19). The term *children* includes John's friend Gaius and all other Christians who have come to know the truth through the preaching and teaching ministry of the apostle.

Why do these spiritual children give John joy and happiness? Because they are walking in the truth. That is, they are walking life's pathway in the light of God's Word (I John 1:7; 2:9). They obey his commands and reflect God's goodness and grace. In short, they are children of the light.

Greek Words, Phrases, and Constructions in 3–4

Verse 3

ἐρχομένων ἀδελφῶν—the genitive absolute construction with the present participle indicates repeated occurrence.

σου τῇ ἀληθείᾳ—the genitive case σου (your) is objective (the truth that affects you), not subjective (the truth that belongs to you).

Verse 4

μειζοτέραν τούτων—the adjective is a double comparison (μείζων, greater) that literally means "more greater." The pronoun τούτων is plural because the plural sometimes may take the place of the singular.[2]

ἵνα ἀκούω—this purpose clause is equivalent to the articular infinitive in the genitive case τοῦ ἀκούειν.[3]

B. A Delightful Report
5–8

After a general tribute to Gaius, John now mentions the hospitality and love Gaius has shown to traveling missionaries. John gives his reaction to the good report he has received.

1. Faithfulness and Love
5–6

5. Dear friend, you are faithful in what you are doing for the brothers, even though they are strangers to you.   6. They have told the church about your love. You will do well to send them on their way in a manner worthy of God.

a. *Address.* Once again John addresses Gaius with the term *dear friend* (see vv. 1, 2). He praises his friend for his faithful conduct, because Gaius has given visible proof of walking in the truth.[4] From traveling missionaries John heard about the kindness Gaius had extended to them. According to the missionaries, Gaius had received them as his spiritual brothers and had provided lodging and food for them. John commends Gaius for his faithfulness toward the brothers.

b. *Hospitality.* Gaius opened not only his heart to the brothers but also his home. He offered hospitality to the brothers, "even though they [were] strangers." The term *strangers* in this context means that the brothers came from other places and were not known to Gaius.

In obedience to the teachings of Scripture,[5] Gaius takes care of the wayfarers. "In the ancient world many a door was opened to a messenger of the new covenant and the host was thus blessed."[6] The traveling missionary depended on the hospitality of fellow believers. Hence Paul asks Philemon to prepare a guest room for him (Philem. 22). The writer of the

---

2. Refer to A. T. Robertson, *A Grammar of the Greek New Testament in the Light of Historical Research* (Nashville: Broadman, 1934), p. 704.

3. Consult Alfred Plummer, *The Epistles of St. John*, Cambridge Greek Testament for Schools and Colleges series (Cambridge: At the University Press, 1896), p. 145.

4. Refer to Raymond E. Brown, *The Epistles of John*, Anchor Bible series (Garden City, N.Y.: Doubleday, 1982), vol. 30, p. 708.

5. Here are a few passages from the Old Testament (Gen. 18:1–8; 19:1–3; II Sam. 12:4; Job 31:32) and from the New Testament (Matt. 25:31–46; Luke 11:5–8; Acts 10:6; 16:15; Rom. 12:13; Heb. 13:2).

6. Hans Bietenhard, *NIDNTT*, vol. 1, p. 690. Also see Gustav Stählin, *TDNT*, vol. 5, p. 22.

Didache (Teaching of the Twelve Apostles), which reflects social and ecclesiastical practices of the first century, states,

> Let every Apostle who comes to you be received as the Lord, but let him not stay more than one day, or if need be a second as well; but if he stay three days, he is a false prophet.[7]

c. *Commendation.* The missionaries told the members of the church, including the apostle John, about the hospitality and care of Gaius.[8] Whether they reported once during one of their visits or more often is inconsequential. The news concerning Gaius's deeds of Christian love is important.

John exhorts Gaius to continue caring for the traveling messenger of the gospel of Christ. He tells him, "You will do well to send them on their way in a manner worthy of God." The phrase *you will do well* is a polite request that is similar to the expression *please.*[9] John's instruction "to send them on their way" means that after Gaius provided lodging, he has to supply the brothers with food, money, and possibly travel companions for their journey (see Titus 3:13).[10] John adds that Gaius must do so "in a manner worthy of God." That is, he ought to provide these services in such a manner that God receives praise (compare Col. 1:10; Phil. 1:27; I Thess. 2:12).

Practical Considerations in 5–6

In most churches during the Sunday morning worship service, worshipers take part in the service by placing their offerings in the offering plate. They do so in harmony with the words of Paul, "God loves a cheerful giver" (II Cor. 9:7). For some people, however, the act of giving relieves their conscience. They think that they have given something to God and are now no longer under any obligation. They forget that God wants us to give our gifts in the context of love.

When we place gifts in the offering plate, we should accompany these gifts with our prayers so that the people who receive them may be blessed. It is our task to care for people, because they need our love. People are of primary importance, and gifts are of secondary importance. "Therefore, as we have opportunity, let us do good to all people, especially to those who belong to the family of believers" (Gal. 6:10).

---

7. *Didache* 11: 4–5 (LCL). Consult I Clement 1:2, where the writer praises the church members of Corinth for their hospitality.

8. In the three epistles, John uses the expression *church* three times (III John 6, 9, 10). The word does not occur in the Gospel of John, but Revelation has it twenty times.

9. Refer to I. Howard Marshall, *The Epistles of John,* New International Commentary on the New Testament series (Grand Rapids: Eerdmans, 1978), p. 85. Also consult Brown, *The Epistles of John,* p. 792.

10. Refer to Bauer, p. 709.

Greek Words, Phrases, and Constructions in 5–6

Verse 5

πιστὸν ποιεῖς—literally these words mean "you are doing a faithful thing." But John is interested more in the character of Gaius than in the work he performs. Therefore, the New International Version has "you are faithful."

ἐργάσῃ—this is the second person singular aorist middle subjunctive of the verb ἐργάζομαι (I work). The aorist is constative. "It takes an occurrence and, regardless of its extent of duration, gathers it into a single whole."[11]

Verse 6

προπέμψας—from the verb προπέμπω (I help on one's journey), the action of the aorist is simultaneous with that of the main verb ποιήσεις (you will do).[12]

---

2. Show Hospitality
7–8

7. It was for the sake of the Name that they went out, receiving no help from the pagans. 8. We ought therefore to show hospitality to such men so that we may work together for the truth.

a. *Cause.* John indicates that missionaries had set out to other places where they proclaimed the name of the Lord Jesus Christ. These messengers were commissioned by the church to bring the gospel. John uses the term *Name* (Acts 5:41; James 2:7; I John 2:12; 3:23).[13] In obedience to Jesus Christ, they left home and family to go to other regions. They knew that if Jesus sent them forth, he unquestionably would provide for their needs (refer to Matt. 10:9–10; Mark 6:8; Luke 10:4).

The missionaries refused to accept aid from people who had never heard the Word of God. John calls these people "pagans" (NIV). The missionaries did not want to hinder the work of the gospel of Christ. They knew that if they accepted help from unbelievers, they would leave themselves open to the charge that they preached for financial gains (I Cor. 9:12). Therefore, John teaches that missionaries should receive help from the church (v. 8).

b. *Help.* "We ought therefore to show hospitality to such men." John contrasts the pagans with the believers. Gentiles have no obligation to help the missionaries, but according to Jesus (Luke 10:7; I Cor. 9:14; I Tim. 5:18), believers do. Thus John emphatically states that we ought to

---

11. H. E. Dana and Julius R. Mantey, *A Manual Grammar of the Greek New Testament* (New York: Macmillan, 1967), p. 196.

12. Refer to Robertson, *Grammar,* p. 861.

13. In the early church, Christians often used the word *Name* as a reference to Jesus Christ. See, for example, Ignatius's epistle to the Ephesians 3. 1, "For though I am a prisoner for the Name, I am not yet perfect in Jesus Christ" (LCL).

show hospitality to the messengers of the Word of God. This passage shows a subtle play on words in Greek which even in English is telling. The missionaries *take* no help from the pagans because the believers have under*taken* to support them.[14] The believers are mindful of Jesus' word, "Anyone who receives a prophet because he is a prophet will receive a prophet's reward, and anyone who receives a righteous man because he is a righteous man will receive a righteous man's reward" (Matt. 10:41).

"So that we may work together for the truth." Another translation is, "that we may be fellow-workers *with* the truth" (NASB, italics added). Is the word *truth* personified (compare v. 12), so that we work with the truth as equals? Hardly. But if we say that John exhorts us to work together with missionaries for the truth, then biblical evidence supports us in this interpretation. For instance, Paul sends the greetings of three companions (Aristarchus, Mark, and Jesus called Justus) to the church in Colosse. He says, "These are the only Jews among my fellow workers *for* the kingdom of God" (Col. 4:11, italics added; also see II Cor. 8:23).[15] John, then, is asking us to help missionaries in the work by spreading the truth, that is, the gospel of Christ.

Greek Words, Phrases, and Constructions in 7–8

Verse 7

λαμβάνοντες—from λαμβάνω (I take, receive), the present tense of this active participle is durative. Furthermore, the use of the present participle discloses that the rule not to accept help from Gentiles was in vogue. The participle denotes manner.

Verse 8

ὀφείλομεν—the verb ὀφείλω (I ought) suggests obligation. By contrast, the word δεῖ (it is necessary) connotes necessity. "The former is moral, the latter, as it were, physical necessity."[16]

ὑπολαμβάνειν—the literal translation of this present infinitive is *"to receive* someone *under* one's roof."

τῇ ἀληθείᾳ—the dative case is a dative of advantage and signifies "for" or "in the interest of."[17]

---

9 I wrote to the church, but Diotrephes, who loves to be first, will have nothing to do with us.   10 So if I come, I will call attention to what he is doing, gossiping maliciously about us.

---

14. Consult Plummer, *The Epistles of St. John,* p. 148.

15. There is a similar construction in I Cor. 3:9. A literal translation of this text is, "For we are God's fellow workers." Some translators understand the genitive case to mean "We are fellow workers with God" (JB). Others think that the use of the preposition *with* is too presumptuous. They prefer to say, "For we are fellow workers for God" (RSV).

16. John Albert Bengel, *Gnomon of the New Testament,* ed. Andrew R. Fausset, 7th ed., 5 vols. (Edinburgh: Clark, 1877), vol. 3, p. 282.

17. Translators generally favor the dative of advantage (consult ASV, GNB, JB, NIV, NKJV).

Not satisfied with that, he refuses to welcome the brothers. He also stops those who want to do so and puts them out of the church.

III. Diotrephes Reproved
9–10

A. A Letter Rejected
9

After exhorting and commending Gaius, John comes to the heart of the matter: his description of Diotrephes. John rejoices to see Gaius walking in the truth. But in Diotrephes, John encounters a person who marks a startling contrast: Diotrephes is conceited and boastful. Notice that although John describes Diotrephes as an arrogant person, he refrains from judging him. Instead John tells him that he will visit the church.

9. I wrote to the church, but Diotrephes, who loves to be first, will have nothing to do with us.

We are unable to ascertain whether the letter which John mentions is his second epistle. We surmise that in addition to the three Johannine Epistles that are extant, John wrote at least one other letter. This letter, however, has not been preserved. If John indeed refers to the second epistle, then the contents of these two documents do not correspond. John's second epistle concerns the teaching of false prophets, but his letter to Gaius is not a rebuke of Diotrephes for spreading false doctrine. Rather, John rebukes Diotrephes because of his behavior in the church. For that reason, we feel that this matter prevents us from identifying the two documents.

John wrote a letter to the church to which Diotrephes belongs. We assume that "the church" of Gaius is another congregation.[18] In the original, John says, "I wrote *something* to the church." By using the term *something*, John diminishes the significance of the letter.

We know little about Diotrephes. His name means "foster child of Zeus,"[19] which suggests that he is of Greek descent. He is a leader within the local church and turns his leadership position to selfish advantage. John writes that Diotrephes "loves to be first." Instead of serving the church, this proud person is egotistic and refuses to recognize superior authority. He himself desires to rule the church. Accordingly, Diotrephes rejects the apostolic supremacy of John. He acts contrary to the injunction of Jesus, "Whoever wants to become great among you must be your servant, and whoever wants to be first must be your slave" (Matt. 20:26–27). Incidentally, even though John introduces himself as "the elder" (v. 1), he exercises authority of a level higher than that of an elder.

---

18. Consult C. H. Dodd, *The Johannine Epistles*, Moffatt New Testament Commentary series (New York: Harper and Row, 1946), p. 161; Marshall, *The Epistles of John*, p. 89.
19. Thayer, p. 152.

John mentions that Diotrephes "will have nothing to do with us." Note that he uses the pronoun *us* possibly to include the friends who send greetings to Gaius. Perhaps some of these friends were leaders with authority (compare, for example, the use of the first person plurals *we* and *us* in I John 1:1–5). However, Diotrephes refuses to respond to John's counsel, ignores his correspondence, and breaks the bonds of Christian fellowship. And if John intends to pay him a visit, Diotrephes will not welcome him. Diotrephes does so not because of a doctrinal dispute but out of personal ambition.

Greek Words, Phrases, and Constructions in 9

ἔγραψα—although John uses this verb in the aorist tense a few times (I John 2:13, 14 [twice], 21, 26; 5:13), in this verse it is not an epistolary aorist. It is the simple past tense because John refers to an earlier letter he has written.

τῇ ἐκκλησίᾳ—the definite article with the noun (see v. 10) points to the church to which Diotrephes belonged.

αὐτῶν—the genitive case is objective, not subjective.

B. John's Warning
10

10. So if I come, I will call attention to what he is doing, gossiping maliciously about us. Not satisfied with that, he refuses to welcome the brothers. He also stops those who want to do so and puts them out of the church.

By writing the short statement, "So if I come," John informs Diotrephes about his impending visit, but he provides no details about the time of his arrival. John intends to visit the congregation to call attention to the behavior of Diotrephes. Indirectly he contrasts the activities of Gaius (v. 5) with those of Diotrephes. Gaius applies the principle of love for God and his neighbor; Diotrephes adheres to the principle of selfish love. John lists the activities of Diotrephes:

a. "[He is] gossiping maliciously about us." That is, Diotrephes is making unjustifiable accusations against John and his companions because he resents John's apostolic authority. Therefore, he tries to undermine John with malicious gossip. In fact, the word *gossip* in Greek is descriptive for bubbles that appear momentarily and disappear. They are useless. The term, then, implies that the evil words Diotrephes utters are empty and meaningless (consult I Tim. 5:13). Nevertheless, the offense is an undisguised violation of God's explicit command, "You shall not give false testimony against your neighbor" (Exod. 20:16; Deut. 5:20). A leader in the local congregation, Diotrephes stands condemned as a violator of God's law.

b. "Not satisfied with that, he refuses to welcome the brothers." Not only are Diotrephes' words vicious; his deeds are equally reprehensible. He will-

fully breaks the rules of Christian hospitality by refusing to receive missionaries sent out to proclaim the gospel. By denying them shelter and food, he
hinders the progress of the Word of God. In brief, Diotrephes is thwarting
God's plans and purposes and consequently he faces divine wrath.

c. "He also stops those who want to do so." Diotrephes goes one step
further and prevents members of the church from showing hospitality to
traveling missionaries. We infer that he is trying to hinder the believers
from receiving the missionaries and attempting to punish them for opening their doors to God's servants.

d. "And puts them out of the church." Diotrephes places before the
believers a choice: either side with me against John or receive the missionaries and be excommunicated. The parallel to this situation is the excom-
munication of the man born blind (John 9:1–34).

Greek Words, Phrases, and Constructions in 10

ἐὰν ἔλθω—the conditional sentence with the aorist subjunctive ἔλθω (from
ἔρχομαι, I come) expresses probability.

ὑπομνήσω—the future active of the verb ὑπομιμνήσκω (I remind) lacks a direct
object. We assume that John will remind the church during his visit.

κωλύει and ἐκβάλλει—these two verbs in the present active indicative may be
conative ("he tries to prevent and put out").

Additional Remarks

The question that has captured the attention of scholars is: "Why does
John inform Gaius about Diotrephes if both men are members of the
same congregation and are in a leadership position?" Granted that we
have only circumstantial evidence, we surmise that with the death of the
apostles in the second half of the first century a power struggle developed
within the church.

Gaius submitted to the authority of the apostle John, but Diotrephes
wanted a leadership position of his own and therefore rejected any supremacy of persons outside his congregation. He wanted nothing to do
with John and his associates because he desired to be first in the church.
Concludes I. Howard Marshall, "Possibly Gaius was a member of a neigh-
boring church, for otherwise it would be strange for John to tell him what
he must already have known."[20]

---

11 Dear friend, do not imitate what is evil but what is good. Anyone who does what is
good is from God. Anyone who does what is evil has not seen God. 12 Demetrius is well
spoken of by everyone—and even by the truth itself. We also speak well of him, and you
know that our testimony is true.

---

20. I. Howard Marshall, "John, Epistles of," *ISBE,* vol. 2, p. 1095.

IV. Exhortation and Recommendation
11–12

John first tells Gaius to do what is good and not to imitate evil deeds, presumably those of Diotrephes. Next he mentions Demetrius as an example of good conduct.

11. Dear friend, do not imitate what is evil but what is good. Anyone who does what is good is from God. Anyone who does what is evil has not seen God.

a. *Exhortation.* Four times in this short letter John uses the address *dear friend* when he refers to Gaius (vv. 1, 2, 5, 11). Three times John appeals to him directly. Here he encourages him to "imitate [not] what is evil but what is good." John is not saying that Gaius is following the example of Diotrephes. Rather, he is stressing the last part of his exhortation: "imitate . . . what is good." And thus by contrast John implies that Gaius should not imitate what is evil.[21]

"Anyone who does what is good is from God." The person who continually obeys God's precepts has his spiritual origin in God and is his child. How do we know the children of God? In his first epistle John gives the norm for determining the difference between the children of God and the children of the devil: "Anyone who does not do what is right is not a child of God" (3:10). Therefore, anyone who continues to do evil, for example, Diotrephes, has not seen or known God (compare I John 3:6). The believer sees God in Jesus Christ. As Jesus told Philip, "Anyone who has seen me has seen the Father" (John 14:9; also see 1:18). When a Christian sees God, he has fellowship with him through Jesus Christ (I John 1:3).

12. Demetrius is well spoken of by everyone—and even by the truth itself. We also speak well of him, and you know that our testimony is true.

b. *Recommendation.* Throughout his epistles John uses the literary device of contrast. After depicting the evil deeds of Diotrephes, John now introduces Demetrius, who "is well spoken of by everyone." This person, then, is well known and needs no further introduction. Although the original readers of John's epistle knew him well, we have no further information beyond that which John gives in verse 12. For instance, we have no evidence that Demetrius, the silversmith of Ephesus (Acts 19:24), was converted and became an exemplary Christian.

Why does John mention Demetrius? John mentions him because of the good report that circulates about Demetrius. Note that three times John states the same thing: everyone speaks well of Demetrius, the truth speaks

---

21. The Greek verb *to imitate* appears four times in the New Testament (II Thess. 3:7 [example], 9 [model]; Heb. 13:7; III John 11).

well of him, and John himself speaks well of him. Demetrius was a person who had gained the trust of the Christian community at large. What was said about him and what particular work he performed is not known.

"And even by the truth itself." What is the significance of the noun *truth?* The context does not call for an identification with God (John 17:3), Jesus (John 14:6), or the Spirit (I John 5:6). Because John writes about "walking in the truth" (v. 4), that is, the truth of the gospel of Christ, we infer that Demetrius lived according to the mandates of God's Word so that his life showed clear evidence of the truth (I John 2:8).

"We speak well of him, and you know that our testimony is true." In this verse the use of the pronoun *we* is probably editorial. John uses the plural to refer to himself and does so with emphasis: "We *too* speak well of him." He assures Gaius that the testimony John has written concerning Demetrius is true (compare John 19:35) because he is personally acquainted with him. Gaius, then, may place full confidence in John.

Greek Words, Phrases, and Constructions in 11–12

Verse 11

μὴ μιμοῦ—this is the second person present imperative of the verb μιμέομαι (I imitate). It is preceded by the negative particle μή (not). The emphasis falls not on the term τὸ κακόν (the evil) but on the term τὸ ἀγαθόν (the good) which stands last in the sentence.

οὐχ ἑώρακεν—the perfect tense with the negative οὐχ (not) signifies that the one who does evil has never seen God in the past and consequently not in the present either.

Verse 12

μεμαρτύρηται—the perfect passive from the verb μαρτυρέω (I testify) indicates action that occurred earlier but continues into the present.

ὑπό—this preposition governs the genitive case of πάντων (all) and ἀληθείας (truth). The grammatical construction is called the genitive of agent.

---

13 I have much to write you, but I do not want to do so with pen and ink.   14 I hope to see you soon, and we will talk face to face.

Peace to you. The friends here send their greetings. Greet the friends there by name.

V. Conclusion
13–14

13. I have much to write you, but I do not want to do so with pen and ink.   14. I hope to see you soon, and we will talk face to face.

These two verses are almost identical to the conclusion of the Second Epistle of John (v. 12). Minor differences do not alter the meaning of the concluding remarks. Their similarity, however, shows that John wrote these two epistles about the same time.

Why John decided not to extend the length of this letter is debatable. The reason may be that John wanted to communicate matters orally. Then he would not run the risk of any misunderstanding that might arise. Also, the matter concerning Diotrephes was delicate and had to be addressed in person.

John expresses the hope that he will meet Gaius soon. He omits the details relating to destination and time because they are unimportant to the recipient. The term *soon* must suffice. When the two friends see each other, they "will talk face to face" (compare Num. 12:8).

Peace to you. The friends here send their greetings. Greet the friends there by name.

The Greek text marks the greeting as verse 15, and many translators and commentators do the same. Others, however, make the greeting part of verse 14.

"Peace to you." The greeting is the equivalent of the Hebrew *shalom*, which is used for both "hello" and "good-by." Jesus and the apostles employ the greeting and give it a New Testament meaning (John 20:19, 21, 26; Gal. 6:16; Eph. 6:23; I Peter 5:14). Consequently, they who receive the greeting have the peace of God in Christ Jesus (Phil. 4:7). The greeting of John is especially for Gaius, because the pronoun *you* is in the singular.

Jesus calls his disciples "friends" (John 15:13–15), yet the Christian community prefers to use the terms *brothers* and *sisters*. John follows Jesus' example by calling the recipients "friends." He sends the greetings of friends who surround him to the friends who receive the letter. In fact, John adds a personal touch; he tells Gaius, "Greet the friends there by name." John, then, implies that the epistle is addressed not only to Gaius but to all the members of the congregation.

Greek Words, Phrases, and Constructions in 13–14

Verse 13

εἶχον—the imperfect tense of the verb ἔχω (I have) shows that John had intended to write more but changed his mind.

καλάμου—"reed." Alfred Plummer observes, "Quills were not used as pens until the fifth century."[22]

Verse 14

ἰδεῖν—the aorist infinitive of ὁράω (I see) indicates that John's visit is a single occurrence.

---

22. Plummer, *The Epistles of St. John*, p. 152.

Summary of III John

After writing the address, John praises Gaius, whom he calls his "dear friend." He expresses the wish that Gaius may receive physical as well as spiritual blessings. John commends him, for he has received a report about the faithfulness of Gaius to the truth, especially in showing hospitality to traveling missionaries. John encourages him to continue to do so.

John informs Gaius about the character and reprehensible deeds of Diotrephes, who has slandered the apostle and hindered the members of the congregation in providing food and shelter for the missionaries. He instructs Gaius not to follow this bad example, but rather to imitate that which is good. Thus he mentions Demetrius, who has a good report in the church.

The epistle has a brief conclusion with the information of a forthcoming visit of John and greetings from friends to friends.

Select Bibliography

Commentaries

Alexander, Neil. *The Epistles of John, Introduction and Commentary.* Torch Bible Commentaries series. London: SCM, 1962.

Alford, Henry. *Alford's Greek Testament, An Exegetical and Critical Commentary.* 4 vols. Vol. 4, part 2, *James–Revelation.* Reprint ed. Grand Rapids: Guardian, 1976.

Barclay, William. *The Letters of John and Jude.* Philadelphia: Westminster, 1958.

Barker, Glenn W. *I John.* Vol. 12, the *Expositor's Bible Commentary,* edited by Frank E. Gaebelein. 12 vols. Grand Rapids: Zondervan, 1981.

Bengel, John Albert. *Gnomon of the New Testament.* Edited by Andrew R. Fausset. 5 vols. 7th ed. Vol. 5. Edinburgh: T. and T. Clark, 1877.

Boice, James Montgomery. *The Epistles of John.* Grand Rapids: Zondervan, 1979.

Brooke, A. E. *A Critical and Exegetical Commentary on the Johannine Epistles.* International Critical Commentary series. Edinburgh: T. and T. Clark, 1964.

Brown, Raymond E. *The Epistles of John.* The Anchor Bible series. Vol. 30. Garden City, N.Y.: Doubleday, 1982.

Bruce, F. F. *The Epistles of John.* 1970. Grand Rapids: Eerdmans, 1979.

———. *The Gospel of John.* Grand Rapids: Eerdmans, 1984.

Bultmann, Rudolf. *The Johannine Epistles.* Edited by Robert Funk. Translated by R. Philip O'Hara et al. Hermeneia: A Critical and Historical Commentary on the Bible. Philadelphia: Fortress, 1973.

Burdick, Donald W. *The Epistles of John.* Everyman's Bible Commentary. Chicago: Moody, 1970.

———. *The Letters of John the Apostle.* Chicago: Moody, 1985.

Calvin, John. *Commentaries on the Catholic Epistles: The First Epistle of John.* Edited and translated by John Owen. Grand Rapids: Eerdmans, 1948.

Conner, Walter Thomas. *The Epistles of John.* 2d and rev. ed. Nashville: Broadman, 1957.

Dodd, C. H. *The Johannine Epistles.* Moffatt New Testament Commentary series. New York: Harper and Row, 1946.

Grayston, Kenneth. *The Johannine Epistles.* New Century Bible Commentary series. Grand Rapids: Eerdmans, 1984.

Greijdanus, S. *De Brieven van de Apostelen Petrus en Johannes, en de Brief van Judas.* Kommentaar op het Nieuwe Testament series. Amsterdam: Van Bottenburg, 1929.

Hendriksen, William. *The Gospel of John.* New Testament Commentary series. Grand Rapids: Baker, 1954.

Houlden, J. L. *A Commentary on the Johannine Epistles.* Black's New Testament Commentaries series. London: Black, 1973.

Lenski, R. C. H. *Interpretation of the Epistles of St. Peter, St. John, and St. Jude.* Columbus: Wartburg, 1945.

Marshall, I. Howard. *The Epistles of John.* New International Commentary on the New Testament series. Grand Rapids: Eerdmans, 1978.

Perkins, Pheme. *The Johannine Epistles.* The New Testament Message. Vol 21. Wilmington: Michael Glazier, 1979.

Plummer, Alfred. *The Epistles of St. John.* Cambridge Greek Testament for Schools and Colleges series. Cambridge: At the University Press, 1896.

Ross, Alexander. *The Epistles of James and John.* The New International Commentary on the New Testament. Grand Rapids: Eerdmans, 1954.

Schnackenburg, Rudolf. *Die Johannesbriefe.* Herder's Theologischer Kommentar zum Neuen Testament. 7th ed. Freiburg: Herder, 1984. Vol. 13, 3.

Smalley, Stephen S. *1, 2, 3 John.* Word Biblical Commentary. Vol. 51. Waco: Word, 1984.

Stott, J. R. W. *The Epistles of John: An Introduction and Commentary.* Tyndale New Testament Commentaries series. Grand Rapids: Eerdmans, 1964.

Westcott, B. F. *The Epistles of St. John, The Greek Text, with Notes and Addenda.* 1883. Grand Rapids: Eerdmans, 1966.

———. *The Gospel According to St. John, The Authorized Version with Introduction and Notes.* 1882. Grand Rapids: Eerdmans, 1964.

Studies

Brown, Raymond E. *The Community of the Beloved Disciple.* New York: Paulist, 1979.

Carson, D. A. "Historical Tradition in the Fourth Gospel: After Dodd, What?" In *Gospel Perspectives, Studies of History and Tradition in the Four Gospels,* edited by R. T. France and David Wenham, vol. 2, pp. 83–145. Sheffield: JSOT Press, 1981.

Culpepper, R. Alan. *The Johannine School: An Evaluation of the Johannine-School Hypothesis Based on an Investigation of the Nature of Ancient Schools.* Society of Biblical Literature Dissertation Series, no. 26. Missoula, Mont.: Scholar's Press, 1975.

de Jonge, M. "An Analysis of I John 1. 1–4." *The Bible Translator* 19 (1978): 322–30.

France, R. T., and David Wenham, eds. *Gospel Perspectives, Studies of History and Tradition in the Four Gospels.* Vol. 2. Sheffield: JSOT Press, 1981.

Guthrie, Donald. *New Testament Theology.* Downers Grove: Inter-Varsity, 1981.

Gutzke, Manford George. *Plain Talk on the Epistles of John.* Grand Rapids: Zondervan, 1977.

Howard, W. F. "The Common Authorship of the Johannine Gospel and Epistles." *Journal of Theological Studies* 48 (1947): 12–25.

Kistemaker, Simon J., ed. *Interpreting God's Word Today.* Grand Rapids: Baker, 1970.

Kotze, P. P. A. "The Meaning of I John 3:9 with Reference to I John 1:8 and 10." *Neotestamentica* 13 (1979): 68–83.

Nauck, Wolfgang. *Die Tradition und der Charakter des ersten Johannesbriefs.* Tübingen: J. C. B. Mohr (Paul Siebeck), 1957.

Pentecost, J. D. *The Joy of Fellowship.* Grand Rapids: Zondervan, 1977.

Robinson, J. A. T. *Redating the New Testament.* Philadelphia: Westminster, 1976.

Scholer, David M. "Sins Within and Sins Without: An Interpretation of I John

5:15–16." *Current Issues in Biblical and Patristic Interpretation*, edited by Gerald F. Hawthorne. Grand Rapids: Eerdmans, 1975.

Torrance, Thomas F. *Christian Theology and Scientific Culture*. New York: Oxford University Press, 1981.

Vaughan, Curtis R. *The Gifts of the Holy Spirit to Unbelievers and Believers*. Reprint ed. Edinburgh: Banner of Truth Trust, 1975.

Wilson, W. G. "An Examination of the Linguistic Evidence Addressed Against the Unity of Authorship of the First Epistle of John and the Fourth Gospel." *Journal of Theological Studies* 49 (1948): 147–56.

Tools

Bauer, Walter. *A Greek-English Lexicon of the New Testament and Other Early Christian Literature*. Second revised and augmented edition by F. Wilbur Gingrich and Frederick W. Danker from Walter Bauer's fourth edition. Chicago and London: University of Chicago Press, 1979.

Berkhof, Louis. *Principles of Biblical Interpretation*. Grand Rapids: Baker, 1950.

Blass, Friedrich, and Albert Debrunner. *A Greek Grammar of the New Testament and Other Early Christian Literature*. Translated and revised by Robert Funk. Chicago: University of Chicago Press, 1961.

Bromiley, Geoffrey W., ed. *The International Standard Bible Encyclopedia*. Rev. ed. 4 vols. Grand Rapids: Eerdmans, 1979–.

Brown, Colin, ed. *New International Dictionary of New Testament Theology*. 3 vols. Grand Rapids: Zondervan, 1975–78.

Dana, H. E., and Julius R. Mantey. *A Manual Grammar of the Greek New Testament*. New York: Macmillan, 1967.

Elwell, Walter A., ed. *Evangelical Dictionary of Theology*. Grand Rapids: Baker, 1984.

Hanna, Robert. *A Grammatical Aid to the Greek New Testament*. Grand Rapids: Baker, 1983.

Kittel, Gerhard, and Gerhard Friedrich, eds. *Theological Dictionary of the New Testament*. Translated by Geoffrey W. Bromiley. 10 vols. Vols. 1–9. Grand Rapids: Eerdmans, 1964–76.

Metzger, Bruce M. *A Textual Commentary on the Greek New Testament*. Corrected ed. London and New York: United Bible Societies, 1975.

Moule, C. F. D. *An Idiom-Book of New Testament Greek*. 2d ed. Cambridge: At the University Press, 1960.

Moulton, James Hope, et al. *A Grammar of New Testament Greek*. 4 vols. Edinburgh: T. and T. Clark, 1908–76.

Nestle, Eberhard, and Kurt Aland, rev. *Novum Testamentum Graece*. 26th ed. Stuttgart: Deutsche Bibelstiftung, 1981.

Robertson, A. T. *A Grammar of the Greek New Testament in the Light of Historical Research*. Nashville: Broadman, 1934.

Strack, H. L., and P. Billerbeck. *Kommentar zum Neuen Testament aus Talmud und Midrasch*. 5 vols. München: Beck, 1922–28.

Thayer, Joseph H. *A Greek-English Lexicon of the New Testament*. New York, Cincinnati, and Chicago: American Book Company, 1889.

Trench, R. C. *Synonyms of the New Testament*. Reprint ed. Grand Rapids: Eerdmans, 1953.

Index of Authors

Index of Scripture

421

Extrabiblical References